MERIDIAN

Crossing Aesthetics

Werner Hamacher

& David E. Wellbery

Editors

D1596663

Translated by
Jan Plug and Others

Stanford

University

Press

Stanford

California

2004

EYES OF THE UNIVERSITY

EYES OF THE UNIVERSITY

Right to Philosophy 2

Jacques Derrida

Stanford University Press
Stanford, California

© 2004 by the Board of Trustees of the
Leland Stanford Junior University

Printed in the United States of America

Assistance for the translation was provided by the French Ministry of Culture.

Eyes of the University: Right to Philosophy 2 was originally published in French in 1990 as
pp. 281–663 of a book entitled *Du droit à la philosophie*, © 1990, Éditions Galilée.

Original Printing 2004

Last figure below indicates year of this printing:
13 12 11 10 09 08 07 06 05 04

Typeset by Tim Roberts in 10.9/13 Adobe Garamond

Contents

Translator's Foreword

Eyes of the University translates the second and third parts of a massive work entitled *Du droit à la philosophie* (Right to Philosophy), which consists of essays, interviews, and talks given by Derrida between 1975 and 1990 on philosophical research, the teaching of philosophy, and the relation between philosophy and institutions, in particular the university. The first part of the book has already appeared under the title *Who's Afraid of Philosophy?*

Part one of *Eyes of the University*, "Transfer *Ex Cathedra*: Language and Institutions of Philosophy," brings together four lectures delivered at the University of Toronto. In the first two lectures Derrida explores the implications of French becoming a State language and of Descartes's writing of the *Discourse on Method* in French for an understanding of the relation between national or natural languages and philosophical discourse. The final two essays examine the conception of the university in Germany at the end of the eighteenth and beginning of the nineteenth centuries. Kant and Schelling are read here as the philosophical forebears of the German model of the university, that model of which current universities are still the heirs.

Part two, "Mochlos: Eyes of the University," brings together texts written and delivered on various occasions, each in its own way returning to questions of the university and its impact upon research and teaching in philosophy: Derrida's talk at the anniversary of the founding of Columbia University's graduate school, his oral defense for the *doctorat d'état*, his inaugural lecture as Andrew D. White Professor-at-Large at Cornell University, an interview with the French newspaper *Libération*, and contributions to conferences and collective works. While these texts often take up philosophical considerations of the university from Kant to Heidegger, they also reflect on the current state of research and teaching in philosophy, on the tendency to orient these toward a programmable and profitable end, and on Derrida's own role, in particular as a member of the Groupe de Recherches sur l'Enseignement Philosophique (Research Group on the Teaching of Philosophy—Greph), in struggles to preserve the teaching of philosophy as a distinct discipline. It should be noted that the political and theoretical struggle for philosophy and its extension, while it took a specific form in France, is not limited to that nation but is being fought in other places as well, in other forms and under different conditions. Indeed, the demand for philosophy, Derrida notes more than once, is felt elsewhere, in North America, for instance, but also in other European countries, in numerous African countries, and so forth.

Greph had its beginnings in a meeting of a small group of teachers and students in 1974 in response to the 1973 CAPES report (published in March 1974), which they judged "scandalous."[1] The group saw this report as part of a larger politics that they felt to be an attack on the teaching of philosophy: a continual decrease in the number of teaching positions available through the CAPES and the agrégation and the devalorization and even the "de facto destruction of the teaching of philosophy" in an educational system that privileged the sciences.[2] In April 1974, the members of Greph approved the group's "Avant-Projet" (published in *Who's Afraid of Philosophy?*); the group was officially founded on January 15, 1975. With the announcement of the Réforme Haby—named after then minister of national education, René Haby—which set out to curtail the teaching of philosophy in French secondary schools, the group's work took on new urgency. Greph fought not only to maintain philosophy in the lycée but to extend it, to have it begin before the final year, or Terminale, in which it had traditionally been taught. As part of this on-going struggle, Derrida and the other members of Greph were among those who called for the Estates General of Philosophy. Held on June 16 and 17, 1979, the Estates General brought together more than 1,200 people from diverse backgrounds, including teachers (of philosophy and other disciplines), scholars, and nonacademics, all concerned about the fate of philosophy. In 1981 François Mitterrand was elected president, and his Socialist government won a parliamentary majority on a platform that included proposals by Greph and the Estates General, in particular the promise that not only would the attack on philosophy end but the teaching of philosophy would be preserved and extended. The promised extension never became a reality, however, and today philosophy continues to be taught in the final year of French lycées.

Nonetheless, as part of a committee established by Mitterrand's minister of research, Jean-Pierre Chevènement, to investigate the possibility of an international college of philosophy, Derrida participated in an initiative that he saw as crucial for the reelaboration of philosophical research and teaching. Founded on October 10, 1983, with Derrida as its first director, the Collège International de Philosophie is funded by the State yet remains autonomous in its operation. Its mission is to provide a place for research, particularly in philosophy, that existing institutions either forbid or marginalize. To this end, the Collège does not require the kind of teaching or research accreditation demanded by other institutions.

The appendices to this volume include Derrida's contribution to a round table held shortly after the Estates General of Philosophy ("Who's Afraid of Philosophy?"); Mitterrand's letter to Greph, in which he promises to maintain and extend the teaching of philosophy; two parts of the report made to Chevènement preparatory to the founding of the Collège International de Philosophie ("Titles" and "Sendoffs"); and the report of the Committee on Philosophy and Epistemology, which, as part of a larger committee formed in 1988 to revise the contents of education, proposed a restructuring of the teaching of philosophy in the lycée and in the university.

Two volumes by Greph, *Qui a peur de la philosophie?* and *États Généraux de la philosophie*, brought together the texts by Derrida translated here and in *Who's Afraid of Philosophy?*, along with the contributions of the other members of the group to these struggles and debates.

It is perhaps appropriate that a book collecting texts written over a fifteen-year period and intended for different audiences and occasions should be translated by many hands. I have had the great pleasure and good fortune to work with and learn from the existing translations, which I have sometimes modified slightly for this volume, recognizing that absolute consistency is no doubt impossible and perhaps not entirely to be wished for.

I would also like to thank Yaël Bratzlavsky, whose patience and good humor in face of the endless task of translation were unfailing.

J.P.

Transfer Ex Cathedra :
Language and Institutions of Philosophy

If There Is Cause to Translate I: Philosophy in its National Language (Toward a "licterature en françois")

> Et si j'écris en français, qui est la langue de mon pays, plutôt qu'en latin, qui est celle de mes précepteurs, c'est à cause que j'espère que ceux qui ne se servent que de leur raison naturelle toute pure jugeront mieux de mes opinions que ceux qui ne croient qu'aux livres anciens; et pour ceux qui joignent le bon sens avec l'étude, lesquels seuls je souhaite pour mes juges, ils ne seront point, je m'assure, si partiaux pour le latin, qu'ils refusent d'entendre mes raisons pour ce que je les explique en langue vulgaire.

> And if I write in French, which is the language of my country, rather than in Latin, which is that of my teachers, it is because I hope that those who use only their pure natural reason will better judge my opinions than those who believe only in old books, and because I am sure that those who combine good sense with scholarship, whom alone I wish to have as my judges, will not be so partial to Latin as to refuse to hear my reasons because I express them in a vulgar tongue.[1]

This, as you know, is the penultimate paragraph of *Discours de la méthode* (Discourse on Method). That it is written in French goes without saying but not without problems. For its present tense ("I write in French") is at once that of a constative (you see what I am doing, I am describing it) and of a performative (I am doing what I say; the constative description is itself written in French; I have committed myself to it; I promise it and am keeping my promise, right now). Now, this simultaneity, this density of the present tenses, points to problems of translation that we will, no doubt, soon encounter. In fact, as I was preparing this seminar in my language, French, knowing that I would have to give it, once translated, in English, I already ran into these problems. But they are not met as accidents or external limits; they reveal the structure and the implications of an event like the one that concerns us now. What happens when, to justify himself, to plead to specific addressees who are also judges, Descartes writes, "And if I write in French, which is the language of my country, rather than in Latin, which is that of my teachers, it is because . . . " and so forth?

The argumentation underlying this defense is more complicated than it may seem at first reading. I even find it cunning. In fact, it is only a weapon, a passage, a passage of arms in the deployment of a rhetorical panoply to justify the recourse to French in other texts, especially—and this is not insignificant —in letters.

French, we would say in the current code, is one *natural language* among others. What Descartes has to do is justify the recourse to a natural language to talk about philosophy, a philosophy that up to this time had been expressed in Greek and, above all, in Latin. As you know, it was Latin that occupied the position of dominant language at the time, particularly in philosophical discourse.

We must not let the word "natural" in the expression "natural language" mislead us. We call "natural" a particular language, a *historical* language as opposed to the artificial, formal language constructed from the ground up to become the universal language. Descartes' argument, as we have just seen in passing, consists in justifying the use of a "natural" language addressed to "those who use only their pure natural reason." But the meaning of the word "natural" in the expression "natural language" is clearly opposed to its meaning in "natural reason." Though it is quite clear, this first paradox must be emphasized: a natural language is native or national, but also particular and historical; it is the least common thing in the world. The natural reason Descartes speaks of is in principle universal, ahistorical, pre- or metalinguistic. We are dealing here with two determinations of naturalness. Between the two, there is a whole history, the historical dimension of a language, the juridical and political, as well as pedagogical, implications that arise the moment a philosophical discourse claiming to be "rational" (by appealing to natural reason as the most common thing in the world) passes from one dominant language to another. What philosophy, what language politics, what psycho-pedagogy, what rhetorical strategy does such an event entail? In what does it consist from the moment it merges with what is called a work, in this instance the *Discourse on Method*, a work in the French language?

We are reading the *Discourse on Method* here in one language or another. I have read it in French; we are reading it in English; I have written about it in French; I am talking to you about it in English. We are distinguishing, then, between the language and the discourse of method. Apparently, we find ourselves here in the distinction, indeed the opposition, between language and discourse, *langue* and *parole*. In the Saussurean tradition, the synchronic system of *langue*, the "treasury of language," would be opposed to the events of *parole* or discourse, which presumably constitute the only actuality of *langage*. This opposition, which would also cover that of the socio-institutional and the individual (discourse would always be individual), raises numerous problems that we will not take up directly here; but you can see already that it is difficult to express the opposition in certain languages. It already resists translation. In German, *Sprache* means at once *langue*, *langage*, *parole*, and discourse, although *Rede* is more strictly reserved for this discursive value. Faced with this difficulty, which he treats rather like an insignificant terminological accident, Saussure says, precisely on the subject of *Rede*, that it is preferable in this case to be concerned with "things" rather than "words."[2] In English, as you know better than anyone, "language" can also mean *langue* and *discours*, even if "tongue" and "discourse" can be used in certain contexts.

If, nonetheless, simply for reasons of temporary convenience, we were to rely on this Saussurean opposition, this model that is more "structural" than it is "generative," we would have to define our problematic as follows: to deal with that which, in a philosophical event as a *discursive or textual* event, is always caught *in* language, and happens *through* language and *to* language. What happens when such a speech act draws from the treasury of the linguistic system and, perhaps, affects or transforms it?

The *Discourse on Method* comes *to* French *through* French, a language that was not so widely used in the world of philosophical discourse. It was not self-evident enough in this type of discourse for the author to dispense with justifying his use of it, rather laboriously and on several occasions, both in the work itself and outside it. This work then also becomes a discourse *on* its own language no less than *in* its own language, indeed a "treatise" on discourse, since the word "discourse" in the title *Discourse on Method* preserves, among other meanings, that of "treatise." The same goes for "method," which, in a title, sometimes had the value of "treatise" or "research" at the time. You will notice already the complexity of this structure, the complexity of the title and the complexity pointed to by the title.

What kind of relations are there, then, between the French language and this discourse? How can one, starting from this example, deal with the general relations between a language and a philosophical discourse, the multiplicity of languages and the universalist claim of the discourse called philosophical? Since it is a question of the language and discourse of method, one could, through an immediate transposition, examine the

hypothesis of a language of method or of language as method. This hypothesis would lead to the formation of a universal language, a project we
will recall from both Descartes and Leibniz, as well as to a mathematical
language, a *langue des calculs*, such as that of Condillac. Before becoming
a *methodical* language, this language could constitute a corpus, a treasury,
a structural and synchronic system of coded elements; this system, this
(programmed-programming) program, would constrain in advance all
possible discourse on method. According to this schema, which is still
Saussurian, each individual subject, each philosopher talking and thinking about method, must draw from this source. He would have to ma-
nipulate this system governed by rules, over which he would have no
power and with which his possibilities would be limited to variations of
combination. And it is often tempting to think that all the specific
philosophies of method, all the systematic discourses on the concept of
method, from Plato to Bergson, from Spinoza to Husserl, by way of Kant,
Hegel, or Marx, could only have been written by combining the types, the
characters coded in a permanent language; they could only have exploited
philosophemes already constituted and caught in a language of philosophy, of method in philosophy, content to make permutations and substi-
tutions in it: an essentially rhetorical implementation of a kind of philosophical grammar over which individual philosophical acts would have no
control. Such a grammar, in the broad sense of the word, would form a
system of concepts, virtual judgments, segments of argumentation, tropo-
logical schemas, and so forth. No invention, then, only a powerful combinatory of discourse drawing from language and constrained by a kind of
pre-established social contract committing individuals in advance. I repeat, it is not for me, at this moment, to give substance to this schema,
Saussurian in its inspiration, and to use this axiomatics as an excuse for a
kind of structural linguistics of philosophy. I am simply naming the opposition *langue/discours* and defining it as the title of a problem, indeed as
an object of inquiry: neither a truth nor a certainty.

It is thus in French, in the language of his country, that Descartes
writes, and he writes that he writes in French. He writes about the language in which he writes, and he does so in the present tense, in that first
person of the present indicative whose privileged status in performative
utterances is stressed by Austin.[3] "Right now I am writing in French"; it

should be impossible to write what I am doing in preparing this lecture in anything but French, and it should defy translation. This grammatical present is even broader and thus goes beyond the performative present: in fact, it comes at the end of the discourse and signifies: I have written, I have just written in French throughout the book, I am forever writing in "the language of my country, rather than in Latin, which is that of my teachers."

Such a present tense, however, marks the clear event of a rupture, but also the continuity of an interminable, and interminably conflictual, historical process. As you know, the imperative of national language, as medium of philosophical and scientific communication, has not ceased to recall itself [*se rappeler*], to call us back [*nous rappeler*] to order, especially in France. Even before the memorandum addressed to all French researchers and academics, even before announcing that the State would not give grants to symposia held in France that did not guarantee the French language its place, at least by means of simultaneous translation, the minister of industry and research specified, in a directive [*Note d'Orientation*] for the great Conference on Research and Technology (1982), that the French language "should remain or become again a privileged medium for scientific and technical thought and information."[4] The language politics defined in this manner justifies itself by threats and responds to necessities that are not without analogy or, indeed, without continuity with certain facts or certain contradictions already felt in Descartes' time. The problematic has remained *relatively* stable since the sixteenth century. *On the one hand*, it is still a question of opposing a national language, which at a given moment has become the language of the State and which preserves in its State legitimacy the traces of a recent and specific formation, to national idioms that are subject to the same State authority and that constitute dissipating or centrifugal forces, risks of dissociation or even subversion, even if, and this is the first contradiction, they are simultaneously encouraged. *On the other hand*, this same dominant national language, the sole language of the State, will be opposed to other natural languages ("dead" or "living") that, for technical and historical reasons that should be analyzed carefully, have become privileged media of philosophical or techno-scientific communication: Latin before Descartes, American English today. We will not be able to deal with the broad implications of these problems. Let us only establish that they are multiple and at the same time socio-political, historical, religious, techno-scientific, pedagogical, and so forth. I need not emphasize this here, in Toronto, at a time when I have to translate into English, in the anglophone part of a bilingual country, a discourse first written in the language of my country, French.

The French history of a problem found in all countries scans to the rhythm of three great historical eras, all closely linked to the violent and interminable constitution of the French State.

1) *In the first place*, it was the great moment of establishing the monarchy as State: a massive if not terminal or decisive progress of a French language imposed on the provinces as administrative and juridical medium. What we are trying to follow in this seminar is the constitution of the legal subject and of the philosophical subject *tout court*, starting from the imposition of a language. As you know, under François I, in 1539, the royal decree of Villers-Cotterêts ordered that legal judgments and other proceedings be "pronounced, recorded, and delivered in the French mother tongue."[5] In 1539: almost a century before the *Discourse on Method*. One century from law to philosophy [*du droit à la philosophie*], one might say. One century for the "French mother tongue" to mark a great philosophical event. For Descartes, who lost his mother when he was one year old, French is a grandmother tongue (he had been raised by his grandmother) that he opposes to that of his teachers, who imposed upon him the law of learning and the law pure and simple *in Latin*. It is the language [*langage*] of the law [*loi*] because Latin, the language of the father if you wish, the language of science and of school, a nondomestic language, is above all a language [*langue*] of right or law [*droit*]. And the greatest resistance to the (natural, maternal, etc.) living language came from the juridical world.

Of course, the decree of Villers-Cotterêts itself represents only the legal form, the scansion, and the juridico-administrative sanction of a broader movement that prepared and followed it, both in the progression of French and in the resistance to Frenchification. The factors of progression and resistance were numerous and diverse. The Reformation, for example, helped the progression of French by fighting against the Catholic Church system: an economic struggle, a struggle for the reappropriation of texts against an *international* church dominated and dominating by Latin. There was a whole "nationalist" dimension of Protestantism that was taken up, after the defeat of the Reformation in France, by a more "Gallic" church in the seventeenth century. The Protestants wanted their New Testament in French: that of Lefevre d'Étaples in 1523, that of Olivetan in

1535, a few years before the decree of Villers-Cotterêts. In 1541, Calvin, theorist of the French Protestants, republished his *Institution de la religion chrétienne* (Institution of the Christian Religion) in French. We do not need to be reminded of the role played by translations of the Bible in other countries during the Reformation: both in the constitution or definitive formation of a language of reference[6] and in the history of a problematics of translation.

The church never stopped, at least in the sixteenth century, resisting this extension of French that can be followed in literature as well, in the Pléiade, Montaigne, Rabelais, and so forth. Du Bellay's book-manifesto *La défense et illustration de la langue française* (Defense and Illustration of the French Language) dates from 1549, that is, ten years after the royal decree of Villers-Cotterêts. We cannot follow this fascinating, rich, and complex history of the French language in depth here without overlooking the other themes that I would like to privilege in this seminar. For a preliminary inquiry, I refer you first to Ferdinand Brunot's *L'histoire de la langue française, des origines à 1900*.[7] Published in 1906, it is already old, but it nevertheless remains an inevitable monument in this area. In Marcel Cohen's book, *Histoire d'une langue: Le français* (1947), content and information are mobilized in a way that is always interesting and usually necessary, through a Marxist inquiry that at any rate makes it possible to show the effects of class struggle, the politico-economic implications, and the link with the history of technologies in these struggles for the appropriation or imposition of a language. For a more modern period in the history of language, particularly in its relationship to the politics of education systems, I refer you to *Le français national* by Renée Balibar and Dominique Laporte, and to Renée Balibar's *Les Français fictifs*.[8] In this short, preliminary, and necessarily incomplete bibliography, I would also like to point out Marcel Bataillon's article "Quelques idées linguistiques du XVIIème siècle, Nicolas Le Gras." This study was published in a collection of texts under the title *Langue, discours, société*[9] in honor of Emile Benveniste, who, like Bataillon, was professor in that very Collège de France created by François I (from 1529 to 1534) and called the *Collège des trois langues* (for the study of Latin, Greek, and Hebrew). Some innovators taught French in this Collège as early as the sixteenth century. If we wanted to immerse ourselves in this enormous history, which we cannot, we would have to problematize simultaneously and methodically all the practices of historians of language. Their system of interpretation, as you can easily imagine, is never neutral: philosophically and politically. It conveys an at least implicit philosophy of language, and itself practices a certain language (rhetoric, writing, etc.), and takes sides, at a specific moment, in a language war. This war continues today, over and within a language in transformation. And this war traverses institutions; the weapons bear its marks (rhetoric, procedures of demonstration, relationships between the disciplines, techniques of legitimation). In this respect, the differences between Brunot's (1906) and Cohen's (1947) histories are spectacular; and they are not limited to political ideology.

Unable to do this work here, let us content ourselves with indicating its necessity and with tracing a few "arrows" to mark directions, supposing that it is possible to trace or to direct arrows in such a labyrinth. These few arrows must in any case retain a certain relationship with the discourse on method, I mean with the question concerning method (*method*: following the road; *odos*, the methodical becoming-road of a path; *odos*, that which is not necessarily methodical),[10] but also with questions of method. One of these directions, at our very point of passage, leads onto the road along which a politics of language also passes, in this instance the State extension of French by a monarchy that had just ensured its power over the provinces and the dialects, gains or confirms control over a territory by imposing linguistic unification upon it. I will not return to the "clearing" [*frayage*], the presumed "metaphor" of method as a figure for the path or *road* (*via rupta*) as language, and not necessarily human language, but also as language, trace, text, mark of what is called animality: tracks, wars for sexual and economic territories.

The imposition of a State language implies an obvious purpose of conquest and administrative domination of the territory, exactly like the opening of a road (for the mares of Parmenides' *Poem*, the horseman Descartes "who took off at such a good pace," the trains of the pioneers of the Far West, for the aerial, maritime, or strangely named "spatial" routes of our century—with their considerable politico-juridical problems). But there is a still more urgent necessity for us, right here: that by which the aforementioned figure of the path to be cleared imposes itself, in a way, *from within*, in order to tell the progress of a language.

I will give only one example. From Louis XII to Henri III, the complicity becomes very visible between the king and numerous writers, storytellers, grammarians, physicians, philosophers, to promote the expansion of the French idiom. Brunot evokes the letters of thanks they

addressed to François I, Henri II, Charles IX, Henri III, the praise bestowed upon them by Du Bellay, Amyot, Henri Estienne, and many others (Brunot 2.27). This sometimes becomes ridiculous; today, at our present moment of the defense and illustration of the French language, we
smile at the idea that it was from the "first François" that our language got
the name *langue françoise*. It is true that the royalty protected *French belles-
lettres*. We would understand nothing of the history of French literature if
we did not pay attention to this language politics. Though François I
never appointed any teachers of French, he appointed a royal printer of
French in 1543, a few years after the decree of Villers-Cotterêts. He re-
warded translators or writers who published in French. And above all, and
here is that delicate and so very current problem (which is also that of a
politics of culture and of publishing): he commissioned, programmed,
and subsidized the work of certain writers. Among those commissions
were works whose purpose seems only too evident: for example, those of
Du Haillan, the history of the kings of France. But there was also some
less immediately profitable programming and planning. These writers
were invited, for example (and this is the example I am choosing from this
enormous corpus, for obvious reasons), to write *philosophy in French*.

It is here, precisely, that you will see a road pass, a French road and
French *marches*, in the French language, in the invitation sent out by
Henri II's chancellery. On August 30, 1556, Henri II sent an invitation—
or an order—to Guy de Bruès for his *Dialogues contre les nouveaux
Académiciens* (Dialogues against the New Academicians, 1557). He did so
in a letter signed by the chancellor. I quote from it the following passage:

> In particular, we wish the path opened by Bruès (doing the great duty of do-
> mesticating and familiarizing philosophy to our subjects in their own lan-
> guage) to be followed by the other good and excellent minds of our kingdom
> and to be led out by them, little by little, from Greece and the country of the
> Latins towards these border regions [*marches*]. (Cited in Brunot 2.28)

It is toward these French *marches* (marks, margins, and so forth, in the
sense of border, here national or military borders, *Marken*; I have insisted
enough elsewhere on this chain of *marche, marge, marque* to go more
quickly here)[11] that Greek or Latin philosophy must be "led out" [*aconduire*], that is, be made to come, diverted, by language, a language that
clears a path toward French. That is what Henri II's chancellor says. We
will not be able to understand Descartes' gesture, less than a century later,

without keeping in mind this political genealogy, even if there is more to it than that.

This political and territorial concern also presupposed that the representatives of the royalty, as well as the people of the court, received the required education. Yet outside the priesthood, people generally were not educated, in particular because they had not learned Latin; books in French therefore had to be made for the benefit of administrators and courtiers; what Claude de Seyssel called for the first time a *Licterature en françois* (literature in French) had to be created. This is the first occurrence of the word in this form and with this meaning. In the Middle Ages it was called "lettreüre." The word and the advice go back to this Claude de Seyssel, extraordinary counsel to Louis XII. He translated Pompei for him. Saddened by the absence of useful works in French, he also translated a good deal (from Latin and Greek, which he did not know and for which he had help); he did so for the nobility and for others who, as he said, "are often more dedicated to the sciences than the nobility." In 1509, in a preface full of morality and politics, he proposed in principle that those who did not know Latin should still learn "many good and lofty things, whether in the Holy Scriptures, moral Philosophy, Medicine, or History," and that therefore there was a need for a "literature in French" (see Brunot 2.29).

Moreover, this same Seyssel directly expressed the political advantage he saw for the royalty, both within and outside of France, in extending the territory of the French language. The extension of the language is a good way, a good *method*, to be precise, to establish or confirm its power over French and foreign territories. Seyssel had visited Italy, and in the course of his travels he had understood at once a Roman model of linguistic-military-political conquest and the chance for France to ensure a certain conquest of Italy in the same way. In a prologue to Justin that he had translated and offered to Louis XII, he gives a piece of advice:

> What did the Roman people and princes do when they held the monarchy of the world and sought to perpetuate it and make it eternal? They could find no more certain means than glorifying, enriching, and making more sublime their Latin language, which, from the beginning of their empire, was indeed meager and rude, and then communicating it to the countries and provinces and peoples they had conquered, together with their Roman laws couched in this language. (Brunot 2.30)

Seyssel then explains how the Romans were able to make Latin as perfect

as Greek, and he encourages the king to imitate these "illustrious con-
querors" and to "enrich" and "glorify" the French language.

You will have noticed in passing the insistence on right and law: it is in
the interest of the central power to "couch" [*coucher*] laws in the dominant
national language. This concern comes up against, in fact it merges with,
the properly philosophical or scientific project: to reduce the ambiguity of
language. The value of clarity and distinctness in the understanding of
words, in grasping significations, will at the same time be a juridical, administrative, police (and therefore political), *and philosophical* value. This
concern is found again in Descartes. If good sense is the most common
thing in the world, and since ignorance of the law is no excuse, the legal
text would still have to be read or comprehended through a linguistic
medium purified of all ambiguity, through a language that is not divisible
or does not dissipate into misunderstanding. The decree of Villers-Cotterêts specifies this in articles 110 and 111, which stipulate that the acts and
proceedings of justice would henceforth be carried out in French:

> And so that there is no cause to doubt the meaning of these decrees [in
> other words, so that the subjects of (the) French language may not use their ig-
> norance of the law, of the language of the law, namely Latin, as an excuse, and
> therefore so that French-speaking subjects in fact may be or become subjects of
> the law and subjects of the king, subjects subjugated to monarchial law with-
> out any possibility of being elsewhere in language, without the possibility of an
> alibi that could make them non-subjects excused by their ignorance of the
> law], we wish and command that they be made and written *so clearly* [my ital-
> ics], that there can be *no ambiguity* or *uncertainty* [I emphasize again these pre-
> Cartesian watchwords], nor any cause to ask for interpretation.
>
> And because such things often take place according to the understanding
> of the Latin words contained in these decrees, henceforth we wish all decrees,
> along with all other proceedings, whether of our sovereign and lower courts,
> or of registers, investigations, contracts, commissions, judgments, testaments,
> and whatever other acts and deeds of justice, or deriving from them, to be
> pronounced, recorded, and delivered in the French mother tongue and not
> otherwise. (Brunot 2.30)

One cannot stress enough the significance of this event, especially its
complicated structure, even though we are still dealing with it in its apparently external and juridical form. One of the complications or overdeterminations stems from the liberating aspect of this act. It appears to be
the release from a violent constraint, that of the Latin language, and to

put into question the privilege of those whose linguistic competence (in Latin) guaranteed them great power. According to this appearance, in a strategy of assuming power, the decree would nevertheless make the concession of moving toward the language that it itself calls the "mother" tongue of the nation's subjects; it seems in fact to move them gently, one might say, into the trap of their *own language*, as if the king were saying to them: in order to be subjects of the law—and of the king—you will finally be able to speak your "French mother tongue" (*langaige maternel françois*); as if they were being given back to the mother in order better to be subjugated to the father.

But not at all. The essential subjugation to the law of the monarchical State that was being constituted went hand in hand with another violence: at the same time as Latin, the provincial dialects were also being abolished. A number of the subjects in question did not understand French any better than Latin. French was so far from being their mother tongue that many did not understand a word of it. That language remained, if you will, paternal and scholarly; after Latin, it became the language of the law [*la langue du droit*], the language by law [*la langue de droit*]—because of the king. A new trap, in a way, put the dialects *before the law*: to plead in favor of a dialect, as to plead in a court *tout court, translation was necessary*; one had to learn French. Once one had learned French, the claim of dialects, the "maternal" reference, was ruined. Try to explain to somebody who holds both force and the force of law that you want to preserve your language. You will have to learn his to convince him. Once you have appropriated the language of power, for reasons of rhetorical and political persuasion, once you master it well enough to try to convince or to defeat someone, you are in turn defeated in advance and convinced of being wrong. The other, the king, has demonstrated through the fact *of translation* that he was right to speak his language and to impose it on you. By speaking to him in his language, you acknowledge his law and authority; you prove him right; you countersign the act that proves him right over you. A king is someone who is able to make you wait or take the time to learn his language in order to claim your rights, that is, to confirm his. I am not sketching the abstract schema of some structural necessity here, a kind of master-slave dialectic as a dialectic of languages rather than of consciousnesses. I am talking about a paradigmatic event. It happened when the representatives from Provence wanted to complain to the king about the obligation forced on them to *pass judg-*

ment in French, under the pretext that judgment must be passed clearly and distinctly. These representatives went up, as they say, to Paris. And here is what happened; I quote Ramus in his *Grammaire* (1572):

> But this gentle king, putting them off from month to month, and having his chancellor tell them he did not like to hear any language other than his own, gave them the opportunity to learn French carefully; then some time later they made their case known in French harangue. This was the ridiculous position of these orators who came to fight the French language, and nonetheless through this fight learned it, and thus showed that, since it was so easy for older people like them, it would be still easier for the young, and that it would only be fit, although the language stayed with the people, for the most notable men, having a public office, to have in their speech, as in their robes, some preeminence over their inferiors. (Brunot 2.31)

In such a dissymmetry is then established what cannot even be called a language contract, but rather the *sharing of a language* in which the subject (the subject subjugated by a force that is not primarily and simply linguistic, a force that consists first of all in the capacity to clear, to trace, to open and to control the road, the territory, the passage, the routes, the borders and border regions [*marches*], to inscribe and preserve its *own* traces there) must speak the language of the more powerful party to protest his rights and therefore to lose or alienate a priori and de facto the right that he claims. And that from then on is meaningless.

What I am suggesting here does not amount to subordinating language or the force of language, or indeed the war of languages as such, in relation to a pre- or nonlinguistic force, to a struggle or more generally to a relationship that is not one of language (a relationship that would not necessarily be one of war but also of love or desire). No, I am only emphasizing that this relationship of language must already, as such, be the power relationship of spacing, a body of writing to clear a path, in the most general and fullest sense of these words. It is on this condition that we have some chance of understanding what happens, for instance when a language becomes dominant, when an idiom takes power, and possibly State power.

Of course, a decree is never enough. Resistances to the juridical act have never ceased. Much more time should be devoted to analyzing them in all their complexity and duration, in all areas, including the university, where law continued to be taught and treatises (particularly philosophical ones) published in Latin. But already at the beginning of the following century, in 1624, it became possible to defend theses in French. It was not until 1680, however, that Colbert instituted the teaching of law in French. A very significant sign is related to this: no doubt in order to convert to Catholicism the children of Protestants who had remained in France, Louis XIV decided in 1698 to create free and compulsory public schools where teaching was essentially religious and where French—or, if that was not possible, patois—would be the only language of instruction. But this decision had no effect.

Not only was there resistance in the face of the act of law, then, a slowing of its effective application, but even the state of the law itself was not simple. It had to come to terms with a historico-linguistic structure that was also a highly differentiated territorial structure. The opposition of Paris or of Île-de-France to the provinces was already marked, and a good many legacies of this situation remain today. Thus, French was not imposed on the recently incorporated provinces (Bretagne in 1532, part of Lorraine in 1559, later, in the seventeenth century, Alsace, Roussillon, Artois, Flanders). Apart from administrative texts, the State had to accept the multiplicity of languages. And still in 1681, when it recognized the authority of the king, the city of Strasbourg was exempted from enforcing the decree of Villers-Cotterêts.

This history cuts across that of the relationships between vulgar and church language, that of the Bible and that of worship, all the debates that developed around these questions (in France and everywhere else in Europe) and whose treasury of arguments is still used today, particularly in regard to the language of worship, to prayer and to song. The Sorbonne declared unanimously in 1523 purely and simply that *translations must be prohibited.* In 1525 it held that it is

> neither expedient nor useful, indeed, given the circumstances, it would rather be injurious, for the Christian republic to authorize the appearance . . . of total or partial translations of the Bible; those that exist already should be suppressed rather than tolerated. (Brunot 2.22)

The Protestants complained:

> Est-ce bien faict qu'un Prince ne consente
> Les faicts du Christ estre à tous relatez
> Et en commun langage translatez? (see Brunot 2.23)

[Is it good that a Prince not consent
To the deeds of Christ being told to all
And translated into common language?]

To measure the complexity of the forces and motivations at stake, one would have to quote Montaigne: although one of the greatest inventors or initiators of French literary language, he nevertheless took a stand *against* popular language in worship and prayer:

> It is not a story to be told, but a story to be revered, feared and adored. Absurd people they are who, because they have put it into the language of the people, think they have made it easy to be understood by the people! . . .
>
> I believe moreover that the liberty given to anyone to disperse so sacred and important a word in so many kinds of idioms is much more dangerous than it is profitable. The Jews, the Mohammedans, and almost all others are wedded to and revere the language in which their mysteries were originally conceived, and any alteration and change in them is forbidden; and not without reason. Can we be sure that in the country of the Basques and in Brittany there are enough men of judgment to establish this translation into their own language?[12]

I suggested a moment ago that this history of the French language, as State institution, went through three great dramatic phases. Such a periodization can only be summary, and I take it as such. Moreover, each of these phases is original enough in itself to render more than problematic the assumption that all these events belong to one and the same history: a homogeneous history of France or of the only "French language." This schema helps us provisionally to pick out a first series of indications and thus to prepare another elaboration. The preliminary investigation of the "first phase," the recognition of a first configuration starting from some unquestionable symptoms, allows us perhaps to begin to read this apparently philosophical event: Descartes writes that he is writing the *Discourse on Method* in French. The philosophical, political, juridical, linguistic, and other implications of this gesture appear perhaps more clearly on the scene that we have just situated, even if this "situation" is still inadequate and only sketched out. And, conversely, by pursuing the "internal" and "philosophical" reading of Descartes' text, we will have a further opportunity to interpret the implications of the historical events that we have just evoked briefly. Not that Descartes talks about them or tells us the truth about them; let's say that they are "talked" about through his text, and it is left to us to translate or decipher it. Not in a conventional relation of text to context, of "internal" reading to "external" reading, but by preparing a redistribution or a recontextualization, that of a *single text*, which does not mean a continuous and homogeneous text.

This is why I have insisted somewhat on these premises and on this "first" phase of the process of French becoming the State language. The other two, of which I will say nothing here, would culminate in the "French Revolution" and in a certain current techno-scientific transformation. In the course of the French Revolution, the movement toward State control once again came up against the juridico-political problem of translation and the intelligibility of decrees. I will refer you here to *Une politique de la langue* by Michel de Certeau, Dominique Julia, and Jacques Revel.[13] Resistance to the Revolution was often interpreted by the revolutionaries as the result of a linguistic force and form. When linguistic politics are hardened, Barère wrote to the convention in a Report of the Committee for Public Safety, "Federalism and superstition speak low Breton; immigration and hatred of the Republic speak German; the counter-Revolution speaks Italian; and fanaticism speaks Basque." A French teacher was appointed in each commune where "the inhabitants speak a foreign idiom" (they were more careful with patois) in order to "enable the people to read and translate orally the laws of the Republic," to teach the language and the Declaration of the Rights of Man. Thus, they move to voice, against writing, which is suspected of "maintaining barbaric jargons."[14] The decree of the second Thermidor prohibited all idioms other than French in any act, even in private agreements. On the XVIth Prairial, Year II, Grégoire presented to the Convention his "Report on the Necessity and Means of Abolishing the Patois and Universalizing the Use of French."[15] No coercive conclusions were drawn from this report; and after Thermidor there was a return to a more tolerant practice. But we would understand nothing of the relation of the French to their language and to their spelling, or of the role of the Republican school in the nineteenth and twentieth centuries, if we did not keep such signals in mind.

Of the "third" great convulsion (and we are in it) I will say nothing. While retaining something of the two legacies we have just talked about, it is characterized in a newer and more specific way, *on the one hand, on the inside*, by a legally recognized reawakening of linguistic minorities (recognized all the more easily as it remains in the order of cultural memory and in no way threatens the linguistic unity of the nation-state), and, *on the other hand, on the outside*, by a struggle against the attempts at monopolization of techno-scientific language, through the techno-linguistic powers that dominate the world (commerce, the telecommunications industry, computerization, software, data banks, etc.). This is well known and I will not insist on it. I will content myself with saying that with regard to this modern problematic, whether it is a question of the complex and measured recourse to a national language, whether it is a question of its linguistics, its discourse on language, or even of a certain project for a universal language of which we will speak later, the Cartesian event of "I write in French, which is the language of my country" is not a past, a simple past, for us. For a reason other than the one I talked about in the beginning, its present is not simply grammatical.

In order to try to think this event since the writing in French of the *Discourse on Method*, what precautions should be taken in its reading and interpretation? One would first have to remember that there are at least three orders and three ranges of texts to consider.

There is the complex and heterogeneous whole, unevenly developed, one might say, of the socio-juridical or politico-religious history of language. We have just made some allusions to this. Others would be tempted to say that they constitute the *outside* of the Cartesian text. But this outside is inscribed *within* the text, and it would be difficult, without taking this inscription into account, to understand what happens when Descartes, justifying with his rhetoric his strategy and choice, decides to write *one* of his texts in French. What little I have said about this history is enough to hint at this: his act is not simply revolutionary, even if it seems relatively singular in the order of philosophy and if it looks something like a rupture. Though he in fact departs from a certain practice and renounces a dominant usage, and though he complicates his relationship with the Sorbonne, he nevertheless follows the tendency of the monarchist State; one might say that he goes in the direction of power and reinforces the establishing of French law. He translates the *cogito* as "je pense" ("I think"), another way of giving speech, but also the law, to the French legal subject. Moreover, and this is a benefit that is perhaps not secondary, he secures a certain clientele in the foreign courts where the use of French was fashionable. This complex strategy was not necessarily commensurate with the consciousness that the subject, beginning with the subject Descartes, could have of it, or with the declarations that this subject could make on this subject.

Yet the second corpus to be considered (the internal reading, one might say this time) is precisely all the utterances through which Descartes explains and justifies his choice. This corpus is divided in two. First, there is, inside the *Discourse* itself, the explicit declaration, the argued justification, the one I read at the beginning. It is rather cunning in itself and we must return to it, at least in our discussions. Then, in this corpus of explicit declarations on the choice of language, there are statements that are not in the *Discourse* itself, particularly in the letters. They concern at the same time a certain pedagogy, a certain pedagogical *facilitation*, aimed at feeble minds and at women (let's not forget that the necessity of, a certain demand for, "facility" is a watchword of Cartesian philosophy): it is a question of a book, he says, which he "wished to be intelligible even to women while providing matter for thought for the finest minds" (*Oeuvres* 1.560). This passage does not directly link the question of vulgar language to the question of women but, as we shall see, its argumentative logic links the two motifs.

The third order or third stratum of the text is the whole of the Cartesian corpus in what at least presents itself as its proper order, its "order of reasons [*ordre des raisons*]," its projected system, the presumed coherence between the linguistic event and the organized whole of its philosophemes. The linguistic event in this case is not limited to the choice of a natural language; it consists in that which links philosophical statements to *some* language (it is the question of the structure of statements such as *cogito ergo sum*, for example) and to a philosophy of language and signs.

Naturally, the treatment we could attempt of these three orders of corpus would be neither equal, equally divided, nor even dissociated or successive. I wanted to mark qualitative or structural boundaries between these orders of texts, even if they are not related to one another as a textual inside to a contextual outside; and even if each of them remains strongly differentiated. We will talk again in particular about the logic of Descartes' explicit declarations, in his letters and in the *Discourse on Method*, beginning with the end that I quoted at the beginning today and that I quote again to conclude:

> And if I write in French, which is the language of my country, rather than in Latin, which is that of my teachers, it is because I hope that those who use only their pure natural reason will better judge my opinions than those who believe only in old books, and because I am sure that those who combine good sense with scholarship, whom alone I wish to have as my judges, will not

be so partial to Latin as to refuse to hear my reasons because I express them in a vulgar tongue.

As you may suspect, this passage *disappears* pure and simple in Étienne de Courcelles's Latin translation, published in 1644, seven years after the original. The great Adam and Tannery edition indicates the omission of this passage. The sentence is sublime: "There was in fact no cause to translate [it]" (*il n'y avait pas lieu de [le] traduire en effet* [*Oeuvres* 6.583]).

Thus, in agreement with Descartes and according to good sense itself, good sense being more common than a language, a translation erases a series of statements that not only incontestably belong to the original, but speak and practice performatively the language in which this original is produced. They speak this language and speak *about* this language. Yet this is where they founder, in their form and their content, body and soul, one might say, at the instant of translation. It is good sense itself: what sense would it make to say in Latin "I am speaking French," as you can see? Or to say and do it, right here, in English?

Thus, when an "original" speaks about its language by speaking its language, it prepares a kind of *suicide by translation*, as one says suicide by gas or suicide by fire. Suicide by fire, rather, for it lets itself be destroyed almost without remainder, without apparent remainder *inside* the corpus.

This tells us a great deal about the status and function of what one could call the self-referential signs of an idiom in general, of a discourse or a writing in its relationship to the linguistic idiom, for instance, but also in its relationship to all idiomaticity. The (metalinguistic and linguistic) *event* is then doomed to be erased in the translating structure. Now, this translating structure does not begin, as you know, with what is commonly called translation. It begins as soon as a certain type of reading of the "original" text is instituted. It erases but also exposes that which it resists and which resists it. It offers up language to be read in its very erasure: the erased traces of a path (*odos*), of a track, the path of erasure. The *translatio*, the translation, *die Übersetzung* is a path that passes over or beyond the path of language, passing its path.[16]

Translation is passing its path, right here.

—*Translated by Sylvia Söderlind*

If There Is Cause to Translate II: Descartes' Romances, or The Economy of Words

Last time, we interpreted a historical sequence in the course of which a certain politics of language asserted itself. We analyzed its logic, its cunning, its dissymmetry. It was one of the three great sequences of a history of French as a State language. In it was inscribed the event entitled *Discourse on Method*, at least insofar as this latter was written "in French . . . the language of my country." We then distinguished the three types of texts that we should discuss, whether successively or simultaneously. We were constantly interested (at the beginning and end of the last session) in the mode of that declaration that is so committed to its own language that it has no chance of lending itself to translation: someone declares, in the first person present indicative, that he is declaring what he declares in such and such a language; this language turns out to be his own language, that of his country or his natural, native, or national language, but this is not essential either to the structure of this utterance or to what in it defies translation. If Descartes had written in Latin, "I am writing in Latin," the problem would have been the same.

Now, we paused for a moment on the fact that this passage ("And if I write in French, which is the language of my country . . . ") was omitted from the Latin translation that Descartes himself revised, as if a sentence given to remarking, in a certain language, that it was written in that language has no meaning that a translation as such could preserve, at least insofar as one relies on a certain concept of translation.

However, this sentence does have a meaning, a meaning that is rather simple and easy, in the end, to translate. Its resistance to translation is not of the same order as that of a poem, at least in its formal effects or its se-

mantic overdeterminations. It has an affinity with the poem only insofar
as the latter, one might say, always implies—even if it does not actually
declare this—an affirmation that it belongs to a natural language, indeed
to the "proper" language of the writer.

But if Descartes' sentence has a clear and distinct meaning, the present
tense of its utterance is irreducibly bound to a language that forms not
only—as goes without saying—the signifying fabric of this *presentation*,
but also the signified theme: to change language is, in this case, to oblit-
erate the very heart of the "signified." It is no longer—as is often the risk
with translations—simply a case of altering the signifier, the signified, or
the structure of their relation in such and such a ratio; it is rather a question of destroying, pure and simple, the essential import of the sentence—and of the whole paragraph, of the whole text itself, which,
whether directly or not, depends on it.

Thus, this sentence is not simply untranslatable. What happens with it
is both more serious and more singular. Others might say that it is less serious and more banal, and with good reasons—the first of which being
that at this very moment I am speaking to you in English, having written
this in French, and apparently no catastrophe has resulted. Also, when I
said that the sentence "And if I write in French . . . " (note this syntax,
and the subtle play of the "if") resisted translation, I was pushing to its
limits a situation that made Adam and Tannery say, more reasonably,
"There was no cause to translate" (*il n'y avait pas lieu de traduire*). The
French expression "il n'y a pas lieu," "there is no cause," crosses several
codes, among others the juridical code of obligation ("one must not," "it
is forbidden"), the code of technical utility (it is not useful or expedient),
and the code of social propriety or decorum (it is not done, it is out of
place). Now, in fact, what would be the counter-indication for a translation *that would present itself as such* and whose reader would know full
well that it refers back to an absent original? We can easily imagine a
Latin translation saying, "Here is why I am writing in a vulgar tongue, in
the language of my country, which happens to be French." And indeed
this is what happened in the translations into living languages (English,
German, etc.). It is enough for these translations to *present themselves* as
translations from French—which is in any case readable and made clear
by this very sentence—for any ambiguity to be lifted. That is why, indeed, this would not be serious: the text then says to you, "I am a translation, you are in the midst of reading a translation that presents itself as

the translation of an original that presents itself as originally written in the language of the writer."

Now, I am claiming that this is precisely what already occurs in the French, in what we are here calling the original. And only this can explain an omission, in the only Latin version there is, of a paragraph that the translations into living languages have never erased. This is because the Latin version of this text, assuming that we should still call it a translation, has an altogether different status. This has to do with the historical and political situation that we discussed last time. Latin is not one foreign language among others. And this translation into Latin is not a translation, at least insofar as a translation presents itself as such by referring back, by contract, to an original. In this case it is less a question of deriving or "leading out" from an original language toward a second language (as the text says, speaking of *leading out* [*aconduire*] from Greek or Latin into these border regions [*marches*])—it is less a question of *aconduire* than of *reconduire, leading back toward* what *should have been*, by rights, the original language. There was cause [*il y avait lieu*], in a situation judged to be *normal and normative*, for books of science, law, and philosophy to be written in Latin. Why did Descartes consent to a Latin translation, to a translation into a "dead" language? Where has it ever been understood that there was cause to translate a living language into a dead language— a language that no one *speaks anymore*? The translation here is that of writing, from a possible speech into writing. If Descartes yielded, it was first of all before a law, a norm, a social contract that was still dominant in certain circles: one had first to write in Latin those texts for which French could only be a vulgarizing language—and that means philosophy. And if by chance, by a deviation or even a transgression, one *made the pretence* of beginning with the vulgar language, if one began in short with the translation, there was still cause [*il y avait lieu*] to return quickly to the supposedly normal language of origin, which should have remained Latin. The Latin version is thus nothing more than a *restitution*, a call to order or a return to order. Only this can explain the embarrassed explanations, indeed the anxious justifications, of Descartes in the French version.

Two remarks here of a very different order.

1. We are speaking of a logic and a topology, also of a phoronomy of translation. A *translatio* goes from one linguistic place to another, from an origin to a nonorigin that *will have* had to be or *should have been, by rights,*

and in the language of right or law [droit] the origin. This movement trans-
ports that which already appeared to be *at work* in translation, and this
path that does not follow a straight line circulates between language, in the
common sense of a spoken language, and the text, in the strict sense of a
written language. To translate the *Discourse* into Latin was to convey it in
writing, or to make it readable under certain conditions and for certain
readers—for all subjects who were competent in certain areas, even if they
were not competent, linguistically speaking, in French. English, Italian,
and German scholars could read, in this language of writing that Latin was,
the *Dissertatio de Methodo* (1644) even if they could not understand the
Discours of 1637. *Discours* sounds closer, moreover, to the spoken, *Dissertatio* to the written. Even if the Latin version is a restoration to writing and
to law [*droit*], let us not conclude too hastily that the vocalization of the
Discourse had the value of transgression or emancipation. We have confirmed that it gives the dignity of writing and of the law to other forces that
are in the course of becoming forces of law, namely those of a monarchic
State. Likewise, during the Revolution, it was in the name of the law that
teachers came into the communes in order to *declare* the laws in French.
We might have been tempted to think these translating itineraries as passages between two poles (law/nonlaw, writing/speech, death/life, dead language / living language, paternal language / maternal language, etc.). But
not at all—and this is perhaps the essential point of what is thus shown:
the violence comes from *both* sides; each term of the opposition is marked
by the *other* side. There are always two forces of breakthrough [*frayage*] and
of resistance, each one bearing life and death at once.

2. In speaking of *restitution*, I was not referring to a virtual and hidden
structure. *In fact*, to a large extent, what discourse of method there is in
the work that bears this title can be read also as the French translation of
the *Regulae ad Directionem Ingenii* (Rules for the Direction of the Mind),
a text that was written in Latin, eight years before the *Discourse*: a hidden
original as it were, since it was not published during its author's lifetime,
but circulated outside of France. We know that Leibniz read it. The *Regulae*, then, would be, in Latin and precisely before its literal writing, a *Dissertatio de Methodo*. The word "method" and the "viatic" vocabulary are
plentiful here, and there is also the issue of rules: technical and ethical pre-
cepts, a deontology of knowledge or of research, in "the search for truth
[*la recherche de la vérité*]" (as the title of Rule IV also puts it). Rules: the

word expresses well what is to be done [*ce qu'il y a lieu de faire*], in a regular, recurrent, repetitive, and thus formalizable manner, in order to be conducted and to conduct oneself well on the path of knowledge when one wants precisely to direct one's mind, to direct oneself, to lead it *straight* (*recte*), on the right path, in the right *direction*, to the right *address*. Thus a Latin treatise will have preceded, almost secretly, the French discourse that henceforth resembles, to an extent that is yet to be determined, a vulgarizing translation, a translating itinerary. As for the *method* and the cartography of the path, as for the motif of the "path" (I prefer "motif" to "figure" or "metaphor" for reasons that I explained or will explain elsewhere, and also because "motif" at least retains the sense of movement; as does "metaphor," you will say—but without any other rhetorical presuppositions)—as for this motif, I will only say a word about it here, saving the longer developments for the discussions and seminar sessions. The motif of the path, of *chemin*, of *via*, as you know, is already determinative in the *Regulae*. This unfinished text also had, in its own adventures, a "viatic" destiny: it returned from its voyage with other papers, in a trunk found at the bottom of the Seine. The boat that brought them from Rouen to Paris sank. The *Regulae* had to be spread out to dry, which, the biographer Baillet says, "could not be done without much confusion in the hands of some servants who did not possess the intelligence of their master for maintaining their order and arrangement."[1] The order of reasons presupposes the intelligence of the master. Clerselier, the French ambassador to Stockholm, Descartes' friend and heir—at least the heir to these papers—had classified the *Regulae* among the texts whose publication was not urgent: no doubt because it was not only unfinished but also written in Latin and thus had little chance of interesting that "general" [*grand*] public to whom Clerselier wanted to introduce Descartes. In his Preface to Volume 2 of the *Letters*, in fact, he notes,

> The booksellers informed me that the large number of letters in Latin in the first volume led several people, who are not conversant with that language, not to buy it and even to tell others that the most beautiful part of the book was hidden from them.[2]

Just like today, then too it was the bookseller who indicated, when questioned, that philosophical books written in a certain language are not in great demand. In order to sell, one must change languages, order one's discourse in relation to the reading capacity of the greatest number of buyers possible. And this gap between ordinary language [*langage*] and a "difficult" (esoteric or formalized) language [*langue*] can be even greater within one and the "same" language than between two separate idioms. We don't even have to transpose it to perceive the present relevance of the problem: pedagogical, academic, editorial, economic, political, and so forth.

By writing in the vulgar tongue, Descartes wanted to facilitate the access to *facility* (a motif we will speak of during the seminar), to avoid the detour through the knowledge archived away in ancient books. So he took into account the philosophical fragility of "weak minds," explaining this with some discomfort in a letter to Silhon (a philosopher and Mazarin's secretary). His letter (of May 1637) begins by saying that he wanted to give reasons that were "easy for everyone":

> I agree, as you observe, that there is a great defect in the work you have seen, and that I have not expounded, in a manner that *everyone can easily grasp* [my emphasis], the arguments by which I think I can prove that there is nothing at all so evident and certain [thus easiest] in itself as the existence of God and of the human soul. But I did not dare to try to do so, since I would have had to explain at length the strongest arguments of the skeptics.[3]

The "weak minds" he addresses in French are not sufficiently equipped by the School, nor experienced in philosophical discipline. Descartes is afraid: they will yield to the arguments of the skeptics, which I will be using in a merely rhetorical, methodical, and provisory way. Because they are weak, they won't know how to make their way or return to what is easiest, to the evidence of clear and distinct ideas, to the *cogito*, to the natural light of "pure reason" by which the existence of God can be proven, and so forth. They will let themselves be impressed by skeptical doubt, by the newly learned argument of the school. The road toward what is easiest— this nonroad, this point of departure, so close to oneself that is intuitive evidence—will be barred to them. A strategic paradox, which stems from the historical and linguistic situation: by writing in French to facilitate matters for the weak minds (insufficiently schooled or scholasticized), Descartes can no longer move with such assurance toward what is easiest and most certain, the absolute value of this philosophical methodology. Later on he says,

> But I was afraid that this introduction [which he has just reconstructed] would look at first as if it was designed to bring in skepticism, and would disturb weaker minds, especially as I was writing in the vulgar tongue.[4] (*Letters* 35; *Oeuvres* 1.353–354).

Choosing to write in a vulgar language in order to appeal more easily to "natural reason," which the School and ancient books have not yet managed to dim and obscure, which dogmatism, intolerant of doubt, has not yet impressed, Descartes finds himself forced to take on a certain facility, in the pejorative sense of the word. This hinders access to "good" facility. This is the fault neither of the vulgar language nor of the weakness of minds, of their natural "imbecility," that of untrained minds. It is institutional, attributable to the School and to the tradition. Weak and not forewarned, these virgin minds that understand only French will let themselves be intimidated by skeptical doubt: the argument of the School, archived, typed, ritualized. And yet *order* must free the mind from sensualism, from the spontaneous dogmatism that prevents one from doubting sense certainties. This order requires the *passage* through skeptical doubt—at least through the schema of its argument, through its language and rhetoric—in order to transform skeptical doubt into methodical doubt. Now, this language and this rhetoric of skeptical doubt are bound, historically, to the language of the School and to Latin. So Descartes dreads the paradoxical and pernicious effects of this order on the "weak minds" that receive it, out of context, in their own mother tongue. Thus he must renounce this bad facility. The recipient of this letter, Silhon, is not part of the society of "weak minds" but rather of that of the scholars whom Descartes "wishes to be [his] judges." He will not let himself be led astray by the vulgar tongue:

> But as for intelligent people like yourself, Sir, if they take the trouble not only to *read* but also to meditate *in order* the same things I say I meditated, spending a long time on each point, to see whether I have gone wrong, I trust that they will come to the same conclusions as I did. (*Letters* 35; *Oeuvres* 1.354; my emphasis)

Language, especially that of the written text, thus remains secondary in Descartes' eyes. He demands that one not be content with merely reading; one must also meditate in order. This order is not that of reading or writing; it is that of reasons—and this is the essential order.

We find the same argument again in the famous letter to Père Vatier (February 22, 1638). But instead of "weak minds," here we read "women."

> It is true that I have been too obscure in what I wrote about the existence of God in this treatise on Method, and I admit that although it is the most important, it is the least worked out section in the whole book. That is partly be-

cause I did not decide to include it until I had nearly completed it and the publisher was becoming impatient [note the modernity of the strategy, the problematic of philosophical vulgarization, of the media, of editorial pressures, etc.]. But the principal reason for its obscurity is that I did not dare [same argument, same wording as in the other letter] go into detail about the arguments of skeptics, nor to say everything which is necessary *ad abducendam mentem a sensibus* [the Latin for coded argument!]: for the certainty and evidence of my kind of argument for the existence of God cannot really be known without a distinct memory of the arguments which display the uncertainty of all our knowledge of material things; and these thoughts did not seem to me suitable for inclusion in a book which *I wished to be intelligible even to women* [my emphasis] while providing matter for thought for the finest minds. (*Letters* 46; *Oeuvres* 1.560)

Always the same strategy: two publics, two destinations, two discourses, indeed two languages, so as to reach as many readers as possible and to train as many philosophers in the "right" facility. Not *everyone* can understand *everything*, especially not women; but let us do something so that they can at least "understand something." We would have to undertake a long and difficult analysis in order fully to understand, in turn, this allusion to the philosopher-women and to the unscholarly women of the era, to those who would like to understand something of the philosophy reserved, like the School, for men: we would have to analyze the situation of women in that period, according to social classes, their relation to education, the premises of "feminist" movements, and so forth. Unable to undertake such an analysis here, I must note, however, that such an inquiry would be essentially insufficient if it did not integrate—letting itself be affected by it as well—the Cartesian problematic of natural (that is, universal) reason and of its relations with language, whether learned or vulgar. This inquiry would thus be inadequate if it did not integrate this immense problem of translation that cannot be separated from it, any more than the event of the *Discourse on Method* can be. The complexity of a "feminist" strategy would be proportionate to the crafty and convoluted complexity of the Cartesian strategy: must women learn Latin and train themselves scholastically in order to claim for themselves philosophical authority and masculine power, with the paradoxical risks that accompany such a claim? Or must they on the contrary demand that one "speak" knowledge, philosophy, law, and in particular, medicine, in one's own mother tongue? You know the record: it is far from being limited to what our schools would have us read by way of Molière's *Les femmes savantes* or *Les précieuses ridicules.*

Descartes wanted to *speak to women*, and to say to them in effect: there is a natural reason; good sense is the most common thing in the world; we must speak a language that is accessible to everyone. This movement, of course, goes against any exclusion of women. It can even lead one to think that by having escaped teachers, Latin and the School, women might be more "virginal" and thus more apt to surrender to what is easiest, most intuitive, most philosophical. The "price to pay" for this "progress" or "process" or "trial" [*procès*] would always be the same: the erasure of sexual difference in and by philosophy. Order, the straight and essential path, that path that goes from what is least easy to what is easiest, would be an *intelligible* order, thus "desexed," without a body. The necessary passages, in the order of demonstrations (the doubt of sensible things, the *I think, I am*, God exists, etc.), are sexually neutral or indifferent. The *cogito* is related, in its thinking as in its utterance, in the grammar of its sentence, to a subject that bears no sexual mark, since it is a *res cogitans* and not a body. As always, this neutralization produces ambiguous effects. It opens up for women access to a universal community and to philosophy (which one might consider progress), but at the cost of a neutralization of sexual difference, now relegated to the side of the body, inessential to the act of the *cogito*, to intuition, to reason, to natural knowledge, and so forth. The subjectivity of the subject that is thus founded in the Cartesian gesture would remain—whether it is a question of the body or of language—sexually undifferentiated. Perhaps it is not even enough, as I have attempted to suggest elsewhere, to deconstruct the Cartesian subject and to propose instead an analytic of *Dasein* in order not to reproduce this "neutralization."[5]

Descartes was nothing less than revolutionary in speaking in such a way as "to be intelligible even to women." He is following a profound movement of the era, a movement born in a certain milieu before him and that developed mainly around him. The reaction against Latin was intense: it was felt to be a pedantic, indeed a barbaric language; it became indecent, indeed impolite, to resort to it in certain situations, and one had to excuse oneself in these cases. The movement did not fade. Several decades later, in his *Doutes sur la langue françoise* (1674), Père Bouhours stages society people who wonder whether one should use the word *inamissibilité*, which "is a little Latin," and which "still smacks a bit of the barbarism of the School."

As for me, interrupted M. le Chevalier, I don't believe it is French; at most, it is a foreigner dressed *à la française*, he added, laughing. Since I don't understand it at all, said Mme la Marquise, I assure you that I would have no difficulty going without it.[6]

In this battle for the French language and against Latin or the School, the place of women is essential, at least in certain social spheres, first and foremost at court. Because they have never been taught Latin and the discipline of the School, women are supposed to have a better rapport with the mother tongue, a better feel for language. They are, in short, the true guardians of the vulgar language. Look at Vaugelas and his famous *Remarques sur la langue françoise* (1647). He wrote that good usage is "the manner of speaking of the soundest part of the court in conformity with the manner of writing of the soundest of the authors of the day."[7] Now, this great chastiser of language also insisted on the fact that "women, like men" were a part of this normative elite. He even added, "In regards to doubts about language, it is ordinarily better to consult women than men and those who have not studied than those who are learned in Greek and Latin."

Yet in his concern to put language at the service of natural reason or natural light, Descartes could not plead, pure and simple, however, for *one* mother tongue, even if it were his own. He also had to invoke his vows for a universal language. He did so. But if we are to take an interest in this related dimension of his thinking on language, we must backtrack, as if returning toward the premises, and at the same time accept a kind of discontinuity in the path we are taking. This is inevitable in so short a time (two talks on such rich problems and such entangled texts). We are only situating preliminary points of reference, and we will attempt, during the lectures and working sessions, to reconstruct some continuity.

I also need a guiding thread for this new stage in the reading of Descartes. Perhaps in order to honor the contract of this lecture, which was supposed to deal also with "literary and poetic language as linked to the problem of their translation," I will choose the romance, the word "roman," as my guiding thread.[8]

Descartes used it several times. I will isolate two occurrences of it. The first is at the end of his famous letter to Mersenne, from Amsterdam, on November 20, 1629 (the period of the *Regulae*, almost ten years before the *Discourse*). He is responding to the proposal of an admirable "new language." An ambivalent response and the counterproposal of a universal language:

> I maintain that this language is possible and that it is possible to discover the science on which it depends: it would make peasants better judges of the truth about the world than philosophers are now. But do not hope ever to see it in use. That would require great changes in the order of things—the whole world would need to become nothing but an earthly paradise, which is worth proposing only in the land of *romance* [*le pays des* romans]. (*Letters* 6; *Oeuvres* 1.81–82; my emphasis)

This is the end of the letter. Everything takes place as if—one can fantasize—Descartes were giving up here on the idea of a universal language for the peasants and was resigning himself to writing, a few years later, in a natural language for women.

The second occurrence is ten years later, in the "Letter from the author to the translator of this book (which can serve here as Preface)." The preface in question is to *Principes de la Philosophie* (Principles of Philosophy), a *real* preface in the guise of a *fictive* preface. Descartes says what he would have said if he had written a preface, which in fact he is in the midst of doing in denying it, that is, in confessing it:

> I would also have added a word of advice concerning the way to read this book, which is that I would like it first read rapidly in its entirety, like a *romance* [*roman*], without the reader forcing his attention too much or stopping at the difficulties which he may encounter in it, simply to have a broad view of the matters which I have treated in it. (my emphasis)[9]

After which he recommends, as you know, reading the book three times.

The word "roman" does not have the same meaning in the two contexts. In the letter, it is a work of the imagination, the fabulous description of an unreal country, a fictitious paradise. The preface, on the other hand, insists on a certain mode of reading: to read a romance is to be taken up in a story, to run through a narration without meditating, without reflecting, and without backtracking. Despite these differences of inflection or accent, the allusion to the romance in both cases touches on the notion of *order*: the order of exposition or of reading in the *Principles*; and the order of things that *should* be—but *cannot* be—changed in the letter ("The whole world would need to become nothing but an earthly paradise, which is worth proposing only in the land of romance").

Now, the romance is not to be confused with the fable. It implies the fabulous but cannot be reduced to this. Let me refer you here to the chapter "Mundus est fabula" in Jean-Luc Nancy's admirable book *Ego sum.*[10] For my own purposes, I will insist on what in the romance is not simply fable.

The fable no doubt has several features in common with the romance. Recall the beginning of the *Discourse*:

> But regarding this Treatise simply as a history, or, if you prefer it, a fable in which, along with the example which may be imitated, there are possibly others also which it would not be right to follow. (*Discourse* 5; *Oeuvres* 6.4)

The fable is a narrative, or *récit,* whose factual truth need not be verified. But it can have the exemplary signification of a truth:

> Many other things would remain for me to explain and I would even be happy to add a few arguments to make my opinions more realistic. But to make the lengthy discourse less tedious, I want to veil part of it in the invention of a fable through which I hope the truth will appear sufficiently and will be no less pleasing to see than if I showed it unadorned.[11]

A fiction that allows the essence to appear, the fable bears truth, exhibits it or displays it in an attractive fashion. It makes the truth desirable. The romance avoids tedium, but the similarity stops there. For in his other uses of the word "roman" Descartes does not seem to acknowledge this value of truth:

> But I considered that I had already given sufficient time to languages and likewise to the reading of ancient books, both their histories and their fables. For conversing with those of other centuries is almost the same thing as traveling. . . . But when one employs too much time in traveling, one becomes a stranger in one's own country, and when one is too curious about things which were practiced in past centuries, one is usually very ignorant about those which are practiced in our own time. Besides, fables make one imagine many events possible which in reality are not so, and even the most accurate of histories, if they do not exactly misrepresent or exaggerate the value of things in order to render them more worthy of being read, at least omit in them all the circumstances which are basest and least notable; it follows from this fact that what is retained is not portrayed as it really is, and that those who regulate their conduct by examples which they derive from such examples are liable to fall into the extravagances of the knights-errant of romance, and form projects beyond their power.
>
> I esteemed eloquence most highly and I was enamoured of Poesy, but I thought that both were gifts of the mind rather than fruits of study. (*Discourse* 6; *Oeuvres* 6.6)

We are thus coming close to the philosophy of language, of *langue* or *langage*, that was announced in the letter of 1629 to Mersenne. Descartes finishes by proposing what I will call a *possible impossible* language, the possibility of an impossible language: "I maintain that this language is possible. . . . But do not hope ever to see it in use. That would require great changes in the order of things—the whole world would need to become nothing but an earthly paradise, which is worth proposing only in the land of romance."

The "land of romance" [*pays des romans*] would have an essential relation with the possible-impossible of language, rather than with a universal philosophical language, something like a completed tower of Babel. Think of Kafka's short story "The City Coat of Arms."[12] This fiction on the theme of the tower of Babel harmonizes ironically with a Cartesian thematic, topic, and rhetoric: the recourse to the figure of a city that is to be constructed from the ground up and raised to the roof (see *Discourse*, Second Part and *passim*), this ascending movement, these stairways, all of this tells of the philosophical enterprise as a systematic edification that is, however, indefinitely deferred, from generation to generation: "At first all the arrangements for building the Tower of Babel were characterized by fairly good order. . . . To this must be added that the second or third generation had already recognized the senselessness of building a heaven-reaching tower; but by that time everybody was too deeply involved to leave the city" (36–39). (The city, it would seem, is Prague: "The city has a closed fist on its coat of arms"; I believe Descartes went there.) We cannot separate this architectonics from a linguistics.

When he replies to Mersenne, who has just informed him of a certain Hardy's proposed project of a new language, Descartes had already written the *Regulae*. He had already conceived the project of a kind of universal characteristic granted to the *mathesis universalis* of Rule IV. In this context, mathematics is the general science explaining everything that can be researched on the subject of order and measure. This is a Platonic and immediately post-Platonic (Speusippus) tradition as well, and is presented in Aristotle's *Metaphysics* (E 1026a, 26–27 and K 1061b, 19, for example): mathematics as the common and universal science, without any particular object. For Descartes, it is both the most necessary and the *easiest* science. The motif of facility is linked essentially with this science. And the project of a universal characteristic, which is outlined in the *Regulae* and announced in the letter to Mersenne, covers the entire axiomatics of facility, of technical power, of the "faculty" that we will be following elsewhere in the course of these lectures. Rule IV:

> As I reflected carefully, it finally became clear to me that only, and all, those matters in which order and measure are investigated are related to mathematics, and that it makes no difference whether we are to seek out this measure in the domain of numbers, figures, stars, sounds, or elsewhere. Consequently I realized that there must be a general science which explains everything it is possible to study which touches on order and measurement without being restricted to any particular subject matter. And I realized that this science was to be called universal mathematics—not an artificial name, but one of long standing which has passed into common use [he had recalled earlier that "it is not enough to consider the etymology of the word; for the word 'mathematics' means nothing more than 'science' . . . " etc.], because this science contains everything by virtue of which the other sciences are called branches of mathematics. We can easily see now how much it surpasses the other sciences in utility and simplicity, by the fact that it applies to the very same objects as these, and many others besides. (*Oeuvres* 10.377–78)

The project of *mathesis universalis*—or, as Husserl will say, of formal ontology—presupposes that the investigation not be stopped by the equivocations of language. In order to formalize and mathematize, all the obscurities, ambiguities, and equivocations of natural language must be overcome. Even before proposing a simple and univocal system of notation, Rule XIII prescribes going from words to things. It would be enough to cross the equivocal thickness of words toward things to dispel philosophical controversies among the learned. This optimism, which later will orient the return to the vulgar language, implies a linguistic instrumentalism, the effects of which we will soon examine. Words, the lexicon, and syntax remain to appoint techniques external to intuitive and deductive thought. It is enough simply to be vigilant as to their condition (univocality, facility, transparency), in order for philosophical communication to erase any misunderstanding. How can we reconcile this optimism—whose logic sustains the project of a universal characteristic—with renouncing the adoption of this universal language, worthwhile only for the "land of romance"? What relation is there between this writing and this land of romance?

Rule XIII recalls that the investigation goes from words to things, from effects to causes, from causes to effects, from parts to whole, or indeed to other parts, or, finally, all these things at once—which opens the philosophy of the simple to its own labyrinth (we will talk, outside this session, about method and the labyrinth in Descartes, about his Ariadne's thread).

> We say that the investigation goes from words to things whenever the diffi-
> culty lies in the obscurity of the expression used: not only do all riddles belong
> to this group—like that of the Sphinx, about the animal which at first has
> four feet, then two feet and finally three feet . . . but in the majority of issues
> which provoke controversy among scholars, it is almost always a question of
> words. . . . These verbal questions arise so frequently that if only philosophers
> could always come to some kind of understanding as to the meaning of their
> terms, we would see almost all controversy disappear. (*Oeuvres* 10. 433–434)

Note Descartes' prudence: he says "almost always" and "the majority of issues."

From the *Regulae* on, an *economy*, a principle of economy, guides the facility of the *mathesis* as well as the facility of an unequivocal language; indeed, beyond language, it guides the facility of a system of notation that
would economize on words—since these themselves can be obscure.
"Faire l'économie des mots": this is an expression in Rule XIV. How can
one designate something that, while necessary to reach a conclusion,
nonetheless does not demand the mind's immediate attention? How can
one come to the aid of memory while avoiding the risks that its weakness
makes us run? One must use "concise signs" (*per brevissimas notas*), always
by *economy*. Since memory is "labile" (*labilis*), we must economize or
spare its efforts: "art" (*ars*) has invented, "most aptly" (*aptissime*), the use
of writing (*scribendi usum*). By committing these economical notations to
paper, to the *charta* (*in charta*), we can free thought for its own movement. One precaution should be taken: in each case we must set aside a
single and arbitrary sign for each single unity, for each *one*, atomic element by atomic element. We will designate by a single sign everything
that must be regarded as *one* for the purposes of resolving a difficulty. This
sign itself will be forged, feigned, invented, arbitrary—whence the recourse to a certain fabulating, if not romanesque or novelistic, *fiction*, in
the invention of this artificial writing: "Per unicam notam designabimus,
quae fingi potest ad libitum" (we shall designate it by a single sign, which
can be constructed as we please; *Oeuvres* 10.455). After giving some examples (letters and numbers), Descartes proceeds:

> By means of this system, not only will we economize on many words but
> moreover—all this is the main point—we shall manage to exhibit the terms of

our difficulty in such a pure and unencumbered way that even though nothing useful will have been omitted, nonetheless nothing superfluous will be found herein, nor anything which might risk preoccupying our mental powers to no avail, since the mind must grasp a number of things at once. (*Oeuvres* 10.455)

Perhaps now we can better understand Descartes' response (both receptive and reserved, both attentive and slightly jealous) to the "Hardy" project for a new language, in 1629, after the completion of the *Regulae*. He calls the project "admirable," but multiplies his objections to the claims that this Hardy—about whom we know nothing—would have made in order to "advertise his drug" (yet another person who proposes a new technique of language or writing, getting himself accused of introducing drugs into a culture),[13] or furthermore, says Descartes, "to praise his wares" or "overcome such a drawback" (*Letters* 3–4; *Oeuvres* 1.77, 78, 79). Reproaching Hardy for not having understood that the language to be sought must depend on "true Philosophy" (*Letters* 6; *Oeuvres* 1.81), Descartes reveals his own project of a universal language, the very one he ends up saying would be worth proposing only in the land of romance.

Here, then, is a letter on the romance of language or on the language of romance, if not on romance languages [*langue romane*]. It introduces us to the philosophy of language that will be proposed later, in the *Discourse*. (By analyzing it during another of these lectures, we will try to specify the import of the *cogito* as an act of thinking *and* as a speech act.)

Right in the first paragraph, Descartes announces plainly that even though he finds the proposal "admirable," he is disappointed when he looks at it more closely. The basis of his criticism falls immediately into place. There are two things to learn in every language, syntax and semantics; or, in the terms Descartes borrows here from the most solid (but also the most problematic) tradition, "the meaning of words and grammar" (*Letters* 3; *Oeuvres* 1.76). On neither of these levels has Hardy proposed anything new or satisfactory. As for "the meaning of words," Descartes has an easy time ironizing on Hardy's fourth proposal, which prescribes "linguam illam interpretari dictionario," which, says Descartes, "a man somewhat versed in languages can do without him in all the common languages" (*Letters* 3; *Oeuvres* 1.76). If it is a question of forging a language that is learned simply by looking up the meanings of words in a dictionary, one can do this for any language, including even "Chinese." If not everyone can do this, it is on account of the difficulty of grammar: "And I believe that is our man's entire secret" (*Letters* 3; *Oeuvres* 1.77). Yet that, according to Descartes, should be very easy, once one forges or configures an absolutely simplified language: just one conjugation, one declension, one construction, without defective or irregular sounds, which "arise from the corruption of use" (*Letters* 3; *Oeuvres* 1.77). This implies an interpretation, on Descartes' part, of the structure and history of language, of its process of degeneration; this process would be linked accidentally to historical usage and not to the original essence of the idiom; degeneration would thus take the form of a useless complication, an irregularity measured against an original regularity or simplicity that is to be restored. Likewise, in Hardy's new language (just one conjugation, one declension, one construction, without defects or irregularities), nouns and verbs will be inflected only by affixes, before or after "primitive words" (*les mots primitives*) (*Letters* 3; *Oeuvres* 1.77). It is impossible to tell whether this expression, "primitive words" (which is Pascal's as well, and indeed common enough), is in Hardy's text or only in Descartes' letter. It is a question of words whose unity of meaning can be neither broken down nor derived. These are simple and originary elements, so many stopping points for analysis. Descartes seems to put forward as his own the hypothesis that such words exist in all languages. Since his project of a universal (possible-impossible), true, and romanesque language presupposes simple ideas, it seems to go without saying that the "primitive words" must correspond to these. Descartes' universal language, which we will come to later, will be constructed on the basis of something like these primitive words. For the moment, the point is to denigrate Hardy, less for the sake of exposing him to difficulties or objections than for the banality—indeed the facility—of his proposal. If one has a new dictionary and such a simplified grammar at one's disposal, "it is no wonder if ordinary people learn to write the language with a dictionary in less than six hours, which is the subject of his first proposition" (*Letters* 3; *Oeuvres* 1.77).

Up to this point, Descartes has been reproaching Hardy only for the extreme banality of his invention: he has reinvented the wheel! It is difficult not to have the impression of bad faith mingled with jealousy or resentment. For after having facilely ironized on the facility of the invention, Descartes paradoxically emphasizes the difficulties there would be in getting the new language accepted and used. Before elaborating on the practical difficulty of this theoretical facility, Descartes drops a few spiteful remarks on the sort of promotional discourse in which Hardy packages a philosophically mediocre product, in order to "advertise his drug" or "praise his wares." These digs tell us more about Descartes' resentment than about what he claims to be discussing. A classic situation.

"To advertise his drug," Hardy proposes—and it is the principle of the second proposal that I find most interesting—considering that, once the new language is known, all languages would end up, would figure, as its dialects. One would *feign* considering natural languages as historical sub-languages, languages that are genealogically derived from this feigned universal language, which has been invented or reinvented. This latter would become, fictively, a reconstructed primitive language. There would thus be a romance of language. It resembles what Descartes would like to substitute for it, with a small difference—a difference that Descartes jealously insists on. This small difference is not slight; he will later call it "true philosophy," but it is not certain that by this name it has all the consistency and all the originality that Descartes once more claims for it—as he will do later for his "I think therefore I am" (against the Augustinian filiation, on the day of his father's death), or for the ontological argument (against Anselm's proof of the existence of God). Here he proves himself to be jealous of the very invention of primitiveness itself, of this putative primitive, archi-paternal or archi-maternal, language. To accuse the inventor of "advertising his drug"—what a burst of venom, surprising enough in a philosophical discussion that should remain serene, and all the more so since the accused is not even there, but only the mediator, in the person of Père Mersenne. The stakes must be serious: this is what we must tell ourselves whenever a philosophical objection takes the violent form of a denunciation or defamation; let us never forget this. Where has Descartes been hit? Let us read.

As if by chance, the only example he can find to sustain his sarcasm, at the point of his nastiest insinuation, is the word "love," "*aimer, amare, philein*, and so forth":

> The second [proposition], that is, *cognita hac lingua, caeteras omnes, ut eius dialectos, cognoscere* [once this language has been learned, the others can be learned as dialects of it] is only to advertise his drugs [*faire valoir sa drogue*]. He does not say how long it would take to learn them, but only that they could be regarded as dialects of his language, which he takes as primitive because it does not have the grammatical irregularities of the others. Notice that in his dictionary, for the primitive words, he could use the words of all languages as synonyms of each other. For instance, to signify *love*, he could use

aimer, amore, philein, and so on; a Frenchman, adding to *aimer* the affix for a noun will form the noun corresponding to *amour,* a Greek will add the same affix to *philein,* and so on.

Consequently, his sixth proposition, *scripturam invenire* [inventing a script], is very easy to understand. For if he put in his dictionary a single symbol corresponding to *aimer, amare, philein,* and each of the synonyms, a book written in such symbols could be translated by all who possessed the dictionary. (*Letters* 4; *Oeuvres* 1.77–78)

Descartes also distrusts the word "arcanum" (secret), which is used by Hardy to "praise his wares." Descartes is in favor of a philosophy without secrets, and as soon as he sees this word appear "in any proposition," and especially in Latin, he "begins to think poorly of it." But his bad faith again resorts to the so-called argument of the kettle ("The kettle I am returning to you is good as new; anyway, the holes were already there when you loaned it to me; furthermore, you never loaned me a kettle"). For he accuses the so-called inventor of labeling with the name *arcanum* a mere pseudo-secret, a recipe that is too easy to teach. And here facility becomes a sin.

In the second part of the indictment, Descartes tries to demonstrate that this overly facile invention is too difficult to implement, although Hardy claims to be able to teach it in six hours. This invention would be useful for the public, Descartes pretends to admit, "if everyone agreed to adopt it. But I see two drawbacks which stand in the way" (*Letters* 4; *Oeuvres* 1.78).

These two "drawbacks" are not of a strictly linguistic order, but are rather historical and social. But does one have the right to make this distinction?

On the one hand, people are used to the sounds of their own language and will tolerate no other. What is easy and pleasant to us becomes harsh and unbearable to Germans. Even if we can avoid this annoyance for one or two languages at the very most, the so-called universal language would be good for only one country: "We do not have to have a new language to speak only with the French" (*Letters* 4; *Oeuvres* 1.79). Another paradox? Another denial? Descartes denounces one utopia, and yet it is another utopia that he will present himself a little later, without making any secret of it. This will not be inconsistent, if the resistance to using the new language must hinge, in Hardy's case, on the fact that the "new language" is not philosophical enough. Descartes' own language, by contrast, will meet with resistance because and insofar as it aspires to being philosophical. And his "romance" will be a philosophical romance.

On the other hand—and this is the second practical drawback—there would be the difficulty of learning the words of this new language. This explanation will be of interest to us to the extent that it touches on the only aspect of the project that is seductive for Descartes: a system of graphic notation, a writing more than a universal language. Descartes uses this as a pretext to advance his own project for a universal language and writing—his own "great method," one might venture to say.

There would be no problem of apprenticeship for the primitive words in everyone's own language. Everyone knows them, or can learn them without effort. But one will be understood only by one's compatriots, unless the other person looks in the dictionary, which is not convenient; and no one will want to learn the primitive words of all languages. Unless, of course, the recourse to writing is the solution, and it is in the course of this argumentation that Descartes acknowledges the only utility of this invention: the possibility of a universal characteristic, the printing of a huge dictionary in all languages, with common characters for each primitive word. We would generally and confusedly call these characters "ideographic," but Descartes does not use this word. They would denote not sounds or syllables, but rather concepts, semantic units. The example of this ideographic writing is, once more, love:

> So the only *possible benefit* that I see from his invention would be in the case of the written word. Suppose he had a big dictionary printed in all the languages in which he wanted to make himself understood, and put for each primitive word characters corresponding to the meaning and not to the syllables, a single character, for instance, for *aimer*, *amare*, and *philein*: then those who had the dictionary and knew their grammar could translate what was written into their own language by looking up all these characters in turn. (*Letters* 5; *Oeuvres* 1.79–80; my emphasis)

Descartes remains cautious. Not excluding the hypothesis of an inadequate deciphering on his own part (the invention is itself a text to be deciphered, and Descartes' only access to it is through the intermediary of a letter, an interpretation itself to be interpreted), he is still afraid that this new technique might be useful only for reading "mysteries and revelations" (*Letters* 5; *Oeuvres* 1.80), remaining too cumbersome for other uses. This allusion to mysteries and revelations points to a whole enthusiastic activity during that period concerning new secret writings. Since I cannot elaborate on this here, let me refer you to the references I make to it in *Of Grammatology*.[14]

Over and above this critique, what is Descartes' counter-proposal? It would be a question of devising a method for instituting primitive words and their corresponding characters. It is indeed a question of institution here, in the strictest sense of the word. This method—artificial intelligence, a translating machine—being at once both language and writing, can be taught in very little time. Its essential mainspring, its novelty, its universality, as much as its economic facility, is the principle of order, the "means of order." Yet another determination of the *odos*, of the path and the passage. It is a question of "the order between all the thoughts that can come into the human mind" (*Letters* 5; *Oeuvres* 1.80). The order and structure of these (linguistic and graphic) marks would be founded on the order of meaning and thought. It is a universal and simple order, which is guaranteed here, once more, by the analogy with mathematics, and in particular with arithmetic. For "just as" "there is an [order]"

> naturally established between numbers. In a single day one can learn to name every one of the infinite series of numbers, and thus to write infinitely many different words in the unknown language. The same could be done for all the other words necessary to express all the other things that fall within the purview of the human mind. If this secret were discovered I am sure that the language would soon spread throughout the world. Many people would willingly spend five or six days learning how to make themselves understood by all men. (*Letters* 5–6; *Oeuvres* 1.80–81)

Hardy has not thought of this. He has not, as a philosopher, begun by thinking order, according to order, the real relation of dependence between this new language and "true" philosophy, which alone permits one to "number all the thoughts of man" (*Letters* 6; *Oeuvres* 1.81), to distinguish them in their clarity and simplicity. Such would be the only *arcanum*, the secret as secret both of method and of language, the secret for acquiring "the true science" (*Letters* 6; *Oeuvres* 1.81).

Now, after boasting not only of the possibility of this language but also of its necessity and, above all, its facility, Descartes, in a sudden and catastrophic turnabout, concludes the impracticability of the thing. Thus, the conclusion:

> If someone were to explain correctly what are the simple ideas in the human imagination out of which all human thoughts are compounded, and if his ex-

planation were generally admitted, I would dare to hope for a universal language that is very easy to learn, to speak, and to write. The greatest advantage of such a language would be the assistance it would give to men's judgment, representing matters so clearly that it would be almost impossible to go wrong. As it is, almost all our words have confused meanings, and men's minds are so accustomed to them that there is hardly anything which they can perfectly understand.

I maintain that this language is possible and that it is possible to discover the science on which it depends: it would make peasants better judges of the truth about the world than philosophers are now. But do not hope ever to see it in use. That would require great changes in the order of things—the whole world would need to become nothing but an earthly paradise, which is worth proposing only in the land of romance [*romans*]. (*Letters* 6; *Oeuvres* 1.81–82)

Here, then, is how the land of romance suddenly becomes the land of the "true science." Philosophy would have undivided dominion there; the arbitrariness of the sign, techno-scientific rationality, and above all the law of language or of writing—for these would be the same thing—would be the law. The map of this land of romance would have some analogy, even if they cannot be confused, with the map of methodological rationality, that of order and of the path become method. I want to insist upon the arbitrariness of the sign. Even if this theme is not explicitly named, it sustains the entire logic of this letter. And especially of the following letter (again to Mersenne, on December 18, 1629), which distinguishes between two kinds of semiotic universalities: on the one hand, that of an absolutely natural language; on the other, that of a totally artificial code that is constructed in an arbitrary fashion. Both are universally intelligible, whether immediately or not. The opposition of nature and art, of *physis* and *techne*, again governs this semiotic: "Voices, crying or laughing, are comparable in all languages. But when I see the heavens or the earth I do not have to name them in one way rather than another; and I believe that would be the case even if there was an original justness" (*Oeuvres* 1.103). The structural difference between the absolutely natural language [*langage*] (which must be distinguished from a merely "natural language" [*langue*]) and the absolutely artificial language remains insurmountable. And since the language said to be "natural," composed of words and names, is founded on the arbitrariness of the sign, it would never be natural, of the naturalness of the cry or the laugh that transcends, according to Descartes, all national borders.

"Natural language" is situated between the two universalities. Peasants, as well as real philosophers (as distinct from the philosopher of the true philosophy), speak this natural language. They are thus at least as receptive to this new rational language, which "would make [them] better judges of the truth than philosophers are now." They are not biased or outwitted by false knowledge and a false idea of science. However, peasants and philosophers today—and one could add here weak minds and women—have in common with this natural language a kind of conservative habit. They will always refuse to change the order of things to call upon the order of thoughts. They will refuse the earthly paradise or the land of romance. One gets the sense that this bad order of things corresponds to the fatality of a fall. An original sin would have expelled us from paradise and imposed this natural language that is no longer *purely* natural and will never be *purely* artificial. The *roman*, the land of romance, would be the language of paradise before the fall: the myth of a pure language *in illo tempore*, purely natural or purely artificial. And these would amount to the same thing. The language of paradise and the language of method would share a universal transparency. There would be no more need even to desire method.

Between the two, there is the method to be constructed and there is history. History [*histoire*] cannot be written as a romance [*roman*]; the romance does not tell a true story [*histoire*]. The philosophical imagination has more affinity with pure rationality; it dreams of a pure language: the true philosophy.

We should now go further and specify the history of romance, of the word "roman," and of the literary genre named thus, of the relations between rhetoric and the *roman* before and after the period of Cartesian discourse.[15]

—*Translated by Rebecca Coma*

Vacant Chair: Censorship, Mastery, Magisteriality

At this point we begin a second journey. No more so than the first will this one lead us toward an overhanging edge from which we could dominate the totality of an epoch or a historical territory. It will be a question of situating some significant points of reference in order to measure a displacement or the transformation of a problematic. This presupposes strategic choices and risks on our part.

I am thus taking the risks of a leap without a clear transition between two great moments in the institutional structures of philosophy in Europe. During the last lectures, Descartes was, for us, the example of a philosopher who, while explaining himself and struggling with all sorts of institutional authorities, never did so as a *teaching* philosopher, as a *professor* and *civil servant* in a State university. He no doubt posed pedagogical questions and analyzed the rhetoric and language of "exposition," but he did so without having to deal with a teaching of philosophy organized by the State and entrusted to teachers who are also servants of the State.

Now, at the end of the eighteenth and beginning of the nineteenth centuries the situation was transformed everywhere in Europe in this respect. We will now focus our attention on the constitution of this new space, that of philosophy in the State university and of the figure of the civil servant–philosopher. Naturally, such a transformation could not remain exterior to philosophical discourse itself, to its procedures and its content. Limiting ourselves here to some exemplary indications, beginning with the *Kantian* figure of this new situation, we will attempt not to isolate the so-called external considerations from analyses of content.

Without further ado, therefore, I will state that the point of departure,

the guiding thread I have taken the risk of choosing for this second journey: the question of *censorship*, as it might be posed between Reason and
the university. We will speak, then, of censorship as institution, of censorship outside the institution, in the university, or at the limits of the university, and of how censorship can operate as academic or State power.

Deployed in its fullest dimension, the question could take a paradoxical form: Can reason be censored? Should it be? Can it in turn censor? Or
censor itself? Can it find good or bad reasons for censorship? *In short,
what is censorship as a question of reason?*

In *The Conflict of the Faculties*[1] for example, Kant seeks to justify (*begründen*), to found in reason, in a critical and discriminating fashion, an
apparently factual situation that must be recalled, at least briefly. In short,
in question is the death of a king, as if to confirm by that event that the
force or the re-enforcement of the law always passes by way of a dead
king. In August 1786, the liberal king, Friedrich II, was replaced, upon his
death, by Friedrich Wilhelm II. The offensive that then developed against
the supporters of the *Aufklärung* has been attributed to the influence of
Woellner, Friedrich Wilhelm II's minister. Censorship was established in
Berlin a few years after the Edict of Religion (July 1788), which prohibited
everything that appeared to oppose the official religion. In December
1788, the law against the freedom of the press was declared. In 1792, after
the French Revolution, a censorship commission was established. In June
1792, this commission prohibited the publication of book two of *Religion
within the Limits of Reason Alone*.[2] Kant protested, addressing himself to
the Faculty of Theology at Königsberg, then to the Faculty of Arts at Jena,
whose dean finally granted the *imprimatur*. In 1793, the publication
earned Kant the king's famous reprimand. Kant responds to this reprimand and explains himself in the preface to *The Conflict of the Faculties*.[3]
It was experts in theology, official theologians authorized by the State,
who, in this situation, had the right and the power to determine what
should or should not be censored. They were the legitimate and recognized trustees of a knowledge; they are supposed to know what does or
does not go against the official religion. Now, in order to obtain a first image of the lines of division, of the critical divisions, of the conflictual
boundaries, and of the interior separations that furrow the territory we are
engaged upon, let us situate, like an emblem, the division a theologian can
undergo, according to Kant, when he must assume two functions as a single person. In the preface to the first edition of *Religion within the Limits*

of Reason Alone (1793), Kant explains the necessity and legitimacy of censorship. The rational sanctity of moral law should be the object *of the greatest respect* (*der größten Achtung*), of an adoration addressed to the Supreme Cause (*Ursache*) that fulfills these laws. Now, what is most sublime shrinks (*verkleinert sich*) in human hands, that is, in the hands of finite beings. Laws of constraint (*Zwangsgesetze*) must therefore be added to the free respect of moral law, the only authentic respect. One must make do with a critique that has force at its disposal, that is to say, with *censorship*. The theologian who censors books (*der Bücher richtende Theolog*) may have been named, placed, charged (*angestellt*), posted, appointed by the State, in agreement with the church, to perform two *functions*, with two purposes. The same individual can belong to two authorities. He can be appointed as a censor, as an ecclesiastic, to see to the well-being of souls (*Heil der Seelen*), or, furthermore, as a scholar (*Gelehrter*), for the well-being of the sciences (*Heil der Wissenschaften*). One must presuppose that these two kinds of well-being do not go hand in hand, at least not immediately.[4] As a scholar responsible for the well-being of the sciences, this theologian in fact belonged (at that time) to a public institution, an institution under the name of a university (*Gliede einer öffentlichen Anstalt, der [unter dem Namen einer Universität]* . . .), to which all the sciences are entrusted. If it is practiced in this institution, censorship should not cause any harm to the sciences and to truth as they are freely cultivated by the university. And I remind you that the guarantor, the guardian of truth for all the faculties (higher and lower) of the university is the philosopher, who also has the right to censor (or should have it, according to Kant) within the entire interior field of the university institution. The theologian responsible for the well-being of souls will therefore be quite distinct, even if within one and the same person, from the university theologian responsible for the well-being of the sciences. Neglecting this rule of bipartition, crossing this boundary, would amount to returning to a pre-Galilean situation; one would reproduce what takes place with Galileo: a biblical theologian who intervened in the domain of the sciences (astronomy, ancient history, history of the earth, etc.), "in order to humble the pride of the sciences and to spare himself the study of them" (*Religion* 8).

Such would be the internal division of the biblical theologian. But there is also the internal division of the theologian in general; he can be a *biblical* theologian (an expert in a positive and revealed religion) but also a *philosophical* theologian, a "rational" theologian.

Before returning to this point, once the motif of censorship has been established, I would like further to justify my choice of and insistence upon this theme. This theme might seem anachronistic to those who would wish to initiate a reflection on *modern* university reason. Today, especially in the regions we inhabit, it seems as though censorship no longer exists in the strict sense we have just evoked: academics are no longer prohibited from publishing a paper, either spoken or written, by a governmental decree (in Kant's case, a royal decree), based on the opinion formulated by a censorship commission composed of other academics appointed by the State. It would nonetheless be naive to conclude from this that censorship disappeared from that time on, even if one refers to Kant's definition of censorship, that is, "*a critique that has power*" (*Religion* 7) and consequently prohibits, reduces to silence, or limits the manifestation of thought, the written or spoken word. What might have changed is the form the use of this force takes, the place and machinery of its application, of its distribution, the complexity, the diversification, and the overdetermination of its pathways. But how can one deny this? There are things that cannot be uttered within the university—or outside of the university. There are certain ways of saying certain things that are neither legitimate nor authorized. There are, quite simply, "objects" that one cannot study, analyze, work on in certain university departments. Moreover, censorship does not consist in reducing something to absolute silence. It is enough for it to limit the range of the addressees, or of the exchanges in general. Censorship exists as soon as certain forces (linked to powers of evaluation and to symbolic structures) simply limit the extent of a field of study, the resonance or the propagation of a discourse. Today, this does not necessarily originate from a central and specialized organism, from a person (the king or his minister), from a commission officially established for this purpose. Through a highly differentiated, indeed contradictory, network, censorship weighs on the university or proceeds from it (for the university is always censured *and* censoring). We find this prohibiting power associated with other instances or agencies, other national or international research and teaching institutions, publishing power, the media, and so forth. The moment a discourse, even if it is not forbidden, cannot find the conditions for an exposition or for an *unlimited* public discussion, one can speak of an effect of censorship, no matter how excessive this may seem. The analysis of this is more necessary and more difficult than ever.

Let us take an example. When an institution (I am thinking here of the recently created Collège International de Philosophie) proposes to give priority to research projects not presently legitimated or insufficiently developed in other institutions (whether French or foreign), what does that signify, if not a challenge to censorship or the plan (clearly formulated in the Report of the Committee established with the aim of creating this Collège) to remove certain forms of censorship? It is a question of privileging the access to those "things" that are not allowed to be uttered or done in current institutions. One should understand the term "current institutions" to mean the totality of the organized field of which I was just speaking: the university and para-university, publishing, the press, the media, the new systems of archiving, and so forth. Not to "legitimize" something, according to this or that criterion, not to give it the means to manifest itself, is already to censor. Of course, since the field of "things" that can be studied, said, or done, is by rights without set limits, the censoring delimitation remains unavoidable in a finite and necessarily agonistic field. At every moment, forces are suppressed, limited, repressed, marginalized, made minor, according to the most diverse ruses. A book of which two thousand copies are published, an untranslated book, remains, today, almost a confidential and private document. By proposing an apparently paradoxical institution that would remove the censorship imposed within the system of other institutions, one must realize that censorship is thereby assigned a regulating idea that in its essence is inaccessible: an idea precisely in the Kantian sense. Such an institution will only see the light of day, become *effective*, in a given (and thus finite) situation, where it will be involved in transactions with the state of the system in place; hence with a certain censoring apparatus, a certain relationship of power between the censored and the censoring, that is, sometimes, a certain relationship of self-censorship. There is never any pure censorship or pure lifting of censorship, which makes one doubt the rational purity of this concept that, however, never exists without reason and without judgment, without recourse to the law. One must also know that a new institution that would propose to lift some forms of censorship should not only permit new "things" to be said and done, but should also devote itself constantly to a theoretico-institutional analysis (an auto- and hetero-analysis), in order to detect within itself the effects of censorship or of nonlegitimation of all kinds. This institution should analyze its own instruments of analysis: for example, this concept of censorship (a bit obsolete today) or that concept of legitimation (of non- or delegitimation) that has taken up its displaced relay and that, having very precise origins in the history of sociological and political thought (for example, in the writings of Max Weber), should include, in its very conceptual structure, some limits and thus its own censoring effects (what is the "legitimacy" of the concept of legitimation?). These concepts of censorship or of legitimation involve theoretical and practical obstacles precisely because of the field into which they have been imported. One can say this a priori and without thereby completely disqualifying them. The field is simply no longer our own. It is in order to begin such a task, very modestly and in a completely preliminary fashion, that I believe it is necessary to return to the constitution of this philosophical concept of censorship in Kant.

I will remind you, then, of the essential features of this concept. The possibility of censorship—its necessity also and its legitimacy—appears in that place where an institution simultaneously intervenes and assures the mediation between pure reason (here in its highest form, pure practical reason) and the disposal of force, force at the disposal of the State. One should not even say that the institution uses censorship or is subjected to censorship: in truth, one cannot construct the concept of the institution without inscribing in it the censoring function. The pure laws of practical reason should only constrain insofar as they are honored through a respect given freely. Since the sublimity of moral law "shrinks" in the hands of man, respect must be imposed from the outside, by "coercive laws" (*Religion* 7). These laws thus depend on the finitude and the fallibility of man. And it is precisely concerning the subject of evil, the possibility of a "radical evil," that the question of the university will reappear along with that of censorship, in an acute, indeed aporetic, form. If we had the right to give in to the facility of such shortcuts, we could say that without the principle of evil in man, there would be no university. Such a statement would not be false, but it is not a good idea to go so quickly.

The Kantian definition of censorship is simple: a *critique* that has force (*Gewalt*) at its disposal. Pure force in itself does not censor and, moreover, would not apply to discourses or texts in general. Nor does a critique without power censor. Evoking force, Kant is obviously thinking of a political force linked to the power of the State. *Gewalt* is legal force. In the majority of cases where censorship was practiced as an official institution, at least since the seventeenth century (with the development of print, the conflicts surrounding religion, censorship in the service of the Catholic Church, or in the famous case of Calvinist censorship in Geneva), censorship was, above all, a matter of the church. This fact always presupposes a theologico-political power, an organic solidarity between the Church and the State. It is thus still a question of censorship as a State institution, with public force at its disposal and working through public acts. Commissions are named, known, centralized. University experts, especially from theology faculties, have always played an essential role in this. Directly or indirectly, the university has always been involved in the definition and formation of qualifications for the professions, in evaluations, the granting or refusal of *imprimatur*, in the seizure or prohibition of books as they are imported, and so forth.

One could interpret all of Kantian politics, that politics implicitly or explicitly implemented by the critical enterprise, through the three great *Critique*s, as a political enterprise whose aim is to *take note* and *delimit*: to take note of a censoring power—and of a legitimacy of State reason as a censoring reason, the power of censorship—but also to delimit this power; not by opposing it with a counterpower, but a sort of nonpower, of reason heterogeneous to power. This would be that of pure reason, or, from the point of view of its institutional translation, that of the Faculty of Philosophy. No doubt, Kant wants this faculty to have, under certain conditions, the right to censor at its disposal (and he uses the word "censorship" in *The Conflict of the Faculties*); but, since he always insists that the Faculty of Philosophy should not have any executive power at its disposal and should never be able to give orders, this amounts to refusing it the right to censor that is inseparable, in its very concept, from the *power* to censor, from force (*Gewalt*).

This is what we will attempt to analyze from this point on. But we will have to narrow our focus to sharpen the analysis. We will not deal directly with all of the problems enveloped in this matter, whether it be a question of reason and faith, or of practical reason and religion, of politics and history, and above all of judgment in general; for the entire politics of censorship, every critique of censorship, is a critique of judgment. Censorship is a judgment. It presupposes a tribunal, laws, a code. Since we are speaking of reason and censorship, we could easily evoke the chain that links *ratio* to accounting, calculation, censorship: *censere* means to evaluate [*réputer*], to count, to compute. The "census," the "cens" is the enumeration of citizens (*recensement*, census) and the evaluation of their wealth by the censors (census takers). But let us leave this chain, even though it is necessary and significant.

Kant intends to legitimize State reason as a censoring reason, supposed to have the right to censor in certain conditions and within certain limits. But he also wants to withdraw pure reason itself from all censoring power. Pure reason should, by rights, exercise no censorship and should be exempt from all censorship. Now, this limit between reason that censors and reason foreign to censorship does not circumvent the university, but passes right through it, right between the two classes of faculties: the higher faculties (theology, law, medicine), linked to the State power they represent, and the lower faculty (philosophy). No power should have a right of inspection [*droit de regard*] over the Faculty of Philosophy, as long as it is satisfied with *saying*, not doing, with saying the truth without giving orders, with speaking *within* the university and *not* outside of it.

This strange limit gives rise to antagonisms that Kant wants to resolve into conflict, into solvable conflicts. He distinguishes precisely between conflict and war: war is savage and natural; it implies no recourse to the law, no institutional access to arbitration. Conflict, however, is a regulated, foreseeable, and codifiable antagonism. It should *regulate itself*; the adversarial parties should be able to appear before an arbitrating body.

Two *remarks* before proceeding further. Both concern this fact or this principle, this principial fact: no censorship without reason. What does that mean?

First remark: There is no censorship without reason (and without given reason) since censorship never presents itself as a brutal and mute repression, reducing to silence what a dominant force has no interest in allowing to be said, proffered, or propagated. In the strict sense Kant wants to delimit, censorship certainly makes use of force, and against a discourse, but always in the name of another discourse, according to the legal procedures that presuppose a right and institutions, experts, authorities, public acts, a State government, and reason. There is no private censorship, even if censorship reduces speech to its condition of "private" manifestation. One does not speak of censorship in the case of repressive acts or of suppression directed toward a private discourse (even less in the case of thoughts without discourse) and thus restricting instances of contraband, translation, substitution, or disguise. Censorship only exists where there is a *public domain*, with state-like centralization. The church can also function as a State power or in cooperation with a State apparatus. When Freud resorts to what one would be a little hasty in terming the "metaphor" of censorship in order to describe the process of repression, this figure is only a figure insofar as psychological "censorship" does not proceed, like censorship in the strict and literal sense, along the public thoroughfare of institutions and the State, even if the State can play a fantasmatic role in the scene. But this figure is "felicitous" only insofar as it appeals to a principle of order, the rationality of a central organization with its discourses, its guardians/experts, and above all its representatives.

Consequently, if censorship is indeed the business of reason, if there is no censorship without reason, one cannot limit the question of repressive or prohibitive force to that of censorship. This would mean being satisfied with analyzing the web of State connections and ignoring all the procedures, techniques, strategies, and ruses that prohibit or marginalize discourse without necessarily being subjected to a process of State reason, or without declaring itself publicly. As a public institution of the State, the university was in Kant's time and remains to a certain extent today a very sensitive place for tracing this limit between censoring and censored reason. This is still a very sensitive area in "totalitarian" countries, where the most massive form of repression passes by way of State censorship. But in industrial societies with supposedly liberal and democratic regimes, even if State censorship is very reduced (I'm not saying nonexistent) for the system in general, there are, on the other hand, mechanisms of prohibition, suppression, repression, *without censorship* (*stricto sensu*): an increasing multiplicity, refinement, and over-determination of marginalization or disqualification, delegitimation of certain discourses, certain practices, and certain "poems."

They already existed, and were already very complex, in Kant's time, and Kant's silence about this would merit analysis. But today this overpotentialization defies all our instruments of analysis. It should mobilize numerous systems of deciphering directed toward places as diverse and diversely structured as the laws of capital, the system of language, the educational machine, its norms and procedures of control or reproduction, technologies, particularly information technologies, all types of politics, particularly cultural and media politics (in the private and public domains), publishing structures, and, finally, all the institutions, including those of "physical and psychological" health, without neglecting to cross all of the systems and subjects that are inscribed or produced in them, with the over-determined complexity of their bio-psychic, idiosyncratic, etc., functioning. Now, even supposing that one mastered the system of these systems and that one made the general diagram of this appear on a giant computer, it would still be necessary to be able to ask it the following question: why for example does such and such a sentence, whatever it be, remain forbidden? Why can't it be uttered? That such a question can be asked, that this forbidden sentence can be said or felt as forbidden, presupposes a lapse, however slight or furtive, in some area of the system, of the organigram of prohibition. The latter includes within it the principle of disturbance, the force or deconstructive counterforce that permits the utterance and even the deciphering of the forbidden sentence. Otherwise it could not even "censor." The censors know, in one way or another, what they are talking about when they say one must not talk about it.

Second Remark. No censorship without reason, we said. This is true in another sense. Within or beyond that which can link the possibility of reason to that of censorship (technical calculation and enforced examination, by force, of that which must and must not be uttered), Kant wants to give the reason for censorship in a discourse on the university. He wants to speak the truth about censorship from the stance of reason. In doing and saying this, he would like to protect reason itself from censorship. How so?

We have seen that Kant legitimizes censorship. He rationalizes the necessity for it. He constructs, as he does elsewhere, a schema of pure a priori rationality in order to justify a state of fact, in this case the fact of the State. He had made the same gesture to justify the division of the university into higher and lower "classes." Kant therefore justifies censorship in reason, censorship as an armed critique, as it were, the critique supported by police. Now, what is the essential argument of this justification? The fallibility of man. And who can understand the evil in man, who can give the reason for it? Who can speak the meaning and truth of it? Who can therefore speak of the meaning, the truth, the possibility and the necessity, the very foundation of censorship? The question "who?" very quickly becomes "what faculty?": what expert, which corporation of experts, which competent authority in the university? This cannot come down to the members of the higher faculties, dependents of the State, subjected to its authority and thus to the power of censorship. Neither the theologian, nor the jurist, nor the doctor can think evil and have access to the very meaning of the censorship that, nevertheless, they represent. The truth of censorship is only accessible to the philosopher, to the Faculty of Philosophy. This "lower" faculty represents the place of pure reason, and in essence, as well as by contract, it has no power. In a moment, we will ask ourselves quite simply if *it takes place*, if it has *a place*, and if the philosopher himself takes place. The three higher faculties all have a specific interpretation of radical evil. But all three fail to understand it, because they deny freedom by conceiving of this evil as simply "hereditary": hereditary disease for the Faculty of Medicine, inherited debt for the Faculty of Law, and inherited sin for the Faculty of Theology.[5]

We must take up this demonstration again, as it is presented a little earlier, at the beginning of book one of *Religion within the Limits of Reason Alone* ("Concerning the Indwelling of the Evil Principle with the Good, or, on the Radical Evil [*das radicale Böse*] in Human Nature"). The problem had already been formulated, in terms of authority and competence, in the preface to the second edition, just before this chapter. Kant reiterates what he had said in the first preface, that is, that what he was undertaking was by right (*mit vollem Recht*) the task of the scholar, of the researcher in religious theory, the task of one who studies religion from a philosophical point of view. By devoting himself to this research, this scholar in no way encroaches upon "the exclusive rights" (*in die ausschließlichen Rechte*) of the biblical theologian, who is competent in positive religion, historically revealed by the Scriptures: "Since then I found this assertion made in the *Moral* (Part 1, pp. 5–11) of the late Michaelis, a man well versed in both departments, and applied throughout his entire work, and the higher faculty did not find therein anything prejudicial to their rights" (*Religion* 12). This juridical vocabulary gives an indication of the fact that these philosophical questions concerning the tribunal of reason should be settled according to a code and before legitimate authorities.

This division of rights and authorities presupposes the establishment of a border, of a line, or of a pure and decidable limit. Kant had just proposed a topological figure to represent this limit. It deserves our consideration for a moment. It proposes a definition of the philosopher as the "teacher of pure reason" (*reiner Vernunftlehrer*), and it prefigures or configures the singular place of the department of philosophy in the Kantian university.

While explaining the title of his book, *Religion within the Limits of Reason Alone*, Kant remarks that revelation (*Offenbarung*) in general can include within it a pure religion of reason (*reine Vernunftreligion*), a religion according to reason alone. This rational religion does not include the historical element of revelation; there is nothing historical about it. However, compatibility, indeed harmony, between the two religions, the rational and the historical, remains thinkable. This is the whole intent and the entire enigmatic difficulty of the book. These two revelations or two spaces, the natural and the historical, form two "spheres" or "circles" (Kant makes use of both words a few sentences apart) that are not exterior to each other, but one inscribed within the other, concentric. Around the same center, the inside circle is that of revealed or historical religion, while the outside circle is that of rational religion. At that moment, instead of situating philosophy, it is the philosopher whom Kant inscribes in the wider circle. He calls the philosopher "the teacher of pure reason."

This signifies at least three things:

1. The teacher of philosophy is outside of the religious domain, at least outside of the historical domain of positive religion. Positive religion *seems in certain respects* not to be within his official competence. I say "in certain respects," since it *seems* to be this way.

2. But, from another point of view, the philosopher, like the Faculty of Philosophy, can be acquainted with the *entire* field of the other faculties, including the Faculty of Theology in its historical knowledge; for the Faculty of Philosophy simultaneously covers the field of knowledge as *historical* knowledge in its entirety (history is part of the Faculty of Philosophy) and all fields concerned with *truth*. Kant says this explicitly in *The Conflict of the Faculties*:

> Now the Faculty of Philosophy consists of two departments: a department of *historical knowledge* (including history, geography, philology and humanities, along with all the empirical knowledge contained in the natural sciences), and a department of *pure rational knowledge* (pure mathematics and pure philosophy, the metaphysics of nature and of morals). And it also studies the relation of these two divisions of learning to each other. It therefore extends to all parts of human knowledge (including, from a historical viewpoint, the teachings of the higher faculties), though there are some parts (namely the distinctive teachings and precepts of the higher faculties) which it does not treat as its own content, but as objects it will examine and criticize for the benefit of the sciences. The Faculty of Philosophy can, therefore, lay claim to any teaching, in order to test its truth. The government cannot forbid it to do this without acting against its own proper and essential purposes. (*Conflict* 45)

The teacher of pure reason is *simultaneously* located in a department, in the exterior space of the larger circle, of the circle that remains exterior to the circle of biblical theology, for example, *and*, by the same token, is able to comprehend in his vision and his critical inspection the entire field of knowledge. He has two places: a circumscribed place and a non-place that is also a panoptical ubiquity. This topology defines the jurisdictional powers. The higher faculties "must put up with the objections and doubts it [the Faculty of Philosophy] brings forward in public" (*Conflict* 45).

3. This philosopher is called "the teacher of pure reason." This is not an insignificant detail. The philosopher is not simply situated as an individual subject (one speaks of the place *of* the philosopher and not only of the place of philosophy and pure reason), but also as a *teaching* subject in an institution, a competent subject and civil servant spreading a doctrine: he is a "Dozent," someone who teaches disciples and whose qualifications are recognized by the State. He has a status, which is no longer the status that dominated in philosophy before Kant. Neither Descartes, nor Spinoza, nor Leibniz, nor Hume, nor any of the philosophers of the eighteenth century had such a status. Between the formulation of the Principle of Sufficient Reason by Leibniz and the Kantian *Critiques*, there is a sort of becoming-institution, more exactly, a becoming-state-institution of reason, a becoming-faculty of reason.

The topological structure of this teaching institution in the Kantian discourse has an essential relation with the architectonics of pure reason. Pure reason, we know, is set out at the *end* of the *Critique of Pure Reason*. This is a famous but seldom examined chapter, at least from the point of view of the teaching institution. In this respect, the chapter is crucial and original. It is singular in that it describes the architectonics of pure reason in its essential relation to the discipline. This is a new development in history. This chapter is undoubtedly well known in French lycées, since parts of it are often extracted to be used as subjects on the French baccalauréat, such as the famous, "one does not learn philosophy, one can only learn to philosophize" (*nur philosophieren lernen*). The very familiarity of this sentence often conceals the dense and difficult context that determines it and gives it meaning.

1. It is a question of a teaching, of the teaching of pure reason. Kant demonstrates that pure reason can be taught, which is not self-evident. And he teaches us this teaching or this original discipline. What is unique about this discipline is that in a certain way one teaches it without learning it. This teaching is a non-teaching. Reason is not learned in the manner in which one learns something, in which one learns historical content. Let us not forget that this famous and often quoted sentence occurs *twice*

in the same chapter. And the emphasis shifts from one occurrence to the other. One of them tells us:

> Mathematics, therefore, alone of all the sciences (*a priori*) arising from reason [those that will be taught in the Faculty of Philosophy next to the historical disciplines that are learned because they are historical], can be learned; philosophy can never be learned, save only in historical fashion; as regards what concerns reason, we can at most learn to *philosophize*.[6]

One can certainly learn philosophy, but not philosophically, only historically. Take a look at the short final chapter, which follows this one, "The History of Pure Reason"; it is a small manual on the history of philosophy or on human reason in a matter that has, up until now, needlessly occupied our "curiosity" and has left edifices in ruins. It is a sort of prehistory of the childhood of philosophy about which Kant claims only to be casting a glance from a transcendental point of view, that is, from the point of view of pure reason.

2. The philosopher, who teaches without learning, who teaches without teaching anything at all, teaches an action, not a content. Nevertheless, he is a teacher (*Lehrer, maître*) and not an artist (*Künstler*), contrary to what one might have thought; for one might consider someone who teaches how to practice the philosophical *act*, rather than Philosophy[7] itself, to be an artist. But:

(a) This *Lehrer*, this *magister*, is a *legislator of reason*. His mastery or his magisteriality has an essential relation to right and to the law.

(b) This teacher of truth does not, in truth, exist. He is nowhere to be found; he does not take place; he is not present, there (*da*); there is no *Dasein* of this teacher-philosopher. As a result: the university, and within it the Faculty of Philosophy that gives it its meaning and its truth, constitutes an institutional place for a teacher of pure reason who in truth remains an ideal and never takes place anywhere. Which amounts to saying that the university itself does not take place: presently.

How does one arrive at this proposition? How do the university, teaching, and the Faculty of Philosophy constitute institutional places allowing a teaching without teaching for a teacher of pure reason who *in fact* does not exist and is nowhere to be found (*aber da er selbst doch nirgend*)? How can one think this corporate body without a body proper?

We will reconstruct the path that leads to this singular proposition. But on the way we will encounter a third theme that I would like to emphasize. In fact, it plays a fundamental role in Kant, but also in the later tradition of this philosophical discourse on the university, in particular that surrounding the founding of the University of Berlin, particularly in Schelling. More than a theme, it is a figural schema.

We see it crossed with, added to, or supplemented by the organic, indeed biological, figure of the living organism as the totality of knowledge, of the (natural) seed from which an academic institution develops. We also see the properly architectonic or architectural figure of the institution as founded and structured edifice, constructed as an artifact. Here, then, are the three themes: 1) The philosopher, teacher of reason, legislator and not artist; 2) this legislator as subject nowhere to be found and as nonplace of the constructed institution or of the organism developed around him, the non-place ruling the topology; 3) the double figure of a bio-architectural totality, nature and artifact, a rationality that can be called, in a manner that is hardly anachronistic, *bio-technological.*

Kant tells us that architectonics is the art of systems (*die Kunst der Systeme*). A system is that which converts vulgar knowledge into science. This also defines the essential function of reason: to go beyond the aggregate, beyond rhapsody, to form the organized whole, and to give it a form (*Bild*). One thus understands the necessity of the organicist "metaphor," at least if it is a metaphor. Reason adds no content; it organizes a system, coordinates and provides the organic *form*; it totalizes according to an internal principle. Architectonics, the art of the system, is nothing other than the theory of the "scientificity" of our knowledge, since this scientificity depends on systemic organicity. All of this takes place—and this figure is no less significant than the others—"under the government of reason," under the regime and the legislation of reason (*unter der Regierung der Vernunft*). The philosophy teacher will be a legislator of human reason (*Gesetzgeber der menschlichen Vernunft*) and not an artist of reason (*Vernunftkünstler*). To speak of the regime, government, or regency of reason is important when considering all of the following concepts together, in their essential relation to one another: the university, the Faculty of Philosophy, and State power. This is also a system of regulated relationships. Royal power will (should) be inspired by reason, by the government of reason, in order to rule the university. It would be in its interest to adjust its political government to the government of reason. This harmony, as regulative idea, as idea of reason, inspires all of the Kantian politics of the university.

The system unifies the organization of various fields of knowledge under one Idea (in the Kantian sense). The fact that the whole does not allow itself to be thought as Idea (in the Kantian sense, that is, in the sense of a certain inaccessibility), as a rational concept of the *form* of the whole, explains indirectly but surely that the teacher of pure reason, the subjective correlate of this idea, is in fact just as inaccessible as it, and therefore as indispensable as he is nowhere to be found. Moreover, the fact that this idea is also that of an organic whole explains that this organic whole, in this case knowledge itself, grows like an animal, from the inside and not by the mechanical addition of parts:

> The whole is thus an organised unity (*articulatio*), and not an aggregate (*coacervatio*). It may grow from within [*innerlich*] (*per intussusceptionem*), but not by external addition (*per appositionem*). It is thus like an animal body [*wie ein tierischer Körper*], the growth of which is not by the addition of a new member, but by the rendering of each member, without change of proportion, stronger and more effective for its purposes. (*Critique of Pure Reason* 653–654)

With this remark, the discourse of the third *Critique* on organic purposiveness [*finalité*] and on the category of the totality of the living being is already implied in this rhetoric (and it is more than a rhetoric) of the *Critique of Pure Reason*, particularly in its architectonics.

Architectonics plays a specific, acute, and irreplaceable role in the process of this development, in the fulfillment of the idea. One cannot think the university institution, as an institution of reason and place of the growth of rational science, without this role of architectonics. No university architecture without architectonics.

The fulfillment of the idea in fact presupposes what Kant calls a schema (*Schema*), a figure, a diversity, and a disposition of parts which is essential to the whole and can be determined a priori, according to the "principle of purpose" (*aus dem Prinzip des Zwecks*). One sets out from a purpose, as in every organic totality. When this schema does not proceed from the purpose as the main purpose (*Hauptzweck*) of reason, when this schema remains empirical and open to unforeseeable accidents, it only provides a "technical," and not an architectonic, unity. The choice of words here is significant. "Technical," here, signifies the order of knowledge as "know-how"; this "know-how" arranges, without referring to principles, a multiplicity of contents in the contingent order in which they present themselves. One can always construct institutions according to technical schemas, with a concern for empirical profitability, without referring to an idea and without rational architectonics. But what we call science, says Kant, cannot be founded technically, that is, by depending on resemblances or analogies of diverse elements, or indeed because of the contingent applications that can be made of science. What today is termed, particularly in France, the *end-orientation* [*finalisation*] of research gives rise to institutional constructions regulated by profitable applications, and therefore, Kant would say, by technical, not architectonic, schemas. This distinction between the technical [*le technique*] and architectonics thus seems to cover, to a large extent, the distinction between end-oriented [*finalisée*] research and "basic" [*fondamentale*] research. This does not mean that such a distinction does not reach its limit at a certain point.[8] If we can distinguish between an idea of knowledge and a project of technical utilization, we should continue to plan institutions that conform to an idea of reason. The Heideggerian interpretation of the *Principle of Reason* puts this principle on the same side as modern technics [*la technique*]; it amounts, then, to limiting, if not contesting, the pertinence of Kant's distinction between the technical and architectonics. It is true that, as interpreted by Heidegger, a certain Beyond-the-Reason-Principle can always find itself reoriented toward an end. This would require recasting the entire problematic, including the "idea" of problem, of science, of research, of *episteme*, and of idea. I will not undertake this here.

The architectonic schema contains the outline of the whole and of its division into parts. This outline, the only one given, Kant calls a *monogram*: an elliptic, enveloped signature, a kind of initial one needs in order to begin to establish a science and thus its institution. An initial outline, an initial outlined, for the idea of science dwells within reason like a seed (*Keim*). All of the parts of a kind of embryo are surrounded and hidden, inaccessible, and barely recognizable when studied under a microscope. There is no radiography, no echography, for the entrails of reason. Further on, Kant compares systems to worms (*Gewürme*) that seem to have a *generatio equivoca* and proceed from a simple collection of united concepts. At first they seem to be truncated, but with time they complete themselves according to their predestined form, which the schema has inscribed in the monogram of reason. Once the organism has developed, all the members of the system appear. The general architectonics of human reason, the system of knowledge of which it is the monogram, can be outlined, Kant says, and this outline today completes the work of the critique of pure reason. Such an outline proceeds from collected materials or from the ruin of ancient, fallen edifices. The outline is a reconstruction:

> We shall content ourselves here with the completion of our task, namely, merely to outline the architectonic of all knowledge arising from *pure reason*; and in doing so we shall begin from the point at which the common root [*die allgemeine Würzel*] of our faculty of knowledge divides and throws out two stems, one of which is reason. By reason here I understand the whole higher faculty of knowledge and am therefore contrasting the rational with the empirical. (*Critique of Pure Reason* 6)

At this very moment, the question of *learning*, the question of didactics and of the discipline as a question of architectonics, is posed. If one disregards the very content of knowledge and its object, knowledge *a parte subjecti* is either *rational* or *historical*. And it is precisely from this *subjective* side of knowledge that the question of the acquisition of knowledge and thus of the teaching institution is posed. In this subjective process, knowledge will be called *historical* when it proceeds from the given (*cognitio ex datis*). It will be called *rational* when it begins where it *must* begin, i.e., with principles, *ex principiis*. A given knowledge is always historical, whether one learns it by immediate experience or thanks to a narrative, the account of a discourse. The same object can be known rationally or historically (in the mode of doxographical narrative, for example). Even a philosophical system, that of Wolff, for example, can be learned historically. One can know everything about it, up to the details of its articulations, but, since the subjective relation with the system is of a historical mode, forgetting an element of it or disputing a simple definition of it is enough to make one incapable of reproducing that definition or of finding another one. There is, then, a simple *historical imitation* of reason as memory or as mnemotechnics. One rediscovers here a rigorously Leibnizian motif.[9] Historical knowledge proceeds from a foreign reason (*nach fremder Vernunft*). The power of imitation (*das nachbildende Vermögen*) is not the power of production or invention (*das erzeugende Vermögen*).

Here, a supplementary distinction arises, the only one from which we can rigorously understand the sentence "one cannot learn philosophy, one can only learn to philosophize." This distinction runs between two types of rational knowledge: the *philosophical*, which operates by pure concepts, and the *mathematical*, which presupposes the *construction* of concepts (and therefore, in the Kantian sense of the word "construction," the recourse to pure sensibility). As we have just seen, taking its mode of acquisition into consideration, an objectively philosophical knowledge can be subjectively historical. Such is the case with schoolchildren when they learn or memorize contents, which can be philosophical systems; and schoolchildren can be schoolchildren at any age. According to Kant at least, throughout one's life one can retain a historical, that is, a scholastic relation with philosophy, which is therefore no more than a history of philosophy or a philosophical doxography.

This distinction between the scholastic-historical and the rational is valid for philosophy, but not for mathematics. Mathematics can be known rationally *and* learned at the same time. The teacher of mathematics cannot draw his knowledge from anything but pure (sensible) intuition, from the pure receptivity of the given. Moreover, it is for this reason that the teacher of mathematics can neither make an error nor remain essentially in a state of illusion. Among all the rational sciences only mathematics can be learned, learned rationally. *Philosophy* can only be learned in the historical mode: "As regards what concerns reason, we can *at most* learn to *philosophize*" (*Critique of Pure Reason* 657).

The system of all philosophical knowledge: this is what is called Philosophy.[10] It is the mere idea of a possible science; nowhere is this idea given *in concreto*. One can thus only find oneself *on the path* toward it. One is never in possession of Philosophy, the teacher of pure reason no more so than anyone else. He is the teacher of philosophizing, not of philosophy. Here we can understand the second occurrence of the phrase "man kann nur philosophieren lernen" ("one can only learn to philosophize" [*Critique of Pure Reason* 657]). This time, the emphasis is on learning (*lernen*), while in the first occurrence it was on philosophizing (*philosophieren*): 1.) One cannot learn philosophy, one can learn *only to philosophize*. 2.) One can *only learn* to philosophize (only learn: for philosophy itself is inaccessible). This is what the progression from one statement to the other would be. The statements remain the same, with the exception of the underlining, which emphasizes the verb *philosophieren* in the first. 1.) One can only learn *to philosophize* (*nur philosophieren*), and not philosophy. 2.) One can only *learn* to philosophize, approach philosophy without ever possessing it; thus without really philosophizing with it. It is a question of translation: in French, the syntactic displacement of the "ne . . . que" (one can learn *only* . . . ; one can *only* learn . . . [on *ne* peut apprendre *que*, on *ne* peut *qu'*apprendre]) allows one to mark the difference clearly. Since in

German the sentence retains the same syntax, *philosophieren* had to be underlined ("to *philosophize*") in the first statement—and the ambiguity remains. It is not out of the question that these two occurrences retained almost the same meaning for Kant.

This same statement, which is repeated, indeed displaced, and, in any case, accented differently, clearly shows that *philosophy* eludes teaching, while *philosophizing* requires it, requires *endlessly and only* teaching. The essence of philosophy excludes teaching; the essence of philosophizing demands it.

It would be enough, if one might say so, to draw the institutional consequences from this. They result from this double bind that knots itself around the sublime body of the teacher of philosophizing, of his evident and unavoidable absence. For in his very withdrawal, he remains unavoidable. He haunts the scene more than he dominates it; he dominates it, indeed, as would a phantom. One could say that he fascinates and seduces, if these connotations were not too closely tied to sensibility and imagination: for reason should break the charm.

Kant says, in short, that there is no philosophy; there is no philosopher. There is the idea of philosophy, there is philosophizing; there are subjects who can learn to philosophize, to learn it from others, and to teach it to others: there are teachers, disciples, institutions, rights, duties, and powers for this; but there is no philosopher, nor philosophy. Nothing of the sort is ever *present, there, here.* Saying "Here I am, me the philosopher, I am a philosopher" [*je philosophe, je suis philosophe*] is not merely the arrogant manifestation of a "braggart" (*ruhmredig*); it is to understand nothing of the difference between an ideal type (*Urbild*) and an individual example. The ideal type of the philosopher as *person* corresponds to the *cosmic* concept, or, put better, the *world concept* (*Weltbegriff*) of philosophy (*conceptus cosmicus*). This concept is opposed to the *conceptus scolasticus*, which is that of a system of knowledge as science, considered uniquely in its systematic unity and logical perfection. The world concept is used as a foundation of the naming of the philosopher, especially when he is personified and *represented* as a model (*Urbild*) in the ideal of the philosopher. We must recall at this point that this ideal philosopher is not an artist of reason (*Vernunftkünstler*), but the legislator (*Gesetzgeber*) of human reason. His object of study is philosophy as *teleologia rationis humanae*, the knowledge of the essential ends of human reason. Here, reason is characterized in its essence as being proper to man, *animal rationale*.

If it was necessary to recall that the ideal philosopher is a legislator and not an artist, it is because not everyone who deals with reason is a legislator. The mathematician, the physicist, and even the logician are only artists of reason. They have instruments and are themselves instruments in the hands of he who is their teacher because he knows the essential ends of human reason: and this is the philosopher, who is nowhere to be found. But the idea of his legislation is found everywhere in man's reason.

Nowhere, everywhere: how to order this topology? How to translate it into an institution? We will see how this paradox unfolds when, in the name of this very logic, Schelling criticizes *The Conflict of the Faculties*. Kant is wrong to wish there were something like a specialized institutional place, a department for philosophy. Since philosophy is everywhere, one must not reserve a place for it. Above all, one must not assign it a place.

There is the teacher [*maître*]—and he is absent. But he has a mistress—metaphysics. Kant presents metaphysics as a cherished lover (*Geliebte*) to whom one always returns after quarrelling. This teacher's mistress [*maîtresse du maître*] is also a censor: in the department or in the (lower) Faculty of Philosophy. She is, therefore, a censor without public force. Perhaps this censor exercises her censorship against the censorship of the State. Censorship against censorship, censorship of reason, serving and not opposing reason.

But, by defining this rational metaphysics as *Censoramt*, one acknowledges a censoring structure of reason.

The debate thus remains that of the best censorship. For a teacher, or for a finite being, there is never any lifting of censorship, only a strategic calculation: censorship against censorship. Is this strategy an art?

—*Translated by Barbara Havercrof*

Theology of Translation

Theology of translation: such a title should start me on a necessary and, on the whole, fairly well-known path. The history and problematics of translation, in Europe, were very early on established on the ground, in fact on the very body or corpus, of holy Scripture. Natural languages were fixed, if it can be put this way, rooted or re-rooted, in the very event of the Bible's translation. For the sake of economy, I will mention only the proper name of Luther; this emblem will suffice. Starting with this event or typical series of events, one could follow what has become in Europe of translation, the discourse on translation, the practice of translation. Other events, other transformations have no doubt affected the structure. But something of this essential relation to sacred writing seems to remain ineffaceable in it—and there is nothing accidental in that. I have tried to show this elsewhere in an essay on Benjamin's "The Task of the Translator."[1] I will not dwell on this here but will simply bring together the conclusion of "The Task of the Translator" and a certain passage from Goethe's *West-Eastern Divan*. In the last sentence of his text, Benjamin speaks of the interlinear version (of the Bible) as the *Urbild*, the prototypical ideal, the originary image or form of translation. (I prefer to retain the German word *Urbild* here, for throughout the lecture I will be speaking of *Bild, bilden, Bildung*.) Now here is what Goethe says, after having distinguished, like Jakobson,[2] though in a completely different sense, three kinds, in fact three epochs, of translation:

> But the reason for which we have called the third period the last, this is what we are going to demonstrate in just a few words. A translation that aims at being identified with the original tends to come close in the final account to the

interlinear version and greatly facilitates the comprehension of the original; by this we find ourselves in a way involuntarily led back to the primitive text, and thus the circle is finally completed according to which the translation from the foreign to the native, from the known to the unknown, is carried out.[3]

I will not speak directly about *this* theological dimension. This title, "Theology of Translation," refers to another historical grouping, to a premodern configuration that, even as it presupposes and contains within itself the "Lutheran" moment, so to speak (as does *every* concept of translation), no less conserves a certain originality, that of a family of events that are irreducible in the history of translation, of its problematics and its practice.

What external and conventional indicators are used to designate this family of events? Roughly speaking, what we call German Romanticism, which was *at once* a moment of intense, restless, tortured, fascinated reflection on translation, its possibility, its necessity, its meaning for German language and literature *and* a moment when a certain thinking about *Bildung, Einbildung,* and all the modifications of *bilden* are inseparable from what one could call precisely the imperative of translation, the task of the translator, the duty-to-translate [*devoir-traduire*]. I have left the words *Bild, bilden, Bildung* and their entire family in their language of origin because they are themselves challenges to translation. *Image, form, formation, culture* are so many inadequate approximations, first of all because they belong to different semantic roots.

Concerning this configuration of *Bildung* and *Übersetzung* (a word that can hardly be translated by *translation* without immediately losing the entire positional dimension of *setzen* [in *übersetzen*]), I will begin by referring to the very fine book by Antoine Berman, *L'épreuve de l'étranger: Culture et traduction dans l'Allemagne romantique.*[4] In a kind of homage to this book, what I will do here is provide perhaps a little supplementary contribution to it, on the subject, moreover, of the structure of *supplementarity* in translation. This modest contribution will concern, first, a certain ontotheological dimension, a problematics of onto-theology that is located at the founding of a certain concept of translation. Berman does not speak of this. I will also try to make visible the link between this onto-theological dimension and speculation in that period on the university institution. Finally, to restrict my analysis and so as not to remain in generalities or metatextual illusions, I will approach a text and author Berman barely names and about whom, in any case, he says almost nothing: Schelling.

In effect, the movement of leaving and returning to itself of Spirit, as it is defined by Schelling and Hegel, but also by F. Schlegel, as we have seen, is also the *speculative reformulation* of the law of classical *Bildung*. What is one's own gains access to itself only by *experience*, namely the experience of the foreign. (162; 258–59)

To this "law of classical *Bildung*" that would dominate the thinking of translation, roughly from Goethe to Hegel, passing by way of Schelling, Berman opposes the thinking of Hölderlin, who would "*explode the simplicity* of the schema of *Bildung.*"

If I have decided to speak to you about Schelling, it is also for another reason that I will not venture to call contingent. This paper on "literary translation" that will speak less about translation and literature "properly speaking" than about a certain Schellingian philosophy of literary translation, a certain onto-theological claim to found poetic translation, this paper is also the concluding session of the course that I gave right here on "Languages and Institutions of Philosophy." You will therefore recognize all the traces of the compromise that I am passing along between that seminar and this colloquium. The last session concerned a certain Kantian apparatus of the philosophy of the university, of philosophy in the university, and it anticipated Schelling's critique of the Kantian proposition. This proposition is indeed called into question again by Schelling in his 1803 *Lectures On the Method of University Studies.*[5] What Schelling reproaches in the Kantian construction and deduction of the university structure (in particular the two classes of faculties, the higher—theology, law, medicine—tied to the power of the State they represent, and the lower, that of philosophy, over which the ruling power has no right of censorship, so long as philosophy speaks *about truth within* the university) is the one-sidedness of Kant's topological perspective, his "Einseitigkeit" (*University* 79).

From the standpoint of institutional architecture, this one-sidedness translates the one-sidedness of Kantian "critique" in its very principle. According to Schelling, all the dissociations, the entire grid of critical limits that chart the Kantian university institution (as it is described in *The Conflict of the Faculties*) only transpose the opposition of sensibility and understanding, of understanding and reason, of sensible intuition and intellectual intuition, of *intuitus derivativus* and *intuitus originarius. Between* the two there is of course the scheme of the imagination (*Einbildungskraft*), a sensitive place for the question of poetry and translation. But there is also, quite simply, thinking. For all the dissociations of Kantian critique must evidently allow themselves to be *thought*. They can do so only from the standpoint of that which makes dissociation itself thinkable and possible, namely *an originary unity*. For Schelling and according to a movement shared by everything that will be referred to as post-Kantian German Idealism, *one must start from that from which we will have had to start in order to think dissociation: originary unity*. And if we start from this, then all differences will only be translations (not necessarily in a linguistic sense) of the *same*, which is projected or *reflected* in different categories. That is what thinking philosophy is: knowing how to start from that from which knowledge will have started, to take note of this originary knowledge presupposed by all critical delimitation. This move is no longer pre-critical; it claims to be post-critical, critique of critique. Schelling's Fourth Lecture clarifies it in a theory of "reflexive" or "reflecting" translation. It concerns the study of the pure rational sciences, mathematics and philosophy. Kant separates these in *The Conflict of the Faculties*. He explains that pure mathematics, unlike pure philosophy (the metaphysics of morals and the metaphysics of nature), *constructs* its pure sensible object. This construction has no meaning in pure philosophy. Schelling calls this dissociation into question again, from the standpoint of the unity of originary knowledge, which precedes the opposition of the sensible and the intelligible. He starts from intellectual intuition. Not that he identifies mathematics and philosophy, but he speaks of their "resemblance." This resemblance makes possible the translation of the one into the other, for they are both founded upon the identity of the general and the particular. The universal triangle is one with the particular triangle that is in turn taken for all triangles, being at once a unity and a totality, unitotality (*Ein- und Allheit*) presented to intuition (*University* 47). For philosophy, intuition is reason; it is an intellectual intuition (*intellektuelle Anschauung*) that is one with its object in originary knowledge (*Urwissen*) (*University* 49). Mathematics *resembles* philosophy. Its intuition is not immediate but rather only reflected (*reflektierte*). It belongs to the world of the reflected image (*abgebildete Welt*) and only manifests originary knowledge in its absolute identity in the form of reflection (*Reflex*) (*University* 48). The analogical translation between the two worlds that in fact are only one is assured by the *symbol* (*Bild*) and this symbolicity is developed in the play of *Abbildung* and *Einbildung*, of imaginative reproduction. Hence the complexity of the relation to Kant, for this privilege extended to *Einbildungskraft* (imagination) also has a Kantian filiation. Hence also the essential role of poetry and of poetic discourse in these lectures. Poetry is at the heart of philosophy; the poem is a philosopheme. The opposition to Kant testifies to the filiation of the *Critique of Judgment*, which Schelling read as a student at Tübingen, only a short time before Fichte (the object of his great admiration) and Goethe helped him get an appointment at Jena in 1798, the very year Kant gathered the texts of the *Conflict of the Faculties*. Very shortly thereafter, as a young professor at Jena (where he stayed for only five years), Schelling produced his *Lectures on the Method of University Studies*. The argumentative strategy he uses to criticize Kant resembles that of the third *Critique* (Hegel will not conceal that he makes an analogous move); he has recourse to the unity of the moments dissociated by the two other *Critique*s. This unity is that of the imagination (*Einbildungskraft*) and of the work of art, which is its product. As *Einbildungskraft*, which Schelling distinguishes from the *Imagination* (false fantasy),[6] the imagination always resolves a contradiction by proposing a mediating, that is to say translating, scheme. This translation by *Einbildung* is also the contract that links philosophy and art, specifically philosophical language and poetic language. Reason and imagination are one and the same thing (cf. The Sixth Lecture), but the one "in the ideal" (*im Idealen*) and the other in the real (*im Realen*) (*University* 61). Only if we remain at the one-sided point of view of understanding do we have any reason to be amazed at this identity or this analogy, this intertranslatability of the rational and the fantastic. If the imagination (*Einbildungskraft*) *is* reason, it is because the internal essence of the absolute, and therefore of originary knowledge, is *In-Eins-Bildung*. Therein lies the fundamental concept of these *Lectures*, and if it ensures the fundamental possibility of translation between the different categories (between the real and the ideal, and therefore between sensible and intelligible contents, and therefore, in languages, between the ideal semantic differences and the formal—signifying—so-called sensible differences), it itself resists translation. The fact that it belongs to the German language and to exploiting the multiple resources of the *Bildung* in *In-Eins-Bildung* remains a challenge. The French translation, *uni-formation*, apart from the fact that it deforms the French language, since the word is nonexistent, erases the recourse to the value of image that is precisely what marks the unity of the imagination (*Einbildungskraft*) and of reason, their cotranslatability. I am not taking the translators to task. Doubtless theirs is the best possible choice. I only wanted to underline a paradox: *the concept of fundamental translatability is linked poetically to a natural language and resists translation.*

But that in fact confirms Schelling's thesis, while at the same time appearing to put it in question. *In-Eins-Bildung*, formation, putting into form and image, gathers together, to be sure, but this gathering together *produces* unity. It is a poetic production, since it uni-forms without uni-formizing [*uni-forme sans uniformiser*]; it preserves the universal *and* the particular in the imprint that it produces. Whence, by virtue of this very particularity, its essential tie to a poetics and to a natural language. The internal essence of the absolute is an eternal *In-Eins-Bildung* that disseminates in profusion; its emanation (*Ausfluß*) traverses the world of phenomena through reason and the imagination (*University* 61). Philosophy and poetry cannot be separated, therefore, an affirmation that Schelling incessantly repeats; they should only be translated into one another, even if the poetic (rooted in the particularity of a language) is the very site of the limit of the translatability that it nevertheless demands.

We find ourselves here in opposition to Kant on a path that he nevertheless opened. Kant opposes the teacher of pure reason, the legislating philosopher, to the artist and even to the rational artist. For Schelling, there is an analogy between the two; the poetic is immanent in the philosophical, and this is fraught with consequences: for philosophical "formation," for *Bildung* as the teaching, cultivation, and apprenticeship of philosophy. This "formation" (*Bildung*) must be thought from the standpoint of *In-Eins-Bildung*, of the internal essence of the absolute, of the uni-formation of the uni-versal and the particular. The *university* must also be thought in the logic of uni-formation, which is also a poetics of translation.

Philosophy is the soul and life of knowledge inasmuch as knowledge has *its end in itself.* Schelling cannot find words harsh enough for those who wish to utilize knowledge, to "end-orient" [*finaliser*] it by making it serve other ends than itself, or subject it to the demands of an "alimentary" professionalization. Nietzsche and Heidegger will do the same. As a "living science" (*lebendige Wissenschaft*), philosophy requires an "artistic impulse" (58). There is (*es gibt*), the Fifth Lecture tells us (*in fine*), "einen philosophischen Kunsttrieb, wie es einen poetischen gibt" (an artistic impulse for philosophy, just as there is a poetical one). The "as" (*wie*) articulates the analogy, the symbolic affinity, the passageway for a translation. This is why Schelling never makes a distinction between the philosophical content, the philosopheme, and the form of its presentation. Every "new" philosophy, he says, has had to make a new "step" in form (*University* 58). Corresponding to a new philosophy there has to be a formal inventiveness, a poetic originality, and therefore a provocation as much as a challenge to translation. In this case there is a problem of philosophical translation, an internal and essential problem that could not have been posed for traditional philosophers, at least insofar as they did not link philosophical rationality, or philosophical semantics in general, to the poetic body, to the "reality" of a form and a language. This is Schelling's originality: it is original (novel) to say that a philosophy can and must possess originality, that formal originality is essential to it, that it is also a work of art.

This originality distinguishes the philosopher from the mathematician (and this explains why there is no problem of translation in mathematics; mathematics is by its very essence the immediate annulling or solution of translation). Like mathematicians, philosophers have a relation to the universal, to be sure, and are united in their science, but they have the originality of being able to be original because they are capable of this "transformation of forms" (*Wechsel der Formen*) that also calls for a transduction or a trans-lation [*une trans- ou une tra-duction*], an *Über-setzung* (one might say: this is not Schelling's word), which *posits* a novelty, imposes and superimposes it inasmuch as it ensures the passage beyond differential particularity (*University* 59).

If there is (*es gibt*) an artistic impulse for philosophy, what conclusion is to be drawn for *Bildung* in the sense of teaching? Can philosophy be learned? This is a question all the thinkers of the period since Kant are obsessed with, as we have seen; they have all became civil servants in public education; they are not sure that this is really the destination, the opportunity, indeed the possibility of philosophy. Can philosophy ever be acquired through practice and study? Is it on the contrary a free gift (*ein freies Geschenk*), an innate (*angeboren*) ability granted by destiny (*Geschick*)? In a certain way the answer is "yes," there is (*es gibt*) a gift or a present (*Geschenk*) bestowed, sent, bequeathed by destiny (*Geschick*); one is thus destined to philosophy insofar as it is an art, an art requiring genius and ruled according to an intellectual intuition that can only be given and give itself its object, while at the same time being linked to the genius of a natural language (*University* 60). That said, if what is essential to philosophy cannot be learned, its particular forms must be learned. That phi-

losophy is a gift does not mean that each person possesses it without practice. The properly artistic aspect of this philosophical science (Schelling
calls it "dialectical art") no doubt cannot be learned, but one can practice
it (*University* 61). Lecture 4 (on mathematics and philosophy) specifies
that if the pure intuition of space and time is only "reflected" in the dimension of the sensible to which mathematics refers, in philosophy intuition is purely and directly in reason. The person who does not possess
this intuition cannot even understand what is said about it; it cannot even
be translated for him (*University* 49). He may appear to understand the
words but he is not thinking what the words say. He is prohibited from
finding a passageway between these two modes of understanding. Philosophical intuition can therefore only be given (in the sense of a gift, a present), and that means that it is incapable of being given (this time in the
sense of being translated or given out by teaching). But this infinite philosophical intuition has a *negative* condition: the consciousness of the
inanity of all finite knowledge (*University* v). This consciousness or this
negative condition can let itself be deepened, clarified, cultivated, formed,
elaborated in a *Bildung*. In the philosopher who knows how to form it, to
cultivate it in himself (*in sich bilden*), to form himself in relation to it, this
consciousness must be *transformed* in character, even to the point of becoming an unalterable organ, an untransformable habitus:[7] the aptitude
for seeing each thing insofar as it is presented (*dargestellt*) in the idea. This
presentation may be precisely the translation or retranslation of the real
into the ideal. The character or type of the translator, of the philosopher
formed in relation to this translation, to this mode or form of presentation (*Darstellung*), can be acquired.

   That originary knowledge that constitutes the last instance of this discourse is the *Urwissen* of God; it is "absolute knowledge"—the expression
is Schelling's. We can therefore speak of a theology of translation. But we
also have the institutional translation of this theology of translation: for
Schelling, in the university he plans, "theology, as the science in which the
innermost core of philosophy is objectified, must have the first and highest place" (*University* 79). This is the objection aimed at *The Conflict of the
Faculties* in the Seventh Lecture ("On Some Conditions Externally Opposed to Philosophy, and in Particular the Opposition of the Positive Sciences"). As the French translators properly note, "positive sciences" does
not carry its modern meaning here, but that of those sciences enjoying an
institutional existence, a body of knowledge and public legitimacy. These

are the sciences that are the object of a discipline, such as the theological, juridical, and medical sciences Kant opposes to the philosophical discipline. The lecture's title indicates clearly that this opposition between philosophy and these "positive" sciences is external, therefore philosophically unjustified, insufficiently thought. It is indeed the system of oppositional limits upon which *The Conflict of the Faculties* is constructed that remains external and unjustified.

The criticism directed at Kant has two imports, the one literal or pointed, that is, strictly institutional, the other more fundamental and serving as the foundation for the preceding one. But the one can be translated into the other. The organizational and intrafaculty critique has for its target the onesidedness of the Kantian point of view: this is the point of view of the finitude that opposes philosophy and theology. It therefore makes of philosophy the field of finite thought. By virtue of this it gives the philosophical discipline at once too little and too much. Too little: it limits it to being only one discipline among others. Too much: it gives it a faculty. Schelling does not beat around the bush and proposes quite simply that there no longer be any department of philosophy. Not so as to erase philosophy from the university map, but on the contrary in order to recognize its true place, which is the entire place: "That which is all things cannot for that very reason be anything in particular" (*University* 79).

Schelling not only says that there should no longer be any department of philosophy. He says that there never is any. When we think we discern one, we are fooling ourselves; that which by usurpation is called by that name is not authentically philosophical. Schelling's "affirmation" (*Behauptung*) appears pointedly anti-Kantian. In fact, it remains faithful to a certain Kantian thesis. Apparently confined in its place, assigned its specific competence, the Faculty of Philosophy is in fact everywhere, according to Kant, and its opposition to the other faculties remains secondary and external. There are in short two Kants, and two times two Kants in this entire scene—which is also a scene of interpretative translation. There is the Kant of *The Conflict*, who wants to bring a department of philosophy into existence and to protect it (in particular from the State). In order to protect it, one must delimit it. And then there is the Kant who grants the Faculty of Philosophy the right of critical and panoptical supervision over all the other departments, in order to intervene in them in the name of truth. And as for critique, there are still two more Kants: the Kant of the two *Critiques* clearly marks out oppositions (and *The Conflict of the*

Faculties, subsequent to the third *Critique*, remains more controlled by the first two); but the Kant of the *Critique of Judgment*, the one who aroused the enthusiasm of the young Schelling, takes himself beyond oppositions and tries to think the living and art. (And let us not forget that for Kant, as we have emphasized, the "teacher of pure reason" is at once everywhere and nowhere. His unavoidable and obvious absence commands the entire field but also *empties* out the space of the philosophy department.)[8]

Now, it is precisely from the point of view of life and art that Schelling himself proposes to *reorganize* the university, to think its organicity, and to resituate philosophy within it. If philosophy is *objectified* in the three positive sciences that are theology, law, and medicine, it is not objectified *in totality* in any one of the three (*University* 79). Each of the three departments is a determinate, partial objectification of philosophy, theology being the highest of them. "Objectification" can be translated as "translation." The same meaning is transposed or transported into another idiom. But what is the total translation, the translation itself that ensures the veritable objectivity of philosophy in its totality? Art. "Philosophy in its totality becomes truly objective only in art" (*University* 79). *And this art is therefore, like this university itself, an art of generalized translation.* Through a rather surprising logic, Schelling concedes that strictly speaking, "for this reason, there can be no Faculty of Philosophy, but only a Faculty of the Arts" (*University* 79–80). This is only a passing concession, for the logic would demand that there no more be a department for this total translation than for omnipresent philosophy.

It is once again the *Bild* that ensures the translating analogy between art, specifically poetry, and philosophy: "Poetry and philosophy, which another variety of dilettantism imagines to be opposites, are alike in that both require a self-produced, original image [*Bild*] of the world" (*University* 74).

This affirmation is political as well. In the Kantian system, the Faculty of Philosophy remains determined and limited by the power of the State, which is still external. Now, art—about which Kant does not speak in *The Conflict*—can never be limited by an external power (*Macht*). It is therefore independent of the State; it has no (external) relation to it; it does not let itself be oppressed, privileged, or programmed by the State (*University* 80). There is no State culture, Schelling seems to be saying. But we will see in a moment that it is not that simple. The positive sciences can be determined in relation to this external (when it is external) State power.

Philosophy alone has the right to demand from the State an unconditional freedom (*Nur der Philosophie ist der Staat unbedingte Freiheit
schuldig*) (*University* 80). A Kantian affirmation, at least as concerns philosophy inasmuch as it is the judge of truth. Since the State could seek to
suppress philosophy only to the detriment of all the sciences, philosophy
should have its place, strictly speaking, in a Faculty of Arts. And for the
arts there are only free associations (*freie Verbindungen*), as opposed to
public State institutions (*University* 80). Such a proposition (philosophy
in the space of the arts) is not revolutionary. Schelling recalls the tradition
of the *Collegium artium*, ancestor of the Faculty of Philosophy to which
Kant refers: a college independent of the State, a liberal institution that
would not appoint *doctores*, professors furnished with privileges in exchange for which they take an oath before the State, but *magistri*, teachers
of liberal arts (*University* 80). Schelling attributes the decadence of philosophy, which has become an object of mockery and ceases to be considered
in the loftiness of its true mission, to the bureaucratic organization of a
corporation (*University* 80). This organization has ceased being a free association in view of the arts—and therefore of poetic translation. Schleiermacher will also say that in relation to the State the Faculty of Philosophy
should keep the status of a private enterprise.[9]

We are now going to draw out the most general foundations of this specific critique of the Kantian university, the grounds of this institutional
translation. The Seventh Lecture challenges the axiomatic principle of
The Conflict of the Faculties, namely the distinction between *Wissen* and
Handeln, knowledge and action. Pure knowledge was part of the Faculty
of Philosophy, which was not to "give orders" or act, while the other
higher Faculties were tied to State power, that is, to action. A historically
marked opposition, Schelling says, a late arrival, constructed and in need
of deconstruction. It is not even modern in a broad sense, but immediately contemporary, "a recent product, a direct offspring of pseudo-en-
lightenment [*Aufklärerei*]" (*University* 71). Schelling reacts violently
against this Enlightenment that, for example in Kant, creates artificial oppositions, separates knowledge from action, politics from ethics (there is
an analogous movement in Heidegger, nor would this be his only affinity
with Schelling). This unhappy separation is transposed into the university
institution of the Enlightenment. Kant, in his theoretical philosophy, was
wrong to have reduced the idea of God or of the immortality of the soul
to "mere ideas" and to have then tried to validate these ideas "in the moral
disposition" (*in der sittlichen Gesinnung*) (*University* 71). Now, the eleva-

tion of ethics to a point beyond determination makes us similar to God, and philosophy translates a similar elevation (*gleiche Erhebung*); it is at one with the ethical (this is again at once Kantian and anti-Kantian). There is "but one world" (*University* 71), Schelling says; there is no hinter-world,[10] no world in itself. Each of us gives a translation of this absolute world, an image (*Bild*) in his own way (*jedes in seiner Art und Weise abzu-bilden strebt*), knowledge as such or action as such (*University* 72). But the one *translates* the other. There is only a reflecting transfer, *Bildung, Abbil-dung* (reflected image, reflection), *Einbildungskraft*. Between knowledge and action, the only difference is between two reflected images or two re-flections of one and the same world, a difference in short in translation (*Übersetzung* and *Übertragung*). The world of action is also the world of knowledge; ethics is as speculative as theoretical philosophy (*University* 72). In order to think the separation, Kant *will indeed have had to think* the originary unity of the two worlds as a single and identical text to be deci-phered, in short, according to the two significations, according to the two versions or two translations of the original text. The unity of the originary world causes us to call into question once again the opposition of philoso-phy and the positive sciences in their institutional translation (theology, law, medicine), since this opposition was founded on the separation of knowledge and action. At the same time, it is the duality of the languages that proves not to be annulled but derived as the result of reflection, of *Re-flex*, of the reflected image, which is also to say, of translating transposition (*Übertragung, Übersetzung*), of transfer. The entire *Conflict of the Faculties* is constructed, we could show, upon the untranslatable multiplicity of lan-guages or, to put it more rigorously, upon dissociations of a discursive type: language of truth (constative) / language of action (performative), public language / private language, scientific (intra-university) language / popular (extra-university) language, spirit / letter, and so forth.

According to a movement typical of all post-Kantiansms, it all takes place as though Schelling, from the standpoint of this idea of reason or of this intellectual intuition, were giving expression to that which is suppos-edly inaccessible: by deeming this intuition inaccessible, you show that you have already acceded to it, you think it, it has already reached you, you have already reached it. You think the inaccessible, and so you accede to it. And in order to think finitude, you have already thought the infi-nite. This is, moreover, the definition of thinking. It would be more con-sistent, more responsible, to arrange everything in relation to this thought that you think, rather than to found your "criticism" in denegation. In the

most different ways, all the post-Kantians, from Schelling to Hegel to
Nietzsche, will accuse Kant of such a denegation. It remains to be seen
what a denegation is when it concerns nothing less than the thinking of
thinking and gives rise to something like the transcendental dialectics of
the *Critique of Pure Reason.*

The logic of this accusation, this negation of denegation or this critique
of critique, has paradoxical political implications. In every case. Let us
consider that of Schelling. He insinuates that Kant subjects the department of philosophy, in a public establishment, to the external power of
the State; and that therefore he does not understand the practice and place
of philosophy in society in a liberal enough way. Kant's liberalism would
not be unconditional. Schelling seems to be calling Kant back to liberalism, for example according to the model of the College of Arts. Inversely,
Schelling's thinking of uni-totality or of uni-formation as generalized
translation, onto-theological translation without a rupture, without opacity, a universally reflecting translation, can lead to a totalizing absolutiza-
tion of the State that Kant in turn would have deemed dangerous and not
very liberal. Liberalism perhaps presupposes separation, the heterogeneity
of codes, and the multiplicity of languages, not crossing certain limits,
nontransparence.

There is, then, a certain Schellingian statism. What is the State? The be-
coming-objective of originary knowledge *in the mode of action.* It is even
the most universal of the ideal productions that objectify and therefore
translate knowledge. The State is a form of knowledge, translated according to the arche-type of the world of ideas. But since it is only the becom-
ing-objective of knowledge, the State itself is in turn transported or transposed into an external organism with a view to knowledge as such, into a
sort of spiritual and ideal State, and these are the positive sciences, in other
words the university, which is in short a piece of the State, a figure of the
State, its *Übertragung,* the *Übersetzungen* that *transpose* the State into the
positive sciences. The State-as-knowledge is here a transposition of the
State-as-action. The higher faculties can therefore no longer be separated
from the lower faculty. The differentiation of the positive sciences is made
on the basis of originary knowledge, in the image of the internal type of
philosophy. The three positive sciences are nothing other than the differentiation, the differentiated translation of originary knowledge, and therefore of philosophy. There is a profound and essential identity between philosophy and the State. It is the same text, the same original text, if one
knows how to read its identity from the standpoint of *Ur-Wissen.*

This grouping (the State and its objectification transposed into the three positive sciences) is a whole, the whole of the objectification of originary knowledge. Originary knowledge forms with philosophy an "internal organism" (*innere Organismus*) (*University* 76) that is projected or transported outward in the external totality of the sciences. It is constructed through divisions and connections so as to form a body (*Körper*) that itself expresses outwardly the internal organism of knowledge and philosophy (*University* 78). The word *organism* is frequent and decisive in this context. It does not translate a biologism, since apparently, at least, we are dealing with a metaphor. The ideal and the real are not yet separable in the unity of originary knowledge. This unity permits one to speak, without trope, of the one as of the other, of the one in the language of the other. There is no metaphor but there is also nothing but metaphor, image in the broad sense (*Bild*). The originary unity of language in originary knowledge allows for rhetoric and at the same time prevents one from considering it only as a restricted rhetoric. It is a generalized rhetoric or translatology. This justifies the fact that, since the beginning of this paper, I have often spoken of translation when it was a question only of transposition, of transfer, of transport in a sense that is not strictly linguistic. One might think I was going too far and was speaking metaphorically of translation (understood in the strictly semiotic or linguistic sense) when there was actually nothing properly linguistic about the transposition of which I was speaking. But the point is precisely that for Schelling, whose onto-theology I wished to present, language is a living phenomenon; life or the living spirit speaks in language; and in the same way nature is an author, the author of a book that must be translated with the skill of a philologist. A motif found at the same period in Novalis in particular, but already in Goethe. Whence Schelling's pedagogy of language, of dead or living languages:

> Nothing forms the intellect so effectively as learning to recognize the living spirit of a language dead to us. To be able to do this is no whit different from what the natural philosopher does when he addresses himself to nature. Nature is like some very ancient author whose message is written in hieroglyphics on colossal pages, as the Artist says in Goethe's poem.[11] Even those who investigate nature only empirically need to know her *language*, so to speak [*so to speak* should be emphasized] in order to understand utterances which have become unintelligible to us. The same is true of philology in the higher sense of the term. The earth is a book made up of miscellaneous fragments dating from very different ages. Each mineral is a real philological problem. In geol-

ogy we still await the genius who will analyze the earth and show its composition as Wolf analyzed Homer. (*University* 40)

We have been led to this pan-rhetoric of translation by apparently political considerations. According to a paradoxical logic, the hyperliberalism set over against Kant always carries the risk of turning into the totalizing—I am not saying necessarily totalitarian—temptation whose consequences can reverse the liberal demand. Whence the impossible strategy of relations between philosophy and politics, specifically between philosophy and the State. It would be a mistake to see in this proposition, according to which the State is the objectifying translation of knowledge into action, one of those speculative statements of a German Idealism that we would today study through the mists like some great philosophical archive. The proposition is no doubt speculative (in a sense that is linked rigorously to a thinking of the reflecting and properly "symbolic" *speculum*), but it is also as "realist" as it is "idealist." It is modern. A politology today cannot construct the concept of the State without including in that concept the objectification of knowledge and its objectification in the positive sciences. A political discourse that would not speak of science would be lost in chatter and abstraction. Today more than ever the determination of the State includes the state of science, of all the sciences, of the whole of science. The way in which State structures (let's not speak of government) function depends essentially and concretely upon the state of all the sciences and techno-sciences. The so-called "basic" [*fondamentales*] sciences can no longer be distinguished from the so-called "end-oriented" [*finalisées*] sciences.[12] And what has rightly been called the military-industrial complex of the modern State presupposes this unity of the basic and the end-oriented. We would also have to connect this "logic" with that of the "performativity" of scientific discourse.

Schelling would no doubt say that the State is not the objectifying translation of knowledge *as knowledge* but of originary knowledge *as action*. It would be all the easier today to show to what extent a modern State is the implementation of a knowledge. Not only because it has a politics of science that it wants to pilot by itself, but because it is itself formed and transformed, in its concept, its discourse, its rhetoric, its methods, and so forth, according to the rhythm of techno-science.

It was necessary to insist, to be sure, on the unity of originary knowledge, on the totalizing gathering-together of the *Ein-Bildung der Vielheit in die Einheit* as general translatability. But that does not mean homogeneity and indifferentiation. There are forms and therefore specific structures. There are differences between philosophy and religion, philosophy and poetry. That is why *one must translate* and this translation stems from the finitude of individuals. Philosophy is indeed the immediate presentation (*Darstellung*), the science of originary knowledge (*Urwissen*), but it is this only in the realm of the ideal and not "really." If the mind could, in a single act of knowledge, *really* grasp (*begreifen*) absolute totality as a system completed in all of its parts, it would overcome its finitude (*University* 75). It would not need to translate. It would conceive the whole as beyond all determination. As soon as there is determination, there is differentiation, separation, abstraction. Schelling does not say "opposition," *Entgegensetzung*. The real presentation of knowledge presupposes this separation, this division and this translation, one could say, of philosophical work. "Originary knowledge" can become "real," be realized in its unity in a single individual, only *in der Gattung*, in the genus or species, which is also to say in historical institutions (*University* 75). History progresses as this becoming-real of the idea.

This schema constructed the First Lecture on the basis of the absolute concept of science. The lecture starts from the idea of *living totality*. From this it deduces the concept of the university, as Kant also deduces it from an idea of reason. We have another indication that Schelling revives the Kantian tradition to which he is opposed as one might be opposed to a philosophy of opposition. The thinking development of the idea of reason leads Schelling to reject the limiting consequences that Kant draws from it.

The specialized training or formation (*Bildung*) of the student must be preceded by the knowledge of this living totality, of this "living unity" (*des lebendigen Zusammenhangs*) (*University* 7). The student must first have access to the organic totality of the university, to the "great tree" of knowledge (*University* 9): one can apprehend it only by starting (genetically) from its originary root, *Urwissen*. On the threshold of his studies, moreover, the "young man" (and not the young girl, of course) has the sense of, and the desire for, this totality (*Sinn und Trieb für das Ganze*) (*University* 8). But he is quickly disappointed. Schelling describes these disappointments, all the damage done by professional training or by the specialization that bars access to the very organization, to the *organicity* of this totality of knowledge, in other words, to philosophy, to the philosophy of the university that constitutes the organic and living principle of this totality. Schelling then makes a proposal from which we have yet to reap the full benefit. "It is imperative," he says, "that universities give general instruction in the aims and methods of academic study, both as a whole and in respect to its particular subjects" (*University* 6). Which is what Schelling does in saying so. His lectures tell us what the orientation, the method, and the totality of the particular objects of a university worthy of the name should be. He defines the final destination (*Bestimmung*) that determines and regulates all the organically interdisciplinary translations of this institution.

This final destination, that of knowledge as well as that of the university, is nothing less than communion with the divine essence. All knowledge tends to enter into this community with the divine being. The philosophical community, as university community, is this *Streben nach Gemeinschaft mit dem göttlichen Wesen* (*University* 11); it tends to participate in this originary knowledge that is one and in which each type of knowledge participates as the member of a living totality. Those whose thought is not regulated and ordered by this living and buzzing community are like sexless bees (*geschlechtslose Bienen*): since they are denied the power to create, to produce (*produzieren*), they multiply inorganic excrements outside of the hives as proof of their own platitude; they attest in this way to their spiritlessness (*Geistlosigkeit*) (*University* 11). This deficiency is also an inaptitude for the great translation that causes the meaning of originary knowledge to circulate throughout the entire body of knowledge.

Man is not a bee. As rational being (*Vernunftwesen*), he is destined (*hingestellt*), placed with a view to, appointed to the task of supplementing or complementing the world's manifestation (*eine Ergänzung der Welterscheinung*) (*University* 12). He completes the phenomenalization of the whole. He is there so that the world might appear as such and in order to help it to appear as such in knowledge. But if it is necessary to complete or supplement (*ergänzen*), it is because there is a lack. Without man, God's very revelation would not be accomplished. By his very activity, man is to develop (*entwickeln*) that which is lacking in God's total revelation (*was nur der Offenbarung Gottes fehlt*) (*University* 12).

That is what is called translation; it is also what is called the destination of the university.

—*Translated by Joseph Adamson*

Mochlos:
Eyes of the University

Mochlos, or The Conflict
of the Faculties

If we could say *we* (but have I not already said it?), we might perhaps ask ourselves: where are we? And who are we in the university where apparently we are? *What* do we represent? *Whom* do we represent? Are we responsible? For what and to whom? If there is a university responsibility, it at least begins the moment when a need to hear these questions, to take them upon oneself and respond to them, imposes itself. This imperative of the response is the initial form and minimal requirement of responsibility. One can always not respond and refuse the summons, the call to responsibility. One can even do so without necessarily keeping silent. But the structure of this call to responsibility is such—so anterior to any possible response, so independent, so dissymetrical in its coming from the other within us—that even a nonresponse a priori assumes responsibility.

And so I proceed: what does university responsibility represent? This question presumes that one understands the meaning of "responsibility," "university"—at least if these two concepts are still separable.

The university, what an idea!

It is a relatively recent idea. We have yet to put it aside, and it is already being reduced to its own archive, to the archive of its archives, without our having quite understood what had happened with it.

Almost two centuries ago Kant was responding, and was responding in terms of responsibility. The university, what an idea, I was just asking. This is not a bad idea, says Kant, opening *The Conflict of the Faculties* (*Der Streit der Fakultäten*, 1798). And, with his well-known humor, abridging a more laborious and tortuous story, he pretends to treat this idea as a find, a happy solution that a very imaginative person would have come up with, as the invention, in sum, of a fairly rational device that some ingenious operator might have sent to the State for a patent. And, in the West, the State would have adopted the concept of this very ingenious machine. And the machine would have worked. Not without conflict, not without contradiction, but perhaps, precisely, due to the conflict and the rhythm of its contradictions.

Here is the opening of this short work that I wanted to invite to our commemoration, with that sense of vague disquiet that arises when, responding to the honor of an invitation from friends, one brings along, as an afterthought, some parasite with poor table manners. But for this symposium, it is not Socrates, it is Kant, and he says:

> It was not a bad idea [*kein übeler Einfall*], whoever first conceived and proposed a public means for treating the sum of knowledge (really the thinkers who devote themselves to it [*eigentlich die derselben gewidmeten Köpfe*]), in a quasi *industrial manner* [*gleichsam fabrikenmäßig*], with a division of labor [*durch Vertheilung der Arbeiten*] where, for as many fields as there may be of knowledge, so many public teachers [*öffentliche Lehrer*] would be allotted, *professors* being like trustees [*als Depositeure*], forming together a kind of common scientific entity [*eine Art von gelehrtem gemeinen Wesen*] called a *university* (or high school [*hohe Schule*]), and having autonomy (for only scholars [*Gelehrte*] can pass judgment on scholars as such); and, thanks to its *faculties* (various small societies into which university teachers are divided, in keeping with the variety of the main branches of knowledge), the university would be authorized [*berechtigt*: Kant is being precise, the university receives its legitimate *authorization* from a power that is not its own] to admit, on the one hand, student-apprentices from the lower schools aspiring to its level, and to grant, on the other hand—after prior examination, and on its own authority [*aus eigner Macht*, from its own power]—to teachers who are "free" (not drawn from the members themselves) and called "doctors," a universally recognized rank (conferring upon them a degree)—in short, creating [*creiren*] them.[1]

Kant underlines the word "creating": the university is thus *authorized* to have the autonomous power of *creating* titles.

The style of this declaration is not merely one of a certain fiction of the origin: the happy idea of the university, that someone comes up with, one fine day, at some date, with something like the fictive possibility of an anniversary—this is what Kant seems to be evoking here. Indeed, further on in his text, after dropping the rhetoric of an introduction, his first move is to set aside the hypothesis of a somewhat random find, of an empirical, even an imaginative, origin to the university. Certain artificial institutions, he goes on to say, have as their foundation an idea of reason. And the university is an "artificial" (*künstliche*) institution of this kind. Kant begins by recalling this fact for those who would like to forget it, believing in the naturalness of the place and the habitat. The very idea of government is founded on reason, and nothing in this respect is a matter of chance.

> For this reason it must be said that the organizing of a university, with respect to its classes and faculties, was not just a matter of chance, but that the government, without showing any special wisdom or precocious knowledge for doing so, was, from a particular need that it felt (for influencing the people through various teachings), able to arrive a priori at a principle of division that happily [*glücklich*] coincides with the principle currently adopted.

And Kant is well aware that he is in the process of justifying in terms of reason what was a de facto organization determined by the government of his day, as if by accident its king were a philosopher. Of this he is evidently aware, since he promptly excuses himself in something of a tone of denial: "But I will not, for all that, speak in its favor as if it had no fault" (*Conflict* 31).

Within the introductory fiction, Kant had multiplied his rhetorical precautions, or rather he had somehow guaranteed the analogical statements with, so to speak, a real analogy: the university is analogous to society, to the social system it represents as one of its parts; and the teaching body represents, in one form or another, the goal and function of the social body—for example, of the industrial society that will give itself, in less than ten years' time, the great model of the University of Berlin; this latter, even now, remains the most imposing reference for what has been handed down to us of the concept of the university. Here, then, is the series of analogies: within the university, one would treat knowledge a little *like* in industry (*gleichsam fabrikenmäßig*); professors would be *like* trustees (*als Depositeure*); together they would form a kind of essence or collective scholarly entity that would have its own autonomy (*eine Art von gelehrtem gemeinen Wesen, die ihre Autonomie hätte*). As for this autonomy, the fiction and hypothesis are more prudent still. In itself, this autonomy is no doubt justified by the axiom stating that scholars alone can judge other scholars, a tautology that may be thought of as linked to the essence of knowledge as to the knowledge of knowledge. When, however, the issue is one of creating public titles of competence, or of legitimating knowledge, or of producing the public effects of this ideal autonomy, then, at that point, the university is no longer authorized by itself. It is authorized (*berechtigt*) by a nonuniversity instance or agency—here, by the State—and according to criteria no longer necessarily and in the final analysis those of scientific competence, but those of a certain performativity. The autonomy of scientific evaluation may be absolute and unconditioned, but the political effects of its legitimation, even supposing that one could in all rigor distinguish them, are no less controlled, measured, and overseen by a power outside the university. Regarding this power, university autonomy is in a situation of heteronomy; it is an autonomy conferred and limited, a representation of autonomy—in the double sense of a representation by delegation and a theatrical representation. In fact, the university as a whole is responsible to a nonuniversity agency.

Kant knew something of this. And if he did not know it a priori, experience recently taught him a lesson. The king of Prussia had just called him back to order. A letter from Friedrich Wilhelm reproached him for abusing his philosophy by deforming and debasing certain dogmas in *Religion within the Limits of Reason Alone*. Among us, perhaps, in 1980, there may be some who dream of receiving such a letter, a letter from a prince or sovereign at least letting us locate the law in a body and assign censorship to a simple mechanism within a determined, unique, punctual, monarchical place. For those who dream, for various reasons, of so reassuring a localization, I will therefore do the pleasure of citing a sentence unimaginable today from the pen of Carter, Brezhnev, Giscard, or Pinochet, barely, perhaps, from that of an ayatollah. The king of Prussia reproaches the philosopher for having behaved unpardonably, literally "irresponsibly" (*unverantwortlich*). This irresponsibility Friedrich Wilhelm analyzes and divides in two. The accused appears before two juridical instances. He bears, in the first place, his inner responsibility and personal duty as a teacher of the young. But he is also responsible to the father of the land, to the sovereign (*Landesvater*), whose intentions are known to him and ought to define the law. These two responsibilities are not juxtaposed, but are instead subordinated within the same system:

> You must recognize how irresponsibly [*wie unverantwortlich*] you thus act against your duty as a teacher of the young [*als Lehrer der Jugend*] and against our sovereign purposes [*landesväterliche Absichten*], which you know well. Of you we require a most scrupulous account [literally, an assuming of your responsibility, *Verantwortung*] and expect, so as to avoid our highest displeasure,

that in the future you will not fall into such error, but rather will, as befits your duty, put your reputation and talent to the better use of better realizing our sovereign purpose; failing this, you can expect unpleasant measures for your continuing obstinancy. (*Conflict* 11)

Kant cites this letter and justifies himself at length, in the preface and finally beyond the preface to *The Conflict of the Faculties*. Whatever one thinks of his system of justification, the nostalgia that some of us may feel in the face of this situation perhaps derives from this value of responsibility: at least one could believe, at that time, that responsibility was to be taken—for something, and before some determinable someone. One could at least pretend to know whom one was addressing, and where to situate power; a debate on the topics of teaching, knowledge, and philosophy could at least be posed in terms of responsibility. The instances invoked—the State, the sovereign, the people, knowledge, action, truth, the university—held a place in discourse that was guaranteed, decidable, and, in every sense of this word, "representable"; and a common code could guarantee, at least on faith, a minimum of translatability for any possible discourse in such a context.

Could we say as much today? Could we agree to debate together about the responsibility proper to the university? I am not asking myself whether we could produce or simply spell out a consensus on this subject. I am asking myself first of all if we could say "we" and debate together, in a common language, about the general forms of responsibility in this area. Of this I am not sure, and herein lies a being-ill [*mal-être*] no doubt more serious than a malaise or a crisis. We perhaps all experience this to a more or less vivid degree, and through a pathos that can vary on the surface. But we lack the categories for analyzing this being-ill. Historical codes (and, a fortiori, historical datings, references to technical events or to spectacular politics, for example, to the great unrest of '68), philosophical, hermeneutic, and political codes, and so on, and perhaps even codes in general, as productive [*performant*] instruments of decidibility, all seem powerless here. It is an im-pertinence of the code, which can go hand in hand with the greatest power, which lies, perhaps, at the source of this being-ill. For if a code guaranteed a problematic, whatever the discord of the positions taken or the contradictions of the forces present, then we would feel better in the university. But we feel bad, who would dare to say otherwise? And those who feel good are perhaps hiding something, from others or from themselves.

Celebrating the anniversary of a university's founding, if one ignores the secondary gains that attend such commemorations, should suppose a confirmation, the renewing of a commitment, and more profoundly, the self-legitimation, the self-affirmation of the university.

I just uttered the word "self-affirmation." Regarding the university, we hear it at once as a translation and a reference. It is the title of Heidegger's sadly famous speech upon taking charge of the Rectorate of the University of Freiburg-im-Breisgau on May 27, 1933, *The Self-Affirmation of the German University* (*Die Selbstbehauptung der deutschen Universität*). If I dare to summon here this great ghost and sinister event, it is not merely because, in doing so, I can avail myself of a pretext here for paying homage to Columbia University, for the welcome it managed to extend to intellectuals and professors emigrating from Nazi Germany. It is also because, however one judges it in terms of political circumstances (necessarily a very complex evaluation, one that I will not attempt at this time), Heidegger's speech on the self-affirmation of the German university undoubtedly represents, in the tradition of *The Conflict of the Faculties* and the great philosophical texts concerning the University of Berlin (Schelling, Fichte, Schleiermacher, Humboldt, Hegel), the last great discourse in which the Western university tries to think its essence and its destination in terms of responsibility, with a stable reference to the same idea of knowledge, technics, the State, and the nation, very close to a limit at which the memorial gathering of a thinking makes a sudden sign toward the entirely-other of a terrifying future. Unable though I am to justify this hypothesis here, it seems to me that Heidegger, after this speech, eventually goes beyond the limits of this still very classical concept of the university, one that already guided him in *What Is Metaphysics?* (1929); or at least that the enclosure of the university—as a commonplace and powerful contract with the State, with the public, with knowledge, with metaphysics and technics—will seem to him less and less capable of measuring up to a more essential responsibility, that responsibility that, before having to answer for a knowledge, power, or something or other determinate, before having to answer for a being or determinate object before a determinate subject, must first answer *to* being, *for* the call of being, and must think this coresponsibility. But, once again, essential as it may seem to me, I cannot explore this path today. I will try, let's say, to keep a constant, if oblique and indirect, link with its necessity.

When one pronounces the word "responsibility" today in the university, one no longer knows for sure with what concept one can still rule it. One hesitates between at least three hypotheses.

1. One can treat responsibility as a precisely academic theme. One would exhume this archived *topos*, whose code would no longer be our own, along the lines of a celebration, an anniversary. In the course of a school exercise, one might, as a historian or philologist, embroider the topic with flowers of rhetoric, paying tribute to a secular institution that, in short, though not entirely of its own time, would, for all that, not have aged altogether badly. Within this hypothesis, that of commemorative aestheticism with all it presupposes of luxury, pleasure, and despair, one would still presuppose that events of the past century, and especially of the most recent postwar era, would have ruined the very axiomatics of a discourse on responsibility—or, rather, of the discourse *of* responsibility. Given a certain techno-political structure of knowledge, the status, function, and destination of the university would no longer stem from the juridical or ethico-political language of responsibility. No longer would a *subject*, individual or corporate, be summoned in its responsibility.

2. A second hypothesis, that of a tradition to be reaffirmed: one would then recall that more than a century ago, when Columbia's graduate school was founded, the question of knowing for what, and to whom, a professor, a faculty, and so forth, is responsible, was posed within a philosophical, ethical, juridical, and political problematic, within a system of implicit evaluations, within an axiomatics, in short, that survives essentially intact. One could posit secondary adaptations as a way to account for transformations occurring in the interval.

3. Keeping its value and meaning, the notion of responsibility would have to be re-elaborated within an entirely novel problematic. In the relations of the university to society, in the production, structure, archiving, and transmission of knowledges and technologies (of forms of knowledge as technologies), in the political stakes of knowledge, in the very idea of knowledge and truth, lies the advent of something entirely other. To answer, what to answer for, and to whom?: the question is perhaps more alive and legitimate than ever. But the "what" and the "who" would have to be thought entirely otherwise. And (a more interesting corollary) they could, starting from this alterity, lead us to wonder what they might once have been, this "who" and this "what."

Would these three hypotheses exhaust, in principle, all possibilities of a typical questioning about university responsibility? I am not certain of this; nothing in this domain seems certain to me. Everything seems obscure, enigmatic, at once threatened and threatening, in a place where the greatest danger today is concentrated. The Western university is a very recent *constructum* or artifact, and we already sense that it is *finished*: marked by finitude, just as, as its current model was established, between *The Conflict of the Faculties* (1798) and the founding of the University of Berlin (October 10, 1810, at the close of the mission entrusted to Humboldt), it was thought to be ruled by an idea of reason, by a certain relation, in other words, with infinity. Following this model, at least in its essential features, every great Western university was, between 1800 and about 1850, in some sense reinstituted. Between that moment and the founding of Columbia's graduate school, less time passed than between the last war and the present day. It is as if, with a minor delay, we were celebrating tonight the birthday of the modern university in general. Whether it is a question of an anniversary or a university, all this turns, as we say in French, very fast.

I was thinking of reopening with you *The Conflict of the Faculties*, because the *fatum* of responsibility seems inscribed there at the origin and on the very eve of the modern university, in its pre-inaugural discourse. It is inscribed there in language receiving from Kant its first great illustration, its first conceptual formalization of great rigor and consequence. There, at our disposal, we find a kind of dictionary and grammar (structural, generative, and dialectical) for the most contradictory discourses we might develop about—and, up to a point, within—the university. I will not call this a Code, precisely because *The Conflict of the Faculties* situates the Code and the written Code (*Gesetzbuch*) (*Conflict* 36ff.) within a very circumscribed and determined part of the university, within the faculties called "higher"—essential instruments of the government (the Faculties of Theology, Law, and Medicine). If *The Conflict of the Faculties* is not a Code, it is a powerful effort at formalization and discursive economy in terms, precisely, of formal law. Here again, Kantian thought tries to attain to pure legitimation, to purity of law, and to reason as the court of final appeal. The equivalence between reason and justice as "law" or "right" [*droit*] finds its most impressive presentation here.

For us, however, most often and in a manner still dominant, the discourse of responsibility appeals, in a mode we find tautological, to a pure ethico-juridical instance, to pure practical reason, to a pure thinking of right [*droit*], and correlatively to the *decision* of a pure egological subject, of a consciousness or an intention that has to answer, in decidable terms, for and before the law. I insist on this: it is thus for us, most often and most prevailingly, though this bond is not indissoluble for all eternity. It is not natural; it has a history. One can no doubt imagine dissolving the value of responsibility by relativizing, secondarizing, or deriving the effect of subjectivity, consciousness, or intentionality; one can no doubt decenter the subject, as it is easily put, without putting into question the bond between responsibility, on the one hand, and freedom of subjective consciousness and purity of intentionality, on the other. This happens all the time and is not that interesting, since nothing in the prior axiomatics is changed: one denies the axiomatics *en bloc* and keeps it going as a survivor, with minor adjustments *de rigueur* or daily compromises lacking in rigor. In so doing, in operating at top speed, one accounts and becomes accountable for nothing: neither for what happens, nor for the reasons to continue assuming responsibilities without a concept.

Conversely, would it not be more interesting, even if difficult, and perhaps impossible, to think a responsibility—that is, a summons requiring a response—as no longer passing, in the last instance, through an ego, the "I think," intention, the subject, the ideal of decidability? Would it not be more "responsible" to try to think the ground, in the history of the West, on which the juridico-egological values of responsibility were determined, attained, imposed? There is perhaps a fund here of responsibility that is at once "older" and—to the extent it is conceived anew, through what some would call the crisis of responsibility in its juridico-egological form and its ideal of decidability—is *still to come*, and, if you prefer, "younger." Here, perhaps, would be a chance for the task of thinking what will have been, up to this point, the representation of university responsibility, what it is or might become, in the wake of upheavals that we can no longer conceal from ourselves, even if we still have trouble analyzing them. Is a new type of university responsibility possible? Under what conditions? I don't know, but I know that the very form of my question still constitutes a classical protocol, of a precisely Kantian type: by posing my question in this way I continue to act as a guardian and trustee responsible for traditional responsibility. Kant in effect tells us the conditions under which a rational university in general will, according to him, have been possible. Reading him today, I see his assurance and his necessity, much as one might admire the rigor of a plan or structure through the breaches of an uninhabitable edifice, about which one cannot decide whether it is in ruins or simply never existed, having only ever been able to accommodate the discourse of its incompletion. This is the uncertainty with which I read Kant, but I will spare you further considerations of the pathos of this uncertainty, the intermittent despair, the laborious or ironic distress, the daily contradictions, the desire to challenge and militate on several fronts at once, so as to maintain *and* to risk, and so forth. From the depths of this uncertainty I still believe in the task of another discourse on university responsibility. Not in the renewal of the contract in its old or barely renewed forms; but since, concerning entirely other forms, I know nothing clear, coherent, and decidable, nor whether such forms will ever be, or whether the university as such has a future, I continue to believe in the interest of light in this domain—and of a discourse measuring up to the novelty, tomorrow, of this problem. This problem is a task; it remains for us *given-to*, to what I do not know, to doing or thinking, one might have once said. I say so not just as a member of the university. It is not certain that the university itself, from within, from its idea, is equal to this task or this debt; and this is the problem, that of the breach in the university's system, in the internal coherence of its concept. For there may be no inside possible for the university, and no internal coherence for its concept. And so I mention this task both as a member of the university taking care not to deny his membership (since the only coherent attitude, for someone refusing all commitment on this point, would amount, in the first place, to resigning) and as a non-academic sensitive to the very fact that, nowadays, the university as such cannot reflect, represent itself, or change into one of its own representations, as one of its possible objects. With a view to this other responsibility, I will hazard a contribution that is modest, preliminary, and above all in keeping with the time at our disposal here, which no one in decency should exceed. With this economy and these rhetorical constraints taken into account, I set myself the following rule: to try to translate *The Conflict of the Faculties* in part, and under the heading of an introductory or paradigmatic essay, so as to recognize its points of untranslatability, by which I mean anything that no longer reaches us and remains outside the usage of our era. I will try to analyze those untranslatable nodes; and the benefits that I anticipate—if not in the course of this brief effort, then at least in the systematic pursuit of this kind of reading—will be an inventory not merely of what was and no longer is, or of certain contradictions, laws of conflicts, or antinomies of university reason, but of what perhaps exceeds this dialectical rationality itself; and the un-translatability we experience will perhaps signal the university's inability to comprehend itself in the purity of its inside, to translate and transmit its proper meaning. Since its origin, perhaps.

Will it suffice today to speak of contradiction in the university? Is the first interest of Kant's text not to recognize the conflict at the university's very interior? Kant foresees the inevitable recurrence of this, a necessity somehow transcendental and constitutive. He classes the different types and places of contradiction, the rules of their return, the forms of their legality or illegality. For he wishes at all costs to *pronounce the law*, and to discern, to decide between legal and illegal conflicts that set into opposition the faculties of the university. Kant's principal concern is legitimate for someone intending to make the right decisions: it is to trace the rigorous limits of the system called university. No discourse would be rigorous here if one did not begin by defining the unity of the university system, in other words the border between its inside and its outside. Kant wishes to analyze conflicts *proper* to the university, those arising between the different parts of the university's body and its power, that is, here, the faculties. He wants to describe the process of these *internal* contradictions, but also to class, to hierarchize, to arbitrate. But even before proposing a general division of the teaching body and recognizing the two major classes of faculties, higher and lower, that can confront each other, Kant encounters a prior, if not a pre-prior, difficulty, one that we today would sense even more keenly than he. As one might expect, this difficulty derives from the definition of a certain outside that maintains with its inside a relation of resemblance, participation, and parasitism that can give rise to an abuse of power, an excess that is strictly political. An exteriority, therefore, within the resemblance. It can take three forms. Only one of these seems dangerous to Kant. The first is the organization of specialized academies or scholarly societies. These "workshops" do not belong to the university; Kant is content simply to mention them. He does not envisage any collaboration, any competition, any conflict between the university and these scientific societies. And yet these do not, as do the private amateurs he mentions in the same passage, represent a state of nature of science. These institutions, which are also among the effects of reason, play an essential role in society. Today, however—and this is a first limit to the translation of the Kantian text in our politico-epistemological space—there can be very serious competition and border conflicts between nonuniversity research centers and university faculties claiming at once to be doing research and transmitting knowledge, to be producing and reproducing knowledge. These problems are no longer isolated or circumscribed when they involve the politics of scientific research, including all socio-technical strategies (military, medical, or other, such limits and categories losing all pertinence today) and all computerization at the intra- or interstate level, and so forth. A whole field is largely open to the analysis of this university "outside" that Kant calls "academic." In Kant's day, this "outside" could be confined to a margin of the university. This is no longer so certain or simple. Today, in any case, the university is what has become its margin. Certain departments of the university at least have been reduced to that condition. The State no longer entrusts certain research to the university, which cannot accept its structures or control its techno-political stakes. When regions of knowledge can no longer give rise to the training and evaluation properly belonging to a university, the whole architectonics of *The Conflict of the Faculties* finds itself threatened, and with it the model regulated by the happy concord between royal power and pure reason. The *representation* of this model remains almost identical throughout the West, but the relation to power and to the research it programs in research academies and institutes differs widely between States, regimes, and national traditions. These differences are marked in the interventions on the part of the State and of public or private capital. They cannot fail to reverberate in researchers' practice and style. Certain objects and types of research elude the university. Sometimes, as in certain Eastern countries, the university is totally confined to the pursuit of a reproducible teaching. The State deprives it of the right to do research, which it reserves for academies where no teaching takes place. This arises most often from calculations of techno-political profitability as figured by the State, or by national or international, State or trans-State capitalist powers, as one might imagine happening with the storage of information and with establishing data banks, where the academic has to surrender any representation as a "guardian" or "trustee" of knowledge. However, this representation *once constituted* the mission of the university itself. But once the library is no longer the ideal type of the archive, the university no longer remains the center of knowledge and can no longer provide its subjects with a representation of that center. And since the university, either for reasons of structure or from its attachment to old representations, can no longer open itself to certain kinds of research, participate in them, or transmit them, it feels threatened in certain places of its own body; threatened by the development of the sciences, or, a fortiori, by the questions *of* science or *on* science; threatened by what it sees as an invasive margin. A singular and unjust threat, it being the constitutive faith of the university that the idea of science is at the very basis of the university. How, then, could that idea threaten the university in its technical development, when one can no longer separate knowledge from power, reason from performativity, metaphysics from technical mastery? The university is a (finished) product. I would almost call it the child of the inseparable couple metaphysics and technics. At the least, the university furnished a space or topological configuration for such an offspring. The paradox is that at the moment this offspring exceeds the places assigned it and the university becomes small and old, its "idea" reigns everywhere, more and better than ever. Threatened, as I said a moment ago, by an invasive margin, since non-university research societies, public, official, or otherwise, can also form pockets within the university campus. Certain members of the university can play a part there, irritating the insides of the teaching body like parasites. In tracing the system of the pure limits of the university, Kant wants to track any possible parasiting. He wants to be able to exclude it—legitimately, legally. Now, the possibility of such parasiting appears wherever there is language, which is also to say a public domain, publication, publicity. To wish to control parasiting, if not to exclude it, is to misunderstand, at a certain point, the structure of speech acts. (If, therefore, as I note in passing, analyses of a deconstructive type have so often had the style of theories of "parasitism," it is because they too, directly or indirectly, involve university legitimation.)[2]

We are still on the threshold of *The Conflict of the Faculties*. Kant has more trouble keeping a second category on the outside. But in naming it, he seems very conscious this time of political stakes. It has to do with the class of the "lettered": *die Litteraten* (*Studirte*). They are not scholars in the proper sense (*eigentliche Gelehrte*); but, trained in the universities, they became government agents, diplomatic aides, instruments of power (*Instrumente der Regierung*). To a large extent, they have often forgotten what they are supposed to have learned. The State gives them a function and power to its own ends, not to the ends of science: "Not," says Kant, "for the great good of the sciences." To these former students he gives the name of "businessmen or technicians of learning" (*Geschäftsleute oder Werkkundige der Gelehrsamkeit*). Their influence on the public is official and legal (*aufs Publicum gesetzlichen Einfluß haben*). They represent the

State and hold formidable power. In the examples cited by Kant, it seems that these businessmen of knowledge have been taught by the three faculties called "higher" (theology, law, medicine). They are ecclesiastics, magistrates, and doctors, who are not educated by the Faculty of Philosophy. Today, to be sure, within the class so defined of businessmen or technicians of knowledge, we would have to inscribe a massively larger variety and number of agents—outside, on the border of, and inside university places. They are all representatives of the public or private administration of the university, all "decision-makers" in matters of budgets and the allocation and distribution of resources (bureaucrats in a ministry, "trustees," etc.), all administrators of publications and archivization, publishers, journalists, and so forth. Is it not, today, for reasons involving the structure of learning, especially impossible to distinguish rigorously between scholars and technicians of learning, just as it is to trace, between knowledge and power, the limit within whose shelter Kant sought to preserve the university edifice? We will return to this question. It is always, in fact, in terms of "influence over the general public" that Kant elaborates his problem. Businessmen of learning are formidable because they have an immediate tie to the general public, which is composed, not of the ignorant, as the term is often rendered in translation, but, as Kant crudely says, of "idiots" (*Idioten*). But since the university is thought to lack any power of its own, it is to the government that Kant appeals to keep this class of businessmen in order (*in Ordnung*), since they can at any time usurp the right to judge, a right belonging to the faculties. Kant asks of governmental power that it itself create the conditions for a counterpower, that it ensure its own limitation and guarantee the university, which is without power, the exercise of its free judgment to decide on the true and the false. The government and the forces it represents, or that represent it (civil society), should create a law limiting their own influence and submitting all its statements of a constative type (those claiming to tell the truth) and even of a "practical" type (insofar as they imply a free judgment) to the jurisdiction of university competence and, finally, we will see, to that within it which is most free and responsible in respect to the truth: the Faculty of Philosophy. The principle of this demand may seem exorbitant or elementary—one or the other, one as well as the other—and it already had, under Friedrich Wilhelm, no chance of being applied, but not for reasons of empirical organization alone, which thereafter would only worsen. One would have to imagine today a control exercised by university competence (and, in the last instance, by philosophical competence) over every declaration coming from bureaucrats, subjects representing power directly or indirectly, the dominating forces of the country as well as the forces dominated insofar as they aspire to power and participate in the political or ideological debate. Nothing would escape it—not a single position adopted in a newspaper or book, on radio or television, in the public practice of a career, in the technical administration of knowledge, in every stage between the research known as "basic" [*fondamentale*] and its civil, police, medical, military, etc., "applications," in the world of students and nonuniversity pedagogy (elementary or high school teachers, of whom Kant, strangely, has nothing to say in this very place), among all "decision-makers" in matters of bureaucracy and university accounting, and so forth. In short, no one would have the authority to use his or her "knowledge" *publicly* without being subject, by law, to the control of the faculties, "to the censorship of the faculties," as Kant literally says. This system has the appearance and would have the reality of a most odious tyranny if (1) the power that judges and decides here were not defined by a respectful and responsible service to *truth*, and if (2) it had not been stripped, from the beginning and by its structure, of all executive power, all means of coercion. Its power of decision is theoretical and discursive, and is limited to the theoretical part of the discursive. The university is there *to tell the truth*, to judge, to criticize in the most rigorous sense of the term, namely to discern and decide between the true and the false; and if it is also entitled to decide between the just and the unjust, the moral and the immoral, this is so insofar as reason and freedom of judgment are implicated in it as well. Kant, in fact, presents this requirement as the condition for struggles against all "despotisms," beginning with the one those direct representatives of the government that are the members of the higher faculties (theology, law, medicine) could make reign inside the university. One could play endlessly at translating this matrix, this model, combining its elements into different types of modern society. One could also therefore legitimately entertain the most contradictory of evaluations. Kant defines a university that is as much a safeguard for the most totalitarian of social forms as a place for the most intransigently liberal resistance to any abuse of power, a resistance that can be judged in turns as most rigorous or most impotent. In effect, its power is limited to a power-to-think-and-judge, a power-to-say, though not necessarily to say *in public*, since this would involve an *action*, an executive power denied the university. How is the combination of such contradictory evaluations possible for a model that is one and the same? What must such a model be to lend itself to this in this manner? I can only sketch out an indirect answer here to this enormous question. Presuppositions in the Kantian delimitation could be glimpsed from the start, but today they have become massively apparent. Kant needs, and he says so, to trace, between a responsibility concerning truth and a responsibility concerning action, a linear border, an indivisible and rigorously uncrossable line. To do so he must submit language to a particular treatment. Language is the element common to both spheres of responsibility, and it deprives us of any rigorous distinction between the two spaces that Kant would like to dissociate at all costs. It is language that opens the passage to all parasiting and simulacra. In a certain way, Kant speaks only of language in *The Conflict of the Faculties*, and it is between two languages, that of truth and that of action, that of theoretical statements and that of performatives (especially of commands) that he wishes to trace the line of demarcation. Kant speaks only of language when he speaks about the "manifestation of truth," of "influence over the people," of the interpretation of sacred texts in theological terms, or, conversely, in philosophical terms, and so forth. And yet he continually erases that in language which breaks open the limits that a criticist critique claims to assign to the faculties, to the interior of the faculties, as we will see, and between the university's inside and its outside. Kant's effort—such is the scope of the properly philosophical project and the demand for a judgment capable of deciding—tends to limit the effects of confusion, simulacrum, parasiting, equivocality, and undecidability produced by language. In this sense, this philosophical demand is best represented by an information technology that, while appearing today to escape the control of the university—in Kantian terms, of philosophy—is its product and its most faithful representative. This is only apparently paradoxical, and it is before the law of this apparent paradox that the ultimate responsibility should be taken today, if it were possible. This force of parasiting inhabits, first of all, so-called natural language, and is common to both the university and its outside. The element of publicity, the necessarily public character of discourse, in particular in the form of the archive, designates the unavoidable locus of equivocation that Kant would like to reduce. Whence the temptation: to transform, into a reserved, intra-university and quasi-private language, the discourse, precisely, of universal value that is that of philosophy. If a universal language is not to risk equivocation, it would ultimately be necessary not to publish, popularize, or divulge it to a general public that would necessarily corrupt it. In his response to the king of Prussia, Kant defends himself thus:

> As a teacher of the people I have, in my writings, and particularly in the book *Religion within the Limits, etc.*, contravened none of the supreme and *sovereign* purposes known to me; in other words I have done no harm to the public *religion of the land*; this is already clear from the fact that the book is not suitable for the public in any way, being, for the public, an unintelligible and closed book, a mere debate between faculty scholars, of which the public takes no notice; the faculties themselves, to be sure, remain, to the best of their knowledge and conscience, free to judge it publicly; it is only the appointed public teachers (in schools and from the pulpit) who are bound to any outcome of such debates as the country's authority may sanction for public utterance. (*Conflict* 15)

It is, then, the *publication* of knowledge, rather than knowledge itself, that is submitted to authority. Reducing this publication so as to save a discourse that is rigorous in science and in conscience, that is a rational, universal, and unequivocal discourse—this is a double bind, a postulation in contradiction with itself, intrinsically in conflict with itself, as if, *within* the Kantian text, it were already not translatable from itself into itself. This contradictory demand was not satisfied in the time of Kant. How could it be today, when the fields of publication, archiving, and mediatization expand as strikingly as have, at the other end of the spectrum, the overcoding and hyperformalization of languages? Where does a publication begin?

There is something still more serious and essential. The pure concept of the university is constructed by Kant on the possibility and necessity of a purely theoretical language, inspired solely by an interest in truth, with a structure that one today would call purely constative. This ideal is no doubt guaranteed, in the Kantian argument itself, by pure practical reason, by prescriptive utterances, by the postulate of freedom on the one hand, and, on the other, by virtue of a de facto political authority supposed by right to let itself be guided by reason. But this in no way keeps the performative structure from being excluded by right from the language whereby Kant regulates both the concept of the university and thus what is purely autonomous in it, namely, as we will see, the "lower" faculty, the Faculty of Philosophy. I let myself be guided by this notion of performativity, not because it strikes me as being sufficiently clear and elaborated, but because it signals an essential topic in the debate in which we are involved here. In speaking of performativity, I think as much of performativity as the output of a technical system, in that place where knowledge and power are no longer distinguished, as of Austin's notion of a speech act not confined to stating, describing, saying that which is, but producing or transforming, by itself, under certain conditions, the situation of which it speaks: the founding, for example, of a graduate school— not today, where we can observe it, but a century ago, in a very determined context. Interesting and interested debates that are developing more and more around an interpretation of the performative power of language seem linked, in at least a subterranean way, to urgent politico-institutional stakes. These debates are developing equally in departments of literature, linguistics, and philosophy; and in themselves, in the form of their interpretative statements, they are neither simply theoretico-constative nor simply performative. This is so because *the* performative does not exist: there are various performatives, and there are antagonistic or parasitical attempts to interpret the performative power of language, to police it and use it, to invest it performatively. And a philosophy and a politics— not only a general politics but a politics of teaching and of knowledge, a political concept of the university community—are involved there every time, whether or not one is conscious of this. A very symptomatic form today of a political implication that has, however, been at work, from time immemorial, in every university gesture and utterance. I am speaking not just of those for which we have to take politico-administrative responsibility: requests for funding and their allocation, the organization of teaching and research, the granting of degrees, and especially, the enormous mass of evaluations, implicit or declared, that we engage in, each bearing its own axiomatics and political effects (the dream, here, of a formidable study, not only sociological, of the archive of these evaluations, including, for example, the publication of every dossier, jury report, and letter of recommendation, and the spectrum analysis, dia- and synchronic, of all codes in conflict there, intersecting, contradicting, and overdetermining one another in the cunning and mobile strategy of interests great and small). No, I am not thinking only about this, but more precisely about the concept of the scientific community and the university that ought to be legible in every sentence of a course or seminar, in every act of writing, reading, or interpretation. For example—but one could vary examples infinitely—the interpretation of a theorem, poem, philosopheme, or theologeme is only produced by simultaneously proposing an institutional model, either by consolidating an existing one that enables the interpretation, or by constituting a new one in accordance with this interpretation. Declared or clandestine, this proposal calls for the politics of a community of interpreters gathered around this text, and at the same time of a global society, a civil society with or without a State, a veritable regime enabling the inscription of that community. I will go further: every text, every element of a corpus reproduces or bequeathes, in a prescriptive or normative mode, one or several injunctions: come together according to this or that rule, this or that scenography, this or that topography of minds and bodies, form this or that type of institution so as to read me and write about me, organize this or that type of exchange and hierarchy to interpret me, evaluate me, preserve me, translate me, inherit from me, make me live on (*überleben* or *fortleben*, in the sense that Benjamin gives these words in "Die Aufgabe des Übersetzers" [The Task of the Translator]). Or inversely: if you interpret me (in the sense of deciphering or of performative transformation), you will have to assume one or another institutional form. But it holds for every text that such an injunction gives rise to undecidability and the double bind, both opens and closes, that is, upon an overdetermination that cannot be mastered. This is the law of the text in general—which is not confined to what one calls written works in libraries or computer programs—a law that I cannot demonstrate here but must presuppose. Consequently, the interpreter is never subjected passively to this injunction, and his own performance will in its turn construct one or several models of community. And sometimes different ones for the same interpreter—from one moment to the next, from one text to the next, from one situation or strategic evaluation to the next. These are his responsibilities. It is hard to speak generally on the subject of what they are taken for, or before whom. They always involve the content and form of a new contract. When, for example, I read a given sentence in a given context in a seminar (a reply by Socrates, a fragment from *Capital* or *Finnegans Wake*, a paragraph from *The Conflict of the Faculties*), I am not fulfilling a prior contract: I can also write and prepare for the signature of a new contract with the institution, between the institution and the dominant forces of society. And this operation, as with any negotiation (precontractual, that is, continually transforming an old contract), is the moment for every imaginable ruse and strategic ploy. I do not know if there exists today a pure concept of *the* university responsibility, nor would I know, in any case, how to express, in this place and within the limits of this lecture, all the doubts I harbor on this subject. I do not know if an ethico-political code bequeathed by one or more traditions is viable for such a definition. But today the minimal responsibility and in any case the most interesting one, the most novel and strongest responsibility, for someone belonging to a research or teaching institution, is perhaps to make such a political implication, its system and its aporias, as clear and thematic as possible. In speaking of clarity and thematization, although these thematizations can take the most unexpected and convoluted pathways, I still appeal to the most classical of norms; but I doubt that anyone could renounce doing so without, yet again, putting into question every thought of responsibility, as one may naturally always wish to do. By the clearest possible thematization I mean the following: that with students and the research community, in every operation we pursue together (a reading, an interpretation, the construction of a theoretical model, the rhetoric of an argumentation, the treatment of historical material, and even a mathematical formalization), we posit or acknowledge that an institutional concept is at play, a type of contract signed, an image of the ideal seminar constructed, a *socius* implied, repeated, or displaced, invented, transformed, threatened, or destroyed. An institution is not merely a few walls or some outer structures surrounding, protecting, guaranteeing, or restricting the freedom of our work; it is also and already the structure of our interpretation. If, then, it lays claim to any consequence, what is hastily called Deconstruction[3] is never a technical set of discursive procedures, still less a new hermeneutic method working on archives or utterances in the shelter of a given and stable institution; it is also, and at the least, the taking of a position, in the work itself, toward the politico-institutional structures that constitute and regulate our practice, our competences, and our performances. Precisely because deconstruction has never been concerned with the contents alone of meaning, it must not be separable from this politico-institutional problematic, and has to require a new questioning about responsibility, a questioning that no longer necessarily relies on codes inherited from politics or ethics. Which is why, though too political in the eyes of some, deconstruction can seem demobilizing in the eyes of those who recognize the political only with the help of prewar road signs. Deconstruction is limited neither to a methodological reform that would reassure the given organization nor, inversely, to a

parade of irresponsible or irresponsibilizing destruction, whose surest effect would be to leave everything as is, consolidating the most immobile
forces of the university. It is from these premises that I interpret *The Conflict of the Faculties*. I return to it now, though in truth I do not believe I
ever left it.

Kant, then, wanted to draw a line between scholars in the university
and businessmen of learning or instruments of government power, between the inside and the outside closest to the university enclosure. But
this line, Kant certainly has to recognize, does not only pass along the border and around the institution. It traverses the faculties, and this is the
place of conflict, of an unavoidable conflict. This border is a front. In effect, by referring himself to a de facto organization that he seeks, in keeping with his usual line of argument, not to transform but rather to analyze
in its conditions of pure juridical possibility, Kant distinguishes between
two classes of faculty: three higher faculties and a lower faculty. And without treating this enormous problem, Kant hastens to specify that this division and its designations (three higher faculties, one lower faculty) are
the work of the government and not of the scientific corporation.
Nonetheless he accepts it; he seeks to justify it in his own philosophy and
to endow this *factum* with juridical guarantees and rational ideals. The
Faculties of Theology, Law, and Medicine are called "higher" because they
are closer to government power; and a traditional hierarchy holds that
power should be higher than non-power. It is true that later on Kant does
not hide that his own political ideal tends toward a certain reversal of this
hierarchy:

> Thus we may indeed one day see the last becoming first (the lower faculty be-
> coming the higher faculty), *not in the exercise of power* [my emphasis, and
> Kant, even with this reversal, remains true to the absolute distinction between
> knowledge and power] but in giving counsel [and counsel, as he sees it, is not
> power] to the authority (the government) holding it, which would thereby
> find, in the freedom of the Faculty of Philosophy and the insight it yields, a
> better way to achieve its ends than the mere exercise of its own absolute au-
> thority. (*Conflict* 59)

Kant's model here is less Plato's philosopher-king than a certain practical
wisdom of the British parliamentary monarchy he mentions in a lengthy,
amusing footnote to the "General Division of the Faculties" (*Conflict* 27).

As long as this ideal reversal has not occurred, that is, in the current state of things, the higher faculties are those that train the instruments of the government and anyone else with whose help the government brings off its "strongest and most lasting influence" over the general public. And so the government controls and oversees those higher faculties that represent it directly, even if it does not itself teach. It sanctions doctrines and can require that some of them be advanced and others withdrawn, whatever their truth may be. This makes up a part of the signed contract between the higher faculties and the government. If, be it said in passing, this sole Kantian criterion were kept (representing the interests of State power and of the forces sustaining it), would one be assured today by a boundary between the higher faculties and the others? And could one limit the higher faculties, as before, to theology, law, and medicine? Would one not find some trace of that interest and that representation of power within the lower faculty, of which Kant says that it must be absolutely independent of governmental commands? The lower (or philosophical) faculty must be able, according to Kant, to teach freely whatever it wishes without conferring with anyone, letting itself be guided by its sole interest in the truth. And the government must arrest its own power, as Montesquieu would say, in the face of this freedom, must even guarantee it. And it should have an interest in doing so, since, says Kant with the fundamental optimism characterizing this discourse, without freedom truth cannot be manifested, and every government should take an interest in the truth manifesting itself. The freedom of the lower faculty is *absolute*, but it is a freedom of judgment and intra-university speech, the freedom to speak out on *that which is*, through essentially theoretical judgments. Only intra-university speech (theoretical, judicative, predicative, constative) is granted this absolute freedom. Members of the "lower" faculty, as such, cannot and should not give orders (*Befehle geben*). In the final analysis, the government keeps by contract the right to control and censure anything that would not, in its statements, be constative, and in a certain sense of this word, representational. Think of the subtleties in our current interpretations of nonconstative utterances, of the effects these would have on such a concept of the university and its relations to civil society and State power! Imagine the training that would have to be undertaken by censors and government experts charged with verifying the purely constative structure of university discourses. Where would those experts be trained? By what faculty? By the higher or the lower? And who would decide? In any case, and for essential reasons, we do not have at our disposal today a truth about performative language, or any legitimate and teachable doctrine on the subject. What follows from this? Every discussion on the subject of speech acts (relations between speech acts and truth, speech acts and intention, "serious" and "nonserious," "fictive" and "non-fictive," "normal" and "parasitic" language, philosophy and literature, linguistics and psychoanalysis, etc.) has politico-institutional stakes that we should no longer hide from ourselves. These concern the power or non-power of academic discourse, or of the discourse of research in general.

The division between the two classes of faculties must be pure, principial, and rigorous. Instituted by the government, it must nonetheless proceed from pure reason. It does not permit, in principle, any confusion of boundary, any parasitism. Whence the untiring, desperate, not to say "heroic" effort by Kant to mark off the juridical borders: not only between the respective responsibilities of the two classes of faculties, but even between the types of conflict that cannot fail to arise between them in a kind of antinomy of university reason. Faculty class struggle will be inevitable, but juridicism will proceed to judge, discern, and evaluate, in a decisive, decidable, and critical manner, between legal and illegal conflicts.

A first border between the classes of faculties reproduces the limit between action and truth (a statement or proposition with truth value). The lower faculty is totally free where questions of truth are concerned. No power should limit its freedom of judgment in this respect. It can no doubt conform to practical doctrines as ordained by the government, but should never hold them as true *because* they were dictated by power. This freedom of judgment Kant takes to be the unconditioned condition of university autonomy, and this unconditioned condition is nothing other than philosophy. Autonomy is philosophical reason insofar as it grants itself its own law, namely the truth. Which is why the lower faculty is called the Faculty of Philosophy; and without a philosophy department in a university, there is no university. The concept of *universitas* is more than the philosophical concept of a research and teaching institution; it is the concept of philosophy itself, and is Reason, or rather the principle of reason *as institution*. Kant speaks here not just of a faculty but of a "department": if there is to be a university, "some such department" of philosophy has to be "founded" (*gestiftet*). Though inferior in power, philosophy ought "to control" (*controlliren*) all other faculties in matters arising from *truth*, which is of "the first order," while *utility* in the service of government is of "the second order."[4] That the essence of the university, namely philosophy, should at the same time occupy a particular place and be one faculty among others within the university topology, that philosophy should represent a special competence in the university—this poses a serious problem. This problem did not escape Schelling, for example, who objected to Kant about it in one of his *Vorlesungen über die Methode des akademischen Studiums* (Lectures on the Method of University Studies; 1802). According to him, there cannot be a particular faculty (or, therefore, power, *Macht*) for philosophy: "Something which is everything cannot, for that very reason, be anything in particular."[5]

The paradox of this university topology is that the faculty bearing within itself the theoretical concept of the totality of the university space should be assigned to a particular residence and should be subject, in the same space, to the political authority of other faculties and of the government they represent. By rights, this is conceivable and rational only to the degree that the government *should* be inspired by reason. And in this ideal case, there should be no conflicts. But there are, and not just contingent or factual oppositions. There are inevitable conflicts and even conflicts that Kant calls "legal." How can this be?

This stems, I believe, from the paradoxical structure of those limits. Though destined to separate power from knowledge and action from truth, they distinguish sets that are each time somehow in excess of themselves, covering each time the whole of which they should figure only as a part or a subset. And so the whole forms an *invaginated pocket* inside every part or subset. We recognized the difficulty of distinguishing the inside from the outside of the university, and then, on the inside, of distinguishing between the two classes of faculties. We are not done, however, with this intestine division and its folding partition inside each space. The Faculty of Philosophy is further divided into two "departments": the *historical* sciences (history, geography, linguistics, humanities, etc.) and the *pure rational sciences* (pure mathematics, pure philosophy, the metaphysics of nature and of morals); within the so-called Faculty of Philosophy, pure philosophy is therefore still just a part of the whole whose idea it nonetheless safeguards. And as *historical*, it also covers the domain of the higher faculties. "The Faculty of Philosophy," writes Kant, "can therefore require all disciplines to submit their truth to an examination" (*Conflict* 45). Because of this double overflowing, conflicts are inevitable. And they must also reappear inside each faculty, since the Faculty of Philosophy is itself divisible. But Kant also wishes to draw a limit between legal and illegal conflicts. An illegal conflict merely sets into opposition, publicly, various opinions, feelings, and particular inclinations. Though always involving influence over the public, such a conflict cannot give rise to juridical and rational arbitration. It primarily concerns a demand from the public, which, considering philosophy to be nonsense, prefers to approach the higher faculties or businessmen of learning to ask them for pleasures, shortcuts, or answers in the form of fortune-telling, magic, or thaumaturgy. The people seek artful leaders (*kunstreiche Führer*), "demagogues." And members of the higher faculties, such as theologians, can, just as well as the businessmen educated by those faculties, answer that demand. In the case of these illegal conflicts, the Faculty of Philosophy as such is, according to Kant, absolutely impotent and without recourse. The solution can only come from beyond—once again, from the government. And if the government does not intervene, in other words, if it takes the side of particular interests, then it condemns the Faculty of Philosophy, that is, the very soul of the university, to death. This is what Kant calls the "heroic" way—in the ironic sense of heroic medicine—that ends a crisis by means of death. Some might be tempted into a headlong recognition of the death of philosophy that others among us oppose in several Western countries, notably in France.[6] But things do not let themselves be taken so simply in this Kantian schema. The "illegal" conflict is only of secondary interest to Kant: putting individual inclinations and particular interests into play, it is prerational, quasi-natural, and extra-institutional. It is not properly speaking a university conflict, whatever its gravity may be. Kant devotes longer analyses to the legal conflicts that properly speaking arise from university reason. These conflicts surge inevitably from within, putting rights and duties into play. The first examples that Kant gives—the ones that obviously preoccupy him the most—pertain to the sacred, faith, and revelation; it is the duty of the Faculty of Philosophy "to examine and judge publicly, with cool reason, the origin and content of a certain supposed basis of the doctrine, unintimidated by the sanctity of the object, for which one presumably feels something, having clearly decided (*entschlossen*) to relate this supposed feeling to a concept" (*Conflict* 55). This conflict (with, for example, the higher Faculty of Theology) reintroduces feeling or history where reason alone should be; it still harbors within itself something natural, since it opposes reason to its outside. It is still a parasiting of the legal by the illegal. But Kant does not wish to recognize this, or in any case to declare it. He imagines instances of interior arbitration, with sentence and judgment pronounced by a judge of reason in view of a "public presentation of the truth" (*öffentliche Darstellung der Wahrheit*). This trial and this arbitration should remain interior to the university and should never be brought before an incompetent public that would change it back into an illegal conflict and feed it to factions, to popular tribunes, in particular to those Kant calls "neologists" (*Neologen*), "whose name, rightly detested, is nonetheless ill understood, when applied indiscriminately to all who propose innovations for doctrines and formulae (for why should the old ways always be taken as better?)" (*Conflict* 57). It is because they *should* by right remain interior that these conflicts *should* never disturb the government, and they have to remain internal *for that reason*: never to disturb the government.

And yet Kant is obliged to recognize that this conflict is interminable and therefore insoluble. It is a struggle that eventually destabilizes departmental regimes, constantly putting into question the borders within which Kant would constantly contain antagonism. Kant further specifies this antagonism of the conflict of the faculties "is not a war" (*kein Krieg*), proposing for it a solution that is properly parliamentary: the higher faculties would occupy, he says, the right bench of the parliament of learning and would defend the statutes of the government. "But in as free a system of government as must exist where truth is at issue, there must also be an opposition party (the left side), and that bench belongs to the Faculty of Philosophy, for without its rigorous examinations and objections, the government would not be adequately informed about things that might be to its own advantage or detriment." Thus, in conflicts concerning pure *practical* reason, the report and the *formal* investigation of the trial would be entrusted to the Faculty of Philosophy. But in matters of *content*, which touch on the most important questions for mankind, the preliminary hearing falls to the higher faculty, and particularly to the Faculty of Theology (see "The Conclusion of Peace and Resolution of the Conflict of the Faculties") (*Conflict* 57–58; on matters of content, see p. 11). And yet, despite this parliamentary juridicism, Kant has to admit that the conflict "can never end," and that the "Faculty of Philosophy is the one which ought to be permanently armed for this purpose." The truth under its protection will always be threatened because "the higher faculties will never renounce the desire to govern" or dominate (*Begierde zu herrschen*) (*Conflict* 55).

I break off brusquely. The university is about to close. It is very late—too late for this Kantian discourse is perhaps what I meant to say. But know that the rest, which I have not discussed, is most interesting and least formal, the most informal. It deals with the very *content* of conflicts among theologians, jurists, doctors, and the technicians or businessmen they train.

You have wondered all along, I am sure, where, as we say nowadays, I was coming from, which side I was on in all these conflicts, (1) to the right of the boundary or (2) to its left, or (3) more probably, as some might (rightly or wrongly) suppose, a tireless parasite moving in random agitation, passing over the boundary and back again, either seeking (no one would know for sure) to play the mediator in view of a treaty of perpetual peace, or seeking to reignite the conflicts and wars in a university that from its birth has been wanting [*en mal de*] apocalypse and eschatology.[7] These three hypotheses, whose responsibility I leave in your hands, all appeal to the system of limits proposed by *The Conflict of the Faculties* and again let themselves be constrained by it.

Here it will have been my responsibility, whatever the consequences, to pose the question of the law of law [*droit du droit*]:[8] what is the legitimacy of this juridico-rational and politico-juridical system of the university, and so forth? The question of the law of law, of the founding or foundation of law, is not a juridical question. And the response cannot be either simply legal or simply illegal, simply theoretical or constative, simply practical or performative. It cannot take place either inside or outside the university bequeathed us by the tradition. This response and responsibility in regard to such a founding can only take place in terms of foundation. Now the foundation of a law [*droit*] is no more juridical or legitimate than is the foundation of a university is a university or intra-university event. If there can be no pure concept of the university, if, within the university, there can be no pure and purely rational concept of the university, this—to speak somewhat elliptically, given the hour, and before the doors are shut or the meeting dismissed—is very simply because the university is *founded*. An event of foundation can never be comprehended merely within the logic that it founds. The foundation of a law [*droit*] is not a juridical event. The origin of the principle of reason, which is also implicated in the origin of the university, is not rational. The foundation of a university institution is not a university event. The anniversary of a foundation may be, but not the foundation itself. Though such a foundation is not merely illegal, it also does not arise from the internal legality it institutes. And while nothing seems more philosophical than the foundation of a philosophical institution, whether a university, a school, or a department of philosophy, the foundation of the philosophical institution as such cannot be *already strictly* philosophical. We are here in that place where the founding responsibility occurs by means of acts or performances—which are not just speech acts in the strict or narrow sense, and which, though obviously no longer constative utterances regulated by a certain determination of the truth, are also perhaps no longer simply linguistic performatives; this last opposition (constative / performative) still remains too closely programmed by the very philosophico-university law—in other words by reason—that is being interrogated here. Such an interrogation would no longer simply belong to a philosophical setting, and would no longer be a theoretical question in the style of Socrates, Kant, Husserl, or others. It would be inseparable from novel acts of foundation. We live in a world where the foundation of a new law [*droit*]—in particular a new university law—is necessary. To call it *necessary* is to say in this case *at one and the same time* that one has to take responsibility for it, a new kind of responsibility, and that this foundation is already well on the way, and irresistibly so, beyond any representation, any consciousness, any acts of individual subjects or corporate bodies, beyond any interfaculty or interdepartmental limits, beyond the limits between the institution and the political places of its inscription. Such a foundation cannot simply break with the tradition of inherited law [*droit*], or submit to the legality that it authorizes, including those conflicts and forms of violence that always prepare for the establishing of a new law [*loi*], or a new epoch of the law [*droit*]. Only within an epoch of the law is it possible to distinguish legal from illegal conflicts, and above all, as Kant would wish, conflicts from war.

How do we orient ourselves toward the foundation of a new law? This new foundation will negotiate a compromise with traditional law. Traditional law should therefore provide, on its own foundational soil, a support for a leap toward another foundational place, or, if you prefer another metaphor to that of the jumper planting a foot before leaping—of "taking the call on one foot" [*prenant appel sur un pied*], as we say in French—then we might say that the difficulty will consist, as always, in determining the best lever, what the Greeks would call the best *mochlos*. The *mochlos* could be a wooden beam, a lever for displacing a boat, a sort of wedge for opening or closing a door, something, in short, to lean on for forcing and displacing. Now, when one asks how to orient oneself in history, morality, or politics, the most serious discords and decisions have to do less often with ends, it seems to me, than with levers. For example, the opposition of right and left, in this originally parliamentary sense, is perhaps largely, if not entirely, a conflict between several strategies of political *mochlos*. Kant serenely explains to us that, in a university as in parliament, there must be a left (the Faculty of Philosophy, or the lower faculty: the left is below for the moment) and a right (the class of higher faculties representing the government). When I asked a moment ago how we should orient ourselves toward the foundation of a new law, I was citing, as you no doubt recognized, the title of another short work by Kant (*How to Be Oriented in Thinking?*; *Was heisst: Sich im Denken Orientieren?* [1786]). This essay speaks, among other things, of the paradox of symmetrical objects as presented in yet another essay of 1768, *Von dem ersten Grunde des Unterschiedes der Gegenden im Raume* (Foundation for the Distinction of Positions in Space), namely, that the opposition of right and left does not arise from a conceptual or logical determination, but only from a sensory topology that can only be referred to the subjective position of the human body. This was obviously related to the definition and perception, perhaps specular, of the left and right sides. But if I quickly displace myself at this point from speculation to walking, well, as Kant will have told us, the university will have to walk on two feet, left and right, each foot having to support the other as it rises and with each step makes the leap. It is a question of walking on two feet, two feet *with shoes*, since the institution is at issue, a society and a culture, not just nature. This was already clear in what I recalled about the faculty parliament. But I find its confirmation in an entirely different context, and I ask you to forgive me this rather rapid and brutal leap; I allow myself to take it by the memory of a discussion I had in this very place more than two years ago with our eminent colleague, Professor Meyer Schapiro, on the subject of certain shoes by Van Gogh. It was a matter, in the first place, of the Heideggerian interpretation of that 1935 painting, and of knowing whether those two shoes made a pair, or two left shoes, or two right shoes, the elaboration of this question having always seemed to me of greatest consequence. Treating the conflict between the Faculty of Philosophy and the Faculty of Medicine, after speaking about the power of the human soul to master its morbid feelings, after involving us in dietetics, his hypochondria, sleep, and insomnia, Kant proceeds to offer the following confidence, to which I shall add, out of respect for your own sleep, not one word. I will only emphasize the *mochlos* or *hypomochlium*:

> Since insomnia is a failing of weak old age, and since the left side is generally weaker than the right, I felt, perhaps a year ago, one of those cramp-like seizures and some very sensitive stimuli. . . . I had to . . . consult a doctor. . . . I soon had recourse to my Stoic remedy of fixing my thought forcibly on some neutral object. . . . (for example, the name of Cicero, which contains many associated ideas . . .). (*Conflict* 193–94)

And the allusion to a weakness of the left side called for the following note:

> It is sometimes said that exercise and early training are the only factors that determine which side of a man's body will be stronger or weaker, where the use of his external members is concerned—whether in combat he will handle the sabre with his right arm or with his left, whether the rider standing in his stirrup will vault onto his horse from right to left or vice-versa, and so forth. But this assertion is quite incorrect. Experience teaches that if we have our shoe measurements taken from our left foot, and if the left shoe fits perfectly, then the right one will be too tight; and we can hardly lay the blame for this on our parents, for not having taught us better when we were children. The advantage of the right foot over the left can also be seen from the fact that, if we want to cross a deep ditch, we put our weight on the left foot and step over with the right; otherwise we run the risk of falling into the ditch. The fact that Prussian infantrymen are trained *to start out* with the left foot confirms, rather than refutes, this assertion; for they put this foot in front, as on a *hypomochlium*, in order to use the right side for the impetus of the attack, which they execute with the right foot against the left.[9]
>
> —*Translated by Richard Rand and Amy Wygant*

Punctuations: The Time of a Thesis

Should one speak of an epoch of the thesis? Of a thesis that would require time, a great deal of time? Or of a thesis whose time would belong to the past? In short, is there a time of the thesis? And even, should one speak of an age of the thesis, of an age for the thesis?

Allow me to begin by whispering a confidence that I will not abuse: never have I felt so young and at the same time so old. At the same time, in the same instant, and it is one and the same feeling, as if two stories and two times, two rhythms were engaged in a sort of altercation in one and the same feeling of oneself, in a sort of anachrony of oneself, anachrony in oneself. It is in this way that I can, to an extent, make sense to myself of a certain confusion of identity. This confusion is, certainly, not completely foreign to me and I do not always complain about it; but just now it has suddenly got much worse and this bout is not far from leaving me speechless.

Between youth and old age, one and the other, neither one nor the other, an indecisiveness of age. It is like a discomfiture at the moment of installation, an instability, I will not go so far as to say a disturbance of stability, of posture, of station, of the thesis or of the pose, but rather of a pause in the more or less well-regulated life of a university teacher, an end and a beginning that do not coincide and in which there is involved once again no doubt a certain gap of an alternative between the delight of pleasure and fecundity.

This anachrony (I am, obviously, speaking of my own) has for me a very familiar feel, as if a rendezvous had forever been set for me with what should above all and with the utmost punctuality never come at its appointed hour, but always, rather, too early or too late.

As to this stage on which I here appear for the defense of a thesis, I have been preparing myself for it for too long. I have no doubt premeditated it, then adjourned it, and finally excluded it, excluded it for too long so that when, thanks to you, it is finally taking place, it is impossible for it not to have for me a slight character of phantasy or irreality, an air of improbability, of unpredictability, even an air of improvization.

It was almost twenty-five years ago now that I committed myself to working on a thesis. Oh, it was scarcely a decision; I was at that time simply following the course that was taken to be more or less natural and that was at the very least classical, classifiable, typical of those who found themselves in a certain highly determined social situation upon leaving the École Normale and after the agrégation.[1]

But these twenty-five years have been fairly peculiar. Here I am not referring to my modest personal history or to all those routes that, after starting by leading me away from this initial decision, then brought me deliberately to question it, deliberately and, I honestly thought, definitively, only to end up, just a very short while ago, by deciding in a context that, rightly or wrongly, I believed to be quite new to take the risk of another evaluation, of another analysis.

By saying that these twenty-five years have been peculiar, I am not first thinking, then, of this personal history or even of the *paths* my own work has taken, even supposing that it could, improbably, be isolated from the environment in which it has moved through a play of exchanges, of resemblances, of affinities, of influences, as the saying goes, but also and especially, more and more indeed, through a play of divergences and of marginalization, in an increasing and at times abrupt isolation, whether as regards contents, positions, let us just say "theses," or whether more especially as regards ways of proceeding, socio-institutional practices, a certain style of writing as well as—regardless of the cost, and today this amounts to a great deal—of relations with the university milieu, with cultural, political, editorial, journalistic representations, there where, today, it seems to me, are located some of the most serious, the most pressing, and the most obscure responsibilities facing an intellectual.

No, it is not of myself that I am thinking when I allude to the trajectory of these twenty-five years, but rather of a most remarkable sequence in the history of philosophy and of French philosophical institutions. I would not have the means here and now, and in any case, this is not the place, to analyze this sequence. But as, for reasons that are due not only to the limited amount of time available to me, there can equally be no question of putting together the works that have been submitted to you in something like a presentation in the form of conclusions or of theses; and as, on the other hand, I do not want to limit the discussion that is to follow by making an overly long introduction, I thought that I might perhaps hazard a few fragmentary and preliminary propositions, indicating a few among the most obvious points concerning the intersections between this historical sequence and some of the movements or themes that have attracted me, that have retained or displaced my attention within the limits of my work.

Around 1957, then, I had *registered*, as the saying goes, my first thesis topic. I had entitled it *The Ideality of the Literary Object*. Today this title seems strange. To a lesser degree it seemed so even then, and I will discuss this in a moment. It received the approval of Jean Hyppolite, who was to direct this thesis, which he did, which he did without doing so, that is, as he knew how to do, as in my opinion he was one of the very few to know how to do, in a free and liberal spirit, always open, always attentive to what was not, or not yet, intelligible, always careful to exert no pressure, if not no influence, by generously letting me go wherever my path led me. I want to pay tribute to his memory here and to recall all that I owe to the trust and encouragement he gave me, even when, as he one day told me, he did not see at all where I was going. That was in 1966 during a colloquium in the United States in which we were both taking part. After a few friendly remarks on the paper I had just given, Jean Hyppolite added, "That said, I really do not see where you are going." I think I replied to him more or less as follows: "If I clearly saw ahead of time where I was going, I really don't believe that I would take another step to get there." Perhaps I then thought that knowing where one is going may no doubt help in orienting one's thinking, but that it has never made anyone take a single step, quite the opposite in fact. What is the good of going where one knows oneself to be going and where one knows that one is destined to arrive? Recalling this reply today, I am not sure that I really understand it very well, but it surely did not mean that I never see or never know where I am going and that to this extent, to the extent that I do know, it is not certain that I have ever taken any step or said anything at all. This also means, perhaps, that, concerning this place where I am going, I in fact know enough about it to think, with a certain terror, that things there are

not going very well and that, all things considered, it would be better not
to go there at all. But there's always Necessity, the figure I recently wanted
to call Necessity with the initial capital of a proper noun, and Necessity
says that one must always yield, always go [*se rendre*] where it calls. Even
if it means never arriving. Even if it means, it says, *to* never arrive. Even so
that you don't arrive. [*Quitte à ne pas arriver. Quitte, dit-elle, à ne pas arriver. Quitte pour ce que tu n'arrives pas.*]

The ideality of the literary object: this title was somewhat more com-
prehensible in 1957 in a context that was more marked by the thought of
Husserl than is the case today. It was then for me a matter of bending,
more or less violently, the techniques of transcendental phenomenology
to the needs of elaborating a new theory of literature, of that very peculiar
type of ideal object that is the literary object, a "bound" ideality Husserl
would have said, bound in so-called natural language, a nonmathematical
or nonmathematizable object, and yet one that differs from objects of
plastic or musical art, that is to say, from all of the examples privileged by
Husserl in his analyses of ideal objectivity. For I have to remind you,
somewhat bluntly and simply, that my most constant interest, coming
even before my philosophical interest, I would say, if this is possible, was
directed toward literature, toward that writing that is called literary.

What is literature? And first of all, what is it to write? How is it that
writing can disturb the very question "what is?" and even "what does it
mean?"? To say this in other words—and here is the *saying otherwise* that
was of importance to me—when and how does an inscription become
literature and what takes place when it does? To what and to whom is
this due? What takes place between philosophy and literature, science
and literature, politics and literature, theology and literature, psychoanalysis and literature? It was here, in all the abstractness of its title, that
lay the most pressing question. This question was no doubt inspired in
me by a desire that was related also to a certain uneasiness: why finally
does the inscription so fascinate me, preoccupy me, precede me? Why
am I so fascinated by the literary ruse of inscription and the whole un-
graspable paradox of a trace that manages only to carry itself away, to
erase itself in re-marking itself, itself and its own idiom, which in order
to take actual form [*arriver à son événement*] must erase itself and produce
itself at the price of this self-erasure.

Curious as it may seem, transcendental phenomenology helped me, in
the first stages of my work, sharpen some of these questions, which at the

time were not as well marked out as they seem to be today. In the 1950s, when it was still not well received, was little known or too indirectly understood in French universities, Husserlian phenomenology seemed inescapable to some young philosophers. I still see it today, in a different way, as a discipline of incomparable rigor. Not—especially not—in the versions proposed by Sartre or Merleau-Ponty, which were then dominant, but rather in opposition to them, or without them, in particular in those areas that a certain type of French phenomenology appeared at times to avoid, whether in history, in science, in the historicity of science, the history of ideal objects and of truth, and hence in politics as well, and even in ethics. I would like to recall here, as one indication among others, a book that is no longer discussed today, a book whose merits can be very diversely evaluated, but which for a certain number of us pointed to a task, a difficulty, and an impasse as well no doubt. This is Tran Duc Tao's *Phénoménologie et matérialisme dialectique.* After a commentary that retraced the movement of transcendental phenomenology and in particular the transition from static constitution to genetic constitution, this book attempted, with less obvious success, to open the way for a dialectical materialism that would admit some of the rigorous demands of transcendental phenomenology. One can imagine what the stakes of such an attempt might have been, and its success was of less importance than the stakes involved. Moreover, some of Cavaillès's dialectical, dialecticist conclusions proved of interest to us for the same reasons. It was in an area marked out and magnetized by these stakes, at once philosophical and political, that I had first begun to read Husserl, starting with a *mémoire* [master's thesis] on the problem of genesis in Husserl's phenomenology.[2] At this early date Maurice de Gandillac was kind enough to watch over this work; twenty-six years ago he alone served as my entire examination committee, and if I recall that he was reduced to one-third of the committee for a thesis for the third cycle (*De la grammatologie* [*Of Grammatology*] in 1967)[3] and to one-sixth of the committee today, I do so not only to express my gratitude to him with that feeling of fidelity that is comparable to no other, but to promise him that henceforth this parceling out, this proliferating division will cease. This will be my last thesis defense.

Following this first work, my introduction to *The Origin of Geometry*[4] enabled me to approach something like the un-thought axiomatics of Husserlian phenomenology, its "principle of principles," that is to say, intuitionism, the absolute privilege of the living present, the lack of attention paid to the problem of its own phenomenological enunciation, to transcendental discourse itself, as Fink used to say, to the necessity of recourse, in eidetic or transcendental description, to a language that could not itself be submitted to the *epoche* (to the epoch)—without itself being simply "in the world"—thus to a language that remained naive, even though it made possible all the phenomenological bracketings and parentheses. This unthought axiomatics seemed to me to limit the scope of a consistent problematic of writing and of the trace, even though the necessity of such a problematic had been marked out by *The Origin of Geometry* with a rigor no doubt unprecedented in the history of philosophy. Husserl indeed located the recourse to writing within the very constitution of those ideal objects par excellence, mathematical objects, though without considering—and for good reason—the threat that the logic of this inscription represented for the phenomenological project itself. Naturally, all of the problems worked on in the introduction to *The Origin of Geometry* have continued to organize the work I have subsequently attempted in connection with philosophical, literary, and even nondiscursive corpora, most notably that of graphic or pictorial works: I am thinking, for example, of the historicity of ideal objects, of tradition, of inheritance, of filiation or of wills and testaments, of archives, libraries, books, of writing and living speech, of the relationships between semiotics and linguistics, of the question of truth and of undecidability, of the irreducible alterity that divides the self-identity of the living present, of the necessity for new analyses concerning nonmathematical idealities, and so forth.

During the years that followed, from about 1963 to 1968, I tried to work out—in particular in the three works published in 1967[5]–what was in no way meant to be a system but rather a sort of strategic device, opening onto its own abyss, an unclosed, unenclosable, not wholly formalizable ensemble of rules for reading, interpretation, and writing. This type of device perhaps enabled me to detect not only in the history of philosophy and in the related socio-historical totality, but also in what are alleged to be sciences and in so-called post-philosophical discourses that figure among the most modern (in linguistics, anthropology, and psychoanalysis), to detect in these, then, an evaluation of writing, or, to tell the truth, rather a devaluation of the writing whose insistent, repetitive, even obscurely compulsive character was the sign of a whole set of long-standing constraints. These constraints were practiced at the price of contradictions, of denials, of dogmatic decrees; they were not to be localized within a limited *topos* of culture, of the encyclopedia, or of ontology. I proposed to analyze the nonclosed and fissured system of these constraints, under the name of logocentrism in the form that it takes in Western philosophy and under that of phonocentrism as it appears in the widest scope of its dominion. Of course, I was able to develop this device and this interpretation only by according a privileged role to the guideline or analyser named writing, text, trace, and only by proposing a reconstruction and generalization of these concepts (writing, text, trace) as the play and work of *différance*, whose role is at one and the same time both of constitution and deconstruction. This strategy may have appeared to be an abusive deformation—or, as some have cursorily said, a metaphorical usage—of the current notions of writing, text, or trace, and have seemed to those who continued to cling to these old self-interested representations to give rise to all sorts of misunderstandings. But I have untiringly striven to justify this unbounded generalization, and I believe that every conceptual breakthrough [*frayage*] amounts to transforming, that is to deforming, an accredited, authorized relationship between a word and a concept, between a trope and what one had every interest to consider to be an unshiftable primary, proper, literal, or current meaning. Moreover, the strategic and rhetorical scope of these gestures has never ceased to engage me in numerous subsequent texts. All of this was grouped together under the title of *deconstruction*, the graphics of *différance*, of the trace, the supplement, and so forth, and here I can only indicate them in an algebraic manner. What I proposed at that time retained an oblique, deviant, sometimes directly critical, relationship with respect to everything that seemed then to dominate the main, most visible, the most spectacular, and sometimes the most fertile outcrop of French theoretical production, a phenomenon that, in its various different forms, was known, no doubt abusively, as "structuralism." These forms were of course very diverse and very remarkable, whether in the domains of anthropology, history, literary criticism, linguistics, or psychoanalysis, in rereadings, as one says, of Freud or of Marx. But regardless of their indisputable interest, during this period that was also in appearance the most static period of the Gaullist republic of 1958–68, what I was attempting or what was tempting me was of an essentially different nature. And so, aware of the cost of these advances in terms of their metaphysical presuppositions, to say nothing of what was, less evidently, their political price, I buried myself from this time on in a sort of retreat, a solitude that I mention here without pathos, as simply self-evident, and merely as a reminder that increasingly in regard to academic tradition as well as to established modernity—and in this case the two are but one—this solitude was and often still is considered to be the well-deserved consequence of a hermetic and unjustified reclusiveness. Is it necessary to say that I do not think this is so and that I interpret in an entirely different manner the reasons for this verdict? It is also true that the living thinkers who gave me the most to think about or who most provoked me to reflection, and who continue to do so, are not among those who break through a solitude, not among those to whom one can simply feel close, not among those who form groups or schools, to mention only Heidegger, Levinas, Blanchot, among others whom I will not name. It is thinkers such as these to whom, strangely enough, one may consider oneself closest; and yet they are, more than others, other. And they too are alone.

It was already clear to me that the general turn that my research was taking could no longer conform to the classical norms of the thesis. This "research" called not only for a different mode of writing but also for a work of transformation on the rhetoric, the staging, and the particular discursive procedures, which, highly determined historically, dominate university discourse, in particular the type of text that is called the "thesis"; and we know how all these scholarly and university models likewise provide the laws regulating so many prestigious discourses, even those of literary works or of eloquent political speeches that shine outside the university. And then, too, the directions I had taken, the nature and the diversity of the corpora, the labyrinthine geography of the itineraries drawing me toward relatively unacademic areas, all of this persuaded me that the time was now past, that it was, in truth, no longer possible, even if I wanted to, to make what I was writing conform to the size and form then required for a thesis. The very idea of a thetic presentation, of positional or oppositional logic, the idea of position, of *Setzung* or *Stellung*, what I called at the beginning the *epoch* of the thesis, was one of the essential parts of the system that was under deconstructive questioning. What was then put forth under the title without any particular claim [*titre sans titre*] of *dissemination* explicitly dealt, in ways that were in the end neither thematic nor thetic, with the value of the thesis, of positional logic and its history, and of the limits of its rights, its authority, and its legitimacy. This did not imply on my part, at least at that particular time, any radical institutional critique of the thesis, of the presentation of university work in order to have it legitimized, or of the authorization of competence by accredited representatives of the university. If, from this moment on, I was indeed convinced of the necessity for a profound transformation, amounting even to a complete upheaval of university institutions, this was not, of course, in order to substitute for what existed some type of non-thesis, nonlegitimacy, or incompetence. In this area I believe in transitions and in negotiation—even if it may at times be brutal and accelerated—I believe in the necessity of a certain tradition, in particular for political reasons that are nothing less than traditionalist, and I believe, moreover, in the indestructibility of the ordered procedures of legitimation, of the production of titles and diplomas, and of the authorization of competence. I speak here in general and not necessarily of the *universitas*, which is a powerful but very particular, very specific, and indeed very recent, model for this procedure of legitimation. The structure of the *universitas* has an essential tie with the ontological and logocentric onto-encyclopedic system; and for the past several years it has seemed to me that the indissociable link between the modern concept of the university and a certain metaphysics calls for the work I pursued in my teaching or in essays that have been published or are in the course of being published on Kant's *The Conflict of the Faculties*, and on Hegel, Nietzsche, and Heidegger in their political philosophy of the university. If I insist on this theme, it is because, given the circumstances and the impossibility in which I find myself of summing up or presenting thetic conclusions, I feel that I should attend first and foremost to what is happening here and now, and I wish to assume responsibility for that as clearly and as honestly as possible: from my very limited place and in my own way.

In 1967 I was so little bent on questioning the necessity of such an institution, of its general principle in any case, if not its particular university structure and organization, that I thought I could make a sort of compromise and division of labor and time, according its share to the thesis, to the time of the thesis. On the one hand, I would have let the work in which I was engaged develop freely, and outside the usual forms and norms, a work that decidedly did not conform to such university requirements and that was even to analyze, contest, displace, deform them in all their rhetorical or political bearing; but at the same time, and on the other hand, the transaction or the epoch of the thesis would have amounted to setting apart one piece of this work, a theoretical sequence playing the role

of an organizing element, and treating it in an acceptable, if not so reassuring, form within the university. This would have involved an interpretation of the Hegelian theory of the sign, of speech and writing in Hegel's
semiology.

It seemed indispensable to me, for reasons I have discussed, especially
in *Marges—de la philosophie* [*Margins of Philosophy*],[6] to propose a systematic interpretation of this semiology. Jean Hyppolite gave me his consent once again, and this second thesis topic was in its turn—registered.

This, then, was in 1967. Things were so intertwined and overdetermined that I cannot even begin to say what the impact was on me, on my
work and my teaching, on my relationship to the university institution
and to the space of cultural representation of that event that one still does
not know how to name other than by its date, 1968, without having a very
clear idea of just what it is one is naming in this way. The least that I can
say about it is this: something I had been anticipating found its confirmation at that time, and this confirmation accelerated my own movement
away. I was then moving away more quickly and more resolutely, *on the
one hand*, from the places where, as early as the autumn of 1968, the old
armatures were being hastily recentred, reconstituted, reconcentrated,
and, *on the other hand*, from a style of writing guided by the model of the
classical thesis, and even directed by a concern for recognition by academic authorities who, at least in those bodies in which were to be found
gathered together, officially and predominantly, their most effective powers of evaluation and decision, seemed to me, after '68, to be both overre-
active and too effective in their resistance to everything that did not conform to the most tranquilizing criteria of acceptability. I had numerous
indications of this; certain concerned me personally, and if I say that politics was also involved it is because, in this case, the political does not take
only the conventional distribution along a left/right axis. The reproductive force of authority can get along more comfortably with declarations
or theses whose encoded content presents itself as revolutionary, provided
that they respect the rites of legitimation, the rhetoric and the institutional symbolism that defuses and neutralizes everything that comes from
outside the system. What is unacceptable is what, underlying positions or
theses, upsets this deeply entrenched contract, the order of these norms,
and that does so in the very *form* of the work, of teaching or of writing.

The death of Jean Hyppolite in 1968 was not only for me, as for others,
a moment of great sadness. By a strange coincidence, it marked at that

date—the autumn of 1968, and it was indeed the autumn—the end of a certain type of membership in the university. Certainly, from the first day of my arrival in France, in 1949, this membership had not been simple, but it was during these years no doubt that I came to understand better to what extent the necessity of deconstruction (I use this word for the sake of brevity, though it is a word I have never liked and one whose fortune has disagreeably surprised me) was not primarily a matter of philosophical contents, themes or theses, philosophemes, poems, theologemes or ideologemes, but especially and inseparably meaningful frames, institutional structures, pedagogical or rhetorical norms, the possibilities of law, of authority, of evaluation, and of representation in its very market. My interest for these more or less visible framework structures, for these limits, these effects of the margin, or these paradoxes of borders continued to respond to the same question: how is it that philosophy finds itself inscribed, rather than itself inscribing itself, within a space that it seeks but is unable to order, a space that opens out onto another that is no longer even *its* other, as I have tried to make apparent in a tympanum[7] as little Hegelian as possible. How is one to name the structure of this space? I do not *know*; nor do I know whether it can give rise to what is called *knowledge*. To call it socio-political is a triviality that does not satisfy me, and even the most necessary of what are called socio-analyses often enough have very little to say on the matter, remaining blind to their own inscription, to the law of their reproductive performances, to the stage of their own heritage and of their self-authorization, in short to what I will call their writing.

I have chosen, as you can see, to confide to you without detour, if not without a certain simplification, all the uncertainties, the hesitations, the oscillations by way of which I sought the most fitting relationship with the university institution, on a level that was not simply political and that concerned not only the thesis. I will thus distinguish between roughly three periods in the time that separates me today from the time I began to abandon the project of a thesis. It was at first a somewhat passive reaction: the thing no longer interested me very much. I would have had to come up with a new formulation, come to an understanding with a new supervisor, and so forth. And as doctorates based on published works, theoretically possible, were obviously not encouraged, to say the very least, I turned away, at first somewhat passively, I repeat, from those places that seemed to me less and less open to what really mattered to me. But I have to admit that in certain situations, most notably those in which I am writing and in which I am writing about writing, my obstinacy is great, constraining for me, indeed compulsive, even when it is forced to take the most roundabout paths. And so beyond the three works published in 1972,[8] I kept worrying away at the same problematic, the same open matrix (opening onto the linked series formed by the trace, *différance*, undecidables, dissemination, the supplement, the graft, the hymen, the *parergon*, and so on), pushing it toward textual configurations that were less and less linear, logical, and topical forms, even typographical forms that were more daring, the intersection of corpora, mixtures of genres or modes, *Wechsel der Töne* [changes in tone], satire, rerouting, grafting, and so on, to the extent that even today, although these texts have been published for years, I do not believe them to be simply presentable or acceptable to the university and I have not dared, have not judged it opportune, to include them here among the works to be defended. These texts include *Glas*,[9] despite the continued pursuit there of the project of grammatology, the encounter with the arbitrary character of the sign and the theory of onomatopoeia in Saussure, as well as with the Hegelian *Aufhebung*, the relation between the undecidable, the dialectic, and the double bind, the concept of generalized fetishism, the pull of the discourse of castration toward an affirmative dissemination and toward another rhetoric of the whole and the part, the re-elaboration of a problematic of the proper noun and the signature, of the testament and the monument, and many other themes besides. All of this indeed was an expansion of earlier attempts. I will say the same thing about other works that I have deliberately left out of this defense, works such as *Éperons: Les styles de Nietzsche* (*Spurs: Nietzsche's Styles*) or *La carte postale* (*The Post Card*),[10] which, each in its own way, nevertheless extend a reading (of Freud, Nietzsche, and some others) begun at an earlier stage, the deconstruction of a certain hermeneutics as well as of a theorization of the signifier and the letter with its authority and institutional power (I am referring here to the whole psychoanalytic system as well as to the university), the analysis of logocentrism *as* phallogocentrism, a concept by means of which I tried to indicate, in my analysis, the essential indissociability of phallocentrism and logocentrism, and to locate their effects wherever I could spot them—but these effects are everywhere, even where they remain unnoticed.

The expansion of these texts dealing with textuality might seem anamorphic or labyrinthine, or both at once, but what in particular made them just about indefensible, in particular as a thesis, was less the multiplicity of their contents, conclusions, and demonstrative positions than, it seems to me, the acts of writing and the performative stage to which they had to give rise and from which they remained inseparable and hence not easily capable of being represented, transported, and translated into another form; they were inscribed in a space that one could no longer, that I myself could no longer, identify or classify under the heading of philosophy *or* literature, fiction *or* nonfiction, and so forth, especially at a time when what others would call the *autobiographical* involvement of these texts was undermining the very notion of autobiography, giving it over to what the necessity of writing, the trace, the *remainder*, could offer of all that was most baffling, undecidable, cunning, or despairing. And since I have just alluded to the performative structure, let me note in passing that, for the same reasons, I have held back from the thesis corpus, along with a good many other essays, a debate that I had in the United States with a speech act theorist, John Searle, in a short work that I entitled *Limited Inc.*[11]

During an initial period, then, from 1968 to 1974, I simply neglected the thesis. But during the years that followed I deliberately decided—and I sincerely believed that this decision was final—not to submit a thesis at all. For, besides the reasons I have just mentioned and that seemed to me to be more and more solid, I have been engaged since 1974 with friends, colleagues, and university and high school students in a work which I should dare to call a long-term struggle that directly concerns the institution of philosophy, especially in France, and first and foremost in a situation whose nature has been determined by a long history, but that was worsened in 1975 by a policy that could—or, one may fear, will—lead to the destruction of philosophical teaching and research, with all that this supposes or implies in the country. For all the women and men who, like me, worked to organize the Groupe de Recherches sur l'Enseignement Philosophique (Greph) and who participated in its Avant-Projet, its research, and its actions, from 1974 until the meeting of the Estates General of Philosophy in this very place just one year ago, for all of us the task was of the utmost urgency, and the responsibility ineluctable.[12] I specify: this task was urgent and ineluctable in the places we occupy—teaching or research in philosophy—the places to which we cannot deny that we belong and in which we find ourselves inscribed. But of course, other things are urgent too; this philosophical space is not the only one available to thinking, nor the first one in the world, nor is it the one with the greatest determining influence on, for example, politics. We dwell elsewhere as well, and this I have tried never to forget; nor indeed is it something that allows itself to be forgotten. What we in Greph were questioning with respect to the teaching of philosophy could not be separated, and we have always been attentive to this point, from all of the other cultural, political, and other relations of forces in this country and in the world.

In any case, as far as I was concerned, my participation in Greph's work and struggles had to be as consistent as possible with what I was trying to write elsewhere, even if the middle terms between the two necessities were not always easy and obvious. I insist upon saying this here: although among the works presented to you I have included neither the texts I have signed or those that I have prepared as a militant of Greph nor, a fortiori, the collective actions in which I have participated or which I have endorsed in that capacity, I consider them to be inseparable, let us say in spirit, from my other public acts—most notably from my other publications. And the gesture I make today, far from signifying that I have abandoned anything in this respect, will, on the contrary I hope, make possible other involvements or other responsibilities in the *same* struggle.

It remains the case that during this second period, beginning around 1974, I thought, rightly or wrongly, that it was neither consistent nor desirable to be a candidate for any new academic title or responsibility. Neither consistent given the work of political criticism in which I was participating, nor desirable with regard to a little forum that was more internal, more private, and where, through a whole endless scenography of symbols, representations, phantasies, traps, and strategies, a self-image recounts all sorts of interminable and incredible stories to itself. So I thought I had decided that, without further changing anything in my university situation, I would continue for better or for worse doing what I had done up to then, from the place where I had been immobilized, and without knowing anything more about where I was going, indeed knowing less no doubt about it than ever. It is not insignificant, I believe, that during this period most of the texts I published placed the greatest, if not the most novel, emphasis on the question of rights and of the proper [*le propre*], on the rights of property, on copyright, on the signature and the market, on the market for painting or, more generally, for culture and all its representations, on speculation on the proper, on the name, on destination and restitution, on all the institutional borders and structures of discourses, on the machinery of publishing and on the media. Whether in my analyses of the logic of the *parergon* or the interlacing stricture of the double bind, whether in the paintings of Van Gogh, Adami, or Titus Carmel, or the meditations on art by Kant, Hegel, Heidegger, or Benjamin (in *La Vérité en peinture* [*The Truth in Painting*]),[13] or again in my attempts to explore new questions *with* psychoanalysis (for example, in exchange with the works, so alive today, of Nicolas Abraham and Maria Torok)[14]—in all of these cases I was increasingly preoccupied with the necessity of re-elaborating, with new stakes, questions said to be classically institutional. And I would have liked in this respect to have been able to harmonize both a discourse and a practice, as the saying goes, to fit the premises of my earlier project. In fact, if not in principle, this was not always easy, not always possible. At times indeed it remained very burdensome in a number of ways.

Of the third and final period, the one in which I find myself here and now, I can say very little. Only a few months ago, taking account of a very wide number of different factors that I cannot analyze here, I came to the conclusion, putting an abrupt end to a process of deliberation that was threatening to become interminable, that everything that had justified my earlier resolution (concerning the thesis, of course) was no longer likely to be valid for the years to come. In particular, for the very reasons of institutional politics that had until now held me back, I concluded that it was perhaps better, and I must emphasize the "perhaps," to prepare myself for some new type of mobility. And as is often, as is always the case, it is the friendly advice of this or that person among those present here, before or behind me, it is others, always others, who effected in me a decision I could not have come to alone. For not only am I not sure, as I never am, of being right in taking this step, I am not sure that I see in all clarity what led me to do so. Perhaps because I was beginning to know only too well not where I was going but where I was, not where I had arrived but where I stopped.

I began by saying that it was as if I was speechless. You recognized, of course, that this was just another manner of speaking; nevertheless it was not false. For the *captatio* in which I have just indulged was not only excessively coded, excessively narrative—the chronicle of so many anachronies—it was also as impoverished as a punctuation mark, rather, I should say, an apostrophe in an unfinished text. And above all, above all, it has sounded too much like the totting up of a calculation, a self-justification, a self-defense (in the United States one speaks of a thesis defense for a *soutenance de thèse*). You have heard too much talk of strategies. "Strategy" is a word that I have perhaps abused in the past, especially as it was always to specify *in the end*, in an apparently self-contradictory manner and at the risk of cutting the ground from under my own feet—something I almost never fail to do—a strategy without any goal [*finalité*]. The strategy without any goal—for this is what I hold to and what in turn holds me—the aleatory strategy of someone who admits that he does not know where he is going. This, then, is not after all an undertaking of war or a discourse of belligerence. I would like it also to be like a headlong flight straight toward the end, a joyous self-contradiction, a disarmed desire, that is to say, something very old and very cunning, but that also has just been born and that delights in being without defense.

—Translated by Kathleen McLaughlin

The Principle of Reason: The University in the Eyes of Its Pupils

How not to speak, today, of the university?

I put my question in the negative (how not to), for two reasons. On the one hand, as we all know, it is impossible, now more than ever, to dissociate the work we do, within one discipline or several, from a reflection on the political and institutional conditions of that work. Such a reflection is unavoidable. It is no longer an *external* complement to teaching and research; it must make its way through the very objects we work with, shaping them as it goes, along with our norms, procedures, and aims. We cannot not speak of such things. On the other hand, the question "how not to" gives notice of the *negative*, or perhaps we should say *preventive*, character of the preliminary reflections I would like to put to you. Indeed, since I am seeking to initiate discussion, I will content myself with saying how one should not speak of the university. Some of the typical risks to be avoided, it seems to me, take the form of a bottomless pit, while others take the form of a protectionist barrier.

Does the university, today, have what is called a raison d'être? I have deliberately chosen to put my question in a phrase [*raison d'être*, literally, "reason to be"] that is quite idiomatically French. In two or three words, that phrase names everything I will be talking about: reason and being, of course, and the essence of the university in its relations to reason and being; but also the cause, purpose [*finalité*], necessity, justification, meaning, and mission of the university; in a word, its *destination*. To have a raison d'être, a reason for being, is to have a justification for existence, to have a meaning, a purpose [*finalité*], a destination. It is also to have a cause, to be explainable according to the "principle of reason" or the "law of sufficient reason," as it is sometimes called—in terms of a reason that is also a cause (a ground, *ein Grund*), that is to say also a footing and a foundation, ground to stand on. In the phrase *raison d'être*, this causality takes on above all the sense of final cause, in the wake of Leibniz, the author of the formulation—and it was much more than a formulation—"the Principle of Reason." To ask whether the university has a reason for being is to wonder "why the university?," but the question "why" verges on "with a view to what?" The university *with a view to* what? What is the university's view? What are its views? Or again: what do we see from the university, whether, for instance, we are simply in it, on board; or whether, puzzling over destinations, we look out from it while in port or, as French has it, "au large," on the open sea, "at large"? As you may have noticed, in asking "what is the view from the university?" I was echoing the title of the impeccable parable James Siegel published in *Diacritics* two years ago: "Academic Work: The View from Cornell."[1] Today, indeed, I shall do no more than decipher that parable in my own way. More precisely, I shall be transcribing in a different code what I read in that article—the dramatic, exemplary nature of the topology and politics of this university, in terms of its views and its site: the topolitics of the Cornellian point of view.

From its first words on, metaphysics associates sight with knowledge, and knowledge with knowing how to learn and knowing how to teach. To be more specific, Aristotle's *Metaphysics* does so, and from its opening lines. I will return later to the political import of its opening lines. For the moment, let us look at the very first sentence: "Pantes anthropoi tou eidenai oregontai phusei" (All men, by nature, have the desire to know). Aristotle thinks he sees a sign (*semeion*) of this in the fact that sensations give pleasure, "even apart from their usefulness" (*khoris tes khreias*). The pleasure of useless sensations explains the desire to know for the sake of knowing, the desire for knowledge with no practical purpose. And this is more true of sight than of the other senses. We give preference to sensing "through the eyes" not only for taking action (*prattein*), but even when we have no praxis in view. This one sense, naturally theoretical and contemplative, goes beyond practical usefulness and provides us with more to know than any other; indeed, it unveils countless differences (*pollas deloi diaphoras*). We give preference to sight just as we give preference to the uncovering of differences.

But is sight enough? To learn and teach, does it suffice to know how to unveil differences? In certain animals, sensation engenders memory, and that makes them more intelligent (*phronimōtera*) and more capable of *learning* (*mathetikōtera*). But to know how to learn, and learn how to know, sight, intelligence, and memory are not enough. We must also know how to hear, and to listen (*tōn psophōn akouein*). I might suggest somewhat playfully that we have to know how to shut our eyes in order to be better listeners. Bees know many things, since they can see; but they cannot learn, since they are among the animals that lack the faculty of hearing (*me dunatai tōn psophōn akouein*). Thus, despite appearances to the contrary, the university, that place where people know how to learn and learn how to know, will never be a kind of hive. Aristotle, let us note in passing, has ushered in a long tradition of frivolous remarks on the philosophical *topos* of the bee, the sense and senses of the bee, and the bee's reason for being. Marx was doubtless not the last to have overworked that topos, when he insisted on distinguishing human industry from animal industry, as exemplified in bee society. Seeking such nectar as may be gathered from the vast anthology of philosophical bees, I find a remark of Schelling's, in his 1803 *Lessons on the Method of University Studies*,[2] more to my taste.

An allusion to the sex of bees often comes to the aid of the rhetoric of naturalism, organicism, or vitalism as it plays upon the theme of the complete and interdisciplinary unity of knowledge, the theme of the university as an organic social system. This is in the most classic tradition of interdisciplinary studies. I quote Schelling:

> The aptitude for doing thoughtful work in the specialized sciences, the capacity to work in conformity with that higher inspiration which is called scientific genius, depends upon the ability see each thing, including specialized knowledge, in its cohesion with what is originary and unified. Any thought which has not been formed in this spirit of unity and totality [*der Ein- und Allheit*] is empty in itself, and must be challenged; whatever is incapable of fitting harmoniously within that budding, living totality is a dead shoot which sooner or later will be eliminated by organic laws; doubtless there also exist, within the realm of science, numerous sexless bees [*geschlechtslose Bienen*] who, since they have not been granted the capacity to create, multiply in inorganic shoots the outward signs of their own witlessness [*ihre eigne Geistlosigkeit*].[3]

(I don't know what bees, not only deaf but sexless, Schelling had in mind at the time. But I am sure that even today such rhetorical weapons would find many an eager buyer. One professor has recently written that a certain theoretical movement ["deconstructionism"] was mostly supported, within the university, by homosexuals and feminists—a fact which seemed very significant to him, and doubtless a sign of asexuality.)

Opening the eyes to know, closing them—or at least listening—in order to know how to learn and to learn how to know: here we have a first sketch of the rational animal. If the university is an institution for science and teaching, does it have to go beyond memory and sight? In what rhythm? To hear better and learn better, must it close its eyes or narrow its outlook? In cadence? What cadence? Shutting off sight in order to learn is of course only a figurative manner of speaking. No one will take it literally, and I am not proposing to cultivate an art of blinking. I am resolutely in favor of a new university Enlightenment [*Aufklärung*]. Still, I shall run the risk of extending my figuration a little farther, in Aristotle's company. In his *De anima* (421b) he distinguishes between man and those animals that have hard, dry eyes (*tōn sklerophtalmōn*), the animals lacking eyelids (*ta blephara*), that sort of sheath or tegumental membrane (*phragma*) that serves to protect the eye and permits it, at regular intervals, to close itself off in the darkness of inward thought or sleep. What is terrifying about an animal with hard eyes and a dry glance is that it always sees. Man can lower the sheath, adjust the diaphragm, narrow his sight, the better to hear, remember, and learn. What might the university's diaphragm be? The university must not be a sclerophthalmic animal, a hard-eyed animal; when I asked, a moment ago, how it should set its sights and adjust its views, that was another way of asking about its reasons for being and its essence.[4] What can the university's body see or not see of its own destination, of that in view of which it stands its ground? Is the university the master of its own diaphragm?

Now that I have opened up this perspective, allow me to close it off for the twinkling of an eye, to allow me to confide in you, to make what in French I could call a *confidence* but in English must call a confession.

Before preparing the text of a lecture, I find I must prepare myself for the scene I will encounter as I speak. That is always a painful experience, an occasion for silent, paralytic deliberation. I feel like a hunted animal, looking in darkness for a way out where none is to be found. Every exit is blocked. In the present case, the conditions of impossibility, if you will, were made worse, for three reasons.

In the first place, this was not to be just a lecture like any other; rather it had to be something like an inaugural address. Of course, Cornell University has welcomed me generously many times since I first came to speak here in 1975. I have many friends here, and Cornell is in fact the first American university I ever taught for. That was in Paris, in 1967–68, as David Grossvogel will undoubtedly remember: he was in charge of a program that had also been directed by Paul de Man. But today, for the first time, I am taking the floor to speak as an Andrew Dickson White Professor-at-Large. In French, "au large!" is the expression a great ship uses to hail a small craft about to cross her course: "Wear off. Give way." In this case, the title with which your university has honored me at once brings me closer to you and adds to the anguish of the cornered animal. Was this inaugural lecture a well-chosen moment to ask whether the university has a reason for being? Wasn't I about to act with all the unseemliness of a stranger who in return for noble hospitality plays prophet of doom with his hosts, or at best eschatological harbinger, like Elijah denouncing the power of kings or announcing the end of the kingdom?

A second cause for worry is that I find myself involved already, quite imprudently, that is, blindly and without foresight, in an act of dramaturgy, writing out the play of that *view* in which Cornell, from its beginnings, has felt so much to be at stake. The question of the view has informed the institutional scenography, the landscape of your university, the alternatives of expansion and enclosure, life and death. From the first it was considered vital not to close off the view. This is what Andrew Dickson White, Cornell's first president, recognized, and I wanted to pay him this homage. At a moment when the trustees wanted to locate the university closer to town, Ezra Cornell took them to the top of East Hill to show them the sights, and the site, he had in mind. "We viewed the landscape," writes Andrew Dickson White. "It was a beautiful day and the panorama was magnificent. Mr. Cornell urged *reasons* on behalf of the upper site, the main one being that there was so much more room for expansion."[5] Ezra Cornell gave good reasons, and since the Board of Trustees, reasonably enough, concurred with them, reason won out. But in this case was reason quite simply on the side of life? Drawing on K. C. Parsons's account of the planning of the Cornell campus, James Siegel observes (and I quote) that

> For Ezra Cornell the association of the view with the university had something to do with death. Indeed Cornell's plan seems to have been shaped by the thematics of the Romantic sublime, which practically guaranteed that a cultivated man in the presence of certain landscapes would find his thoughts

drifting metonymically through a series of topics—solitude, ambition, melancholy, death, spirituality, "classical inspiration"—which could lead, by an easy extension, to questions of culture and pedagogy. ("View" 69)

A matter of life and death. The question arose again in 1977, when the university administration proposed to erect protective railings on the Collegetown bridge and the Fall Creek suspension bridge to check thoughts of suicide inspired by the view of the gorge. "Barriers" was the term used; we could say "diaphragm," borrowing a word that in Greek literally means "partitioning fence." Beneath the bridges linking the university to its surroundings, connecting its inside to its outside, lies the abyss. In testimony before the Campus Council, one member of the faculty did not hesitate to express his opposition to the barriers, those diaphragmatic eyelids, on the grounds that blocking the view would mean, to use his words, "destroying the essence of the university" ("View" 77).

What did he mean? What is the essence of the university?

Perhaps now you can better imagine with what shudders of awe I prepared myself to speak to you on the subject—quite properly sublime—of the essence of the university. Sublime in the Kantian sense of the term. In *The Conflict of the Faculties*, Kant averred that the university should be governed by "an idea of reason," the idea of the whole field of what is presently teachable (*das ganze gegenwärtige Feld der Gelehrsamkeit*). As it happens, no experience in the present allows for an adequate grasp of that present, presentable totality of doctrine, of teachable theory. But the crushing sense of that inadequacy is precisely the exalting, desperate sense of the sublime, suspended between life and death.

Kant also says that the approach of the sublime is first heralded by an inhibition. There was a third reason for the inhibition I myself felt as I thought about speaking to you today. I was resolved of course to limit myself to preliminary, preventive remarks,[6] to speak only of the risks to be avoided, the abyss, and bridges, and even boundaries as one struggles with such fearful questions. But that would still be too much, because I wouldn't know how to pick and choose. In my teaching in Paris I have devoted a year-long seminar to the question of the university. Furthermore, I was recently asked by the French government to write a proposal for the establishment of a Collège International de Philosophie, a proposal that for literally hundreds of pages considers all of the difficulties involved. To speak of such things in an hour would be more than just a challenge. As I sought to encourage myself, daydreaming a bit, it occurred to me that I didn't know how many meanings were conveyed by the phrase "at large," as in "professor at large." I wondered whether a professor at large, not belonging to any department, nor even to the university, wasn't rather like the person who in the old days was called *un ubiquiste*, a "ubiquitist," if you will, in the university of Paris. A ubiquitist was a doctor of theology not attached to any particular college. Outside that context, in French, an *ubiquiste* is someone who travels a lot and travels fast, giving the illusion of being everywhere at once. Perhaps a professor at large, while not exactly a ubiquitist, is also someone who, having spent a long time "au large" (in French, more than English, the phrase is most often used as a nautical term meaning on the high seas) occasionally comes ashore, after an absence that has cut him off from everything. He is unaware of the context, the proper rituals, and the changed environment. He is given leave to consider matters loftily, from afar. People indulgently close their eyes to the schematic, drastically selective views he has to express in the rhetoric proper to an academic lecture about the academy. But they may be sorry that he spends so much time in a prolonged and awkward attempt to capture the benevolence of his listeners (*captatio benevolentiae*).

As far as I know, nobody has ever founded a university *against* reason. So we may reasonably suppose that the university's reason for being has always been reason itself, and some essential connection of reason to being. But what is called the principle of reason is not simply reason. We cannot plunge into the history of reason here, its words and concepts, into the puzzling scene of translation that has shifted *logos* to *ratio* to *raison, reason, Grund*, ground, *Vernunft*, and so on. What for three centuries now has been called the principle of reason was thought out and formulated, several times, by Leibniz. His most often quoted statement holds that "nothing is without reason, no effect is without cause" (*Nihil est sine ratione seu nullus effectus sine causa*). According to Heidegger, the only formulation Leibniz himself considered authentic, authoritative, and rigorous is found in a late essay, *Specimen inventorum*: "There are two first principles in all reasoning, the principle of noncontradiction, of course . . . and the principle of rendering reason" (*Duo sunt prima principia omnium ratiocinationum, principium nempe contradictionis . . . et principium reddendae rationis*). The second principle says that for any truth—for any true proposition, that is—a reasoned account is possible. "Omnis veritatis reddi ratio potest." Or, to translate more literally, for any true proposition, *reason can be rendered.*[7]

Beyond all those big philosophical words—reason, truth, principle—that generally command attention, the principle of reason also holds that reason *must be rendered.* [In French the expression corresponding to Leibniz's *reddere rationem* is *rendre raison de quelque chose*; it means to explain or account for something.—Trans.] But what does "render" mean with respect to reason? Could reason be something that gives rise to exchange, circulation, borrowing, debt, donation, restitution? But in that case, who would be *responsible* for that debt or duty, and to whom? In the phrase *reddere rationem, ratio* is not the name of a faculty or power (*Logos, Ratio, Reason, Vernunft*) that is generally attributed by metaphysics to man, *zoon logon ekhon,* the *rational animal.* If we had more time, we could follow Leibniz's interpretation of the semantic shift that leads from the *ratio* of the *principium reddendae rationis,* the principle of rendering reason, to reason as the rational faculty—and in the end, to Kant's definition of reason as the faculty of principles. In any case, if the *ratio* in the principle of reason is not the rational faculty or power, that does not mean it is a thing, encountered somewhere among the beings and the objects in the world, which must be rendered up, given back. The question of this reason cannot be separated from a question about the modal verb "must" and the phrase "must be *rendered.*" The "must" seems to cover the essence of our relationship to principle. It seems to mark out for us requirement, debt, duty, request, command, obligation, law, the imperative. Whenever reason can be rendered (*reddi potest*), it must. Can we, without further precautions, call this a moral imperative, in the Kantian sense of pure practical reason? It is not clear that the sense of "practical," as it is determined by a critique of pure practical reason, exhausts the meaning, or reveals the origin, of this "must" that, however, it has to presuppose. It could be shown that the critique of practical reason continually calls on the principle of reason, on its "must," which, although it is certainly not of a theoretical order, is nonetheless not simply "practical" or "ethical" in the Kantian sense.

A responsibility is involved here, however. We have to respond to the call of the principle of reason. In *Der Satz vom Grund* (*The Principle of Reason*), Heidegger names that call *Anspruch*: requirement, claim, request, demand, command, convocation; it always entails a certain addressing of speech. The word is not seen; it has to be heard and listened to, this apostrophe that enjoins us to respond to the principle of reason.

A question of responsibility, to be sure. But is answering *to* the principle of reason the same act as answering *for* the principle of reason? Is the scene the same? Is the landscape the same? And where is the university located within this space?

To respond to the call of the principle of reason is to render reason, to explain effects through their causes, rationally; it is also to ground, to justify, to account for on the basis of principles (*arche*) or roots (*riza*). Keeping in mind that Leibnizian moment whose originality should not be underestimated, the response to the call of the principle of reason is thus a response to the Aristotelian requirements, those of metaphysics, of first philosophy, of the search for "roots," "principles," and "causes." At this point, scientific and technoscientific requirements lead back to a common origin. And one of the most insistent questions in Heidegger's meditation is indeed that of the long "incubation" time that separated this origin from the emergence of the principle of reason in the seventeenth century. Not only does that principle constitute the verbal formulation of a requirement present since the dawn of Western science and philosophy, it provides the impetus for a new era of purportedly "modern" reason, metaphysics, and technoscience. And one cannot *think* the possibility of the modern university, the one that is restructured in the nineteenth century in all the Western countries, without inquiring into that event, that institution of the principle of reason.

But to answer *for* the principle of reason (and thus for the university), to answer *for* this call, to raise questions about the origin or ground of the principle of foundation (*Der Satz vom Grund*), is not simply to obey it or to respond *in the face of* this principle. We do not listen in the same way when we are responding to a summons as when we are questioning its meaning, its origin, its possibility, its goal, its limits. Are we obeying the principle of reason when we ask what grounds this principle that is itself a principle of grounding? We are not—which does not mean that we are disobeying it, either. Are we dealing here with a circle or with an abyss? The circle would consist in seeking to account for reason by reason, to render reason to the principle of reason, in appealing to the principle in order to make it speak of itself at the very point where, according to Heidegger, the principle of reason says nothing about reason itself. The abyss, the hole, the *Abgrund*, the empty "gorge" would be the impossibility for a principle of grounding to ground itself. This very grounding, then, like the university, would have to hold itself suspended above a most peculiar void. Are we to use reason to account for the principle of reason? Is the

reason for reason rational? Is it rational to worry about reason and its principle? Not simply; but it would be over-hasty to seek to disqualify this
concern and to refer those who experience it back to their own irrationalism, their obscurantism, their nihilism. Who is more faithful to reason's
call, who hears it with a keener ear, who better sees the difference, the one
who offers questions in return and tries to think through the possibility of
that summons, or the one who does not want to hear any question about
the reason of reason? This is all played out, along the path of the Heideggerian question, in a subtle difference of tone or stress, according to the
particular words emphasized in the formula *nihil est sine ratione*. This
statement has two different implications according to whether "nihil" and
"sine" or "est" and "ratione" are stressed. I shall not attempt here, given
the limits of this talk, to pursue all of the decisions involved in this shift
of emphasis. Nor shall I attempt—among other things, and for the same
reasons—to reconstruct a dialogue between Heidegger and, for example,
Charles Sanders Peirce. A strange and necessary dialogue on the com-
pound theme, precisely, of the university and the principle of reason. In a
remarkable essay on "The Limits of Professionalism," Samuel Weber
quotes Peirce, who, in 1900, "in the context of a discussion on the role of
higher education" in the United States, concludes as follows:

> Only recently have we seen an American man of science and of weight discuss
> the purpose of education, without once alluding to the only motive that ani-
> mates the genuine scientific investigator. I am not guiltless in this matter my-
> self, for in my youth I wrote some articles to uphold a doctrine called prag-
> matism, namely, that the meaning and essence of every conception lies in the
> application that is to be made of it. That is all very well, when properly un-
> derstood. I do not intend to recant it. But the question arises, what is the ul-
> timate application; and at that time I seem to have been inclined to subordi-
> nate the conception to the act, knowing to doing. Subsequent experience of
> life has taught me that the only thing that is really desirable without a reason
> for being so, is to render ideas and things reasonable. One cannot well de-
> mand a reason for reasonableness itself.[8]

To bring about such a dialogue between Peirce and Heidegger, we
would have to go *beyond* the conceptual opposition between "conception"
and "act," between "conception" and "application," theoretical view and
praxis, theory and technique. This passage *beyond* is sketched out briefly
by Peirce in the very movement of his dissatisfaction: what might the ultimate application be? What Peirce only outlines is the path where Hei-

degger feels the most to be at stake, especially in *Der Satz vom Grund*. Unable to follow this path myself here in the way I have attempted to follow it elsewhere, I will merely draw from it two assertions, at the risk of oversimplifying.

1. The modern dominance of the principle of reason had to go hand in hand with the interpretation of the essence of beings as *objects*, an object present as representation (*Vorstellung*), an object placed and positioned *before* a subject. This latter, a man who says "I," an *ego* certain of itself, thus ensures his own technical mastery over the totality of what is. The "re-" of *repraesentatio* also expresses the movement that accounts for—renders reason to—a thing whose presence is *encountered* by *rendering* it present, by bringing it to the subject of representation, to the knowing self. This would be the place, if we only had the time, to reconstruct the way Heidegger makes language do its work (the interaction between *begegnen*, *entgegen*, *Gegenstand*, *Gegenwart* on the one hand, *Stellen*, *Vorstellen*, *Zustellen* on the other hand).[9] This relation of representation—which in its whole extension is not merely a relation of knowing—has to be grounded, ensured, protected: that is what we are told by the principle of reason, the *Satz vom Grund*. A dominance is thus assured for representation, for *Vorstellen*, for the relation to the ob-ject, that is, to the being that is located *before* a subject that says "I" and assures itself of its own present existence. But this dominance of the being-before does not reduce to that of sight or of *theoria*, nor even to that of a *metaphor* of the optical (or indeed sklerophthalmic) dimension. It is in *Der Satz vom Grund* that Heidegger states all his reservations on the very presuppositions of such rhetoricizing interpretations. It is not a matter of distinguishing here between sight and nonsight, but rather between two ways of thinking sight and light, as well as between two conceptions of listening and voice. But it is true that a caricature of representational man, in the Heideggerian sense, would readily endow him with hard eyes permanently open to a nature that he is to dominate, to rape if necessary, by fixing it in front of himself, or by swooping down on it like a bird of prey. The principle of reason installs its empire only to the extent that the abyssal question of the being that is hiding within it remains hidden, and with it the very question of the ground, of grounding as *gründen* (to ground, to give or take ground: *Boden-nehmen*), as *begründen* (to motivate, justify, authorize), or especially as *stiften* (to erect or institute, a meaning to which Heidegger accords a certain pre-eminence).[10]

2. Now this institution of modern techno-science that is the university *Stiftung* is built both on the principle of reason and on what remains hidden in that principle. As if in passing, but in two passages that are important to us, Heidegger asserts that the modern university is "grounded" (*gegründet*), "built" (*gebaut*) on the principle of reason; it "rests" (*ruht*) on this principle.[11] But if today's university, locus of modern science, "is grounded on the principle of grounding" (*gründet auf dem Satz vom Grund*), nowhere do we encounter within it the principle of reason itself; nowhere is this principle thought, scrutinized, interrogated as to its origin. Nowhere, within the university as such, is anyone wondering from where that call (*Anspruch*) of reason is voiced, nowhere is anyone inquiring into the origin of that demand for grounds, for reason that is to be provided, rendered, delivered: "Woher spricht dieser Anspruch des Grundes aus seine Zustellung?" (57). And this dissimulation of its origin within what remains unthought is not harmful, quite the contrary, to the development of the modern university; indeed, Heidegger in passing makes certain laudatory remarks about that university: progress in the sciences, its militant interdisciplinarity, its discursive zeal, and so on. But all this is elaborated above an abyss, suspended over a "gorge"—by which we mean on grounds whose own grounding remains invisible and unthought.

Having reached this point in my reading, instead of involving you in a micrological study of Heidegger's *Der Satz vom Grund* or of his earlier texts on the university (in particular his inaugural lecture of 1929, *Was ist Metaphysik?*, or the Rector's Speech of 1933, *Die Selbstbehauptung der deutschen Universität*)—a study which I am attempting elsewhere, in Paris, and to which we will no doubt refer in the discussions that will come after this talk—instead of meditating at the edge of the abyss—even if on a bridge protected by "barriers"—I prefer to return to a certain concrete actuality in the problems that assail us in the university.

The framework of grounding, or foundation, and the dimension of the fundamental impose themselves on several counts in the space of the university, whether we are considering the question of its reason for being in general, its specific missions, or the politics of teaching and research. Each time, what is at stake is the principle of reason as principle of grounding, foundation, or institution. A major debate is under way today on the subject of the politics of research and teaching, and on the role that the university may play in this arena: whether this role is central or marginal, progressive or decadent, collaborative with or independent of that of other research institutions sometimes considered better suited to certain purposes [*finalités*]. The terms of this debate tend to be analogous—I am not saying they are identical—in all the highly industrialized countries, whatever their political regime, whatever role the State traditionally plays in this arena (and, as we all know, even Western democracies vary considerably in this respect). In the so-called developing countries, the problem takes shape according to models that are certainly different but in all events inseparable from the preceding ones. Such a problematic cannot always—cannot any longer—be reduced to a political problematic centered on the State, but on multinational military-industrial complexes or techno-economic networks, indeed international techno-military networks that are apparently multi- or trans-national in form. In France, for some time, this debate has been organized around what is called the "end-orientation" [*finalisation*] of research. "End-oriented" research is research that is programmed, focused, organized in an authoritarian fashion *in view of* its utilization (in view of "ta khreia," Aristotle would say), whether we are talking about technology, economics, medicine, psycho-sociology, or military power—and in fact we are talking about all of these at once. There is no doubt greater sensitivity to this problem in countries where the politics of research depend closely upon state-managed or "nationalized" structures, but I believe that conditions are becoming more and more homogeneous among all the technologically advanced, industrialized societies. We speak of "end-oriented" [*finalisé*] research where, not so long ago, we spoke—as Peirce did—of "application." For it is growing more and more obvious that, without being immediately applied or applicable, research may pay off, be usable, end-oriented [*finalisable*], in more or less deferred ways. And what is at stake is not merely what sometimes used to be called the techno-economic, medical, or military "by-products" of pure research. The detours, delays, and relays of "end-orientation," its random aspects as well, are more disconcerting than ever. Hence the attempt, by every possible means, to take them into account, to integrate them in the rational calculation of programmed research. A term like "end-orient" is preferred to "apply," in addition, because the word is less "utilitarian"; it leaves open the possibility that noble aims may be written into the program.

You may wonder what is being advocated, in France, in opposition to this concept of end-oriented research. The answer is basic, "fundamental" research, disinterested research with aims that would not be pledged in advance to some utilitarian purpose. It was once possible to believe that pure mathematics, theoretical physics, philosophy (and, within philosophy, especially metaphysics and ontology) were basic disciplines shielded from power, inaccessible to programming by the agencies or instances of the State or, under cover of the State, by civil society or capital interests. The sole concern of such basic research would be knowledge, truth, the disinterested exercise of reason, under the sole authority of the principle of reason.

And yet we know better than ever before what must have been true for all time, that this opposition between the basic and the end-oriented is of real but limited relevance. It is difficult to maintain this opposition with thoroughgoing conceptual as well as practical rigor, especially in the modern fields of the formal sciences, theoretical physics, astrophysics (consider the remarkable example of the science of astronomy, which is becoming useful after having been for so long the paradigm of disinterested contemplation), chemistry, molecular biology, and so forth. Within each of these fields—and they are more interrelated than ever—the so-called basic philosophical questions no longer simply take the form of abstract, sometimes epistemological questions raised after the fact; they arise at the very heart of scientific research in the widest variety of ways. One can no longer distinguish between the technological on the one hand and the theoretical, the scientific, and the rational on the other. The term technoscience has to be accepted, and its acceptance confirms the fact that an essential affinity ties together objective knowledge, the principle of reason, and a certain metaphysical determination of the relation to truth. We can no longer—and this is finally what Heidegger recalls and calls on us to think through—we can no longer dissociate the principle of reason from the very idea of technology in the realm of their modernity. One can no longer maintain the boundary that Kant, for example, sought to establish between the schema that he called "technical" and the one he called "architectonic" in the systematic organization of knowledge—which was also to ground a systematic organization of the university. The architectonic is the art of systems: "Under the government of reason, our knowledge in general," Kant says, "should not form a rhapsody, but must form a system in which alone it can support and favor the essential aims of reason."[12] To this pure rational unity of the architectonic, Kant opposes the scheme of the merely technical unity that is empirically end-oriented, according to views and ends that are incidental, not essential. It is thus a limit between two ends [*finalités*] that Kant seeks to define, the essential and noble ends of reason that give rise to a basic [*fondamentale*] science, and the incidental and empirical ends that can be systematized only in terms of technical schemas and necessities.

Today, in the end-orientation [*finalisation*] of research—forgive me for presuming to recall such obvious points—it is already impossible to distinguish between these two ends [*finalités*]. It is impossible, for example, to distinguish programs that one would like to consider "worthy," or even technically profitable for humanity, from other programs that would be destructive. This is not new; but never before has so-called basic scientific research been so deeply committed to ends that are at the same time military ends. The very essence of the military, the limits of military technology and even the limits of the accountability of its programs are no longer definable. When we hear that two million dollars a minute are being spent in the world today for armaments, we may assume that this figure represents simply the cost of weapons manufacture. But military investments do not stop at that. For military power, even police power, and more generally speaking the entire defensive and offensive security establishment benefits from more than just the "byproducts" of basic research. In the advanced technological societies, this establishment programs, orients, orders, and finances, directly or indirectly, through the State or otherwise, the front-line research that is apparently the least "end-oriented" of all. This is all too obvious in such areas as physics, biology, medicine, biotechnology, bio-programming, data processing, and telecommunications. We have only to mention telecommunications and data processing to assess the extent of the phenomenon: the end-orientation of research is limitless; everything in these areas proceeds "in view" of technical and instrumental security. At the service of war, of national and international security, research programs have to encompass the entire field of information, the stockpiling of knowledge, the workings and thus also the essence of language and of all semiotic systems, translation, coding and decoding, the play of presence and absence, hermeneutics, semantics, structural and generative linguistics, pragmatics, rhetoric. I am accumulating all these disciplines in a haphazard way, on purpose, but I will end with literature, poetry, the arts, and fiction in general: the theory that has these disciplines as its object can be just as useful in ideological warfare as it is in experimentation with variables in all-too-familiar perversions of the referential function. Such a theory may always be put to work in communications strategy, the theory of commands, the most refined military pragmatics of jussive utterances. (By what token, for example, will it be clear that an utterance is to be taken as a command in the new technology of telecommunications? How are the new resources of simulation and simulacrum to be controlled? And so on.) One can just as easily seek to use the theoretical formulations of sociology, psychology, even psychoanalysis in order to refine what was called in France during the Indochinese or Algerian wars the powers of "psychological action"—alternating with torture. Consequently, so long as it has the means, a military budget can invest in anything at all, in view of deferred profits: "basic" scientific theory, the humanities, literary theory, and philosophy. The Department of Philosophy, which covered all this, and which Kant thought ought to be kept unavailable to any utilitarian purpose and to the orders of any power whatsoever in its search for truth, can no longer lay claim to such autonomy. What is produced in this field can always be used. And even if it should remain apparently useless in its results, in its productions, it can always serve to keep the masters of discourse busy: the experts, professionals of rhetoric, logic, or philosophy who might otherwise be applying their energy elsewhere. Or again, it may in certain situations secure an ideological bonus of luxury and gratuitousness for a society that can afford it *as well*, within certain limits. Furthermore, when certain random consequences of research are taken into account, it is always possible to have in view some eventual benefit that may ensue from an apparently useless research (philosophy or the humanities, for example). The history of the sciences encourages researchers to integrate that margin of randomness into their centralized calculation. They then proceed to adjust the means at their disposal, the available financial support, and the distribution of funding. A State power or the forces that it represents no longer need to prohibit research or to censor discourse, especially in the West. It is enough that they can limit the means, can regulate support for production, transmission, and diffusion. The machinery for this new "censorship" in the broad sense is much more complex and omnipresent than in Kant's day, for example, when problematics and the entire topology of the university were organized around the exercise of royal censorship. Today, in the Western democracies, this form of censorship has almost entirely disappeared. The prohibiting limitations function through multiple channels that are decentralized, difficult to bring together into a system. The unacceptability of a discourse, the noncertification of a research project, the illegitimacy of a course offering are declared by evaluative actions: studying such evaluations is, it seems to me, one of the tasks most indispensable to the exercise of academic responsibility, most urgent for the maintenance of its dignity. Within the university itself, forces that are apparently external to it (presses, foundations, the mass media) are intervening in an ever more decisive way. University presses, particularly in the United States, play a mediating role that entails the most serious responsibilities, since scientific criteria, in principle represented by the members of the university corporation, have to come to terms with many other aims. When the margin of randomness has to be narrowed, restrictions on support affect the disciplines that are the least profitable in the short run. And that provokes, within the professions, all kinds of effects, certain of which seem to have lost any direct relation to that causality—which is itself still largely overdetermined. The shifting determination of the margin of randomness always depends upon the techno-economic situation of a society in its relation to the entire world arena. In the United States, for example (and it is not just one example among others), without even mentioning the economic regulation that allows certain surplus values—through the channel of private foundations, among others—to sustain research or creative projects that are not immediately or apparently profitable, we also know that military programs, especially those of the Navy, can very rationally subsidize linguistic, semiotic, or anthropological investigations. These in turn are related to history, literature, hermeneutics, law, political science, psychoanalysis, and so forth.

The concept of information or informatization is the most general operator here. It integrates the basic into the end-oriented [*finalisé*], the purely rational into the technical, thus bearing witness to that original intermingling of metaphysics and technics. The value of "form"—and that which in forms maintains to be *seen* and *done*, having to see with *seeing* and to do with *doing*—is not foreign to it: but let us drop this difficult point for now. In *Der Satz vom Grund*, Heidegger locates this concept of "information" (understood and pronounced as in English, he says at the time when he is putting America and Russia side by side like two symmetrical and homogeneous continents of metaphysics *as* technics) in a dependence upon the principle of reason, as a principle of integral calculability. Even the principle of uncertainty (and he would have said the same thing of a certain interpretation of undecidability) continues to operate within the problematics of representation and of the subject-object relation. Thus he calls this the atomic era and quotes a popularizing book entitled "We shall live thanks to atoms" with prefaces both by Otto Hahn, Nobel Prize winner and "fundamentalist" physicist, and Franz Joseph Strauss, then minister of national defense. Information ensures the insurance of calculation and the calculation of insurance. In this we recognize the period of the principle of reason. Leibniz, as Heidegger recalls, is considered to have been the inventor of life insurance. In the form of information (*in der Gestalt der Information*), Heidegger says, the principle of reason dominates our entire representation (*Vorstellen*) and delineates a period for which everything depends upon the delivery of atomic energy. Delivery in German is *Zustellung*, a word that also applies, as Heidegger points out, to the delivery of mail. It belongs to the chain of *Gestell*, from the *Stellen* (*Vorstellen, Nachstellen, Zustellen, Sicherstellen*) that characterizes technological modernity. "Information" in this sense is the most economic, the most rapid, and the clearest (univocal, *eindeutig*) stockpiling, archiving, and communication of news. It must instruct men about the safeguarding (*Sicherstellung*) of what will meet their needs, *ta khreia*, Aristotle said. Computer technology, data banks, artificial intelligences, translating machines, and so forth, all these are constructed on the basis of this instrumental determination of a calculable language. Information does not inform merely by delivering an information content, it gives form, "in-formiert," "formiert zugleich." It installs man in a form that allows him to ensure his mastery on earth and beyond. All this has to be pondered as the effect of the principle of reason or, more rigorously, of a dominant interpretation of this principle, of a certain emphasis in the way we heed its summons.[13] But I have said that I cannot deal with the question of such stress here; it lies outside the scope of my topic.

What, then, is my topic? What do I have in view that has led me to present things as I have done so far? I have been thinking especially of the necessity of awakening or of resituating a responsibility, in the university or in face of the university, whether one belongs to it or not.

Those analysts who study the informative and instrumental value of language today are necessarily led to the very limits of the principle of reason thus interpreted. This can happen in any number of disciplines. But if the analysts end up for example working on the structures of the simulacrum or of literary fiction, on a poetic rather than an informative value of language, on the effects of undecidability, and so on, by that very token they are interested in possibilities that arise at the limits of the authority and the power of the principle of reason. On that basis, they may attempt to define new responsibilities in the face of the university's total subjection to the technologies of informatization.[14] It is obviously not a question of refusing these technologies. Nor, moreover, of accrediting too quickly and too simply an opposition between the instrumental and some pre-instrumental ("authentic" and properly "poetic") origin of language. I have often tried to show elsewhere, long ago, that this opposition remains of limited relevance and that, as such, it perhaps remains within Heidegger's interrogation. Nothing precedes technical instrumentalization absolutely. It is thus not a matter of opposing some obscurantist irrationalism to this instrumentalization. Like nihilism, irrationalism is a posture that is symmetrical to, thus dependent upon, the principle of reason. The theme of extravagance as *irrationalism*—there is very clear evidence for this—dates from the period when the principle of reason was being formulated. Leibniz denounced it in his *New Essays on Human Understanding*. Raising these new questions may sometimes protect an aspect of philosophy and the humanities that has always resisted technologization; it may also preserve the memory of what is much more deeply buried and ancient than the principle of reason. But the approach I am advocating here is often felt by certain guardians of the "humanities" or of the positive sciences as a threat. It is interpreted as such by those who most often have never sought to understand the history and the system of norms specific to their own institution, the deontology of their own profession. They do not wish to know how their discipline has been constituted, particularly in its modern professional form, since the beginning of the nineteenth century and under the watchful vigilance of the principle of reason. For the principle of reason can have obscurantist and nihilist effects. They can be seen more or less everywhere, in Europe and in America among those who believe they are defending philosophy, literature, and the humanities against these new modes of questioning that are also a new relation to language and tradition, a new *affirmation*, and new ways of taking responsibility. We can easily see on which side obscurantism and nihilism are lurking when on occasion great professors or the representatives of prestigious institutions lose all sense of proportion and control; on such occasions they forget the principles that they claim to defend in their work and suddenly begin to heap insults, to say whatever comes into their heads on the subject of texts that they obviously have never opened or that they have encountered through a mediocre journalism that in other circumstances they would pretend to scorn.[15]

It is possible to speak of this new responsibility that I have invoked only by sounding a call to practice it. It would be the responsibility of a community of thinking for which the border between basic and end-oriented research would no longer be secured, or in any event not under the same conditions as before. I call it a community of thinking in the broad sense—"at large"—rather than a community of research, of science, or of philosophy, since these values are most often subjected to the unquestioned authority of the principle of reason. Now, reason is only one species of thinking—which does not mean that thinking is "irrational." Such a community would interrogate the essence of reason and of the principle of reason, the values of the basic, of the principial, of radicality, of the *arche* in general, and it would attempt to draw out all the possible consequences of this questioning. It is not certain that such thinking can bring together a community or found an institution in the traditional sense of these words. It must rethink what is meant by community and institution. This thinking must also unmask—an infinite task—all the ruses of end-orienting reason, the paths by which apparently disinterested research can find itself indirectly reappropriated, reinvested by programs of all sorts. That does not mean that "end-orientation" is bad in itself and that it must be combated, far from it. Rather, I am defining the necessity for a new training that will prepare students to undertake new analyses in order to evaluate these ends and to choose, when possible, among them all.

As I mentioned earlier, along with some colleagues I was asked last year by the French government to prepare a report in view of the creation of an International College of Philosophy. I insisted, in that report, on stressing the dimension that in this context I am calling "thinking"—a dimension that is not reducible to technique, nor to science, nor to philosophy. This International College would not only be a College of Philosophy but also a place where philosophy itself would be questioned. It would not only be open to types of research that are not perceived as legitimate today, or that are insufficiently developed in French or foreign institutions, including some research that could be called "basic." We would go one step further, providing a place to work on the value and meaning of the basic, the fundamental, on its opposition to end-orientation, on the ruses of end-orientation in all its domains. As in the seminar that I mentioned earlier, the report confronts the political, ethical, and juridical consequences of such an undertaking. I cannot go into more detail here without keeping you much too long.

These new responsibilities cannot be purely academic. If they remain extremely difficult to assume, extremely precarious and threatened, it is because they must at once keep alive the memory of a tradition and make an opening beyond any program, that is, toward what is called the future. And the discourse, the works, or the position-taking that these responsibilities inspire, as to the institution of science and research, no longer stem solely from the sociology of knowledge, from sociology or politology. These disciplines are no doubt more necessary than ever; I would be the last to want to disqualify them. But whatever conceptual apparatus they may have, whatever axiomatics, whatever methodology (Marxist or neo-Marxist, Weberian or neo-Weberian, Mannheimian, some combination of these or something else entirely), they never touch upon that which, in themselves, continues to be based on the principle of reason and thus on the essential foundation of the modern university. They never question scientific normativity, beginning with the value of objectivity or of objectification, which governs and authorizes their discourse. Whatever their scientific value—and it can be considerable—these sociologies of the institution remain in this sense internal to the university, intra-institutional, controlled by the deepseated norms, even the programs, of the space that they claim to analyze. This can be observed, among other things, in the rhetoric, the rites, the modes of presentation and demonstration that they continue to respect. Thus I will go so far as to say that the discourse of Marxism and psychoanalysis, including those of Marx and Freud, *inasmuch* as they are standardized by a project of scientific practice and by the principle of reason, are intra-institutional, in any event homogeneous with the discourse that dominates the university in the last analysis. And the fact that this discourse is occasionally proffered by people who are not professional academics changes nothing essential. It simply explains, to a certain extent, the fact that even when it claims to be revolutionary, this discourse does not always trouble the most conservative forces of the university. Whether it is understood or not, it is enough that it does not threaten the fundamental axiomatics and deontology of the institution, its rhetoric, its rites, and its procedures. The academic landscape accommodates such types of discourse more easily within its economy and its ecology; however, if it does not simply exclude those who raise questions at the level of the foundation or nonfoundation of the university, it reacts much more fearfully to those who address sometimes the same questions to Marxism, to psychoanalysis, to the sciences, to philosophy, and to the humanities. It is not a matter simply of questions that one *formulates* while submitting one-self, as I am doing here, to the principle of reason, but also of preparing oneself thereby to transform the modes of writing, the pedagogic scene, the procedures of academic exchange, the relation to languages, to other disciplines, to the institution in general, to its inside and its outside. Those who venture forth along this path, it seems to me, need not set themselves up in opposition to the principle of reason, nor need they give way to "irra-tionalism." They may continue to assume *within* the university, along with its memory and tradition, the imperative of professional rigor and compe-tence. There is a double gesture here, a double postulation: to ensure pro-fessional competence and the most serious tradition of the university even while going as far as possible, theoretically and practically, in the most abyssal thinking of the university, to think at one and the same time the entire "Cornellian" landscape—the campus on the heights, the bridges, and if necessary the barriers above the abyss—and the abyss itself. It is this double gesture that appears unsituatable and thus unbearable to certain university professionals in every country who join ranks to foreclose or to censure it by all available means, simultaneously denouncing the "profes-sionalism" and the "antiprofessionalism" of those who are calling others to these new responsibilities.

I will not venture here to deal with the debate on "professionalism" that is developing in your country. Its features are, to a certain extent at least, specific to the history of the American university. But I will conclude on this general theme of "professions." At the risk of contradicting what I have been urging here, I would like to caution against another kind of precipitous reaction. For the responsibility that I am trying to situate can-not be simple. It implies multiple sites, a stratified terrain, postulations that are undergoing continual displacement, a sort of strategic rhythm. I said earlier that I would be speaking only of a certain rhythm, for exam-ple that of the blinking of an eye, and that I would only be playing one risk off against another, the barrier against the abyss, the abyss against the barrier, the one with the other and the one under the other.

Beyond technical ends, even beyond the opposition between technical ends and the principle of sufficient reason, beyond the affinity between technology and metaphysics, what I have here called "thinking" risks in its turn (but I believe this risk is unavoidable—it is the risk of the future it-self) being reappropriated by socio-political forces that could find it in their own interest in certain situations. Such a "thinking" indeed cannot be produced outside of certain historical, techno-economic, politico-institutional, and linguistic conditions. A strategic analysis that is to be as vigilant as possible must thus, with its eyes wide open, attempt to ward off such reappropriations. (I would have liked to situate at this point certain questions about the "politics" of Heideggerian thought, especially as elaborated prior to *Der Satz vom Grund*, for example in the two inaugural discourses of 1929 and 1933.)

I will limit myself, however, to the double question of "professions." First: does the university have as its essential mission that of producing professional competencies, which may sometimes be external to the university? Second: is the task of the university to ensure within itself—and under what conditions—the reproduction of professional competence by preparing for pedagogy and for research professors who have respect for a certain code? One can answer the second question in the affirmative without having done so for the first, and seek to keep professional forms and values internal to the university outside the marketplace and the ends of social work *outside of the university*. The new responsibility of the "thinking" of which we are speaking cannot fail to be accompanied, at least, by a movement of suspicion, even of rejection with respect to the professionalization of the university in these two senses, and especially in the first, which regulates university life according to the supply and demand of the marketplace and according to a purely technical ideal of competence. To this extent at least, such "thinking" can, at a minimum, result in reproducing a highly traditional politics of knowledge. And the effects can be those that belong to a social hierarchy in the exercise of techno-political power. I am not saying that this "thinking" is identical with that politics, and that it is therefore necessary to abstain from it. I am saying that under certain conditions it can serve that politics, and everything then comes down to the analysis of those conditions. In modern times, Kant, Schelling, Nietzsche, Heidegger and numerous others have all said as much, unequivocally: the essential feature of academic responsibility must not be professional education (and the pure core of academic autonomy, the essence of the university, is located in the Faculty of Philosophy, according to Kant). Does this affirmation not repeat the profound and hierarchizing political evaluation of metaphysics, I mean of Aristotle's *Metaphysics*? Shortly after the passage that I read at the beginning (981b and following), one sees a theoretico-political hierarchy being put into place. At the top, there is theoretical knowledge. It is not sought after in view of its utility; and the holder of this knowledge, which is always a knowledge of causes and of principles, is the leader or *arkhitekton* of a society at work, is positioned above the manual laborer (*kheiroteknes*) who acts without knowing, just as a fire burns. Now this theoretician leader, this knower of causes who has no need of "practical" skill, is in essence a *teacher*. Beyond the fact of knowing causes and of possessing reason or *logos* (*to logon ekhein*), he bears another mark (*semeion*) of recognition: the "capacity to teach" (*to dunasthai didaskein*). To teach, then, and at the same time to direct, steer, organize the empirical work of the laborers. The theoretician-teacher or "architect" is a leader because he is on the side of the *arche*, of beginning and commanding. He commands—he is the premier or the prince—because he knows causes and principles, the "why" and thus also the "in view of" of things. Before the fact, and before anyone else, he answers to the principle of reason, which is the first principle, the principle of principles. And that is why he takes orders from no one; it is he, on the contrary, who orders, prescribes, lays down the law (982a 18). And it is normal that this superior science, with the power that it confers by virtue of its very lack of utility, is developed in places (*topoi*), in regions where leisure is possible. Thus, Aristotle points out, the mathematical arts were developed in Egypt owing to the leisure time enjoyed by the priestly caste (*to tōn iereon ethnos*), the priestly folk.

Kant, Schelling, Nietzsche, and Heidegger, speaking of the university, premodern or modern, do not say exactly what Aristotle said, nor do all three of them say exactly the same thing. They also do say the same thing. Even though he admits the industrial model of the division of labor into the university, Kant places the so-called "lower" faculty, the Faculty of Philosophy—a place of pure rational knowledge, a place where truth has to be spoken without controls and without concern for "utility," a place where the very meaning and the autonomy of the university meet—Kant places this faculty *above and outside professional education*: the architectonic schema of pure reason is above and outside the technical schema. In his *Lectures on the Future of our Educational Establishments*,[16] Nietzsche condemns the division of labor in the sciences, condemns utilitarian and journalistic culture in the service of the State, condemns the professional ends of the university. The more one *does* (*tut*) in the area of training, the more one has to think (*denken*). And, still in the first lecture: "Man muß nicht nur Standpunkte, sondern auch Gedanken haben!" (One must not have viewpoints alone, but also thoughts!) As for Heidegger, in 1929, in his inaugural lecture, entitled "What is Metaphysics?,"[17] he deplores the henceforth technical organization of the university and its compartmentalizing specialization. And even in his *Rector's Speech*, at the very point where he makes an appeal on behalf of the three services (*Arbeitsdienst, Wehrdienst, Wissensdienst*, the service of work, the military, and knowledge), at the very point where he is recalling that these services are of equal rank and equally original (he had recalled earlier that for the Greeks *theoria* was only the highest form of *praxis* and the mode, par excellence, of *energeia*), Heidegger nevertheless violently condemns disciplinary compartmentalization and "exterior training in view of a profession," as "an idle and inauthentic thing" (*Das Mussige und Unechte ausserlicher Berufsabrichtung*).[18]

Desiring to remove the university from "useful" programs and from professional ends, one may always, willingly or not, find oneself serving unrecognized ends, reconstituting powers of caste, class, or corporation. We are in an implacable political topography: one step further in view of greater profundity or radicalization, even going beyond the "profound" and the "radical," the principial, the *arche*, one step further toward a sort of original an-archy risks producing or reproducing the hierarchy. "Thinking" requires *both* the principle of reason *and* what is beyond the principle of reason, the *arche* and an-archy. Between the two, the difference of a breath or an accent, only the *enactment* of this "thinking" can decide. That decision is always risky; it always risks the worst. To claim to eliminate this risk through an institutional program is quite simply to erect a barricade against a future. The decision of thinking cannot be an intra-institutional event, an academic moment.

All this does not define a politics, nor even a responsibility. Only, at best, some negative conditions, a "negative wisdom," as the Kant of *The Conflict of the Faculties* would say: preliminary cautions, protocols of vigilance for a new *Aufklärung*, what must be seen and kept in sight in a modern re-elaboration of this old problematics. Beware of the abysses and the gorges, but also of the bridges and the barriers. Beware of what opens the university to the outside and the bottomless, but also of what, closing it in on itself, would create only an illusion of closure, would make the university available to any sort of interest, or else render it perfectly useless. Beware of ends; but what would a university be without ends?

Neither in its medieval nor in its modern form has the university disposed of its own absolute autonomy and of the rigorous conditions of its own unity. For more than eight centuries, "university" has been the name given by our society to a sort of supplementary body that at one and the same time it wanted to project outside itself and to keep jealously to itself, to emancipate and to control. On this double basis, the university was supposed to *represent* society. And in a certain way it has done so: it has re-produced society's scenography, its views, conflicts, contradictions, its play and its differences, and also its desire for organic union in a total body. Organicist language is always associated with "techno-industrial" language in "modern" discourse on the university. But with the relative autonomy of a technical device, indeed that of a machine and of a prosthetic body, this university artifact has *reflected society* only in giving it the chance for reflection, that is, also, for *dissociation.* The time for reflection, here, sig-nifies not only that the internal rhythm of the university system is rela-tively independent of social time and relaxes the urgency of command, ensures for it a great and precious freedom of play. An empty place for chance: the invagination of an inside pocket. The time for reflection is also the chance for turning back on the very conditions of reflection, in all senses of that word, as if with the help of a new optical device one could finally see sight, could not only view the natural landscape, the city, the bridge, and the abyss, but could "view" viewing. As if through an acousti-cal device one could "hear" hearing, in other words, seize the inaudible in a sort of poetic telephony. Then the time of reflection is also an other time; it is heterogeneous to what it reflects and perhaps gives time for what calls for and is called thinking. It is the chance for an event about which one does not know whether or not, presenting itself *within* the uni-versity, it belongs to the history of the university. It may also be brief and paradoxical: it may tear up time, like the instant invoked by Kierkegaard, one of those thinkers who are foreign, even hostile to the university, who give us more to think about, with respect to the essence of the university, than academic reflections themselves. The chance for this event is the chance of an instant, an *Augenblick,* a "wink" or a "blink"; it takes place "in the blink of an eye." I would say, rather, "in the twilight of an eye," for it is in the most crepuscular, the most westerly situations of the Western university that the chances of this "twinkling" of thinking are multiplied. In a period of "crisis," as we say, a period of decadence and renewal, when the institution is "on the blink," provocation to think brings together in the *same* instant the desire for memory and exposure to the future, the fi-delity of a guardian faithful enough to want to keep even the chance of a future, in other words the singular responsibility of what he does not have and of what is not yet. Neither in his keeping nor in his purview. Keeping the memory and keeping the chance—is this possible? How is one to feel *accountable* for what one does not have, and is not yet? But what else is one to feel *responsible* for, if not for what does not belong to us? For what, like the future, belongs and comes down to the other? And chance—can it be kept? Is it not, as its name indicates, the risk or the event of the fall, even of decadence, the falling-due that befalls you at the bottom of the "gorge"? I don't know. I don't know if it is possible to keep both memory and chance. I am tempted to think, rather, that the one cannot be kept without the other, without keeping the other and being kept from the other. Differently. This double keeping or guarding would be assigned, as its responsibility, to the strange destiny of the university. To its law, to its reason for being, and to its truth. Let us risk one more etymological wink: truth is what keeps, that is, both preserves and is preserved. I am thinking here of *Wahrheit*, of the *Wahren* of *Wahrheit* and of *veritas*—whose name figures on the coat of arms of so many American universities. It institutes guardians and calls upon them to watch faithfully—truthfully—over itself.

Let me recall my *incipit* and the single question that I raised at the outset: how not to speak, today, of the university? Will I have said it, or done it? Will I have said how one should not speak, today, of the university? Or will I have rather spoken as one should not do today, within the university?

Only others can answer. Beginning with you.

—*Translated by Catherine Porter and Edward P. Morris*

"In Praise of Philosophy"

Introduction Proposed by *Libération*

The initiatives taken by the minister of research, Jean-Pierre Chevènement, are today shaking up the world that has generally been insulated
from the exact and the social or human sciences. We do not yet know
what, good or bad, will come of this "construction site": debates, projects,
counterprojects, polemics, discussions are in progress. Yet one thing is obvious: philosophy has been quite forgotten. We remember, however, the
"quarrel over philosophy" and the debates about philosophy that gave rise
to the (bad) intentions of the previous governments. Mobilized, philosophers met, in June 1979, at the Estates General of Philosophy, during
which they accepted the idea not only, of course, of a defense of philosophy and of what it represents, but also of an extension of the teaching of
philosophy.[1] At the time, the Socialists, who a priori are not to be classified among those who are "afraid of philosophy," listened favorably to the
proposals born of the Estates General. François Mitterrand himself, before
the elections, assured us that, with the Socialists in power, the teaching of
philosophy would be "preserved and developed."[2] The Socialists are now
in power. What about the promises, then? Contrary to his colleague in research, the minister of national education, Alain Savary, is quite silent. We
asked Jacques Derrida, who as leader of Greph has always been on the
front line of the fight "for philosophy," to make his contribution—which
could sound the note of a necessary questioning.

The Proposals of Greph

Greph proposes that a decision in principle confirm and enact the promises of the president of the republic: at the soonest possible date, the teaching of philosophy, preserved in all sections of the Terminale, should be introduced beginning in the Seconde.[3] Once this date and this decision have been determined, different kinds of work should bring together all the interested parties; and most of all, experimentation should be multiplied, not only in a few pilot lycées specializing in experimentation, but wherever possible and desired, it being understood that the ministry should encourage and officially favor the conditions for such experimentation. Greph proposes, moreover—but these are points to be discussed with all the instances and agencies concerned—that, on the one hand, philosophy be introduced in the Seconde in the form of a recognized discipline, with its demands and its classical norms. For example, at a rate of two hours per week, and with the rights accorded every other basic [*fondamentale*] discipline. The philosophy teacher would teach what we agree to call, in the strict sense, institutional philosophy. But on the other hand, together with the representatives of other disciplines, something like thinking at the limits of philosophy would be practiced as well as taught, in novel forms, on contents that are new and still little or poorly represented in the current distribution of the fields of teaching, if possible outside any program and with the greatest possible sense of innovation, of invention in common. In this space still to be cleared, philosophers and philosophy (in the broadest and most novel sense possible) would have their part, a part that would not be predominant, in an ensemble that would be available to all teachers and all students. This assumes a profound overhaul of the system and of normal practice, in education and elsewhere.

J. Derrida

On all these questions, one can read *Qui a peur de la philosophie?* and *Les États Généraux de la philosophie.*[4]

Interview with Jacques Derrida

Libération: Twice, François Mitterrand took up the question of the extension of the teaching of philosophy. Yet this theme has been on the agenda for you since the Estates General of Philosophy.

Jacques Derrida: In fact, since the beginning of 1975, it has been for us much more than and different from a particular (technical, pedagogical, even corporative) demand. Such a transformation would affect everything, before and after secondary school, within and outside of education. Since it is above all not a matter of propagating a discipline, even less the same discipline (the same contents, the same methods, and so forth) in identical conditions, and since we are calling for a profound transformation of the entire system of education in its relations to society, we knew that we were talking about a true political mutation. And we did not hide the fact that with a left-wing government the space of the debate or fight would of course be more open, more favorable, but the resistance would remain lively, and work and struggles would still be necessary. What we ran into is in fact older, more deeply rooted, and thus more tenacious than the political themes, programs, and codes the electoral majorities clash over—or agree upon—in this country.

Libération: But we have nonetheless seen a certain political change. Are these changes such that they will get rid of certain obstacles?

J.D.: Apparently the systematic political obstacle has been removed; it seems to have disappeared formally. I am not speaking only of the feeling of deliverance, of the immense hope to which the Left's coming to power has given rise. I am not speaking only of what could, let's hope, bring an end to the most sinister historical sequences since the war, particularly, it must be stressed, in the university. No, I am referring very precisely, since it is the sole theme of our interview, to François Mitterrand's formal promises during his presidential campaign. Like all his promises during this time, they ought to form the charter of the government's action. There were, in the first place, ten proposals in the Évry speech, then the letter to Greph (since published in *Le Monde*, May 28 [1981]): "the teaching of philosophy should be preserved and developed"; it "could be extended within secondary education" and "should obligatorily figure in all sections of the long second cycle."[5] These promises respond precisely to the demands of the Estates General. We will not allow them to be forgotten or neglected. It is urgent that we remember them today. For the problems remain.

There is still no sign from the Ministry [of Education] of the slightest initiative in this area. No official reference has been made to François Mitterrand's promises. Not even the hypothesis of a discussion, of a preliminary project for study or exploration, has been put forward. Nothing. The suppression (by Saunier-Séité)[6] of certain habilitations[7] vital for philosophy in certain universities is even being maintained. We can attest to the surprise or outrage of many teachers and students faced with this. Repeatedly, this summer and autumn, Greph proposed participating at least in this indispensable preparatory work. All the interested parties should be brought together: the ministry and the Inspection Générale;[8] students' parents; and the representatives of the other disciplines, unions, and corporative associations, such as the Association of Teachers of Philosophy (which is not "the only representative association" any more than it "has been devoted for more than thirty years to the extension of the teaching of philosophy," as it has just claimed: certain of its members even admit to fearing the extension of the teaching of philosophy to technical sections). In any case no action that would merely adjust the timetable in the Terminale would be adequate for the problems we are debating, with which we are struggling.

Libération: This question of the technical sections is very important in your eyes?

J.D.: Yes, and revealing. With it, we are getting, too quickly, at the properly historical difficulty that we skimmed over a moment ago. Why, in this area precisely, does the new majority risk pursuing, with a barely different language, a politics it seems to have fought against for decades? When the forces that supported past governments, within and outside of education, tended to limit the teaching of philosophy, their concern was not only to forbid or suppress a certain barely controllable politicization, through certain immediately political (in the immediately coded sense of the term) discourses, texts, or themes. One could recall the numerous and serious proofs of the role that this immediately political anxiety has no doubt played, especially after 1968. But there was above all the powerful constraint of a market, techno-economic imperatives, a certain concept— others would say an ideology or simply a philosophy—of immediate adaptation to the apparent urgencies of productivity in national and international competition.

There is nothing more "natural," in short, than this technologism, which is also a productivism and a positivism. For the philosophy that supports them (it is also a philosophy, a great tradition of philosophy, a philosophy of philosophy), the training of philosophers was not to be extended to the point of a certain democratization, beyond a social class that had a de facto monopoly over it and marked philosophical discourse with its own features. The extension of such training was not profitable, was not sufficiently "productive" [*performant*].⁹ By the training of philosophers, I mean that of citizens (first of all pupils and students, sometimes teachers or researchers) trained in the rigor of a discipline (as they must be in that of other disciplines or fields of knowledge) but also opened by it and beyond it to ways of questioning or putting into question that are difficult to program.

Libération: What is happening today? Are we, in this respect at least, in a truly new situation?

J.D.: I'm not certain of that. The project, the socialist "idea," has to work its way through numerous and essential contradictions. For example, it must at once respond to and avoid the techno-economic programming of the market, of production; must respond to and avoid the very strict urgencies of national and global competition in its current state. It must respond and not respond to the laws of this machinery, satisfy them and attempt to displace them. A no doubt inevitable contradiction whose effects can be followed in the details of Socialist management and discourse. In itself this is not an absolute evil, a vice, an accident, or a weakness. But there is cause to think this contradiction, to analyze it, without ignoring or denying it.

Libération: Do you think the National Conference on Research and Technology, organized by Jean-Pierre Chevènement, is indicative in this regard?

J.D.: In principle, it is a very favorable initiative. How not to approve of it? But since its official protocols and its first preparatory work, we have been called upon to facilitate the "passage" between, on the one hand, the imperatives of technology or production (very obscure notions, no matter what is said about them) and, on the other hand, teaching, science, or culture (no less problematic notions that, today, as yesterday, are often treated as though they were self-evident). We are called upon to "adapt" "interdisciplinary modes of training" "to the new needs of the economic and social sector (industry, agriculture, etc.)." Nothing could be more legitimate, of course, nothing more necessary, but where is the innovation concerning the idea of science, culture, technology, research, and teaching?

Although there is, fortunately, consideration of increasing certain budgets, of further realizing a social and humanist democracy that previously remained formal and insufficient, the system of evaluation, the aims [*finalités*], remain the same, as do the discourse and the idea of culture. Within this continuity, of course, enormous progress can be made, and I am among those who hope for this. But must one not question oneself once again about this continuity and realize, in all domains, the possibility of this questioning? Was it not in the name of this same discourse, of the same "passages," of the same "adaptation," that some not long ago wanted to evacuate philosophy and everything that did not respond to the criteria of productive "performance," to the so-called "social needs"? This final notion is indeed ambiguous, and it is being made the supreme authority. What is a social need? Who defines it? What does it mean to adapt to a supposedly prior social need, especially for research, science, culture, and, *a fortiori*, philosophy, which is something altogether different again?

Libération: Yes. But it is not enough to say that it is "altogether different." It is perhaps this artistic vagueness that fuels the diatribes against philosophy.

J.D.: You're right, but I am not going to improvise a definition of "philosophy" here. Limiting myself to the immediate preoccupations we share, I will say that "philosophy" today names at least two things.

On the one hand, obviously, a very rich tradition, texts, a wealth of discourse, of argumentation, of (precritical, critical, and more than critical, other than simply critical) questions, metaphysics, regional ontologies, epistemology in the broadest sense, politics, and so forth. These elements of a discipline, these powerful instruments, are not only instruments and techniques, although they are also that, and although their indispensable tradition must be ensured. As such, already, philosophy does not derive from either the exact sciences or the social or human sciences, whose "underdevelopment" (an enormous question that I merely evoke in passing) the minister of research believes he can observe or regret. Scientificity and the object of these sciences are also questions for philosophy. Formerly, it was also in order to make room for the "human sciences" that some wished to reduce or dilute the teaching of philosophy. Nor is philosophy simply a productive activity, and I would even say that its belonging to what is called "culture" is not self-evident. Without opposing them, philosophy is different from science, technology, culture. And one can bet that in these domains no transformation can arise that does not take shape on the borders of philosophy. I prefer to say "on the borders," on either side of a limit that looks at once toward the inside and toward a beyond of philosophy.

On the other hand, the name of philosophy finds itself rightly associated with every "thinking" that no longer lets itself be determined, by rights, by techno-scientific or cultural programs, that troubles them sometimes, interrogates and affirms them, yes, affirms, beyond them, without necessarily opposing or limiting them in the "critical" mode. The value of "critique" is only one of the philosophical possibilities; it has its history and its own genealogy. What is called "deconstruction," for example, is not limited to one of those so-called critical operations whose virtue and incontestable necessity have inspired all those who defend philosophy, "critical" reflection before the powers that be. What interests me in this "deconstruction" is in particular the affirmative thinking that, while neither techno-scientific nor cultural, nor even philosophical through and through, maintains an essential affinity with the philosophical, which it works—in every sense of the word—in its discourse as well as in its institutional, pedagogical, political, etc., structures. This "thinking" can find itself at work in all the disciplines, in the sciences and in philosophy, in history, literature, the arts, a certain manner of writing, of practicing or studying languages, without the obsession of techno-economic performativity. If there is any, this thinking is incalculable and marks the very limit of technocratism.

These strange and apparently fragile questions, these unusual breakthroughs [*frayages*] that must be given their chance, are not necessarily sterile speculations. What is more, why not let them run this risk of being unproductive? Those worried about calculable profitability should know that through these marginal and random wanderings transformations sometimes take shape, the encoded future of a discovery that in advance cracks [*lézarder*] with its signature the heaviest and surest programming machines. We know it well: unheard-of thoughts, groundbreaking scientific discoveries have sometimes resembled unpredictable blows [*coups*], throws [*coups*] of the dice or blows [*coups*] of force.

Libération: But is there not, in the texts preparatory to the Chevènement conference itself, a protest against technocratism, even if it is very timid?

J.D.: Certainly. And that is why I neither criticize nor denounce that conference. On the contrary, as you can see, I am making my modest contribution to it, even if that contribution appears a bit dissonant. The problem is that in those preparatory texts the protest against technocratism is nearly lost in the midst of a hymn to that techno-democratic humanism that is most certain of its legitimacy, its necessity, its optimism, and its progressism. Well, the stronger this discourse grows, the more it appears irrefutable, the more we will need (now there is a "need"!) to question its ultimate foundations, its limits, its presuppositions, its old and its new history. We will be able to do so only from isolated places or non-places, with minority, out-of-the-ordinary discourses and gestures, uncertain of their immediate admissibility, and according to forms of questioning that will not let themselves be dominated or intimidated by this powerful program.

For me, philosophy, or rather "thinking," would be this mobile non-place from which one continues or begins again, always differently, to ask oneself what is at stake in technology, the positivity of the sciences (exact or not), production, yes, and above all, productivity. This "philosophy," we must recognize, has no site that could be assigned it in a Conference on Research and Technology. It might be named in passing among "multiple forms of research that are philosophical, historical, sociological, economic, or political in nature," but it does not belong to the *series* of such research.

Libération: It is thus the entire structure of the university and of higher education that is to be questioned?

J.D.: Institutions that leave space, and breathing room, for what does not yet have an identifiable face would have to be created: a paradoxical, apparently contradictory, and yet vital task. I am not referring only to philosophy in its recognized form as the theory of science or epistemology, as the discipline dealing with the foundations of science or technology, politics or ethics. Philosophy is that, of course; but a certain "thinking," differently philosophical, can also question the genealogy and presuppositions of this very fundamentalism, this appeal to foundations, and even an ontologico-encyclopedic hierarchy (general or fundamental ontology, regional ontologies, forms of knowledge and positivities, and so forth).

Let us not forget that this hierarchy has constructed the model of the university we have been living by since the beginning of the nineteenth century. This model is itself very weakened today, and irreversibly, I believe. All states, in the East and in the West, are letting or making it die, preferring more "productive" [*performant*] (from the point of view of scientific, industrial, and, always, military technology) research institutions, ones that are more closely dependent and that are cut off from all teaching. One would have to pause for a long time over this evolution. We cannot do so here. In a word, the paradox would be the following: according to the model that could be called "modern," and first of all German, since the nineteenth century in Europe this university has indirectly represented an old, condemned State rationality, but it could become, curiously, in its very old age, a kind of refuge of liberalism, in the sense that one can also speak of the "liberal arts." It could become, perhaps, a solution of withdrawal and urgency for a thinking that would still like to avoid the constraining planning we spoke of a moment ago and that is spreading to all the places of research (which in Kant's time and that of *The Conflict of the Faculties* were few and marginal and were called "academies" and "learned societies").

I do not believe that we have to choose between these two possibilities. As antithetical as they appear, they join up in the same system. No, one would have to reconstruct from top to bottom all the relations (and sometimes even interrupt all relation) between the State and knowledge, technology, culture, philosophy, thinking, whether in their institutional form or not. Perhaps this is in the process of happening, even if it is not very obvious. But seriously speaking, one should at least recall the entire history of this problematic, reread among other things *The Conflict of the Faculties*, rewrite it completely differently today, rewrite completely differently the best and the worst of what Kant, Schleiermacher, Hegel, Humboldt, Fichte, Schelling, but also Cousin, Heidegger, and a few others have handed down to us on these subjects. We still have to be left the time and the means to do so.

—*Translated by Jan Plug*

The Antinomies of the Philosophical Discipline: Letter Preface

My friends, I am afraid that the letter I promised will be too long. But I prefer to restrict myself to a letter. It will tell you first of all that I am far away, and I regret that: you know how much I would have wished to take part in your work and your discussions—and to show my solidarity. With whom? With what? That is a question I would like not to elude, in a moment. Yet if I prefer to entrust what I have to say to the genre of the letter, it is especially because one can allow oneself to manifest there, with less embarrassment, something like a "mood." I don't know exactly what a mood is; I don't believe in it very much; I don't believe it is opaque, insignificant, indecipherable. It speaks, and there is always room to analyze it. But the *language of mood*, like the code of the letter, allows one to act *as if*, for lack of time and space, the affected language of the affect could gather everything up economically in an "it cannot be explained," "it goes without saying"—everything, the premises, the mediations, and even the conclusions of an interminable analysis.

And a letter, even a philosophical letter, dates the "as if" of the mood, of a fabled mood: once upon a time, one day, I had the feeling that...

So what is my mood, today, with regard to something—already a myth in itself—called "School *and* Philosophy"? Let's not even talk about a "bad mood" against this word "school," the place of so many confusions and abuses. It remains a little mythic because overly marked and too little marked, historically too determined and too undetermined, too French in its universal guises. Like any word, you'll say. Yes, but I find that the possibilities of this equivocation are exploited a little too much today, in France, especially when one is talking about philosophy.

But as I see it, that is not the essential thing. My mood might be bad, but it is not a bad mood. My mood would translate, rather, a certain despair. It is not new, and no doubt I have found there the strength or the reason for a certain philosophical *affirmation* (which has nothing to do with a philosophical position or assurance; quite the contrary) and even, along with others, along with some of you, the reason and the strength to demonstrate, testify, "militate," as one says, *for* the teaching of philosophy. One would need a lot of philosophical ingenuousness to read nothing but an incoherence in this relation of affirmation to despair. But let's not go into that. It is true that the thing remains enigmatic for me, still today (hence philosophy!), no doubt more than ever, and the questions remain wide open, whether one is talking about the link between philosophizing, philosophy, and their discipline or the link between the necessity of a certain writing, which to go quickly we'll call deconstructive writing, and a reaffirmation of philosophy. It is something more and something other than a link, a logical connection or a coherency in a system; it is an essential *alliance.* That is why I prefer to speak of affirmation rather than of position, in other words of what demands commitment, yes, beginning from its provenance and for the future. And this is what is still not understood, what remains inaccessible first of all to those who do not know how or do not want to read, who are in a rush either to caricature or to falsify; and since we are talking about the school and philosophy, I think of the stupefying dogmatism that, for a while now, has authorized some to distort the proposals of Greph or of the Estates General of Philosophy: imperturbably, without reference, without analysis, without quotation, without demonstration. I will come back to this below.

No, the despair could not even look like what it is; it could not assume its figure of despair if there were not this basic fund of philosophical reaffirmation. And I feel this despair today in the face of a certain obviousness of *repetition,* a distressing obviousness.

What repetition?

There is first of all the *surface repetition,* if you want to call it that for the sake of convenience. Below, I will spell out my reservations concerning such a distinction between two sorts of repetition, in which one would be the surface of the other. This apparently superficial repetition would be that of political action and discourse, the compulsive trotting out of the same thing as concerns the philosophical discipline. Oh, I am very well aware that still in 1979, at the time of the Estates General, my friends in

Greph and I said—and published—that although the essential transformations we were calling for presupposed a profound political mutation, a change of government would not be enough. It might lighten the atmosphere; it would allow an opening for debate, put an end to threats that were too openly declared, make room for symbolic experiments, perhaps a certain change in the tone of official discourse or the presentation of measures undertaken. But, as we were already saying then, the constraints that urge the reproduction of the *type* and the reduction of the *field* of the philosophical discipline would remain the same. People would continue to believe that the training of technical competencies, a submission of knowledge to a certain kind of profit-making, the "end-orientation" [*finalisation*] of research, economic competition, the race for production, a certain concept of the relations between industrial or military techno-science and philosophy, between the social sciences and philosophy, all of this required that a discipline as untouchable as it is useless be maintained within its limits (thought to be natural). That discipline should remain (and this is the best scenario!) confined to one year in the lycées or little cells in the university where life is becoming increasingly difficult. There is no point in elaborating upon these things we are all very well aware of. Besides a few symbolic and precarious initiatives—which, however, I do not want to minimize (such as experimental attempts to teach philosophy other than in the Terminale, the extension of philosophy to the last year of technical lycées, a certain support, however insufficient it may be, for the Collège International de Philosophie and for everything it may represent today in France and outside of France)—things have not changed very much. Here or there, they will instead have gotten worse: I am thinking in particular of what is taking shape in the university. This growing confinement reinforces the power of certain institutions of the press and publishing, sometimes in the direction of credulity or cynicism, even of incompetence *and* of immediate self-interest.

But let's not pursue this debate any further. This tireless repetition may be discouraging, but we will not find the strength or the desire to analyze it, much less to try to interrupt it, unless, as philosophers, we ask ourselves questions about another order, another place, another dimension of the repetition, the one I hesitated to call "profound." Which one? The one that encloses the discourse, logic, rhetoric of all those who, speaking "for philosophy"—as *we* are doing—reproduce *types* whose matrix is well known and whose combinatory grid is more or less exhausted. The most serious thing is certainly not the finitude, always irreducible, of the reserve of arguments or figures, or the necessity to draw endlessly from that reserve with sometimes the illusion of inventing something. No, the most serious thing is, *in the first place*, the structure of this matrix: it holds us to an apparently insurmountable contradiction, one might say a "nondialecticizable" contradiction. One can also see in it a divided law, a double law or a double bind, an *antinomy*. It imposes itself not only on us but also on our partners or adversaries, outside of education, if not outside of philosophy (since there is no simple exteriority here, no outside-philosophy or nonphilosophy; as was said for whoever could or wanted to hear it at the Estates General of Philosophy, there is no nonphilosophical barbarity, and we never fight against nonphilosophical barbarity; the fights or the debates we are talking about always oppose different philosophies, forces represented by different philosophies). That is why I would not maintain for too long the merely convenient distinction I proposed a moment ago between two repetitions. But it would be even more serious if, *in the second place*, we did not try to think this antinomy *as such*, to analyze it, interrogate it, situate it, and so forth, in the structure of its authority, in the aporias it endlessly reproduces, in its provenance or its future.

To think it: will this still be a philosophical act? Philosophical through and through, simply philosophical? Can it give rise to institutions and discipline? I am not sure. This question already belongs, as we will see in a moment, to the program of antinomies.

Yet, while it may not be certain that this thinking is philosophical through and through, it certainly implies philosophy and philosophical knowledge. It perhaps is not limited to philosophical knowledge, but it is impossible without that knowledge.

The only thing that seems to me clear and desirable today (you see, I am still talking about my "mood") is a community that would take charge of such thinking, the community of a responsibility that no longer has simply the figure given it by Husserl (responsibility in the face of the infinite task of philosophy, transcendental community of a rational "we," and so forth, in the face of the "crisis") or Heidegger (responsibility for the response to the call of Being). These two figures belong to the space of repetition that comprises us and pre-comprehends us, to which we are already destined and that it would be a matter of thinking: not *against* Husserl or Heidegger, of course, which would be a bit foolish, but rather *beginning with* them, and no doubt otherwise.

If, among all the differences and disagreements that may separate those who will have taken part in these meetings, there is still the chance for an "us" and a community, I would not know where to situate it outside of this *responsibility*. I *would not know*; however, it is not certain that this community still has to be a community of *knowledge*, a community of the *consciousness of knowledge*. Within such a community, *polemos* is possible, sometimes necessary, but it excludes petty battles and mediocre polemics, the mere displacement of pawns in an interminable game.

How is one to define the poles of this contradiction without dialectic? What would be the two essential but contradictory requirements we do not want to renounce? If the double law of an antinomy reproduces, directly or indirectly, all the types of our arguments, defenses, or accusations, what is its axiomatics?

Since this letter is already too long, I will restrict myself to the barest outline. For the convenience of the demonstration, I will distinguish *seven* contradictory *commandments*.

First Commandment

On the one hand, we must protest the submission of the philosophical (its questions, programs, discipline, etc.) to any external purpose: the useful, the profitable, the productive, the efficient, "high performance" [*performant*], but also whatever belongs in general to the techno-scientific, the techno-economic, the end-orientation [*finalisation*] of research, even ethical, civic, or political education.

But, on the other hand, we should on no account give up the critical, and therefore evaluative and hierarchizing, mission of philosophy, philosophy as the final instance of judgment, as constitution or intuition of final meaning, last reason, thinking of ultimate ends. It is always in the name of a "principle of finality," as Kant would say, that we mean to save philosophy and its discipline from any techno-economic or sociopolitical end-orientation [*finalisation*]. This antinomy is indeed philosophical through and through since "end-orientation" always appeals to some philosophy, at least implicitly. Once again: there is never any "nonphilosophical" barbarity.

How is one to reconcile these two orders of finality [*finalité*]?

Second Commandment

On the one hand, we must protest the enclosure of philosophy. We legitimately refuse house arrest, the circumscription that would confine philosophy to a class or a curriculum, a type of object or logic, a fixed content or form. We stand opposed to whatever would prohibit philosophy from being present and insistent outside its class, in other disciplines or other departments, from opening itself up to new objects in a way that knows no limit of principle, from recalling that it was already present there where no one wanted to acknowledge it, and so forth.

But, on the other hand and just as legitimately, we should claim the proper and specific unity of the discipline. We should be very vigilant on this score, be ready to denounce, as Greph has been doing incessantly, anything that might come along to threaten this integrity, dissolve, dissect, or disperse the identity of the philosophical as such.

How is one to reconcile this localizable identity and this ubiquity that exceeds all bounds?

Third Commandment

On the one hand, we feel we have the right to demand that philosophical research and questioning never be dissociated from teaching. Is that not the theme of our colloquium, confronted as we are with the return of the same threat?

But, on the other hand, we also feel we are authorized to recall that some aspect of philosophy, perhaps the essential part of it, is not limited to, has not always been limited to, teaching acts, to educational events, to its institutional structures, indeed to the philosophical discipline itself. That discipline can always be overrun, sometimes provoked, by the unteachable. Perhaps it has to accept teaching the unteachable, to produce itself by renouncing itself, by exceeding its own identity.

How is one to maintain, within the same now [*maintenant*] of the discipline, the limit and the excess? How to maintain that one must teach this very thing? That it cannot be taught?

Fourth Commandment

On the one hand, we consider it normal to demand institutions adequate to this impossible and necessary, useless and indispensable discipline. We consider it normal to demand new institutions. In our view, this is essential.

But, on the other hand, we postulate that the philosophical norm is not limited to its institutional appearances. Philosophy exceeds its institutions; it even has to analyze the history and the effects of its own institutions. It finally has to remain free at every moment, obeying only truth, the force of the question or of thinking. It is legitimate for it to break every institutional tie. The extra-institutional has to have its institutions without, however, belonging to them.

How is one to reconcile the respect and the transgression of the institutional limit?

Fifth Commandment

On the one hand, in the name of philosophy, we require a teacher or master [*maître*], the presence of a teacher. There must be a teacher for this discipline that cannot be disciplined, for this teaching that cannot be taught, for this knowledge that is also nonknowledge and more than knowledge, for this institution of the an-institutional. The concepts of this mastery or this magisteriality can vary. Its figures may be as diverse as those of the All High [*Très Haut*] or the inaccessible Altogether Other, of Socrates, of the Preceptor, the civil-servant Professor, the instructor in the university or the Terminale[1] (the first and the last of all), a little bit of all of the above at once: in every case, there must be a teacher or master [*maître*] and some magisterial alterity. Consequence: they must be trained; there must be students, teaching positions; there will never be enough; and all of this is controlled from outside the philosophic community.

But, on the other hand, although the teacher or master [*maître*] must be another, trained and then appointed by others, this heteronomic asymmetry ought not infringe on the necessary autonomy, indeed the essentially democratic structure of the philosophic community.

How can that community bring about an agreement within itself between this heteronomy and this autonomy?

Sixth Commandment

On the one hand, the philosophical discipline, the transmission of knowledge, the extreme wealth contained there normally require time, a certain rhythmic duration, indeed as much time as possible: more than a flash, a month, a year, more than the time of a course, always more time. Nothing can justify the extraordinary artifice that would consist in fixing this duration at nine months (here I refer you to the analyses of Greph).

But, on the other hand, the unity, even the architecture of the discipline requires a certain organized gathering up of this duration. One has to avoid spreading things out in a disordered way, one has to avoid dissolution and make room for the experience of the "at a single blow," of the "all at once" (here too I refer to what was said above and once again to the analyses of Greph).

How is one to reconcile this duration and this quasi-instantaneous contraction, this nonlimitation and this limit?

Seventh Commandment

On the one hand, pupils, students, like teachers, have to see themselves as having been granted the possibility—in other words the conditions—of philosophy, just as in any other discipline. These include what we'll call, to save time, the external conditions (time, place, positions, etc.) as well as the essential and "internal" condition, the access to the philosophical as such. A teacher has to initiate, introduce, train the disciple in the philosophical. The teacher, who will have to have been first of all trained, introduced, initiated himself, remains an other for the disciple. Guardian, guarantor, intercessor, predecessor, elder, he has to represent the speech, thought, or knowledge of the other: *heterodidactics.*

But, on the other hand, on no account do we want to give up the autonomist and *autodidactic* tradition of philosophy. The teacher is only a mediator who must efface himself. The intercessor has to neutralize himself in the face of the freedom of philosophizing. This freedom *trains itself,* however grateful may be its relation to the necessity of the teacher, the necessity for the magisterial act to *take place.*

How is one to reconcile the taking-place and the no-place of the teacher [*maître*]? What incredible topology do we require in order to reconcile the heterodidactic and the autodidactic?

These antinomies sometimes configure aporias. The number 7 is a little arbitrary. One could shorten or extend the list, given the coimplicating or overdetermining structure of these commandments. I have not accumulated them in order to accuse anyone of incoherence, still less in order to derive from them some argument to be exploited here and there against those who speak *for philosophy,* in the name of philosophy and its discipline. These contradictions place a constraint not only on philosophers and advocates of philosophy but also on whoever treats of philosophy today, for or against, and not just philosophers by profession. It is out of the question, especially in a letter, to draw out all the consequences of these contradictions. But regarding this fatal axiomatics and this double constraint, I will say three sorts of things, still very schematically.

1. By hypothesis (it is only my hypothesis), this matrix provides the types of all the utterances producible today on the subject of "School and Philosophy." It gives them also to be read; it prescribes them; it inscribes them under this terrible law of duplicity.

2. The only livable community (for me—and I say livable so as to speak at the same time of a faithfulness to the spirit of philosophy and of a living faithfulness, without dogma, without murder, without idiotic polemic, without hateful distortion) would be a community that, far from shunning or denying this double law, tries to measure itself against it, to think what it is that comes with it, where it comes from and what its future [*avenir*] is, what *to come* [*venir*] means or does not mean, what to come involves for philosophy (see above).

3. One of the questions (just one, and I will restrict myself to it for the space of this letter) that could lead into such thinking would concern the history of this axiomatics, of this program with seven entryways. Does it have a history, or rather does it order the history of its figures on the basis of an ahistorical deal of the cards or permanency? And if there is a history or a distribution of these figures, what is its law, its progressive articulation (period, epoch, moment, paradigm, *episteme*, continuity, discontinuity)? This question is made all the more difficult by the fact that the opposition history/ahistory is part of the matrix! Thus it overdetermines each of the seven commandments.

To conclude, I will take an example and open here a long parenthesis. This will be my little scholarly and philosophical contribution to your colloquium. It concerns a situation, more precisely a *topical* structure, and the more than paradoxical place assigned by Kant to the "teacher of pure reason." Is this our situation? To what extent does the configuration in which *we* today experience these double commandments still suppose the Kantian topical structure? Or at least that which, within philosophical discursivity, one might call the Kantian topical structure of the teaching of philosophy; for what I am going to recall in a moment about the Kantian text is only one determination, whatever importance or status it may be granted, of a device or a general text that does not wholly belong to the inside of philosophical discursivity or to any kind of discursivity: all of history, the history of Europe in particular, the relations between the State

and the university, between church and State, and so forth. If our configuration supposes something of the Kantian topical structure, what are the
modes of this supposition? An enormous problem that I must set aside
here. That which, coming from Kant, marks our situation and our discourses passes through trajectories that are so complex I do not even have
the will to outline them in a letter. It is the whole history of French post-
Kantianism, the modes of appropriation, translation, exploitation of Kantianism, of this Kant or that Kant, in philosophy and literature, in
"French ideology," in the "French school." This history is under way,
more restless than ever; our interpretations of it would come to be inscribed in that history and perhaps inflect it. Why is it to Kant that one
looks so easily in France whenever the subject is the teaching of philosophy? Why this obligatory reference, here as well? What services does it
render? What limitations does it impose? Etc.

Who is Kant? What if he occupied that unlocalizable place that he himself assigns to the "teacher of pure reason"?

I am getting to the point: the teacher of pure reason and the singular
topology prescribed by this idea. For it is an Idea.

Among other premises, and to take a shortcut, I must recall this: Kant
justifies a certain rational necessity of *censorship*. Now, what justifies censorship in the final analysis? The fallibility of man, his finitude, the existence of evil. Here I refer to *Religion within the Limits of Reason Alone* to
economize a long commentary. The question then becomes: if there is
evil, and radical evil, who can understand this evil in man? Who can account for it to reason? Who can say what its meaning and truth are? That
is, the meaning and truth of censorship, namely, of a critique that relies on
force, an armed judgment, an evaluation shored up by the police? Who
then can say the possibility and the necessity, the very foundation of this
censorship, of this institution legislating what can be said or is prohibited
to be said about the truth, of the truth?

*I will not reproduce here the rest of this long parenthesis, which corresponds
in fact very closely to the argument developed in "Vacant Chair: Censorship,
Mastery, Magisteriality" (see above).*

(. . .)

I close the parenthesis and this overly long letter.
To all of you, in friendship,

                                                              J.D.

                                         —*Translated by Peggy Kamuf*

Popularities: On the Right to the Philosophy of Right

I would like to take a moment first of all to express gratitude, mine as well as that of all the members of the Collège International de Philosophie, to the organizers of the meeting from which the following work is extracted and to all those who participated in it.

The Collège International de Philosophie owed it to itself to take part in these reflections devoted to the "Auto-Emancipation of the People and the Teaching of Proletarians in the Nineteenth Century" and to contribute, as best it could, to their planning. I am not going to improvise here a presentation of the Collège. Still young and precarious, this new institution nevertheless has a history and structures too complex for me to venture saying anything about them except this: it is a place that we would like first of all to open up to forms of knowledge, research, and philosophical practice that seem to us insufficiently legitimized, even delegitimized, by present institutions in France and elsewhere. Because this delegitimation or this disqualification passes by way of frequently invisible paths, indirect or overdetermined trajectories, our attention to it ought to be active, anxious, vigilant—whether it is a matter of relations with the State as such or with some forces of what is called civil society, to take up that convenient distinction. Our first priority should be to interest ourselves in all the ruses of marginalization, occultation, repression. At stake is the access to philosophy and to learning, the right to philosophy and to learning. It is particularly from this point of view—which is not, however, the only one by a long shot—that we felt this work to be something like a chance and a necessity.

Du droit à la philosophie, of the right to philosophy: that was the title of a college seminar last year.[1] There is nothing fortuitous about that, nothing fortuitous in the fact that the question of the *popular* (popular philosophy, popular knowledge) held our attention for a long time. What does *popular* mean? Allow me, as an epigraph, to place here, in a modest way and at the edge of what will be constructed in the following pages, a few pebbles, a few souvenirs I have of last year's seminar. On a certain day, our considerations took off from a story told by Diogenes Laertius, the one about Theophrastus, whom Agonides, I believe, dared to accuse of impiety, just as Meletus had accused Socrates. Now, Theophrastus was so "popular" among the Athenians that the accusation almost caused the downfall of the accuser. What, we wondered, did the "popularity" of a philosopher mean?

What is a "popular" philosopher? The word is very equivocal. Its overdetermination exposes it to all sorts of uses, misuses, and hijackings. I suppose that in the course of your work, approaching it in multiple ways, some instruments of critical vigilance (I mean that in both the philosophical and the political sense) will refine its meaning but also the uses of this concept, if it is one, and will determine the different contexts in which it has served as well as what causes it will have served. When one speaks, for example, of a "popular" philosopher, one may understand by that today at least two things. On the one hand, a "popular philosopher," who hails from the people or is a militant for the people, may very well not be popular. He may be deprived of any legitimacy as recognized by the legitimating agencies that dominate the scene (in the seminar to which I am referring, we also proceeded to examine this concept of *legitimization*, its genealogy, the uses and misuses to which it can be put, its critical *or* dogmatic value, etc.). On the other hand, a "popular philosopher" may also not belong to the people, may be totally unknown to them or even opposed to them. But does anyone know today what one is saying when one says "people," "popular," "popularity"? From "people" to "popular" to "popularity," the kernel of meaning can change far beyond what is determined by the passage from an adjective to a noun or a noun to an adjective.

What is more, a philosopher can be *for* what he thinks he can call "popular philosophy" without being himself either of the people or otherwise popular. One may also say (and naturally I am thinking of Kant, and I will come back to this) that one is *for* a "certain" popular philosophy and be oneself popular in a "certain" way, even as one remains, in another way, totally inaccessible to a certain "people."

And since we are talking here about "popular" knowledge, the right to philosophy, philosophical teaching and practice, we could also take a look at the manner in which the questions of right, of the right to philosophy and to its teaching, and finally of the "popular" in all the ambiguity of its meaning got knotted together at a moment that is perhaps not altogether *past*, a past for us.

I will limit myself to a few indications about this "Kantian" moment, still by way of epigraph. In the preface to the *Metaphysics of Morals*, Kant poses the question of a "popular" philosophy.[2] He has just proclaimed that after the critique of practical reason must come the system. The system is the metaphysics of morals, which is itself divided into metaphysical first principles of the doctrine of *right* and metaphysical first principles of the doctrine of *virtue*. Now (and here is where the question of the "popular" gets posed), the concept of right has to be a *pure* concept. But it has to rely on practice and apply to cases that occur in experience. The metaphysical system should, then, take into consideration the empirical multiplicity of all cases, until it has exhausted all possibilities. Such a culmination is an essential requirement for the elaboration of a system of reason, but one knows that it is empirically impossible. One will therefore have to be content (hence the title) with the *first* metaphysical principles of a doctrine of right, just as one was for the *first* principles of a metaphysics of nature (freedom/nature). What is here called *right* refers to a system outlined a priori, and it will be *the text*: it will be inscribed *in the text* (*in den Text*), by which is meant the principal text. On the other hand, *rights*, adjusted to experience and to particular cases, will be found in detailed *remarks* so as to distinguish clearly the metaphysics of right from empirical practice. Here, then, is posed the question of the obscurity of philosophical language and of what risks making it hardly *popular*. It is highly significant that this question is posed on the subject of right (and, in the seminar to which I am referring in this improvisation, we worked a long time on this conjunction). Everything conspires to suggest that the question of the people's access to philosophical language, the right of the people to philosophy, was first of all most manifestly put in play as regards the theme of right, the philosophy of right, the right to the philosophy of right.

Kant then answers the reproach of obscurity (*Vorwurf der Dunkelheit*) that had been put to him. He says that he agrees with Garve, a philosopher in the authentic sense ("authentic" is his word, I believe) who tells the writer-philosopher to be popular, to attain "Popularität" without obscurity. Agreed, says Kant, except where it is a matter of the system and, in philosophy, the system of the critique of the power of reason itself. This system supposes the distinction of the sensible from the intelligible in our knowledge. The supersensible belongs to reason. Now, the system of this reason, the system capable of thinking the supersensible, *can never become popular*. Kant does not explain what seems here to go without saying, as if it were understood within the very concepts of the supersensible, on the one hand, and of the "popular," on the other. The supersensible, which is to say reason *as such*, cannot be accessible to the people *as such*. This conventional and dogmatic conception situates the popular on the side of the sensible, the empirical, and the sentimental—the nonrational and the nonmetaphysical, or at least, and this is a central nuance on which Kant is immediately going to play, the metaphysical that does not pose itself or think itself *as such*, the unwittingly metaphysical. And in fact, although one cannot exhibit to the people, in a popular way, the metaphysics of pure right *itself* in its first principles and its formal structures, one ought to be able to exhibit clearly the *results* of this pure systematics. These ought to be accessible to "healthy reason" (*gesunde Vernunft*) of which the people have not been deprived. Healthy reason is the reason of "an unwitting metaphysician" (*eines Metaphysikers, ohne es zu wissen*). Nevertheless, in this exhibition of the results themselves, without the principles, one must not try to use the language of the people (*Volksprache*), one must not seek *Popularität*. One must impose "scholastic precision" even if its tedious character is regrettable. That is normal, says Kant; it is a language of the schools (*Schulsprache*), and he seems to think that a school language has to be, cannot but be, tedious—even, if not especially, for the people.

    In this way, a certain device of philosophical schooling or the philosophical discipline is outlined. It is also a relation between philosophical discourse and popular language. Once again, it is symptomatic that this is put first of all in terms of right. The popular is on the side of the sensible. And having just said that a philosopher ought to be able to be popularized, Kant adds in parentheses: it should be sensible enough, with, so to speak, a sufficient sensibilization to achieve communication (*einer zur allgemeinen Mitteilung hinreichenden Versinnlichung*).[3] Now, the metaphysician of right, the man of system, cannot "sensibilize," popularize, teach the very principles that are themselves not sensible. But he can and he ought to exhibit the concrete results of this system in a clear, scholarly, and not necessarily imagistic language once the people have "a healthy reason" at their disposal. The people, "unwitting metaphysicians," can

thus learn, learn to know, to know knowledge, even if given only its conclusions without the principle. All of pedagogy has its place, its proper
site, outside the thinking of pure principles, those that are reserved for the
metaphysicians as such, who know what they are doing and what they
think. The place of pedagogy is thus only a place of passage: access to the
results of a thought elaborated elsewhere by metaphysicians who know
that is what they are, but access also as a possible coming to consciousness.
The unwitting metaphysicians can become conscious and organized
metaphysicians. Although the people do not spontaneously and from the
first have access to reason, although they cannot, *by themselves*, approach
the distinction between sensible and intelligible, a scholarly and rigorous
exhibition of the results can awaken their sleeping reason. Easily recognizable (still today in all of its consequences), this pedagogical outline
seems to fit with everything on which the Kantian architectonic depends—that is, the art of systems, of reason determined on the basis of
the distinction between sensible and intelligible, between pure and impure. Along with everything it presupposes (and which it is not a question
of reviewing here), the relation between critique and metaphysics in the
Kantian sense is also a *socio-pedagogic scenography* through and through. It
is also a determined thinking of the right to philosophy as philosophy of
the right to the philosophy of right.

If, just to stay with this epigraph on a preface, one added that Kant responds *no* to the question of "whether there could really be more than one
philosophy," then one would fix a coherent image of the principles of a
pure pedagogy of philosophy—and of the right to philosophy as right to
access by way of discipline. At stake is a certain concept of *popularity*: of
the people, of popular philosophy, of popular knowledge—which is also
to say of knowledge regarding the "people" and what one thinks one can
call by that name by thus calling it to learning and philosophy.

Kant recognizes that there are different *ways* of philosophizing. But
these are not different philosophies; they are different styles of *going back*
to the first principles of philosophy. The difference remains pedagogical.
There are only different paths for leading toward principles, for *leading
back* to the principles of unwitting metaphysicians. Yet this multiplicity of
philosophers is not a multiplicity intrinsic to philosophy; it merely divides
the pedagogical analytic, the regression toward the principle. As soon as
there is only one human reason, there can be only one true rational system possible.

All of this was concerned with first principles and the system of meta-physics in general, that of morals and nature, even if, in this preface, the "pedagogical" pretext and the question of the "popular" found themselves bound up with the problem of right. The schema I have just sketched is specified even as it generalizes itself when one considers the metaphysics of morals in general, of which the doctrine of right is only one of the two parts. As you know, the metaphysics of morals is an a priori system of knowledge by simple concepts. Such is the definition of metaphysics for Kant. The object of the metaphysics of morals is everything having to do with freedom, not nature. Speaking to us of rights and duties, such a metaphysics is itself a duty. To possess it is a duty (*Eine solche [Metaphysik] zu haben ist selbst Pflicht*). But Kant has to add to this prescription, or he has to provide as the elementary medium within which to describe this prescription, a kind of statement within the same sentence: "Every human being also has it within himself, though in general only in an obscure way."[4] How can one make it a duty to have in oneself something that one already has anyway and a priori? Here once again, a sort of prescription, an order having a performative structure, would get mixed up in a con-fused way with descriptive constatition if there were not precisely this dif-ference between the consciousness called obscure and the consciousness called clear. Such a difference is the very medium of this pedagogy and of the obscure relation to the people that it has to suppose. It is not separated from this obscure concept of "popularity" as obscure consciousness that must be *made to come* into the light.

Everyone, whether of the people or not, has this metaphysics and thus this duty. This is a *Faktum*. The duty that is here implied is to render *this duty itself* clear as such, in its metaphysical purity. This is still the place of pedagogic mediation. Kant gets around to it a little further on, and what he says might interest us from the point of view of the topical structure, in a certain way, of the pedagogical scene.

Just as the metaphysics of nature has to apply its supreme and universal principles to nature, so too the metaphysics of morals has to take as its ob-ject the particular nature of man, such as it can be known from experi-ence, in order to *indicate* (*zeigen*, Kant underlines this important word) there the consequences of moral principles. This it must do without al-lowing the purity of the principles to suffer, without rendering their a pri-ori origin doubtful. Now, this indicative monstration has an anthropo-logical dimension, which concerns consequences and which can neither

merge with the metaphysics of morals as such, in its principles, nor especially claim to found that metaphysics. Even before being divided into the
doctrine of right and the doctrine of virtue, the metaphysics of morals in
general cannot be *founded* (*gegründet*, justified by right: the vocabulary of
foundation is always, already, a juridical vocabulary) on anthropology,
even though it can and in fact must apply to anthropology. The *Zeigen*
thus concerns anthropological consequences, but its discourse (which will
be the pedagogical discourse), as anthropological discourse, cannot found
moral and juridical discourse, the metaphysics of morals itself.

Kant has then to define what he calls *moral anthropology*, that is, the
discipline (in the strong sense of the word) containing the subjective conditions that either hinder or favor the fulfillment (*Ausführung*) of the laws
of practical philosophy in human nature. Practical philosophy would thus
include a metaphysics of morals and a moral anthropology. Moral anthropology could not found a metaphysics of morals. As defined by moral
anthropology, the conditions of the "fulfillment" of the moral laws suppose the production, propagation, and strengthening of moral principles
through education in schools and popular instruction (*in der Erziehung,
der Schul- und Volksbelehrung*). If I understand this last distinction correctly, Kant would take into account a popular instruction that does not
necessarily go on in schools. One would have to read this text more closely
than we are able to do here in improvising. It seems that there are finally
three places for pedagogy, three disciplinary instances shaped by the same
concept of pedagogy and consequently by the same concept of the "popular" that is inscribed in it: 1. the return to principles for unwitting metaphysicians: pedagogy as a *coming to consciousness of metaphysics*; 2. pedagogy as monstration (*Zeigen*) or indication of the relation between moral
principles and their anthropological consequences: a sort of *theoretical instruction*; 3. propaedeutic pedagogy, introduction to the conditions of application or fulfillment of principles: *moral education* in the field of moral
anthropology.

These three pedagogical instances are distinct, to be sure, but as an educational system, they are, one could say, all situated *between* the pure and
the impure, principle and consequence (or result), the intelligible and the
sensible. They go from one to the other, sometimes in one sense, sometimes in the other. But as to the sense of this sense, as to what by right
comes first, and the order of foundation and legitimization, no confusion
ought to be possible. That is what the people have to learn. Moral anthro-

pology is certainly indispensable, it ought not be set aside, but it cannot, by right and on the level of principles, precede the metaphysics of morals, that is, the principles (by definition one does not precede principles), and it cannot even be *mixed up* with that metaphysics. (But can one say that the concept of the "popular" thus constructed or implied does not do just that, and do so surreptitiously?)

What does this mean? Not only that anthropology (like the social sciences that presuppose it) implies some philosophy, but that this philosophy is not itself pure philosophy. It does not attain its own philosophical principles. It also means that culture is not philosophy (a system of pure principles). It means finally that pedagogy, the discipline of philosophy, is not a purely philosophical act or moment. Here one would have to situate what Kant says, in a frequently cited but finally little-read text, about the "teacher of pure reason" and about what it means to learn to philosophize. I am trying to do that elsewhere,[5] and I do not want to prolong any more this foreword whose only function is to introduce.

—*Translated by Peggy Kamuf*

Appendices

"Who's Afraid of Philosophy?" (1980)

The Estates General of Philosophy

1. To begin to explain an event like the Estates General, one would have to deploy and prudently link together several types of analyses. One would have to deal with all the roots of the situation of philosophy in France today, the "sociology" (let's call it, to be quick) of intellectuals, French instructors and students, the structures of French teaching in the university, in the lycées, before the lycées, and so forth. We will not be able to tackle these problems in the course of a discussion. The nearest and most obvious, also the shortest, sequence takes us back to the implementation of the Haby Reform, beginning with the approval of the Reform plan of the education system that elicited such great opposition in the country, in particular among those interested in philosophy, who believe in the necessity of philosophical research and debate in our society. . . . Since the struggle was undertaken against this Reform, certain threats have not ceased to become more serious and specific. Tampering with the baccalauréat is being prudently avoided for the moment: the problem is too delicate to be taken up before the 1981 election. But the effects of a politics aiming to restrict the field of philosophical research and teaching have been accentuated at any rate. Conditions are more and more difficult and are getting worse by the year. The massive reduction of the number of teaching positions available through the competitive examinations is only one sign of this, but was even more spectacular last year, when, moreover, a large number of philosophy teachers in the écoles normales lost their positions.[1] Last year the Haby Reform had not yet reached the phase of its applica-

tion that concerns the Terminales.[2] We are waiting for the decrees that should make clear the consequences of the Reform for this level of the curriculum. We have not been waiting for them in order systematically to oppose the *principles* that must inform them throughout the school system, but we do not yet know precisely what the decrees as to philosophy will be. The rumors around this subject—as was said and as has now been published in the proceedings of the Estates General—were disturbing, even beyond what we had first feared. We thought this would alarm not only teachers and students but all those concerned about the future of something like philosophy in this country. A certain number of teachers (whether philosophers or not) came together to issue the Appeal you are familiar with.[3] They did so in a language in which they could acknowledge the concern they share beyond philosophical, political, or other differences, which it was never a question of ignoring. Thus, more than 1,200 people participated in those Estates General on June 16 and 17 [1979], in the big amphitheater at the Sorbonne. This massive and exceptional crowd was in itself already an event, a sign, and a warning. All the more so since, it must be insisted, the participants were not only philosophers by profession, teachers or students, and were not only academics. One can get a first impression of what happened there by reading the transcript of the debates.

2. The great diversity of those who took the responsibility to call for the Estates General must be insisted upon. In France, this is a very rare and therefore all the more significant phenomenon. The twenty-one member committee was formed, in part, of philosophers who, in other contexts, are not so close. . . . We had no prior agenda. We wanted to favor a broad debate (without excluding anyone, without hierarchical references, with no imposed code, without phenomena of authority or competence), a broad open debate. And it was undertaken in a place and even an atmosphere that, many observed, recalled certain moments of 1968, when people spoke as freely as possible, to discuss, question, make proposals, work, inform. In large part, what we hoped for in this regard took place. How the event will be interpreted in the long term, I do not know. At any rate, it was a question, it seems to me, of not investing it in advance with this or that historical meaning. The immediate assessment [*bilan*] (since you pose the question of the "assessment") would be at least double: on the one hand, the gathering took place (and it could be duplicated; everyone should take this into account and be informed of it), information circu-

lated, awareness increased, groups formed and continue to work, in Paris and in the provinces. Without this limiting us to a corporatist point of view (and many nonprofessional questions were posed and discussed broadly during these two days), resolutions were passed that concern, for example, the extension of the teaching of philosophy outside the Termi-nale.[4] (Such resolutions were then taken up and confirmed by other in-stances: this is the case of the motion on extension, passed a few days later by the assembly of the graders of philosophy for the baccalauréat in the academy of Paris-Versailles.) The meeting of other Estates General was contemplated and will take place immediately if the governmental threats reappear. The evening of the first day of the Estates General, a televised declaration by the minister [of education] made itself out to be reassuring on this subject, but we are waiting for the decrees to be able to judge.

3. What shows in an objective and verifiable fashion that these were not the Estates General of Greph is that the members of Greph were a minor-ity on the Planning Committee and even more so during the Estates Gen-eral themselves. This quantitative point of view, which is not always con-vincing, is convincing, in any case, every time there is a vote, and all the resolutions were voted on democratically. It is true that the idea of the Es-tates General was first evoked by certain members of Greph (first of all by [Roland] Brunet, as I reminded everyone at the opening of the Estates General), but we thought that the broadest possible gathering was neces-sary for everything that set this event under way as well as for its agendas, resolutions, and so forth. Everything that has now been published bears witness to this: Greph no doubt brought the event about but has not wished to appropriate or dominate it—and has not done so. We no doubt defended the positions of Greph in the discussions, but what could be more legitimate? The members of other associations did the same, and that is as it should be. That Greph is more mobilized and has been so for longer on positions of struggle that sometimes, and more and more, carry conviction is also true. The best example was the resolution adopted on the subject of the extension of philosophy beginning in the Seconde, but one must not forget that this resolution still does not go far enough in re-lation to our own perspectives.

4. Let us clarify again that Greph is neither a union nor a corporative association. Since 1975 it has brought together a large number of teachers and students, whether philosophers or not, determined to question them-selves about the philosophical institution, its history and current func-

tioning, but also to intervene in it by posing new questions and behaving
differently within it. Concerning Greph's research program and perspectives for action, its founding "Avant-Projet" and the first stands it took, I
can only refer you here to the texts published in *Qui a peur de la philosophie?*[5] Currently, everywhere in France, without any centralization and
avoiding every orthodoxy and hierarchy, numerous groups are working to
transform philosophical teaching and research. They are doing so in conditions that vary greatly from one group to another. All the questions
taken up in the Estates General are obviously questions privileged by
Greph, whether they concern the media or the situation of philosophy in
France today, programs or evaluative sanctions, publishing or the pedagogical scene in all its elements, the problem of women in philosophy, but
also many other questions that were not brought up in the Estates General as well. Although we take militant stands on the immediate problems
(for example, in order to counter the Haby Reform with a new and offensive watchword that was no longer that of the traditional defense of the
Terminale, or when a large number of philosophers were excluded from
the écoles normales, and so forth), we view our work as long-term, working toward what certain people consider dangerous utopias (this was already the case for the extension of the teaching of philosophy outside the
Terminales: things have changed in a few years in the minds of many).

5. The commitment was made, in the Estates General, to broaden and
renew this experience. Within every academy, offices should be set up that
would in no way compete with union and corporative organizations but
that would set things in motion, that would propose new problematics
and new modes of action.

6. Slowing the growing rate of decrease in positions available through
the competitive examinations is not simply corporatism. The effects of
this measure are widespread, and well beyond problems of recruitment.
Once all professional future is blocked, the number of students of philosophy decreases continually and the students become more and more dis-
couraged, demobilized. This deteriorates the conditions of research, to say
nothing of the conditions for philosophical debate outside of the places of
teaching. In this regard, the supposedly appeasing ministerial declarations
the day after the Estates General are far from satisfying us.

7. Extending the teaching of philosophy would have such consequences
on the whole educational system that it absolutely cannot be considered a
fallback position. It is difficult to elaborate upon these consequences here,
but the work of Greph (see *Qui a peur de la philosophie?*, for example) can
give an idea of them. Everything that was said in a programmatic form in

the Estates General is far from corresponding to a fallback. But of course it was only a matter of a preliminary phase there.

Philosophy and Its Teaching

8. It seems desirable to us to extend philosophy (according to modes to be invented and forms that of course would not amount to "dispensing" elsewhere a teaching that is already known and established) not only upstream from the Terminale but also downstream, in the universities, outside philosophy departments. Moreover, this corresponds to a very lively demand from scientists, jurists, literary scholars, doctors, technicians, and so forth. In comparison with European systems that do not include the teaching of philosophy before university, our demand might in fact initially appear unusual or exorbitant. But we are fighting in a French context that has its own history. Moreover, it is worth noting that the questions raised by Greph interest many people (and for essential reasons, which stem from traits common to all industrial societies in their current phase) outside of France, in Europe and the United States. It is at a time when certain people outside of France are demanding more philosophy, and beginning before university, that we in France are considering taking the opposite path. We have numerous signs of this interest and this concern wherever sociopolitical forces attempt to limit certain types of research (philosophy is not the only one, and we are very mindful here of what exceeds the unity of a "discipline"). These questions are relevant in numerous European or American countries, in North Africa and in more than one sub-Saharan African country. Groups analogous to Greph and in relation with it are being formed there and are working with us. One of the principles of Greph is that it not enclose itself within the limits of one discipline but instead attempt to rethink the relations between philosophical and other practices. We never propose anything that does not imply a fundamental reelaboration in this regard, and this reelaboration can be undertaken only by working together with researchers, teachers, and students in other disciplines.

9. Any answer to this question[a] already deploys *a* philosophy. There are many philosophical differences and fundamental disagreements [*différends*] among those who fight today to extend the teaching of philoso-

a. Guy Coq's question: "What might teaching be in a secondary school today, that is, a school proposing to adolescents a minimal relation to the cultural traditions of their historical collectivity? This is the essential question that no one has taken up (except Greph)."

phy. The common conviction, for the moment, is that the question, the type of question, you are posing can be elaborated seriously only once the material and technical conditions of teaching and research are improved and are more open. But to struggle for that is already to take a stand—and to do so philosophically. We all agree that this broad philosophical debate should develop; today, despite certain appearances, it is hindered from all sides. The more active and lively philosophical work is within the institution, the more active and lively it will be outside it.

10. There has never been a pure unity of philosophical discourse, no doubt for essential reasons. It is difficult to enter into this problem here. Nonetheless, at certain periods (of history and of this or that society) a *representation* of this relative unity of the philosophical code and debate was able to impose itself. At the price of powerful exclusions, naturally. Today, what is called philosophy is the site of the greatest disparity in discourses. One indication of this—an indication that should not be lamented and that must be taken into account: I believe I am barely exaggerating in saying that one teacher of philosophy resembles another teacher of philosophy less than he does any other teacher. If one could hear simultaneously all the discourses and all the teachings that are being produced today under the title of philosophy, one would, I believe, be stunned not only by the difference in content, which can legitimately be expected, but by the difference in elementary codes, by the untranslatability of the languages, of the most decisive evaluations (for example, in determining the "questions" and "texts" that preliminary work should not skirt, in determining what would formerly have been called a "fundamental training": this very expression poses problems and is yet another indication). Thinking this profound disturbance,[6] which does not come to us by chance or from the outside, is no doubt one of our tasks.

Of Some Criticisms and Misunderstandings

11. We can move on to the criticisms, if you wish. First, it could never be a question of wanting to shelter the Estates General from criticism; on the contrary, we wanted to open the broadest and most contradictory discussions, and two days of improvised debates neither could nor should have given rise to an unattackable corpus of absolutely coherent and satisfactory proposals, of a doctrinal or dogmatic form. That said, not every criticism is just. For example, the criticism that points to a gesture of self-defense. There would be nothing illegitimate about a defense of their own working conditions by teachers who are conscious of their responsibility.

We have mounted such a defense, but we did not limit ourselves to this, as the proceedings of the Estates General, which I can only refer to here, testify. As you know, the proportion of nonphilosophers and even of non-teachers among the participants in the Estates General was quite considerable. The questions posed were very broad; they concerned the place and modes of philosophical practice in society and outside the institution, the meaning of philosophical thinking today, and the general purpose of teaching. All of that carried well beyond the professional horizon. And at no time, nor to anyone, did it appear desirable to fall back toward the old conditions of philosophical practice. The proposed transformations and extension concerned research and teaching in general, beyond philosophy, as well as philosophy outside the institution.

Let us come to the supposedly "hasty" character of the discourse on the media. The question of the media (their function and current functioning, their role in culture, their effects on teaching, and so forth) held an important place, and this was not a "false debate." If by "hasty" one wanted to emphasize that this debate was in part improvised, that would not be entirely wrong, although the necessity of the problematic of the media was recognized from the beginning of the first day (in terms that I believe were prudent, differentiated, and programmatic) and although those who took part most actively in the work group on the media (I think in particular of Debray)[7] brought the results of significant research to the debate. We can be pleased that for the first time, even if relatively improvised, questions of a type that I believe is fundamental and to this point insufficiently acknowledged in scholarly and university circles were taken up. That is why I thought it necessary to call attention to them from the first meeting on.

That said, were the talks "hasty"? An honest evaluation must not content itself with the scandalous simplifications some indulged in during the following days (I think in particular of a certain review, if it can be called that, full of hate—which is indeed the right word—in *L'Express* and of a certain note in *Le Nouvel Observateur*). One must rather return to what was actually said (which has now been published),[8] which was prudent, complicated, and, I believe, for such a brief debate, quite well elaborated. The group on teaching and the media worked long hours; it brought together a considerable number of participants; there was a long discussion preceding the approval of the report. Reading the transcript of the debates at the Estates General, one will see (if one were determined to doubt this) that they contain no criticism of the media as such and in general, only certain technical or political conditions of their current functioning, and of the general effects this inevitably has on discourse, teaching, research, and so forth. All kinds of precautions were taken so that this would in no case resemble a summary trial of the media in general. Let us reread; let us read. Since the stakes are serious, the investments numerous and diverse, one cannot question the press and the media without giving rise to a great deal of nervousness. The reactions are powerful and come by definition from places armed massively in this domain. Certain people would like to forbid posing these questions freely and in the open, as we have done. For example, that is no doubt why, Sunday afternoon, a very determined small troop tried to make it impossible for us to work and tried to interrupt our debates: continually making a racket, whistling, yelling aggressively to drown out or muffle every speech, in short, the well-tried technique of the small terrorist commando. The troop was led by B. H. Lévy and D. Grisoni. They were given the opportunity to take the floor at the microphone like every other participant. When they began to do so, certain people in the room, no doubt exasperated by the sabotage under way and by the fanatical obstruction, protested. Near the platform where the microphone was located, two or three unknown people even *started a brief and minor scuffle* (I am weighing my words). But the organizers, who moreover invited B. H. Lévy, saw to it that he could take the floor freely. Which is what happened, and this speech has now been published. I would not linger over this incident, which, by the way, is very illuminating, if I had not just learned that, if we are to believe an interview between P. Sollers and B. H. Lévy, the latter claims to have been "beat up" at the Estates General. "Beat up"! One can hope that such an eloquent defender of human rights knows the meaning of and weighs this expression, which he had already used, in reference to the same incident, during one of his appearances on television (an interview, this time, with J.-L. Servan-Schreiber). This is an instance of the most appalling slander on the part of B. H. Lévy. During this *brief and minor scuffle* (I stress) no punches were thrown by anyone; there were people shouting in the confusion, pushing around a microphone, or pulling one another by the jacket: these are the facts; more than a thousand people can testify to them. Knowing like everyone that B. H. Lévy is hardly concerned with distinguishing between falsity and truth (although he wears the Truth, the Law, and the Ethical on his sleeve), I would have abandoned these symptoms to their context, at once sinister and derisory; I would not have brought up a contemptible slander if the falsity, this time, were not an affront to all those who were present at the Estates General, to *everyone* and not merely to the auxiliary teachers [*maîtres-auxiliaires*] whom B. H. Lévy, with the same outburst, so comfortably sends back to their little problems.

Spread and accredited by public instruments (television, periodicals), this falsity constitutes too serious and massive an attack to go unanswered, no matter how much one dislikes such exchanges. If the cause of human rights were defended only by people this quick to insult and falsify, we should be more anxious than ever. I close this parenthesis.

12. This is where a patient and multiple analysis, moving in numerous directions, should explain that a *given* critique of totalitarianism—of a *given* totalitarianism—had access to television, in a *given* form, only at a specific moment in the history of this country, although elsewhere it had for a long time been clearly formulated, well informed, made more pointed, and had long justified certain people in taking unequivocal stands.[b] I believe that what is at issue is not the difficulty of the discourse alone but rather a whole group of lateral evaluations that go along with a given content (for example, what you call the critique of totalitarianism, which is far from summing everything up). But one should not indulge in improvisation in this area, which already suffers from too many stereo- types and manipulations when we need subtle, differentiated work that does not give in to any intimidation. And I wonder whether the form of a discussion, which is so useful and illuminating from another point of view, does not risk hurrying us toward simplifications. In place of an analysis that is difficult to reconstruct in these conditions, I will merely in- dicate a very clear stand, while referring to the published texts: no one, I believe, at the Estates General, no one at Greph attacked something like the media as such and in general, but rather, as I said a moment ago, they criticized a certain state and a certain use today, in France, of this or that instrument of the "media" type. As for me, I stated perfectly clearly my mistrust of any reactionism against the media, and I will add, in a word, that I simply believe that *there are not enough* media. The media suffer rather from monolithism, concentration, monopolization, violent and controlled uniformization. In short, the most glaring symptom is of an oligarchic type. Why, then, so few players, and why these specific ones? That, perhaps, is a question we can begin with.

—Translated by Jan Plug

b. This paragraph responds to a comment by Olivier Mongin: "One must go fur- ther and ask whether TV necessarily denaturalizes philosophical work. One would have to ask what the role of the new philosophy in relation to the criticism of totali- tarianism was. One would have to ask if it appeared on TV because its discursive form lent itself to it, while Lefort's or Castoriadis's discourse was less likely to come off. This isn't so certain. At any rate, one goes into exile and exiles cultural work if one thinks it is not communicable outside those who already know how to read."

Letter from François Mitterrand to Greph (1981)

Le Monde, May 28, 1981

The Groupe de Recherches pour l'Enseignement de la Philosophie [*sic*] (Greph) has just made public the response addressed to it by Mr. François Mitterrand this past May 8. The new president of the republic, at the time a candidate, made two promises in relation to the place of philosophy in secondary education.

"1. The teaching of philosophy should be preserved and developed. At issue, in fact, is a critical discipline that should better allow everyone to understand the world and their place in it in order to live and act in that world."

"2. The teaching of philosophy could be extended in secondary education, as the teachers of philosophy wish. The precise modalities of this extension will be the object of discussion during the definition of the programs. At least, the teaching of philosophy should obligatorily figure in all sections of the long second cycle."

[To be sure, the "ten proposals for education" formulated by the candidate François Mitterrand already included the development of the teaching of philosophy. But the promise made here to Greph is more precise and more radical: in the end, philosophy, the learning of the critical viewpoint, should therefore be brought out of the ghetto of the Terminale classes and be taught in the Seconde. This was an old demand of the philosophers. It implies an effort at recruitment, a greater number of positions on the competitive examinations, and the creation of [teaching] positions in the classes at issue.]

—*Translated by Jan Plug*

Titles (for the Collège International
de Philosophie) (1982)

Philosophy

By now justifying the titles of this new institution, beginning with the
name we propose to give it, we want to emphasize its titles to exist.

Why philosophy? Why philosophy today? And why would this new
college be first of all a college of philosophy?

Of course, we are not proposing to invent or restore philosophy in
France. It has its modes of existence and its institutional conditions there,
for example, in the university, in the Terminale classes in the lycées, at the
Collège de France and the CNRS.[1] There are also philosophy societies in
Paris and the provinces.

We will define the necessity of adding another institution to these, an
institution that will be structured completely differently and that will in
no way compete with or threaten the existing systems. On the contrary, we
have in mind, rather, a new resource, and a force for proposals and incentives, a place very open and favorable to experimentation, on the order of
philosophical exchanges, research, and teaching, as well as to debates in
which the representatives of all current institutions could join. According
to modalities that we will specify later, all the philosophical institutions in
the country could be represented, take responsibility, and discuss their
work and projects in this Collège. As a matter of principle, we exclude
every hypothesis that would tend to duplicate possibilities already present
elsewhere in the country. Moreover, we abstain from judging previous
policies here, whatever their effects, and even if certain of them remain
overwhelmingly negative as we see it. We are not implicating those who

represented these policies. Our intention here is above all essentially affirmative; moreover, such a critical evaluation, which is out of place here, has already been initiated; it would call for extensive, complex analyses putting into play the essence and destination of philosophy as well as a considerable number of sociopolitical determinations and overdeterminations. That ought to constitute one of the fields of study intended for the new Collège ("for example, what about philosophy and institutions in France, in the twentieth century, and especially since the Second World War?"). Such a study is too big to be undertaken here and is not what we intend. Pleading for a certain future, we will limit ourselves to a few *axioms*.

One sees taking shape today, on all sides, what could be called an *awakening of the philosophical* or a *return to philosophy*. These expressions involve no simplifying evaluation. They indicate roughly a new, powerful, and singular phenomenon that greatly exceeds academic limits and all the traditional places reserved for philosophical exchange and research (that is to say, in France, the field, increasingly reduced over the last decades, of the university, the CNRS, its specialized publications, or the very threatened space of the Terminale classes in the lycées). Such a return to philosophy is in no way a recession, even if it must, in certain of its forms, run this risk here or there. The constraints that could explain these regressive forms, as well as the value of regression itself, would in this case merit a complex and prudent analysis. There again, we must limit ourselves to making a few indications: so many problematics, among others, to be entrusted to the new Collège.

This return of the philosophical is not a "return of the repressed" either, or not simply so, at any rate, even if philosophy today must perhaps avoid a kind of repression whose sequences and different modes are explained in part by a certain techno-political concept of education: it was believed that the extent of philosophical training (and of training in the "humanities" in general), thought to be at once too critical, too negative, and too unproductive, had to be limited. This, in its more abstract form, is the theme that has been analyzed widely by those who, over the last years, have struggled against the stifling of philosophy.

The "return" of which we are speaking does not necessarily imply the erasure or omission of what, in diverse perspectives, has been said or thought about the end of metaphysics. In its most original and rigorous forms, this "return" announces on the contrary a new relation to philosophy as such, to a philosophy whose limits are understood differently:

philosophy does not rule the encyclopedic field of knowledge from a hegemonic position any more than it is "dead" or doomed to disappear pure and simple. Let's not forget that everything that has been said or thought about philosophy over the last two centuries is also explained by what here forms a paradoxically indissociable couple: the hegemony/death of philosophy.

It is no doubt the system of this alternative that is displaced and made obsolete today, and with it a concept of the *universitas* that always assumes it: the model of the university that has dominated, in the West, since the University of Berlin and the beginnings of industrial society is constructed on State-philosophical foundations conferring upon philosophy a kind of absolute juridical authority (fundamental ontology or the tribunal of pure reason legislating on the totality of the theoretico-practical field) while refusing it, in principle, the least bit of effective power or the slightest chance of intervening outside the university enclosure. (In this regard, see Kant's exemplary *The Conflict of the Faculties* and many other philosophical discourses on the destiny of the university.)

Therefore, if we propose the creation of a college *of philosophy*, it is not first of all to signal that this institution belongs integrally to what we might believe we can determine in advance as its *philosophical* destination or essence. It is, *on the one hand*, to designate a place of thinking in which the *question of philosophy* would be deployed: the question *about* the meaning or destination of the philosophical, its origins, its future, its condition. In this regard, "thinking" for the moment designates only an *interest for philosophy*, in philosophy, but an interest that is not philosophical first of all, completely and necessarily. It is, *on the other hand*, to affirm philosophy and define what it can be and must do today in our society as regards new forms of knowledge in general, of technics, culture, the arts, languages, politics, law, religion, medicine, military power and strategy, police information, and so forth. The experience of thinking *on the subject of the philosophical*, no less than philosophical research, is what might be the task of the Collège. A task at once classical (what philosophy has not begun by seeking to determine the essence and destination of philosophy?) and to be deployed today in singular conditions. Later, we will say the same for the values of research, science, interscience, or art.

Practicing new research, engaging in interferential movements and interscientific spaces, does not mean (on the contrary) that one is settled in a secure concept of "scientificity" and of "scientific research." What are the historical meaning and the future of these concepts? In its most differentiated forms, this question would be on the Collège's program.

This "philosophical awakening" today takes diverse and remarkable forms in all the Western societies and in all the regions of the world that are open to scientific and technological development. Certain francophone African countries provide a particularly spectacular example in this regard: the demand from the new generations and a certain historical situation have already led this or that country to extend the teaching of philosophy in lycées *before the Terminale*, with explicit reference to demands formulated in France itself (notably by Greph), where these demands have not yet been sufficiently heard. Whether or not this forms the essential unity of an epoch, it is no doubt more than a fortuitous conjuncture. That the motifs that determine this urgency and this convergence remain heterogeneous, even contradictory, only makes this common recourse to philosophy as such more enigmatic and significant.

Let us recall briefly a few of these motifs as exemplary indications. Refusing to engage this project in a preinterpretation of this phenomenon, we will content ourselves with accumulating incontestable symptoms, those that allow for a definition, at least, of a demand and an expectation.

1. The formerly dominant discourses on the "end of philosophy" or the "overcoming of metaphysics" have everywhere called, in response or in reaction, for a new relation to the entire Western philosophical tradition. This tradition is neither rejected, like an outdated heritage, nor seen as natural or indestructible. The discourses on *the limit of the philosophical* have established models of reading that are barely comparable, despite certain appearances, to those that were the norm for philosophical discourse and research even twenty-five years ago. In France more than elsewhere (we will stress this below), this transformation has been profound, even if philosophical institutions *as such* have not adapted to it. This failure to adapt makes the demand for philosophy outside the institution still more impatient, and the diversity of its forms alone constitutes a phenomenon of the greatest interest.

2. The return of the philosophical often takes the form of a new configuration of *ethico-juridical* problems. This stems in particular from the memory and the anticipation of global cataclysm, from the forerunners of humanity's self-destruction, from phenomena of totalitarianism, of physical and psychological torture, from the withdrawal of certain philosophico-ideological securities, from techno-scientific powers (in particular,

over life—organ transplants, genetic manipulation, etc.), from the questioning, by philosophy and psychoanalysis, of the traditional axioms of morality and of the law (the value of the subject, of consciousness, of the responsible I, of freedom, etc.). In short, in the three areas that, with reference to a certain model of the university (still with us although we inherited it from the nineteenth century in Germany), were situated outside the traditional Faculty of Philosophy in the broad sense of the word,[2] that is, theology, law, and medicine, disturbances[3] are calling, once again and completely differently, for philosophy. A new problematic of right (for example, of what are called the "rights of man"), of the experience of illness or health, of the relations between the political and the religious, and so forth, is taking shape and everywhere calls for a different encounter with the philosophical as such. Consequently, the philosophical can neither disappear nor play the role of an arbitrating instance that it was previously accorded or refused without leaving room for any other possibility.

3. A certain massive and recent withdrawal of Marxist orthodoxies has given rise in Western democracies to two apparently contradictory movements, both of which, however, take the form of a sort of philosophical upsurge:

a. Simply returning to philosophical axiomatics that such Marxist orthodoxy seemed to have rendered obsolete, discredited, or at least reduced to an intimidated silence.

b. Considering this withdrawal of Marxism and of its political conditions as a significant phenomenon, to be sure, but one that, far from being recorded as a death certificate or a page that has been turned in a magazine of philosophical fashions, should bring about a rigorous reelaboration of Marx's heritage and a larger opening to the modern problematics against which it often protected itself. These reexaminations and this new debate, with Marxism or within it, can and must take original forms in France today.

4. Another paradox: the powerful and obvious resurgence of religious movements all over the world and the political force they represent. Two apparently contradictory and concurrent motifs come together in the same philosophical effect.

On the one hand, this resurgence goes *together* with a renewed interest in ethico-metaphysical or theological themes that were previously indissociable, in the West, from the history of religions.

On the other hand, and elsewhere, it dictates, by way of response or re-

action, a recourse to the "Enlightenment" and to modern forms of rationalism that are held *also* to be congenital to philosophy inasmuch as it is
supposed to resist mysticism, mystagogy, and obscurantisms. Through the
extreme simplifications the genre and speed of the present considerations
impose upon us, one can see that it is the *question of reason* that here finds
a new form and a new urgency. But in the two "situations" we have just
recalled, as contradictory as they are, a new interest for philosophy is thus
mobilized.

5. Finally and most of all, techno-scientific research is in the process of
entering into a new relation with the philosophical, which would not be
reduced merely to its classic forms:

a. Coextensivity and immediate communication between the encyclopedia, the totality of knowledge, and philosophy.

b. Subordination (in principle) of the regions of knowledge to a general
ontology or to a transcendental instance.

c. The (later) demand for the autonomy of each scientific field seeking
to found and formalize itself by excluding every philosophical instance.

d. Recourse to the philosophical in the properly epistemological moment of research.

e. The always-philosophical form of experiences of so-called "crisis": the
crisis of "foundations," concern regarding the ethico-political goals of science and technics (military or police use of techno-scientific power, genetic manipulation, the role of information technology and telematics:
once again, the new problems of "law, medicine, and religion").[4]

These typical forms, moreover, are neither necessarily nor equally outdated. But a different philosophical practice and a different relation to the
philosophical are being sought, within and at the limits of all these types of
knowledge. As an alternative to the philosophical all-or-nothing, to philosophical hegemony *versus* nonphilosophy or independence regarding all
philosophemes, one sees, today, a tendential succession of a multiplicity of
transversal exchanges, original at once in their local character and in the re-
nunciation of a *classical* recourse to philosophy (a "radical," fundamentalist, ontological, or transcendental recourse, an always-totalizing recourse).

On the one hand, questions of a philosophical type traverse spaces that
were previously unknown, excluded, or marginalized. Let us cite them, in
no particular order: psychoanalytic practice and theory, the psychoanalytic movement, the new facts of military strategy, of international law in
dealing with space and information, urbanism, the media, the new technological conditions of the relation to disease, to death, to torture, the

theoretical exploration of languages, writings, grammars, discourse, the transformation of "artistic" media and thus forms—and therefore of artistic institutions and classifications, of the concept of the "fine arts," verbal or nonverbal, and so forth.

On the other hand, and reciprocally, these new incursions compel the philosopher, who sometimes accepted a relative exteriority (and thus a certain incompetence) in regard to this or that field of particular knowledge, to question once again a certain type of authority (fundamentalist, transcendental, or ontological); they compel the philosopher to change styles and rhythms in any case, sometimes languages, without, however, renouncing philosophy and without believing that it is invalid pure and simple. Without ceasing to question the meaning and destination of philosophy and of what continues to affirm itself under this name, philosophers seem today to have to transform their modes of questioning to respond to provocations and expectations from still-unknown places, most often from philosophical institutions, excluded by the problematics they recognize and legitimate.

Freedom, mobility, resourcefulness, diversity, even dispersion: such would be the characteristics of these new philosophical "formations." By "formations" we mean the new philosophical "objects" and the process of their constitution, as well as the "social formations" (groups of philosophers, institutional communities, research and teaching structures) that would correspond to them. By definition difficult to situate in what previously would have been a "system" or a model of the *universitas*, they in any case require institutions that are as light, permeable, and mobile as possible. We will draw the conclusions from this below.

What we have just outlined schematically might give the feeling of a simple "global" conjuncture, in other words, of a contingency or an accidental unity. What might be the essential destination shared by these motifs that all seem to lead back to philosophy or at least to intersect at a site said to be philosophical, even though they appear to be contradictory?

We do not want to determine this presumed *unity* here. We do not want to propose a philosophical or metaphilosophical preinterpretation of it. At least we are doing everything possible to abstain from that. Hence we deliberately accept the risk of a prephilosophical, empiricist, rhapsodic discourse. We do so for several reasons, all of which stem from the type of text we are proposing here and from the mission entrusted to us. We think it would be useful to state these reasons briefly.

1. We believe that reaching a consensus on the approximate location of

all these signs and symptoms would be rather easy, but the same is not necessarily true for their interpretation as a whole. Each sign presents itself as a discourse and a philosophical preinterpretation of the totality of the global field. In a given situation (for the sake of brevity, let's call it France's chance today), we think it is possible to found an institution on this first consensus, but we insist upon not linking the project itself to a preinterpretation or to being put in a philosophical perspective, ours or that of any one of us. That is our responsibility. We insist upon assuming it as rigorously as possible, knowing that the absolute neutralization of all preinterpretation would ultimately be unattainable and absurd: it would make this very discourse irresponsible.

What will finally have helped us in this difficulty is a hypothesis or question. Suspending, in effect, as long as possible, all philosophical preinterpretation, we not only conform to the neutrality and reserve required for the mission entrusted to us, but perhaps also put forward the hypothesis (one or the other among us will gladly claim it as his own) that no discourse that can be delimited today according to the academico-institutional models or criteria of the tradition is, as such, capable of such an interpretation: neither a (regional) scientific discourse nor a philosophical discourse (fundamental ontology or transcendental philosophy, and so forth). This is barely more than a question, a hypothesis. If one could still claim to recognize it as having an identity and a unity, *the* question or *the* type of question for this Collège would thus concern precisely the theoretico-institutional limits within which it has been possible up to this point to attempt to appropriate this interpretation. This interpretation traverses and exceeds, perhaps, without disqualifying them, however, all the discourses and all the thematics that claim to dominate it, for example, philosophy (in all its forms, in particular the philosophy of language, the philosophy of history, hermeneutics, the philosophy of religion), the human sciences (for example, sociology in all its forms, up to and including the sociology of knowledge; history, up to and including the history of the sciences and of technologies, politology or political economy, psychoanalysis, and so forth), and the so-called natural sciences, supposing this final distinction still withstands analysis. In other words, the charter of such a Collège should not exclude the possibility that the thinking that would measure up to this unity of the epoch, if there are an "epoch," a unity, and a measure, is perhaps no longer scientific or philosophical, in the sense in which these words can be determined today. It is in fact this indetermination and this very opening that we designate, in this context, by the word "thinking." This word is not nothing, but it is nothing else: not philosophy but what questions it.

2. This "thinking" will be precisely the horizon, the task, and the destination of this Collège, its adventure as well. Its adventure because it is a matter of the future, as we have said, but also because it will be a question of taking risks: in the way of ambitious speculations on the most wide-ranging subjects as well as in the form of experimental incursions in unexplored areas. The speculative attitude and traditional [*artisanal*] experimentation will here find the most welcoming place for their cohabitation.

This Collège would not be an *establishment*, an immobilized institution in which we would seek to cover areas recognized by programs certain of their efficiency, their performance, and their productivity. It will be, rather, a place of provocation, of incentives for research, of speculative or experimental exploration, of proposals and stimulation in new directions.

The themes we have just evoked to situate the awakening of the philosophical today are known and treated (directly or indirectly, but always separately) by this or that specialized group in this or that institution. The Collège must not, of course, replace or compete with this activity, still less contest these specialists. Moreover, it could not do so. On the other hand, it will be able to make converge or cross, in the style we defined a moment ago (incisive incentive, speculative or experimental exploration, establishing intercommunication, etc.), problematics that are too often separated or isolated. In the strongest and most spectacular moments of its existence (and one can reasonably anticipate them), the Collège will bring about essential debates between the most diverse and significant thinkers from all countries, on the decisive stakes we evoked above.

In this regard, one can say in all neutrality, this unique opportunity can be given in France, to France, and by France. Our country's situation is singular today. Let's limit ourselves to what is best known and briefest.

Over the last twenty-five years, many French researchers (philosophers, scholars, artists), without ever having been given the means, have no doubt shown the greatest originality, that originality, at any rate, that is most easily recognized as theirs abroad in ways and according to a style that prefigures precisely what would be an international college of philosophy. For it is abroad that the consciousness of this is no doubt the most acute: it is in France that a good number of intellectuals with different training have transgressed established theoretico-institutional limits or academic territories better than elsewhere. We will refrain from naming the individuals here; but it is well known that, for example, the French philosophers who are most renowned and who are sometimes the only ones known abroad are those who have done their work in the margins of university programs and norms, opening philosophy to the sciences, literature, psychoanalysis, the visual arts, and so forth. And they have done so in difficult conditions—conditions made more difficult by the French institutional system and by its traditional politics, which foreign countries, always ready to welcome them, have a good deal of difficulty understanding.

A strange situation, an opportunity not to be missed. There is today, in a kind of marginal or inter-institutional territory, a space that no other national culture has been able to create. And, *stricto sensu*, according to established criteria, this space is neither purely philosophical, nor purely scientific, nor purely aesthetic.

It happens that the wealth and singularity of this quarter of a century have often given rise to conflicts, to doctrinal or dogmatic exclusions, to establishing cliques and clienteles, and to exploiting small differences that foreigners more attentive to the general unity of the French scene find laughable. The history and sociology of these phenomena would also merit systematic study that could be undertaken or pursued by the Collège. But it is just as important to observe today a kind of break in this war that was no doubt made worse, sometimes created, by the structures of institutional power, as much in the university as in the media and publishing. Certain signs lead one to think that this type of conflictuality without any meeting or debate could to a certain extent leave room for discussions that are at once more direct and more tolerant. Without this amounting to facileness, eclecticism, or ecumenism, the Collège could offer in these conditions one of the principal sites of meeting, research, and debate. One can reasonably anticipate the interest it could therefore stir as such. The quality and number of thinkers it would attract would make this Collège a site of high attendance and heavy traffic, a possibility for highly intense creation. Its creation alone would be an event, and not only a spectacle: we are already certain that it would be greeted, in France and abroad, in the spirit of the great hopes it has already occasioned. Every day new signs confirm this.

One could also expect a great wealth of proposals and incentives for the future of the teaching of philosophy in France "at a time when the government is preparing to extend the study of philosophy in secondary education" (Jean-Pierre Chevènement, *Lettre de mission*).

The mission confided in us is therefore situated expressly in the perspective of a development of this teaching: in secondary and higher education, in specialized sections and classes, but elsewhere as well. If, as we hope, the teaching of philosophy is extended to reach the proportions of every other basic [*fondamentale*] discipline, if in order to be extended it must transform and enrich itself, the Collège will be able to play an invaluable role in this perspective. That does not mean that it will centralize or bring together all the research undertaken to this effect. But, on the one hand, very spontaneously and naturally, all the activities of the Collège will be so many openings, hypotheses, and proposals for a new teaching of philosophy that is as rigorous as possible, in its traditional demands as well as in its innovations. And, on the other hand (a decisive task that we will clarify below), from the moment of its creation the Collège will organize systematic research and experimentation in this direction. It will thus prepare a set of new and coherent proposals (pedagogical procedures, programs, methods, contents, but also freeing up space for other breakthroughs [*frayages*] and for more innovative practices, and so forth) in view of the extension of the teaching of philosophy before the Terminale and outside philosophy departments in the university.

Of course, all those, in secondary and higher education, at the CNRS and elsewhere, who would like to participate in it will join in this work, which will consist only of proposals and incentives. The wish that was widely expressed during the Estates General of Philosophy will finally be implemented; and to do so we will be able to consult the work published by those Estates General, as well as those of Greph. But this is only a possibility and an example.

Interscience and Limitrophe

Why link, along with "sciences" and "arts," the subtitle "interscience" with the title "philosophy"?

Certain of the preceding considerations have no doubt prepared for our response. We should now clarify the contours of a concept that, while having no theoretical legitimacy within, precisely, an already determined field of objectivity, appears no less necessary once one takes into account a certain theoretico-institutional topology of knowledge. There again, it is a matter of what happens, can and must happen, between the domains of already legitimated fields when borders allow themselves to be exceeded or displaced. Taking up Einstein's word, we will name "interscientific"[5] any thematic, any field, any research activity (later we will say any performativity) that the map of institutions, at a given moment, does not yet grant stable, accredited, habitable departments. These zones of instability might appear wild and uninhabitable in the eyes of a certain social representation of organized research. They are in fact sites of great traffic, privileged sites for the formation of new objects or rather of new thematic networks. These paths, which are in the course of being cleared, establish connections between institutional roads already open for traffic, with their code of signals and signs and their programmed (productive and reproductive) flow. The clearing of these new paths can have begun already or be totally to come. One can prepare for it or let oneself be surprised by it, since it depends not on the initiative of a subject (who is either "free" or "trained" [*formé*] in terms of education programs) but rather on the much more complex relation to the new information and communications technology, and so forth. In both instances, we will speak of the interference of knowledge or of "interscience," since what is at issue are new objects arising on oblique or transversal paths establishing communication between previously separate areas.

It is the privilege accorded these interferences that will give the life of the Collège a character all its own: exploration, experimentation, innovation, invention, proposal, a throw of the dice and a bet in spaces that are still quite unknown or unacknowledged; and especially *transference*, in every sense of the word. We will draw the conclusions of this for the status, organization, form, and rhythm of the Collège later. For a considerable portion of the research to be undertaken it will be a question of formulating new problematics and new fields that, once they are recognized in their necessity and stabilized in their unity, will have to emigrate, be transferred and taken in elsewhere, in another existing institution or in an institution still to be created. It will therefore be a matter of inventing the best conditions and the best rhythm for these interferences and transferences. We know how difficult it is for a research establishment, certain of its field and competence, of its legitimacy and its productivity, to be hospitable to themes and questions that at first appear to disorganize or exceed its general program.

These difficulties are very diverse in origin and manifestation. They obey an ordered inertia that, in the great theoretico-institutional mobility that must be accepted today, calls for systematic study. This study will be privileged in a Collège that will once again have to question, directly or indirectly, its own conditions of possibility. And this questioning will not only be a reflexive sociology of knowledge, although it could be that as well.

All this confirms the necessity of uniting philosophy, in the sense we have attempted to define, with multiple and active intersections, for several reasons.

Performativity

Once again, in the context we are defining here, the fields of "knowledge" *between* which new paths are to be recognized are not limited to what are commonly called the "sciences" (mathematics, logic, natural science, the human or social sciences). They extend to all fields of activity or competences, whatever the area. Therefore, by virtue of the same trans- or interferential necessities, the Collège will have to open itself to artistic experiments and to all their languages (the "theory and practice" of literature, the visual arts, music, theater, cinema, all audiovisual techniques, and so on).

These possibilities are accepted as self-evident and are empirically organized in many universities; this is common in the United States, for example. It is a matter of making official, of enriching, and of systematizing this research, of making room, under certain conditions, not only for theoretical work *on* arts and techniques of all kinds, but for so-called "creative" research. . . . The fields of activity or competences we are calling for would not only be theoretical; they would also define a know-how [*savoir-faire*] or a knowing-how-to-produce [*savoir-produire*] and, therefore, as is self-evident when speaking of a competence, the capacity for *performance*. We must stress this point, for it no doubt defines one of the most original stakes for the Collège, the high risk and the difficulty of calculation. Stressing performance does not, of course, amount to valorizing the "high-performance" [*performant*][6]—as the saying goes—character of techniques or operations that can be programmed and made profitable. We have insisted upon indicating, on the contrary, that the Collège should avoid the dominant modes of calculation in this regard, which does not destine it to being unproductive but rather requires that other rhythms, very heterogeneous qualitative structures, and probabilistic or aleatory phenomena avoiding classical institutional calculation be taken into account. Let us note in passing that this could also be one of the research themes to be privileged in the Collège, with all the effects of the technological transformations under way on knowledge (competence and performance), in particular those concerning archiving, the stocking and communication of information, computerization, telematics, databases, the problematics of so-called "artificial intelligence."[7] One of the missions of the Collège will be "research training": we will therefore have to see develop at once *technical competence* in the access to this new instrumentalization of knowledge and a new reflection of an original "philosophical" kind on this new technological condition of knowledge and communication, on the role of the "media," on the politics of science, on the new responsibilities involved in this, and so forth.

We therefore propose that the "performative" possibility and exigency be recognized by rights as one of the essential marks of the Collège. They have never been recognized, *as such*, in any research and teaching institution, for structural, philosophical, and political reasons. No doubt, every philosophical or, more generally, theoretical language implements, under its apparently "constative" or descriptive appearance and norms, "performative" forces that have in general been ignored, or rather denied, in any case, deprived of all legitimacy in the institutions of "knowledge." This therefore excluded any *legitimate* possibility of seeing a speech act as an event provoking an event, which does not amount, in accordance with the trivial and long-recognized possibility, to inducing events or actions with words. Let us recall briefly that it is a matter of speech acts whose very structure, in certain given contexts, is the immediate cause of certain events. This is not the place to enter into the current problematic of performative statements and of "pragmatics" in general. Its field is being extended and complicated with increasing speed. The performative dimension of language covers, in differentiated fashion, an enormous mass of typical statements. Let's consider, for the moment, only the institutional effect of this fact, which concerns philosophy, linguistics, logic, literature, the arts, political discourse, and so on: by itself it should at once constitute a very broad and differentiated field of research for the Collège and a structural transformation in the history of the systems of knowledge and their legitimation. For the first time, an institution will expressly take up a dimension of language that had been excluded or denied to this point. The effects of this transformation can be wide-ranging, if one wants to follow this principle in all its consequences, and the very creation of such an institutional space will already be an unprecedented inaugural "performative," with (we will never hide this) all the risks that a "blow" [*coup*] of this type can entail. But whatever the risks, this event will by itself have a "philosophical" meaning. It will first of all necessitate a reconsideration of all the hierarchical theorems and principles upon which the systems of research and teaching are constructed, whether the structure of speech acts, their relation to the technology of communication and to *techne* in general, relations between theory and practice, knowledge and power, philosophy, science, and arts. In addition to the wide-ranging and long-term consequences, such an inauguration will immediately allow for the open admission that the Collège is giving itself, among other missions, that of favoring certain performances, in particular in the fields of the so-called arts (verbal or not), once they have the status of an experimental exploration and the effect of "intersection" we evoked above. Each of these experiments would have "philosophical" import capable of giving rise to a new thematic.

Beyond Interdisciplinarity

It should be clarified here that this transversal intersection of fields of knowledge could not be reduced to what is conventionally called "interdisciplinarity": a programmed cooperation between the representatives of the established sciences that would study a common object, itself already defined in its contours, with the help of different methods and complementary approaches. As necessary as it remains within its very limits, interdisciplinarity thus understood does not institute a novel problematic and does not invent new objects. As such it does not claim to modify the structure and recognized borders of the fields of research, and of the protocols and approaches that are proper to them. On the other hand, the intersections that we believe need to be made and multiplied should tend to free up problematics and speech acts that the established disciplines, as such, must in general inhibit or marginalize—sometimes even because of their strength, their legitimacy, their efficiency.

It is thus less a matter, for the Collège, of mobilizing several fields of activity or competences *around* an already discovered theme than of bringing forth new themes and new modes of research and teaching. To be sure, it would remain more necessary than ever to call upon established fields of knowledge at the intersection of existing "disciplines." But this will be done here in order to create research groups and then to propose their stabilized theoretico-institutional system and form to other agencies, in France and throughout the world.

This motif of intersection or crossing would be a kind of charter for the Collège. It would inform its criteriology, particularly in the orientation of research, the definition of responsibilities, the selection of projects, and the evaluation of results.

The transversal breakthroughs [*frayages*] will be, to put it very schematically, of *two types*, which could naturally intersect in turn.

"EXTERNAL" LIMITROPHE

Such an advance will first of all be able to bring to the fore a place or a theme that no specific discipline, as such, will to this point have recognized and treated. Of course, this does not mean that this new topic has in principle been inaccessible to already established and legitimized research; and it will be objected precisely that the normal progress of a discipline consists in discovering and analyzing new objects or new properties within an already identified field of objectivity. Every scientific contribution, from the most modest thesis to the most ambitious elaborations, conforms in principle to this norm, and this is what we call "research."

We therefore have to specify what kind of transversal breakthroughs [*frayages*] are to be privileged systematically. First of all, a quantitative criterion that we believe is pertinent: certain breakthroughs can be accepted in principle by this or that institution and immediately deprived, in fact, of any future; without sufficient support, original work is immediately marginalized, contained in a narrow space, held back in a kind of under-development. Insufficient support is never insignificant or purely aleatory. It reflects politico-institutional motivations, interests, and structures that are always worth questioning the moment one attempts to compensate for it, and in this very movement. Each time, one must ask oneself: why has this or that research not been able to develop? What is getting in the way? And who? And how? Why? With what aim? Up to a certain point, the Collège could play a telling theoretico-institutional role. Sometimes, turning this question back toward its own limits, it would multiply questions of this type and develop them in the most consistent fashion.

It is by definition impossible to give a priori a well-thought-out list of these exclusions, foreclosures, interdictions, or marginalizations (whether discreet or violent). By definition, the examples we could give of them would be partly outdated. Over the course of work that we do not want to predetermine here, this "unlocking" will appear and we will propose different models of general interpretation or of particular intervention regarding it. For the moment, we can only identify its abstract form and most open criteriology.

This first type of *limitrophe* would by itself lead to an analysis of a philosophical type. Putting several orders of "knowledge" into communication in a mode that is not simply interdisciplinary always poses general questions. In this case, the recourse to philosophy no longer takes its classical and hierarchizing form: the arbitrating of an ontological or transcendental authority or instance legislating on questions of possibility, and so forth.

What is being sought now is perhaps a different philosophical style and a different relation of philosophical language to other discourses (a more horizontal relation, without hierarchy, without radical or fundamental re-centering, without an architectonics, and without an imperative totalization). Will this still be a philosophical style? Will philosophy survive the test of these new fields of knowledge, of this new topology of limits? This will be the test and the very question of the Collège.

"INTERNAL" LIMITROPHE

Another kind of *limitrophic* work could define the mission of the Collège. This time it is *within a single discipline*, within an already organized theoretico-institutional system, that the question of limits could arise. This happens the moment a given positive knowledge encounters in its autonomous field difficulties or limits that its own axiomatics and process do not allow to be raised. A science or a *techne* in general then questions its own presuppositions, displaces, deforms the framework of its problematic, submits it to other configurations. This moment—which is typical and normal for all research—is not necessarily that of an "epistemological crisis" or of a "questioning of foundations," and so forth. These models of the so-called "critical" moment can be transformed, and although they are first of all philosophical in appearance, they can also trouble the philosophical certainty upon which they are still constructed. This philosophical certainty has a history; it has taken many forms, and "the philosopher" cannot avoid questioning it in all its forms, from the classical questioning of the essence of metaphysics, the limits and destination of philosophy, of philosophical research and teaching, to perhaps novel questions, born at the limits of new fields of knowledge, powers, and technical systems with which philosophy had never before associated.

It is not for us to propose models for the elaboration of these questions here, still less typical responses to them. We are only indicating the urgent necessity of giving them a place and an opportunity worthy of them. All the problematics and all the proposals that depend upon them (they are innumerable) will find a privileged greeting in the new Collège. Not that all approaches of this kind must constitute the *program* of the Collège; that would be excessive and out of proportion with the dimensions of such an institution, and no doubt of every institution in general. The idea of saturation has no pertinence here, and a program cannot be constructed according to what by definition problematizes every programmatic contract. Let us merely say that the rule of the Collège will be to give priority to these limitrophic problematics and above all to those that concern the limits as such of the philosophical. Priority will also be given to certain styles of approach: exploration at the limits [of philosophy],[8] singular or out-of-the-ordinary incursions. To be sure, the out-of-the-ordinary, the limitrophic or aleatory, would not be valorized by themselves and as such. But alongside other elements of assessment, they should be to the credit of the research projects submitted to the Collège.

The schema we are proposing leads one to question—and perhaps to displace—the relation between philosophy and the fields of knowledge as this relation has been established in the model of the university institution that has dominated in the West since the beginning of the industrial age: a vertical ontologico-encyclopedic structure that tends to immobilize all recognized borders of knowledge. In the university, philosophy is supposed to organize and order the entire space of knowledge and all the regions of the encyclopedia. But in terms of power this hierarchical principle is immediately inverted: the department of philosophy (the "Faculty of Philosophy" that Kant speaks of in *The Conflict of the Faculties*)[9] is subjected to the disciplines representing the power of the State.[10] All-powerful and powerless: this was the destiny assigned philosophy in a system subordinating all the university languages to statements of (theoretical) truth *within* the university, and the whole of this university to representatives of State power for everything that was not a "constative" judgment. Philosophy was everything and nothing (using the same logic, Schelling objected to the idea of a "department" of philosophy, since philosophy had to be everywhere, and thus nowhere, in no determinate place).[11] Since then, all speculations on the death or survival of philosophy have maintained an essential relation with this institutional projection. Throughout many variations, this Kantian paradigm has illustrated powerfully the logic of the relations between the State, philosophy, and nonphilosophical fields of knowledge.

It is this concept of the *universitas* that, directly or not, leads to these still-current paradoxes: a certain hegemony of the philosophical goes hand in hand with civil society or the State system confining, even repressing, philosophical teaching and research. To limit ourselves to this very significant example, what happened in France stems from this logic: the philosophy class ("queen of disciplines," "crowning moment of studies") is also an enclosure in which philosophy is penned up, deprived of the treatment and dignity given other disciplines (see the works of Greph).[12]

The transformation and extension of the teaching of philosophy (before the Terminale classes in lycées and outside university departments [*Unités d'enseignement et de recherche, UER*] of philosophy) will again put into question the space that is hierarchized in this way and all the theoretico-institutional limits that structure it. If, in accordance with the promises of the president of the republic, the extension of the teaching of philosophy is to become a political reality in the immediate future, the creation of the Collège International de Philosophie must move in the same direction.[13] The economy of our project supposes this in any case. It outlines an entirely different topology: a multiplicity of transversal, horizontal, heterogeneous relations will tend to be substituted for what we will call, for the sake of convenience, *univerticality* (radical unity of the foundation, onto-encyclopedic hegemony, centralism, maximal identification, and hierarchy). But this will be only a tendency—and an experiment to be attempted. Numerous signs suggest that it is time for this.

The Collegiate and International Dimension

Why a *college*? Why an *international* college? If we have recourse to the historical name "college," it is first of all to take into account premises that we have attempted to justify: this new institution must be neither a school nor a university. Nor will it merely be a research center in the traditional sense of the expression. Second, it is to propose its *autonomous* and *liberal* operation: in its mode of recruiting and of administration, in its relation to the State, the nation, and the regions.

In the following chapters, we will multiply the proposals intended to guarantee this collegiality. Sticking to generalities here, let us say that the regulatory authority should not impede but on the contrary favor this autonomy, the possibility of initiatives that would lead to decentralization,

of turning (in certain conditions) to private resources, of contracts with
regional and international agencies.

Other collegiate characteristics: the free and pluralistic style of the relations between members of the institution, the necessity of excluding all
stabilized hierarchization, every phenomenon of the "school," of authority and doctrinal intolerance, rapidly renewing the *active* members of the
Collège, the ease of movement [*passages*] between the Collège and other
institutions of research and teaching (lycées, universities, CNRS, Collège
de France, EHESS [École des Hautes Études en Sciences Sociales], foreign
institutions, and so on), and a broad and lively community among the *active* members of the Collège and all others.

This collegiate structure will no doubt facilitate welcoming foreign students, researchers, and artists. For the *international* dimension of the Collège must appear as one of its essential characteristics. The statutes of the
Collège will be very explicit in this regard: it is a matter of the originality,
strength, and influence of this institution, the only one of this kind in
France and perhaps the world.

It must be recognized that up to this point France has not given itself the
means for large-scale international cooperation, in particular in the spaces
we have outlined. This is a well-known fact for foreign researchers and for
the French researchers who are often welcomed in other countries, especially the United States. University structures make the steps in preparation
for welcoming a foreign researcher or artist in good conditions cumbersome, difficult, often discouraging. We are not speaking here of the values
of intellectual hospitality that France respects in principle concerning this
or that great writer (though the history of the emigrants we have not been
able to keep is sometimes rather sad). Beyond individual hospitality, it
seems to us urgent and vital to open new, rich, and very clear, even spectacular, possibilities for international exchanges and organic cooperation
with foreign institutions. This should be done in all directions but giving a
certain priority to exchanges with African, Asian, and Latin American
countries, and more generally with developing countries. Experimentation
in new forms of cooperation, particularly concerning research training,
would be desirable. Without neglecting relations with the United States
and with Eastern and Western European countries (on the contrary), we
should avoid making the Collège a new Eurocentric institution.

a. French intellectuals who are known for their work and who are generously received abroad will have to be allowed to take reciprocal initiatives.

b. It is important for French students and researchers to maintain lasting relations with foreigners who would stay in France long enough to exhibit the state of their research here but also to pursue the most creative activities.

c. It would be desirable for the Collège to become a place of international exchange (linguistic, cultural, scientific, artistic) in keeping with its specificity and not limited to bilateral communication. The problematic of national languages in scientific communication (and taking new information technologies into account) must become an important and permanent theme for all those who participate in the life of the Collège.[14]

d. Most of all, this international openness must allow, in a more traditionally philosophical field, for the multiplication of original initiatives whose historical necessity is more obvious than ever today. We know that the "philosophical world," assuming it still has a unity, is not only divided into "schools" and "doctrines" but also, beyond and independently of philosophical contents and positions, divided according to linguistico-national borders that are more difficult to cross than political borders. These traditional differences in "style," "rhetoric," "method," and so on are sometimes more serious than differences in doctrine. Although they cannot be reduced to national languages and traditions, they nonetheless remain part of these. These philosophical areas between which passages are rare, whether in the form of critique or polemics, are a historical—and philosophical—challenge to philosophy. Whether one sees it as an enigma or a scandal, this is a phenomenon that we should give ourselves the means of studying; otherwise we reduce it systematically, with new costs.

This would be one of the most difficult and necessary tasks of the Collège, which can play an irreplaceable role here. For the reasons evoked above, numerous French and foreign philosophers expect a great deal from this immense project and think that France can today give it its best chances.

—*Translated by Jan Plug*

Sendoffs (for the Collège International de Philosophie) (1982)

Foreword

I

The propositions advanced in this chapter claim, certainly, a certain coherence. But it will be neither the coherence of a *system*—even less that of a philosophical *doctrine*—nor even that of a *program*, in the technical and institutional sense we give this word in our report.

What is called a *philosophical system* constitutes in fact a certain type of coherence or continuous cohesion, a form of *ontological* ordering that has appeared historically, and, we can even say, as linked to the essence of the history of philosophy. In the form of *doctrine* the system has always linked philosophy to its discourses and its pedagogical institutions. But every consistent discourse, organized or simply gathered together with itself, does not necessarily have the form of a system (perhaps it is even destined to break with this form from the moment it addresses itself to the other). Since the Collège will be directed toward making the *systemic* idea or project (in general) *one of its themes*, one of the problems to be considered, and since, correlatively, the Collège should never neglect the questions of teaching, pedagogy, education, doctrinal effects, and all their sociopolitical aims [*finalités*], and so on, it could not be a question of imposing the form of a "system" on this research, this history, this "thinking." For this very reason, however, the nonsystemic coordination we are going to propose will have nothing of the rhapsodic or the empirical about it either.

Nor will it sketch out a *program*. First, because everything will not be undertaken there in the form of a prescription, with its "objectives" and its end-oriented [*finalisée*] production. Furthermore because, without being necessarily kept there, several research groups—called "programs" in the first part [called "The Regulating Idea"] of this report—will eventually be able to cooperate, communicate, try to cross with, confront, and translate each other there, *but above all without ever renouncing their most precise specificity, their autonomy, and their internal necessity.*

II

These propositions claim a demonstrative value, a demonstrativity both intraphilosophical and with regard to certain singular borders of the philosophical. But this demonstrativity cannot be constantly *exhibited as such* here. This is in keeping with the limits of such a report, whether it is a matter of the material limits of this chapter or, especially, of those that come with the genre, with the *aim* [*finalité*] or with the *destination* of such a text, with the very nature of the *mission* assigned to it. There is nothing fortuitous in this, for the values of *aim*, of *destination*, like the entire semantics of the mission (placing, emitting, missive, missile, sendoff [*envoi*], etc.), will form one of the essential foci of my propositions or "projections." Referring implicitly but without dissimulation to other work (my own included), drawing directly or indirectly on the lessons of all the discussions in which the mission has engaged over the course of the last months, I will try to limit myself to practical or technical *conclusions* concerning the research to be instituted in the Collège, to what in any case seems to me as though it should be given priority. *But the necessity of these conclusions should be capable of imposing itself on the basis of other premises.* My rule here will be: project the necessity of certain research, but always in such a way that one could be convinced of it on the basis of other perspectives or other premises about which nothing will be said, and even without any general "perspective" or "premise" other than the intrinsic merit of such research. The nonsystematic unity of this "projection" or "setting into perspective," the possibility of coordination which it might present, should thus be considered here only as a *supplementary interest*, a *premium* to which one might attribute all the values one wishes (philosophical, aesthetic, economic, reason, poem, painting, history, etc.).

Contenting myself often with naming or titling, with situating some "topoi," I will naturally have to leave implicit both the reference to a great deal of work, French and foreign, and the essentials of an analysis of the philosophical, technoscientific, poietic, etc., "fields." We will retain only some indices of these macro- or micro-analyses, which we practice constantly and which orient our approach here: those which have guided us in the definition of the Collège, its project, its regulating idea, its constitution; those which have been spectacularly confirmed in the course of the mission; those which have helped us discover or better situate new orientations; and finally all those which have taken the form of commitments or of research projects (we attach them to this report and we will refer to them at the right moment).[1] But we neither could nor should have gone beyond this in the course of this mission. It was not a question for us of drawing a map of French or world philosophy, for example, nor of proposing a general interpretation of it, even if complete abstention or reserve on this matter was impossible. We strove for this, however, for obvious reasons, which are recalled in the first part of the report. Without proposing any sectioning or cartography of the philosophical terrain, we have made use of many works which could have helped us do so, whether we cite them or not. That is the case, notably, with the recent report by Maurice Godelier and his collaborators on *Les sciences de l'homme et de la société.*[2] We were only able to take account of it at the end of our mission, but the "upshot" and the recommendations we encountered there were already known to us, at least partially (concerning philosophy, for example). Although the objects of these two reports are very different, certain convergences appeared to me remarkable and encouraging. We should nevertheless, for obvious reasons, limit ourselves to this general reference, and presume that our reader will be aware of the "Godelier Report."

III

Let us recall once and for all: for reasons already stated in the first part of the report, we will too often be making use of words that we would like to see received without assurance and without tranquility. For it is without assurance and without tranquility that I will speak, for example, of proposals for *research*, properly *philosophical, scientific, theoretico-practical, poietic*, etc., research, or research on a *theme*, or *problematics*, or *field*. Now, it is understood: all these words remain for the moment inevitable, but they are for the Collège titles of problems and problematic titles, including the values of title and of problem: the laws and the procedures of *le-*

gitimation, the *production of titles and of legitimate problems*, these are also what the Collège will study, analyse, transform all the time, notably in its own space. The concept of *legitimation* itself, which has become so useful and so "legitimate" in so many sociological discourses (sociology of research and teaching institutions, sociology of the arts and culture, etc.), should not remain out of range of this questioning. How has it been constructed? What are its presuppositions and its limits? What is sociology today, the aim and strategy of its "usage"?, etc. We will return to these questions. What we have provisionally and within quotation marks called "thinking," in the first part, should mark the style and the site of such an approach. It proceeds to the limits "on the subject" of all these current values, called "philosophy," "science," "art," "research," "technique," "theory," "practice," "problem," "law," "legitimacy," "title," and so forth. These precautions are not purely formal. Evidently they do not concern only the vocabulary in which one generally speaks of research and teaching institutions. We will not be able to avoid this lexicon, but we will give it, for anyone who wants to hear, a certain interrogative inflection: what are these things we're talking about—"philosophy," "science," "inter-science," "art," "technique," "culture," "production," "theory," "research," and so forth? What is an "object," a "theme," a "problem," a "problematic"? How to think the question "what is" concerning them?

These forms of interrogation will assign to the Collège its greatest and most permanent opening, which it must never suture with the assurance of a body of knowledge, a doctrine or a dogma. Whatever the abstract generality of this axiom, we believe it is necessary to inscribe it in the very charter of the institution, as a sort of founding contract. That will not prevent—on the contrary—further analysis of the values of *contract*, of *foundation*, and of *institution*.

IV

Despite the measureless unfolding and the infinite reflection in which these preliminaries might seem to engage, the concrete propositions I will present in this chapter are strictly delimitable: *a four-year sendoff*. During the *first four years* of the Collège, a large number of activities—*we are not saying all the activities*—can be coordinated in a supple and mobile fashion, without ever being constrained by some general and authoritarian planning. *Without being kept there and without renouncing its most precise specificity*, each of the research groups I am going to define will be able to refer to a general and common theme. We could call it a "title," "category," "regulating idea," "problematic," or "working hypothesis." Its unity would be only *presumed*, according to different modes, and it will assure, at least during this initial period, a common reference, a principle of *general translation or of possible transfer(ence)* for the exchanges, debates, cooperations, transversal or oblique communications.

    v

Despite these limits, the propositions that follow will traverse an immense and differentiated terrain. But it goes without saying that this territory does not have to be covered or saturated by the Collège's research. Conforming to the style proper to this institution, that of *pathbreaking* [*frayage*] or *trailblazing* [*fléchage*], it will be a matter only of *bringing about new research* and of selecting *inaugural incursions*. I will not return to what was laid out in the first part, namely the necessity of interrogating and displacing in this respect the ontological encyclopedic model by which the philosophical concept of the *universitas* has been guided for the last two centuries.

Destinations

Without all this amounting either to *giving the word* or to saying everything *in a word*, from now on I will make all of these proposals converge toward their most simple, most economical, and most formalizable statement, namely the category or the theme of DESTINATION.
    What does this mean?

    For the reasons announced in the Foreword, I will dispense with the exercise (which would otherwise be necessary) destined to show that it is not a matter here either of a *theme* or a *category*. The philosophical or "thinking" history of the theme, the *thesis* or the *kategoreuein*, would make it clear that the meaning of "destination" won't allow itself to be subordinated to them. But this is not the place for that development. Let's speak in a more indeterminate fashion of a *scheme* of destination, and content ourselves with a single question, in its elementary unfolding: What of destination? What does "to destine" mean? What is "to destine?" What happens to the question "what is?" when it is measured against that of destination? And what happens to it with the multiplicity of idioms?

Let's not unfold this problematic in its most easily identifiable dimensions yet (destination and destiny, all the problems of the end and thus of limits or of confines, ethical or political aim, teleology—natural or not— the destination of life, of man, of history, the problem of eschatology (utopian, religious, revolutionary, etc.), that of the constitution and the structure of the sender / receiver system, and thus of the dispatch or sendoff and the message (in all its forms and in all its substances—linguistic or not, semiotic or not), emission, the mission, the missile, transmission in all its forms, telecommunication and all its techniques, economic distribution and all its conditions (producing, giving, receiving, exchanging), the dispensation of knowledge and what we now call the "end-orientation" [*finalisation*] of research or of techno-science, etc.

Let's content ourselves for the moment with situating the strategic force of this question schematically, with situating what constitutes, it seems to me, its most unavoidable philosophical necessity as well as its performing and performative value as a "lever." The word "strategy" does not necessarily imply calculation or warlike stratagem, but the question of calculation, including its modern polemological aspect (the new concepts of war, strategy and game theory, weapons production, military techno-science, the economy of military-industrial complexes, relations between the armed forces and research in all domains, etc.), should be included in this problematic network and accordingly be fully welcomed in the Collège. We will return to this.

The "lever," then: having been gathered and identified in these still "classical" forms (destination and end of philosophy, of metaphysics or of onto-theology, eschatological or teleological closure), the problematic of the limits of the philosophical as such seems to have arrived at a very singular point.

On the one hand, the modern sciences ("human or social sciences," "life sciences," and "natural sciences") are continuing or beginning again to adjust themselves to the problems we have just redirected toward that of destination (aim, limits, teleology of systems). And their irreducibly philosophical dimension is often there, at the moment when philosophy returns, whether or not we want it, whether or not we hold on to the representation of a post- or extra-philosophical scientificity.

On the other hand—and above all—the recourse to a thought of the *sendoff,* of *dispensation* or the *gift* of being, signals today one of the most singular and, it seems to me, most powerful—in any case one of the last—attempts to "think" the history and structure of onto-theology, even the history of being in general. However we interpret them, and whatever credit we grant this thought or this discourse, we should pause before this marker: the "destinal" significations (sending or sendoff, dispensation, destiny of being, *Schickung, Schicksal, Gabe, "es gibt Sein," "es gibt Zeit,"* etc.) do not seem to belong to the *within* of onto-theological philosophemes any longer, without being "metaphors" or empirical or derived concepts either. There is a sense here that is thus not reducible to what the sciences can and should determine of it, whether it is a matter of the empirical sciences, the natural or life sciences, so-called animal or human societies, techniques of communication, linguistics, semiotics, and so forth. Another thought of the "sendoff" thus seems necessary to the unfolding of the "great questions" of philosophy and of science, of truth, of meaning, of reference, of objectivity, of history.

Let us emphasize the very visible reference that has just been made to the Heideggerian *path*, and not simply to one or another of its scholastic effects. It seems clear enough that the meditation on the history of being, after the existential analytic, opens the question of the ontological difference onto what it always seems to have "presupposed"—in a sense not purely logical—implicated, enveloped, namely a *thinking of the sendoff,* of *dispensation,* and of the *gift* (note, by the way, that it is a matter here of another great text on the gift, which should be read in—very complex—connection with Mauss's "Essai sur le don,"[3] that is to say, with an enormous corpus of French ethnology and sociology over the last six or seven decades, in its scientific but also in its politico-historical dimensions; no doubt we would have to encounter and analyze, in the course of that trajectory, the *Collège de Sociologie,*[4] whose title was often recalled during this mission). The thought of the gift and the sendoff, the thought of "destining" *before* the constitution of the sentence or of the logical structure "X gives or sends Y to Z," Y being an *object* (thing, sign, message) between two "*subjects,*" the sender or the emitter and the receiver or receptor (ego, conscious or unconscious, unconscious), *before* this subject/object constitution and in order to take account of it, and so forth. The same necessity appears, even if in another manner, *mutatis mutandis,* for what I have tried to demonstrate under the heading of *différance* as sendoff, differentiation, delay, relay, delegation, tele- and trans-ference, trace and writing in general, destination and undecidability, and so forth. These indices should naturally be multiplied. For obvious reasons, I limit myself to the most schematic ones and, openly, to what is closest to me. If I hold to declaring these limits and this proximity, it is, contrary to what one might be tempted to think, in order to lift the limits, to distance them and to dis-appropriate them. It is in order to call for critical debate about them, for open disagreements and explications, for other approaches, and in order to avoid the disguised recentering or the hegemony of a problematic, a discourse or a history. These risks should be avoided with thoroughgoing vigilance. The translating, transversal, and transferring coordinations we are proposing will operate without a pyramidal effect, in a lateral, hori-zontal, and nonhierarchial way. The scheme I have just designated, at the limits of the "destinal," seems to me capable of putting into question and displacing precisely the topological principles that have dominated all of onto-theology, invested its space and commanded its traditional forms of univerticality, in philosophical discourse as much as in research and teach-ing institutions. It is already clear that one should not accord this general "schematic" and its entirely presumed unity the status of a new general ontology, and even less that of a transcendental phenomenology, an ab-solute logic, a theory of theories, dominating once again the encyclopedia and all its theoretico-practical regions. But let's go further: this "schematic" should not even be admitted as a new *organon*. By one of the singular contracts without which no opening of thought and no research would be possible, the Collège should consider this "schematic" as itself problematic, as *debatable*: through and through, in a fundamental debate that would certainly assume its deliberately "fundamentalist" dimension, as one sometime says, but would also go so far as to question the motifs of "depth," "foundation," of "reason" [*Grund*] in all of its possible transla-tions—and in particular in relation to the distinction between so-called "basic" ["*fondamentale*"] and so-called applied or even "end-oriented" [*fi-nalisée*] research. It is useless to insist on this here: it is a matter of an es-sential stake touching on the axiomatic and the very future of the Collège, and its relations to the State (to States), nationalities, "civil societies." A singular and paradoxical contract, we were saying, as well might be a com-mitment never to leave the very terms of the instituting contract out of the question, analysis, even transformation, resting in some dogmatic slumber. Doesn't this transform such a contract into a fiction and the reg-ulating idea of the Collège into an "as if" (let us act *as if* such a community were possible, *as if* the priority granted to "still not legitimated path-breakings" could have been the object of a consensus *in fine, as if* a "general translation" could at least have been attempted, beyond the classical systems and the onto-encyclopedic uni-versity whose totalizing model was imposed—even if in its "liberal" variant, that of Schleiermacher and Humboldt—at the moment of the creation of that Western paradigm, the University of Berlin)? And doesn't this *as if* give such an engagement, and all the legalized contracts it calls for, a touch of the simulacrum? To which we will respond, at least elliptically, this way: on the one hand, far from being absolutely new, this type of singular contract will have characterized *every* philosophical or scientific institution worthy of the name, that is to say, which has decided never to leave anything out of the question, not even its own institutional axiomatic. On the other hand, the reflection on what could link a fictional structure to, for example, such performative utterances, promises, contracts, engagements, founding or instituting acts, will be one of the tasks of the Collège, and the richness of these implications is inexhaustible. I will say the same for the reflection on the history and the stakes of the concept of the university since the eighteenth century.

In what follows, my only ambition will be to project some hypotheses. Without being bound by them, those responsible for the Collège in the future might, if they agree with them, also refer to them as *points of order* for a first movement: a broad discussion, a broad introduction which would also be a four-year "translation." Points of order or of pause, rather than of a planned and uni-totalizing organization. Points of pause, *fermata*, if we want to name precisely those signs destined less to mark the measure than to suspend it on a note whose duration may vary. Rhythms, pauses, accents, phases, insistences—it is with these words and these values that I propose to describe, in their diversity, the possibilities and compossibilities of the Collège, certain of them at least, during the four years of its instauration.

I. THINKING DESTINATION: ENDS AND CONFINES FOR PHILOSOPHY, THE SCIENCES, AND THE ARTS

Under this title, whose slight determination is deliberate, it is a question of designating that research called, in a code that no longer fits here, "basic" [*fondamentale*]. It is indispensable that it be developed broadly, and to the point of questioning the fundamentalist scheme, such as it has so often been able to regulate philosophy's relation to itself and to other regions of the encyclopedia. Even if we had not been convinced of it in advance, our consultations have provided us with an eloquent proof: the demand for this type of research is very marked today, and it is capable of mobilizing great forces and taking original forms. For reasons and following routes that must be analyzed, this "fundamentalist" thought has given in to a sort of intimidation before the sciences, all the sciences but especially the human and social sciences. It can and should find a new legitimacy and cease being somewhat ashamed of itself, as has sometimes been the case over the last two decades. This can happen without regression and without inevitable return to the hegemonic structure we alluded to in the first part of this report. Furthermore, this movement is underway. The Collège should permit it to affirm itself in all of its force: to affirm philosophy and the thinking of philosophy. It is not only philosophers by profession who ask this but also a great number of researchers engaged in their scientific or artistic practices.

In the perspective which is thus opening up here, the first "themes" of this "basic" or "fundamental" research will be organized around this series: *destination* (destiny, destining, sender/receiver, emitter/transmittor/receptor) and *gift* (giving/receiving, expenditure and debt, production and distribution).

The necessary development of semantic, philological, historical, etc., inquiries will apply itself to the "great questions" of which the following list constitutes only an indication.

How can a thinking of "destination" concern philosophy, more precisely its own contour, its relation to a thinking which would not yet or no longer be "philosophy" or "metaphysics," nor for that matter "science" or "technics"? What of the limits or the "ends" of philosophy, of metaphysics, of onto-theology? What of their relation to science and technics? This enormous network of questions can, we will say (and this goes for everything we advance here), be unfolded for itself, independently of any reference to the scheme of destination. So why not do without the proposed guiding thread? Response: Why not, in fact, if possible? We ought to be able to try that in the Collège, which is why I proposed that this "scheme" never become a "program" or an obligatory "theme," even if I am convinced that it is more and something other than one "guiding thread" among others.

In all cases, foci of reflection should be instituted wherever the question of the *end and ends* of the philosophical as such can *take place*, wherever the limit, the borders, or the destination of philosophy is at stake, wherever *there is cause or space* to ask: Philosophy *in view of what? Since and until when? In what and how? By whom and for whom?* Is it *decidable* and within what limits? In fact and by rights, these *topoi* will also be sites of the Collège's vigilant reflection on itself: on its own aim, on its destination (today and tomorrow) as a *philosophical* site, on what legitimates it and then confers on it its own power of legitimation, on what decides its politics and its economy, on the forces it serves and the forces it makes use of, on its national and international relations with other institutions. *Destination* and *legitimation*, thus, of the Collège itself: these are not problems to be treated secondarily or to be dissociated (in the space of a sociological analysis, for example) from the major interrogations on the essence and the destination of the philosophical. Furthermore, as we noted above, the concept of "legitimation," so common today, calls for a reelaboration in its construction and its usage. Starting with the "open letter" [of May 18, 1982] through which we made public the object of our mission and opened a discussion, we have emphasized ways of research whose *legitimacy* has not yet been recognized. It remained to be specifed, which a simple letter of this type could not do, that the Collège would not keep itself simply outside any process of legitimation, that is, within the illegitimable. Even were we to want it, this seems absolutely impossible. The most ruthless critique, the implacable analysis of a power of legitimation is always produced in the name of a system of legitimation. It can be declared or implicit, established or in formation, stable or mobile, simple or overdetermined—one cannot not know it, one can at most deny it. This denegation is today the most common thing in the world. Making it a theme, the Collège will try to avoid this denegation, insofar as this is possible. We already know that the interest in research not currently legitimated will only find its way if, following trajectories ignored by or unknown to any established institutional power, this new research *is already underway and promises a new legitimacy* until one day, once again . . . and so on. We also know—and who wouldn't want it?—that if the Collège is created with the resources it requires and, above all, if its vitality and richness are one day what we foresee, then it will become in its turn a legitimating instance that will have obligated many other instances to reckon with it. It is this situation that must be continuously analyzed, today and tomorrow, to avoid exempting the Collège as an institution from its own analytic work. In order to track without complacency the ruses of legitimating reason, its silences and its narratives, it would be better to begin in the knowledge that we do so from an authorized, that is to say accredited, site; and from one that is accredited to confer accreditations, even if in a form or according to procedures and criteria completely different from—indeed incompatible with—current practices. Not telling (itself) too many stories about its own independence from this or that power of legitimation (dominant forces of society, institutions, university, State, etc.) is perhaps the *first* condition of the greatest possible independence, though that does not preclude looking for others. What we propose is not the utopia of a wild non-institution apart from any social, scientific, philosophical, etc., legitimation. It is a new apparatus, the only one capable of freeing, *in a given situation*, what the current set of apparatuses still inhibits. Not that the Collège is today the only or even the best form of institution possible in this respect. But to us it appears indispensable to the given set. And it is, moreover, for that reason that the necessity has been able to make itself felt, even as a symptom.

What I have just said about *legitimation* is easily transposed in terms of *orientation*. The ruses of the orientation of research must give rise to a new strategy of analysis. The opposition between end-oriented research and basic or fundamental research has no doubt always been naive and summary. It is today, in all domains, startlingly obvious. We must yet again reelaborate this problematic from the fundamentals up, and that is finally what I propose here, at the same time as I insist on the *topoi* of a "fundamentalist" research-style. Which ones?

A

The questions of metaphysics and of onto-theology everywhere they can be recast: new approaches or connections. The interpretations of the "entire" history of philosophy (teleology, periodization, "epochalization," historical and systematic configurations).

B

The problematic of the *completion or of the limit of philosophy* (teleological or genealogical interpretations, critique, deconstruction, etc.). With the proper names appearing here only as indices, we can thus recommend coordinated and intertwined work on Kant, Hegel, Feuerbach, Kierkegaard, Marx, Comte, Nietzsche, Husserl, the Vienna Circle, Wittgenstein, Russell, Heidegger, and so forth. There is a great deal of room for original research in these directions, especially if it practices grafting, confrontation, or interference. This is almost never done rigorously and deliberately in France; it would break with homogeneous traditions and with institutions closed in on themselves.

This research would put "major," that is to say already recognized and well-known, sites into "configuration." We will recommend later initiatives of another style; they will have in common a concern to analyze— even sometimes to put in question—the processes by which philosophical problematics and traditions become dominant. How and under what conditions are discourses, objects, and philosophical institutions formed? How do they become "philosophical" and how are they recognized as such? Under what conditions do they impose themselves (and on whom?) in order to minoritize or to marginalize other ones?

Each time one of these questions finds an original, interesting, and necessary determination, a *research group* might be created, of greater or lesser dimensions, for a longer or shorter duration. The example I am going to specify was imposed on me primarily by the *scheme of destination*, but it should be able to be translated, transposed, and multiplied. Research organized into one or many seminars, one or many programs, short-lived or long-term, should be able to correspond to each of the "proper names" just listed and to the movements of thought they represent.

C

Take the example of *Heidegger.* Around his work and its "problematic" (like those of the other thinkers listed), a program could be organized by the Collège, then transformed into a relatively independent research center, linked by contract to the Collège under conditions to be studied. In this case as in others, the Collège would have the role of provocation and initial organization. In the process, which would make the program into a research center, the work would first off be magnetized by these questions about the limits, ends, and destinations of onto-theology. It would treat, among others, each of the following "themes," which are all strongly marked in the Heidegerrian text:

— The interpretation of the history of Being. Meaning and truth of Being.

— Thinking, philosophy, science.

— Thinking, philosophy, poetry.

— Technics and metaphysics.

— The work of art.

— Language, languages, translation (beginning with the theoretical and practical problems of translating the corpus being considered). Technics and translation (formal and natural languages, problems of metalanguage and translation machines).

— The political: what, *for example*, of Heidegger's political thought, its relations with his thought in general and with his political engagements on the other hand? (The same questions impose themselves, naturally, for other thinkers.) As for Heidegger, what of his "reception" in France? What will have been its singular destiny? We would thus follow the history and the course of his "legacy" over the last fifty years, during which it will have, in one way or another, traversed all of French philosophy in an alternation of eclipses and reappearances, different each time and always highly significant, even today. Such research should naturally be coordinated with research that takes a fresh look at this century's history, at the constitution of a thematic of modernity or postmodernity in Germany and elsewhere, and at the analysis of the phenomena of totalitarianism, Nazism, fascism, Stalinism, without limiting itself to these enormities of the twentieth century. There again, we might see the originality of the paths to be broken, the specific necessity that will impose them on the Collège, especially in the active and intense crossings between all these different research efforts. Although we have proposed the example of Heidegger, such crossings should traverse other problematics, past or contemporary, around the destinal limit of philosophy (Hegel, Feuerbach, Marx, Kierkegaard, Comte, Nietzsche, Husserl, the Vienna Circle, Wittgenstein, Heidegger, the Frankfurt School, etc.), as well as work on the genealogy of these dominant problematics, of their domination itself. In all these efforts, the rigorous distinction between internal and external reading should not be disregarded, but neither should it be treated as a dogma. This problematic, like that of "context" and of contextualization in general, requires a new elaboration.

— The reason of the university. All these "philosophies" carry with them,

whether thematically (Hegel, Nietzsche, Heidegger, at least) or implicitly,
a discourse on reason which is also a discourse on the university, an evaluation of or a prescription for the destiny of the modern university, its politics (notably in its relations with the State and with the nation), and the
organization of relations between philosophical and technoscientific research. The constant reflection of the Collège on its own mission, its aims
or its eventual "orientation," should pass by way of, among other things,
an encounter with these thoughts which are all thoughts of the university.

Such research communities exist nowhere, as far as I know, neither in
France nor anywhere else. Outside of informal groups and dispersed initiatives, the only organized research depends on narrowly specialized centers, most often incapable of the opening, the mobility, and the intertwined or diagonal approaches we are proposing here. The difficulty for
them (and this stems more often from institutional mechanisms than
from people) is to *mobilize* this research, which sometimes becomes pure
philology, without philosophical ambition, even if it is armed here or
there with modern technology; the difficulty is to measure this research
against the most serious stakes, today's and tomorrow's. No one should
read in these last remarks a will to discredit historicizing attitudes or interest in the past as such, rather the contrary. The paradox is that, in
France at least, historical, philological, even "archival" work—despite the
premium of positivity which it receives in many institutions—remains
very deficient in the domain we have just invoked. In any case, for reasons
that the Collège should analyze, there are enormous and inadmissable delays here—beginning with that of the publication and translation of the
fundamental corpus of the twentieth century. Its translation remains
largely incomplete, dispersed, heterogeneous. This deficiency is not only
serious in itself, but also in what it signifies or entails for philosophical or
scientific research. To cite only these examples, we know that this is the
situation of the works of Freud, Wittgenstein, and, precisely, Heidegger,
which need a complete and, insofar as possible, homogeneous translation,
based on the scientific and complete edition of his writings (now underway). In all these tasks, the Collège could associate its initiatives with
those of other research institutions (CNRS[5] and universities).

D

Numerous indications permit us to affirm that such programs and centers would be active and efficacious, that they would attract many researchers and would bring together many specialties—those of philosophers, but also of philologists, historians, poeticians, linguists, logicians, political scientists and theorists, sociologists, translators, writers, and so forth. They ought thus to be structured in their own identity and at the same time traversed by all the other axes of research. But this should be able to be said of all the research groups we will be led to determine. Another indicator, particularly exemplary in this respect, would be that of "women's studies"—even though, at least at first glance, it does not have a direct relation with the preceding example. I consider this relation essential, but without attempting to demonstrate it here I will recall only a few obvious things. The institutional underdevelopment of these studies in our country is scandalous (in comparison, for example, with the United States, as regards the university, and with the richness and force of these "studies" in France outside of public institutions).

As the "Godelier Report" recalls, in France there is only one "women's studies" research group accredited by the former government (directed by Hélène Cixous, at the University of Paris VIII). On the other hand, it is too evident that if women's studies should, for this very reason, be developed extensively in the Collège, they should also expand, without dissolving, into all the other sites of research.

II. DESTINATION AND ORIENTATION

The "themes" we will situate under this title should by right not be dissociated from the preceding ones, with which they can cross at many points. But an original inflection will mark their treatment. It will be a matter of reactivating or reactualizing categories said to be classical by adjusting them, if possible, to new objects, putting them to the (transforming or deforming) test of situations which may seem unprecedented or specific. All the themes and problems which organize the great philosophical tradition, from Aristotle to Kant, from Leibniz to Hegel and to Marx, from Nietzsche to Bergson, and so forth, around *teleology* and *eschatology, ends* and *aims*, will have to be mobilized in directions as numerous and different as modern biology and genetics, biotechnology, biolinguistics, and "biotics." A new reflection on law in relation to the techno-scientific mu-

tations of medicine will open as well onto the ethical and political dimensions of a thinking of destination. As examples, we suggest engaging in
very precise research at the intersections of the following paths:

A

The philosophical implication *of the life sciences.* In this "domain" of uncertain frontiers, the richness and the acceleration of "discoveries" *engages*
philosophy more than ever in its most essential and most critical ques-
tionings. We say "implication" and "engagement" in order to mark the
fact that it is no doubt a matter of something other than an epistemological reflection which *follows on* scientific production. Without disputing
the necessity of such an epistemology, in this domain and in all others,
must we not also take into account the possibility of "philosophical decisions" opening and orienting new scientific spaces? Here it would not necessarily be a matter of spontaneous or dogmatic philosophy, of residues of
precritical philosophy in the activity of scientists, but of inaugural philo-
sophico-scientific approaches productive, as such, of new bodies of knowledge. While this possibility can claim a noble history in all domains of scientific theory, it seems particularly rich and promising today in all the
spaces which put the life sciences in communication with other sciences
and emerging technical mutations (sciences of language, physics, com-
puting, etc.). The dissociation between all these investigations and all
these resources, like that between philosophy and these techno-sciences,
has to do more often with socio-institutional effects of the scientific or
technical community than with the intrinsic nature of the objects. The
Collège could play a vital role in this regard.

B

*The philosophical, ethico-political, and juridical problems posed by new med-
ical technologies.* The foundations of a new *general deontology.* Whether it
is a matter of demography (in all its dimensions, from the distribution of
nutritional resources to birth control worldwide), gerontology (the science of aging in general and not only of "old age"—of which theoretical
and institutional developments have a worldwide breadth often disregarded in France), genetic manipulation, the enormous problematic of
prostheses and of organ transplants and grafting, biotics (biocomputers
with synthetic genes, constitution of "artificial senses"), or euthanasia—

each time the philosophical stake is obvious. It is not posed simply in terms of knowledge or of mastery but, demanding in this regard the highest competence, it calls as well for ethical interpretation, for taking sides and decisions. It also supposes putting back into play the whole fundamental axiology concerning the values of the body, the integrity of the living, "subject," "ego," "conscience" or "consciousness," individual and community "responsibility." Linked with these are all the questions of a politics of "health" (society's rights and duties with regard to what we call "health," but also the reelaboration of its very concept) and those of a politics of research in this domain (priorities, orientations, articulations with military-industrial research).

C

Psychiatry and psychoanalysis. Certainly we will be attentive here to link them to the research we have just situated, to link them to each other, but also to dissociate them in their most jealous and irreducible originality. This said, in both cases, whether it is a matter of knowledge, "theoretical" discourse, technique, or institution, the necessity of a philosophical discussion is widely recognized and called for by the "practitioners" with whom we have been in contact during our consultations, most widely by those—and they are very numerous in every domain of research—who "deal" today with psychoanalysis in one way or another. Whether we interrogate literature or linguistics, history, ethnology or sociology, pedagogy or law, the very axiomatic of research finds itself transformed in every way by it. Let's not insist here on something so obvious. I will only emphasize a point on which the future directors of the Collège should remain particularly vigilant. This has recently been verified on the occasion of the discussion organized by Maurice Godelier and Gérard Mendel: many psychoanalysts are very concerned to preserve what is in their eyes the irreducible singularity of their discourse and their practice. The majority of psychoanalysts want to maintain the greatest independence with regard to social public health organizations or public research institutions. Whatever one thinks of these very complex problems, with which I prefer not to engage here, it seems to me desirable in any case that the Collège never consider them "resolved" in any way; in other words, that it maintain a policy of reserve and abstention with regard to them, which does not mean that it not pose them in a theoretical mode, rather the contrary. But it should not seek to determine some social inscription of psychoanalysis, for example by means of some kind of link between the Collège and a group of analysts or an analytic institution as such. All research contracts will be made with individuals or with groups *interested* in the psychoanalytic problematic, but not with psychoanalysts *as such* (even if they are that in fact and if their work in the Collège concerns the institution or history of the analytic movement). There is nothing paradoxical in this. The recommendation which I am formulating here, in the interest of everyone and first of all the Collège, addresses a request often formulated by psychoanalysts. A good number among them have told us that they prefer to work in these conditions rather than in a space which would be reserved for them by statute, in the CNRS, for example, or in other research institutions. Whether wrongly or rightly, they fear being too (theoretically) hemmed in and too (sociopolitically) engaged there, and they prefer more open and more multiple exchanges with philosophers, researchers in the social sciences and also—it must be strongly emphasized—in the life or "natural" sciences as well, in France and abroad. This international dimension takes on certain particular aspects here to which some of our correspondents have repeatedly drawn our attention.

D

Law and philosophy of law. There is a spectacular deficiency in the French field here, something of which we were convinced at the start of our mission and which has received the most emphatic confirmation. Many philosophers and jurists regret it and propose that a special effort be launched in this domain. This effort might first be undertaken in the directions we have just indicated by taking account of the legal problems posed by certain modern (technical, economic, political, artistic) mutations. The themes of destination, the gift, and thus exchange and debt lend themselves to this in a particularly privileged way. We should not speak only of the "comparative," ethnosociological, and historical approaches this requires, but also of certain less classical ones, for example, those based on "pragmatic" analyses of the structure of juridical utterances. Inversely, we will also study the juridical conditions of the constitution of works of art or of the production and reception (or destination) of works. Not to mention all the possible connections with a political, even theologico-political, problematic. To limit ourselves to a few indica-

tive examples, here are some "modern" provocations to this new philo-
sophico-juridical reflection, accumulated in their apparent diversity: the
phenomena of the totalitarian society, new techniques of physical and
psychic torture, new conditions of the investment and occupation of
space (urbanism, naval and air space, "space research"), the progress of
computerization or informatization, the ownership and transfers of technology, the ownership, reproduction, and distribution of works of art under new technical conditions and given new materials used in production
and archiving. All these transformations in progress call for a thorough
reelaboration of the conceptuality and axiomatics of law, international
law, public law, and private law. A *new* problematic of human rights is also
under way, progressing slowly and laboriously within the major international organizations. It seems that French philosophy has not been terri-
bly interested in this so far. This deficiency is often dissimulated behind
the classical eloquence of declarations in favor of human rights. However
necessary they are, such declarations no longer take the place of philosophical thought. Such thinking has to measure itself today against a situation without precedent.

E

The police and the army, warfare. Here too, technological mutations in
progress are profoundly transforming the structures, modes of action,
stakes, and aims. Philosophical reflection seems to be keeping too great a
distance from research already under way on this subject in numerous
French and foreign institutes.

The Collège should make possible confrontations between experts (on
the police, different police forces, prison institutions, armies, modern
strategy, and polemology) and other researchers, especially philosophers.
The directions of research are numerous and diverse, as important projects which have come from France and abroad remind us. There is practically no theme evoked by this "projection" that should not, in one way
or another, cross with the problematics of the police, the army, and warfare. Warfare in all its figures, which are not metaphors (ideological warfare, economic warfare, broadcast warfare). Biocybernetics, so-called
smart weapons, and self-guided missiles would here be only the most con-
spicuous and determined paradigms of a problematic of the "sendoff" or
"launch" and of the "destination" in this domain. In fact the field extends

to the regions of game theory, the politics of (military-industrial) research, psychoanalysis, semiotics, rhetoric, law, literature, and the "status of women."

III. LANGUAGES OF DESTINATION, DESTINATIONS
OF LANGUAGE

"Language"—the word is understood here in its most open sense, beyond the limits of the linguistic and the discursive proper, in their oral or graphic form. The values of "information," "communication," "emission," and "transmission" will be included here, certainly, in *all* their forms, yet they will not exhaust it. That is to say directly that, under the title of "language," the study of all "destinal" significations or operations (destining, sending, emitting, transmitting, addressing, giving, receiving, etc.) can and should in turn traverse *all* the Collège's fields of activity. And we have laid down the principle, in the first part of this report, that this activity would not only be theoretical study but also, connected to it, "creation" and performance. Referring for convenience to classical categories, let us indicate the titles and the principal paths of these intertwined research efforts.

A

Philosophy of language. What can its specificity be, if it is neither simply an epistemology of linguistics nor a linguistics? How is this "specificity" constituted? History and analysis of its problematic and its categories in relation to all the forms of *teleology*. What is a sender, a receiver, an emitter, a receptor, a message, and so forth? How are their "pragmatic" unity and their conceptual identity constituted? Across all the dimensions of this analysis (metaphysical, psycho-sociological, psychoanalytic, techno-economic), we will encounter the problems of decidability and undecidability. We will recognize them in their logical or semantic forms, in pragmatic paradoxes, or again in the interpretation of "works of art."

B

Linguistics. As with all the "immense domains" which I am naming here, it is a question of signaling what the Collège's precise angle of approach should be. We will not cover all the territory of linguistic research there, nor will we teach all of linguistics, even supposing that this could be done anywhere. We will try, rather, while providing an "introduction" to linguistic research in its newest directions, to interrogate linguists, during debates with other researchers, philosophers or not, on the subject of philosophy in linguistics and linguistics in philosophy. Not only in terms of the dogmatic presuppositions on each side. Other modes of implication are at least as interesting, as much from the historical as from the systematic point of view. We can interrogate anew, for example, the inscription of philosophical discourse in a natural language and in the "philosophy of language" it tends to entail; we can interrogate the philosophical decisions, assumed or not, of every linguistics. These decisions are not inevitably negative ("epistemological obstacles"), and not necessarily to be confused with the philosophical discourse or reference *exhibited* by linguistics ("Cartesian linguistics," "Rousseauist linguistics," "Herderian," "Humboldtian"). In medieval thought, so neglected by French academic philosophy, these explorations would doubtless be among the most fruitful. But these are only examples.

c

Semiotics. We can transpose here what has just been said about the philosophical stakes of linguistics. The field will be larger since it covers not only linguistic systems but also nonlinguistic sign systems. We will be particularly interested in *intersemiotic* functionings (speech and gesture, formal graphs and natural or ordinary language, works of art with multiple inscriptions: text, painting, music, etc.). The reflection will thus extend— in a nonencyclopedic but incursive mode, let's not forget—to all systems of signals and all codes, beginning with those of genetic information. As for the necessary problematic of "artificial intelligence," we will not consider as secured or guaranteed any of the philosophical axiomatics with which all the research in progress is engaged, beginning with the opposition between the "artificial" and the whole series of its others.

Likewise, we will not be content to sift and orient, at the start, the impressive range of this "field" by reference to questions of "destination." We will leave open, and constantly reopen, the question of knowing whether the thought of language depends on "philosophy," semiotic theory, or linguistic theory, and whether it is limited by their horizon.

D

Pragmatics. Despite everything it can share with a linguistics, a semiotics, a general semantics, or a philosophy of language, pragmatics is developing today, especially outside France, as a relatively original discipline. Whether it concerns enunciation ("speech acts") or a more complex semiotic context (including, for example, gestural behavior), it seems to me that it is effecting a general redistribution of great consequence today. Besides its own rich results, it entails an essential coimplication of "disciplines" that formerly compartmentalized or protected themselves in the name of their own scientificity. That is why pragmatics seems to me to require a particularly sensitive place in the Collège, that of a "crossroads" of heavy traffic (philosophy, semantics, linguistics, semiotics, artistic theory and practice, interpretation of juridical performatives). Given the importance of the stakes, given the place that the Collège should grant to the "performative" dimension (cf. the first part of this report), and given as well that dispersed work is proliferating today without specific institutional resources (based on Austin's theory of speech acts and its tradition, but sometimes deviating from them to the breaking point), the Collège should create a site of coordination and, later, a real research center which, though outside the Collège, would remain associated with it. Numerous proposals in this direction, sometimes highly elaborate ones, have come to us; we foresaw that, and we sought out and called for them.

E

Technology of telecommunications. "Fundamental" reflection on the concepts of "communication" and "long-distance communication," on the no doubt structural and thus irreducible links between *techne* in general and "telecommunications," from its "simple" and "elementary" forms. In other words, the technology of telecommunications is not one technology among others; whence the link between this problematic and that of distance, of oriented spacing and thus of destination. Among all the possible foci of this reflection, let us signal these, which are among the most necessary today (and tomorrow).

1. Aims, structures, and putting into practice of all *modes of archiving*—and thus of communication (philosophical, scientific, artistic, etc.). Since the necessity of this work and these experiments is too obvious with re-

gard to new techniques (microfilm, data banks, telematics, video), I prefer to insist on the *book* (history of writing and history of the book; the model of the book and its effects on the structure of works and discourses, especially philosophical discourses; the technical and political problems of the culture of the book; the crisis and the future of publishing in general, and of scientific, philosophical, or literary publishing in particular; national and international dimensions of the problem—dominant languages and minority cultures, etc.). Of course, these questions can no longer be considered today as annexes in a research institution such as the Collège. They will thus be treated in all their breadth and acuity, with the special help of experts (experts in the new techniques of archiving and distribution, printers, publishers, librarians, etc.). These initiatives will be coordinated with those which can be undertaken elsewhere (for example in CESTA, CREA, the Ministry of Culture, and the Direction du Livre).[6]

2. The *mass media.* Philosophical and scientific reflection, theoretical, empirical, and experimental "mediology." Among the countless tasks required in this domain, the Collège could first of all privilege the "cultural," artistic, scientific, and philosophical aspects. This will lead it to a much closer analysis of the relations between "media" culture, research, and teaching. Without a "reactive attitude, without "rejection" (which is in any case doomed to powerlessness), faced with the extension of the mass media, the Collège will pose the "deontological," "ethico-juridical," or "ethico-political" problems associated with such an extension. It will attempt to propose new uses for these technical possibilities (public or private) and will seek to arrange access to them. What goes for the mass media goes as well for other more diverse and less widespread modes of communication, for example the private or "free radio" stations, or for all the techniques of telecommunication. A great deal of work is under way in foreign universities and in other French institutions: the Collège should associate itself with it while maintaining the originality of its own approach.

3. *Computer science, telematics, robotics, biotechnologies.* In liaison with other research centers, particularly with the whole CESTA network, the Collège should participate, in its style and with its resources in the ongoing scientific and philosophical reflection on "orientation," the modes of production and appropriation of new techniques, whose spectacular acceleration is transforming the whole of culture and knowledge. This work

should, as much as possible, connect technical initiation—the provision of basic proficiency—with philosophical analysis (ethical, juridical, political) of the stakes.

F

Poietics. In what may be a somewhat conventional manner, we choose this term to regroup everything that concerns, in classical terms, theories of art and artistic practices. The title "poietics" at least has the merit of recalling a double dimension: theoretical and necessarily discursive research on the one hand, and experimental, "creative," and performative research on the other.

The Collège's projects (at least such as they have been interpreted and represented by our mission) have elicited spectacular interest in these domains. The research proposals in this domain have been more numerous and more eager than in any other, above all, we must note, on the part of French researchers or artists. We could have expected this. It confirms, among other things, the difficulty these initiatives have in finding a site—and support—in this country's theoretico-institutional topology.

We insist that, whenever possible, the Collège seek in these domains to associate itself with the numerous initiatives under way in Paris and above all, regionally and abroad, whether public (for example, those sponsored or supported by the Ministry of Culture) or private. Privileged attention will be accorded to those which bring "theorists" together with "creators"—who are sometimes one and the same.

Besides all the "great questions" to be reactivated (origin of the work of art, meaning, reference, art and truth, art and national culture, etc.), what all this research will have in common will concern primarily:

— The structures of destination and orientation ("aim of the beautiful," with or "without a concept"): Who produces what? Destined for whom? Theories of reception, "taste," the art market, phenomena of evaluation, legitimation, distribution, and so forth.

— The thematic of destination (destiny, law, chance and necessity) within works and on the "production" side.

— The interpretation of works and the philosophy or hermeneutics involved there. Transformation of "art criticism" in the new audiovisual spaces of the press and publishing.

—Mutation of the arts (of forms and materials) following scientific and technical advances.

—Critique and transformation of the customary classification of the arts.

While the necessity of a different philosophical questioning is perceptible in all the arts, and while it is primarily the "creators" who have insisted on this, the urgency is no doubt most marked in literature or poetry and music. During the last two decades, proliferating work has mobilized great resources (philosophy, human sciences—linguistics, psychoanalysis, etc.—logico-mathematical sciences), generally outside academic institutions or their customary divisions. An entity which we could call "literature and philosophy," for example, while it is practically recognized in foreign universities (especially in the United States), remains contraband in our country. We have received important projects leading in this direction; others, just as new and as necessary, bring together music and philosophy, musicians, music theorists, and philosophers in an original way. But without a doubt, analogous attempts might be made with the visual arts, the so-called spatial arts, the theater, the cinema, and television.

IV. TRANSLATION, TRANSFER(ENCE), TRANSVERSALITY

Under this title we will indicate and recommend all the transferential proceedings that, *as such*, define the precise specificity of an *international* Collège open first of all to *diagonal* or *transversal* interscientific research. Translations, then, in the triple sense, whose division we borrow for convenience from Jakobson: *intralinguistic* (phenomena of translation—commentary, reformulation, transposition—within the same language), *interlinguistic* (in the common or "proper" sense of the word, says Jakobson: from one language to another), *intersemiotic* (from one semiotic medium to another, for example speech/painting), but translations also in the larger sense of the transfer of a model or paradigm (rhetoric, art, sciences).

Here are some exemplary directions. It is understood that they should cross with other paths situated under other titles and orient themselves according to the general scheme of "destination."

A. "Basic" or "fundamental" research on language, the multiplicity of languages, and the general problematic of translation. History and theories of translation, in its linguistic, philosophical, religious, and political, poetic dimensions. Contemporary problems of State languages and minority languages (extinction and reawakening, participation in the international scientific and philosophical community, domination and appropriation of techno-science by language).

B. Setting up specialized *centers for linguistic training*, for French or foreign researchers, inside the Collège or in association with it.

C. *The modern technology of translation: theoretical problems.* Translation machines, "artificial intelligences," programming—in a determined language—of data banks and other modes of archiving or communication.

D. *Languages and philosophical discourse.* The role of natural (national) languages in the constitution of the philosophical as such; history of "philosophical" languages; the political, theologico-political, and pedagogical dimensions: how does a philosophical language become dominant? This work will be coordinated closely with work in the so-called comparatist problematic and on the philosophical institution (see below). Each time, the question already posed will be recast: that of the processes by which "philosophical objects" are formed and legitimated.

E. *"Comparatism" in philosophy*: an empirical and uncertain title, but research whose necessity admits of no doubt. The urgency, especially in our country, makes itself felt massively, and the testimonies here are numerous and eloquent. Everywhere it has imposed itself, for better or worse, the word "comparatism" has certainly covered approaches that are difficult to delimit, not quite sure of the existence of their object, and even less of their method.

Nevertheless, as is sometimes the case, this fragility or this empiricism has not prevented some work from imposing itself in strange institutional conditions which would justify an entire study. It is doubtful that "comparatism" *as such* has much meaning in philosophy, but the very critique of this vague notion should itself be produced in the course of analyses which are today too underdeveloped in the West, and particularly so in France (we are speaking of philosophical analyses and not only of "culturological" ones). Let us situate this schematically.

a. *On the difference between thought (in general) and philosophy.* On systems of thought which are not necessarily limited to the "philosophical" form as it was born and has developed under this name in the West. All of these "thoughts," if not strictly philosophical, are not necessarily reducible to what, from a philosophical standpoint, we name with categories like "culture," "worldview," ethico-religious "system of representations," in the West and elsewhere. Often the attempts to think beyond the philosophical or beyond what links metaphysics to Western techno-science bring to light affinities with non-European (African or Far Eastern) thought. Systematic work and exchanges at these frontiers should cross with others, which we might entitle:

b. *Philosophical systems and religious systems*, within and outside the West. Renewal of theological research (to link up with the renaissance of religious and theologico-political movements all over the world).

c. *Philosophical systems and mythological systems.*

d. *Philosophy and ethnocentrism. Problematic of ethnophilosophy* (a wide and exemplary debate which has developed in Africa starting from the critique, by Paulin Hountondji, of Tempels's *Bantu Philosophy*.[7]

This could be developed in relation to the questions posed by a (semantic, linguistic, ethno-culturological) study of the significations attached to gestures and discourses of destination (giving/receiving, emitting, transmitting, sending, addressing, orienting).

e. *Philosophical "transcontinentality."* On the difference (intraphilosophical and intra-European in its manifestations, even if it affects philosophical institutions that are non-European yet constructed on a European model) between philosophical traditions. What does this difference consist in, once it is no longer determined on the basis of objects or "contents" alone, nor simply of national languages, nor finally of doctrinal conflicts? Over the centuries what I propose to call *philosophical continents* have been constituted. This movement has accelerated and its traits have made themselves apparent in the last two centuries. "Continent": the metaphor, if it were simply geographical, would not be rigorous; it is justified to the extent that geographical or geographico-national limits have often surrounded traditional entities and institutional territories (French, German, Anglo-Saxon philosophy, etc.). Today it is just as difficult to get through the "customs" and the "police" of these philosophical traditions as it is to situate their borderline, their essential trait. An analysis (which we cannot undertake here) would show, it seems to me, that these frontiers do not depend strictly on language, nationality, the types of objects privileged as philosophical, rhetoric, the socio-institutional modalities of the production and reproduction of philosophical discourse (in the educational system and elsewhere), or general historico-political conditions. And yet the accumulation and intrication of all these conditions have engendered these "continental" formations so closed in on themselves. Their effects are multiple and already interesting in themselves. This original quasi-incommunicability does not take the form of a simple opacity, of a radical absence of exchange; it is rather the delay and disorder of all the phenomena of translation, the general aggravation of all the misunderstandings. These do not obtain only or essentially between countries or national philosophical communities. To the extent that each of the great traditions is also represented within each national community, the borders are reconstituted inside each country, in diverse configurations.

Inversely, following a process that is also interesting, this situation is slowly beginning to evolve. Certain philosophers are more and more sensitive to it here and there. Movements are beginning to reflect on and transform this "babelization." An urgent, difficult, original task, without a doubt that of philosophy itself today, if some such thing exists and has to affirm itself. It is in any case the first task for an International College of Philosophy, and the most irreplaceable. Even if the Collège had been created only to this end, its existence would be completely justified.

Starting with its first four years, the Collège should prepare the following initiatives:

Setting up international working groups, including each time French and foreign researchers. They will work in France (in Paris and as much as possible outside of Paris) and abroad. Their competencies will be not only philosophical, but also, for example, linguistic. They will seek the cooperation of other experts, in France and abroad. All of them will work to analyze and transform the situation we have just been describing. They will take initiatives and multiply proposals concerning exchanges, cooperation, meetings, contracts of association, translations, and joint publications, in all the domains of interest to the Collège. As the Collège's constant perspective, this thematic and problematic of "intercontinental" difference will be a high-priority program during the first years. Everywhere such groups can be constituted, each time according to original modalities, they will be—in (Eastern and Western) Europe and outside Europe, whether it is a matter of philosophy in the strictly occidental sense or (see above) of nonphilosophical "thought."

A program of large international colloquia will be organized as soon as the Collège is created, as its inaugural act. It will not be a matter of colloquia in the traditional form (formal juxtaposition of large lectures and panels). Those organized by the Collège will be the culmination of two or three years of intense work, in France and abroad, with their active preparation entrusted to specialized philosophers. Periods of study in residence toward this end should be the object of agreements and support in France and abroad: study in residence at the Collège for several foreign philosophers, abroad for as many French philosophers. It seems to me that the first large meetings of this type should concern first of all French and German thought, French and Anglo-Saxon thought. We will make sure that the most diverse currents of thought are represented there. But particular attention will naturally be given to what is most alive and what is most specific, whether it is dominant in academic institutions or not. And starting with the preparation of these two large colloquia, setting up other groups should give rise to future meetings (Italy, Spain, Latin America, India, the Arab countries, Africa, and the countries of the Far East, etc.).

V. THE INSTITUTIONAL ORIENTATIONS OF PHILOSOPHY (RE-SEARCH AND TEACHING)

These too are oriented, to begin with, by the problematic of *destination* (constitution of senders and receivers—individual or collective "subjects"—units and legitimation of messages, structures of transmission and reception, etc.). Research of great breadth will be brought to bear on the history and system of philosophical institutions, whether of teaching or research, French or foreign. On the one hand "theoretical" (much, if not everything, remains to be done in this domain), they will also be largely practical and experimental. They will aim to develop and enrich philosophical research and teaching. The president of the republic invited this and expressly committed himself to it in his letter of May 8, 1981 to Greph. This necessity was recalled by the minister of research and industry, in his letter to the mission of May 18, 1982: "At a time when the government is preparing to extend the study of philosophy in secondary education, it is important that research devoted to this discipline be assured of the conditions and instruments best suited to its scope." And the minister specified further on that the Collège should be "inclined to favor innovative initiatives, open to the reception of unprecedented research and pedagogical experiments."

The reference I make here to the projects and early work of the Groupe de Recherches sur l'Enseignement Philosophique (Greph) and to the États Généraux de la Philosophie (1979) has only an *indicative value*.[8] Other paths are possible, and the Collège should vigilantly maintain an opening for them.

Everyone who wants to participate in this research should be provided with the means to do so, particularly secondary school teachers, university and lycée students.

In order to give a schematic idea of such research, I will cite the opening of Greph's "Avant-Projet"[9] in the hope that this group be associated with the Collège, under conditions that guarantee at once maximum cooperation and strict independence on the part of both.

Avant-Projet:
For the Constitution of a Research Group
on the Teaching of Philosophy

Preliminary work has made it clear that it is today both possible and necessary to organize a set of research investigations into what relates philosophy to its teaching. This research, which should have both a critical and a practical bearing, would attempt initially to respond to certain questions. We will define these questions here, under the rubric of a rough anticipation, with reference to common notions, which are to be discussed. Greph would be, first of all and at least, a place that would make possible the coherent, lasting, and relevant organization of such a discussion.

1. What is the connection between philosophy and teaching in general?

What is teaching in general? What is teaching for philosophy? What is it to teach philosophy? In what way would teaching (a category to be analyzed in the context of the pedagogical, the didactic, the doctrinal, the disciplinary, etc.) be essential to philosophical practice? How has this essential indissociability of the didacto-philosophical been constituted and differentiated? Is it possible, and under what conditions, to propose a general, critical, and transformative history of this indissociability?

These questions are of great theoretical generality. They obviously demand elaboration. Such would be, precisely, the first work of Greph.

In opening up these questions it should be possible—let us say only *for example* and in a very vaguely indicative way—to study:

(a) models of didactic operations legible, with their rhetoric, logic, psychagogy, etc., within *written* discourses (from Plato's dialogues, for example, through Descartes' *Meditations*, Spinoza's *Ethics*, Hegel's *Encyclopedia* or *Lectures*, etc., up to all the so-called philosophical works of modernity), as well as

(b) *pedagogical practices* administered according to rules in fixed places, in private or public *establishments* since the Sophists: for example, the *quaestio* and *disputatio* of the Scholastics, etc., up to the courses and other pedagogical activities instituted today in the collèges, lycées, grade schools, universities, etc. What are the forms and norms of these practices? What effects are sought and obtained from them? Things to be studied here would be, for example: the "dialogue," maieutics, the master/disciple relationship, the question, the quiz, the test, the examination, the competitive examination, the inspection, publication, the frames and programs of discourse, the dissertation, the presentation, the *leçon*, the thesis, the procedures of verification and of control, repetition, etc.

These different types of problematics should be articulated together, as rigorously as possible.

2. How is the didactico-philosophical inscribed in the so-called instinctual, historical, political, social, and economic fields?

How does it *inscribe itself there*, that is, how does it operate and represent—(to) itself—its inscription, and how is it *inscribed* in its very representation? What are the "general logic" and specific modes of this inscription? Of its normalizing normativity and of its normalized normativity? For example, at the same time as they prescribe a pedagogy indissociable from a philosophy, the academy, the lycée, the Sorbonne, preceptorships of every kind, the universities or royal, imperial, or republican schools of modern times also prescribe, in specific and differentiated ways, a moral and political system that forms at once both the object and the actualized structure of pedagogy. What about this pedagogical effect? How to delimit it, theoretically and practically?

Once again, these indicative questions remain too general. They are above all formulated, by design, according to current representations and therefore must be specified, differentiated, criticized, and transformed. They could in fact lead one to believe that essentially, indeed uniquely, it

is a matter of constructing a sort of "critical theory of philosophical doc-
trinality or disciplinarity," of reproducing the traditional debate that philosophy has regularly opened about its "crisis." This "reproduction" will itself be one of the objects of our work. In fact, Greph should above all
participate in the transformative analytics of a "present" situation, questioning and analyzing itself in this analytics and displacing itself from the
position of what, in this "situation," makes it possible and necessary. The
preceding questions should thus be constantly reworked by these practical motivations. Also, without ever excluding the importance of these
problems outside of France, we would first of all insist strongly on the
conditions of the teaching of philosophy "here-and-now," in today's
France. And in its concrete urgency, in the more or less dissimulated violence of its contradictions, the "here-and-now" would no longer be simply a philosophical object. This is not a restriction of the program, but the
condition of Greph's work on its own field of practice and in relation to
the following questions:

A. What are the past and present historical conditions of this teaching
system?

What about its power? What forces give it its power? What forces limit
it? What about its legislation, its juridical code and traditional code? Its
external and internal norms? Its social and political field? Its relation to
other (historical, literary, aesthetic, religious, scientific, for example) kinds
of teaching? To other institutionalized discursive practices (psychoanalysis
in general and so-called training analysis in particular—for example, etc.)?
From these different points of view, what is the specificity of the didactico-philosophical operation? Can laws be produced, analyzed, and tested
on objects such as, for example (these are only empirically accumulated
indications): the role of the Ideologues or of a Victor Cousin? Of their
philosophy or of their political interventions in the French university?
The constitution of the philosophy class, the evolution of the figure of the
philosophy professor since the nineteenth century, in the lycées, in the
khâgne,[10] in the écoles normales, in the university, the Collège de France;
the place of the disciple, the student, the candidate; the history and functioning of:

   (a) the examinations and competition programs, the form of their tests (the
       authors present and those excluded, the organization of subjects, themes,
       and problems, etc.);

(b) the juries, the *inspection générale*, advisory committees, etc.;

(c) the forms and norms for assessment or sanction (grading, ranking, comments, reports on competitions, examinations, and theses, etc.);

(d) so-called research organisms (CNRS, Fondation Thiers,[11] etc.);

(e) research tools (libraries, selected texts, manuals of the history of philosophy or on philosophy in general, their relations with the field of commercial publishing, on the one hand, and with the authorities responsible for public instruction or national education, on the other);

(f) the places of work (the topological structure of the class, the seminar, the lecture hall, etc.);

(g) the recruiting of teachers and their professional hierarchy (the social background and political stances of pupils, students, teachers, etc.).

B. What are the stakes of the struggles within and around philosophical education, today, in France?

The analysis of this conflictual field implies an interpretation of philosophy in general *and*, consequently, taking stands. It *therefore* calls for action.

As far as France is concerned, it will be necessary to connect all this work with a reflection on French philosophy, on its own traditions and institutions, especially on the different currents that have traversed it over the course of this century. A new history of French thought in all its components (those which have dominated it and those which have been marginalized or repressed) ought to orient an analysis of the present situation. We will trace these premises as far back as possible, while insisting on the most recent modernity, on its complex relation to the problematics of philosophy and its limits, to the arts and sciences but also to French sociopolitical history and to the country's ideological movements, as much those of the French right, for example, as those of French socialisms.

—Translated by Thomas Pepper;
edited by Deborah Esch and Thomas Keenan

Report of the Committee on Philosophy and Epistemology (1990)

Preamble

The Committee on Philosophy and Epistemology, cochaired by Jacques Bouveresse and Jacques Derrida, and composed of Jacques Brunschwig, Jean Dhombres, Catherine Malabou, and Jean-Jacques Rosat, met over a period of six months, from January to June 1989. Its work was carried out in two phases: First was a phase of preparatory reflection and of discussion and consultation with representatives from diverse bodies and associations, such as the Inspection Générale de Philosophie, the Inspection Générale de la Formation des Maîtres, unions (SGEN, SNES, SNESUP),[1] the Association des Professeurs de Philosophie (Association of Professors of Philosophy), Greph, the Association des Bibliothécaires (Association of Librarians—FADBEN). The second phase involved the elaboration and composition of the present report, which includes four general principles and seven detailed proposals. These are preceded by five summary points intended to synthesize the basic orientations of the committee's consideration of the situation and future of the teaching of philosophy in France—in secondary education, in the first cycle of the universities, and in the future Instituts Universitaires de Formation des Maîtres.[2]

Five Fundamental Points

(REPORT SUMMARY)

1. Philosophy should constitute an indispensable part of every coherent

and structured program of intellectual training with a critical dimension, starting from a certain level of knowledge and culture.

Since nothing in the current organization of knowledge and culture could justify philosophy's having a position overhanging the other disciplines, philosophy must be understood not as occupying a position superior to those of the other disciplines taught, but as following their approaches by formulating its own questions. Such a conception implies:

A. That the teaching of philosophy, like that of the other disciplines, should be progressive and yet respect the specificity of its own approach, which would obviously in no case be reduced to a simple cumulative process of the acquisition of philosophical knowledge.

B. That the connections between the teaching of philosophy and that of the other disciplines should be systematically reinforced, developed, and considered as constitutive of every practice of philosophy.

C. That philosophy should consider it one of its obligations and one of its opportunities to facilitate the transition, interaction, and communication not only between literary culture and scientific culture but equally, more generally, among the different sectors of knowledge and culture, whose dispersal poses so many problems for students today.

2. Like every basic discipline, philosophy must give rise to teaching that respects its identity, articulates it with other disciplines, and extends over several years the cycle of *introduction, training,* and *specialization.*

A. The *period of introduction* will begin at least in the Première, with two mandatory hours of philosophy per week distributed according to different models during the year. The philosophy teacher will organize the introduction to philosophy *as such* in collaboration with teachers representing three groups of disciplines: philosophy/sciences (mathematics, physics, and biology), philosophy / social sciences (sociology, history, geography, economics), philosophy/languages / arts and literatures. Among the benefits to be expected from this innovation and from the intersections that, in any case, should never dissolve the unity of the disciplines, this new practice would allow for a balanced philosophical training that to this point has too often, indeed exclusively, been dominated by literary models or opposed to the models of the social sciences or the sciences in general.

B. The *period of training*, or the "high point," will remain that of the Terminale. Now taught in all sections of the classical and technical lycées, philosophy must retain a timetable sufficient for effective training, which excludes dilution, fragmentation, or reduction. This timetable should in no case be inferior to the present one.

C. The *period of specialization* will belong to the cycle of the universities, not only in literary but also scientific, legal, medical, and other studies. In each case, it will be possible to link this in-depth *general* philosophical culture to a critical reflection more specifically adapted to professionalization (for example, for future doctors, the study of questions of medical ethics, of the history and epistemology of biology).

3. Given the organizing role the stage of the baccalauréat plays, the system of our proposals assumes a prudent, but determined, innovation on this level. The credibility of the philosophy part of the baccalauréat implies a clear *contract* with the candidates as regards the skills demanded of them, and a *diversification* of the exercises that *relativize the role of the essay*; a set of measures will have to guarantee that students will be faced only with *questions with which they have previously been able to acquire real familiarity*.

In the current conditions, most of the baccalauréat exams do not meet the minimal demands of a philosophy essay, and the test is not a reliable instrument for the evaluation of the skills actually acquired by students. For many reasons—the limitless diversity of subjects; their extreme generality and the lack of direct connections between them and what was studied during the year; the call for rhetorical capacities beyond those of the majority of current students, particularly those in technical education; and so on—it seems mysterious and random to the candidates; not being masterable, it elicits anxiety, cramming, or giving up, and little by little puts the teaching of philosophy itself into question.

In the general baccalauréat, we propose that the four-hour written test combine two exercises:

—a series of questions to evaluate the assimilation of basic philosophical vocabulary and elementary conceptual distinctions, as well as the knowledge of points of reference in the history of philosophy (for example, six questions would be proposed in the framework of the general program, students choosing three; one hour in length);

—an essay test (or the choice of a *commentaire de texte*) exclusively on the notions, problems, and texts determined by the special program (three hours in length).

For the technical baccalauréat, we propose that the test be made oral and that it consist in questions based on a dossier established by the student during the year.

4. The Programs

The precise definition of the programs would of course come from the Conseil National des Programmes d'Enseignement (National Council on Education Programs). However, the principles stated and the reforms proposed above imply a profound transformation of their conception, structures, and content.

The most salient consequence is no doubt the distinction that will have to be made (with the necessary differentiations for each type of Terminale class) between:

4.1. a *general* program, defined long-term at the national level, and

4.2. a *special* program, defined annually at the level of each of the academies.[3]

The general program should include:

4.1.1. A group of notions chosen from the most fundamental in the tradition and practice of philosophy. This group of "contents" should be significantly more restricted than that of the current programs.

4.1.2. A group of methodological notions corresponding to the basic [*fondamentaux*] tools of theoretical reflection; it would be more a question of learning to use these correctly than of defining them without any context.

4.2. The special program would be made up of two or three basic philosophical problems, formulated on the basis of the group defined in 4.1.1. The teachers in each academy will have to be present or represented at the agencies responsible for choosing these.

4.3. As for the texts to be studied, a list of (two or three) philosophical works will also be put on the program annually, according to the same modalities, in every academy. The group from which these works will be chosen could be expanded considerably in relation to the current programs, in particular the contemporary works. The philosophical significance of the works should nonetheless remain beyond question in every case.

5. Teacher training: All teachers in primary and secondary education, no matter what discipline they are preparing to teach, should have the benefit, during their training, of instruction in philosophy.

Teacher training should have as its objective, in addition to acquiring the professional qualities required to fulfill the task of education successfully, that of a constructive and critical reflection on teaching itself. All teachers should be able to question themselves about the necessarily problematic aspect of their practice, which of course cannot be limited to the application of pedagogic recipes.

Moreover, a pluridisciplinary conception of teaching, like that developed here, implies that all teachers be able to have the means of constructing a reflection on the historical and logical connections between diverse fields of knowledge taught in schools and the lycées. That is to say that, on the basis of the demand for such a transversality, in all the branches of teacher training, instruction in philosophy is necessary.

Future teachers of philosophy, in addition to their basic training, should be prepared: (1) to keep up with the significant evolutions in contemporary knowledge; (2) to master the new pedagogical practices called for by the preceding proposals.

Principles

FIRST PRINCIPLE: **To extend the teaching of philosophy by structuring it in three stages, with a high point in the Terminale.**

A. Learning philosophy takes time, more than the current eight months of teaching in the Terminale. More time is needed to familiarize oneself with an approach, problems, a vocabulary, and authors. Philosophy is the only discipline students are expected to learn in a single year. *From the point of view of students*: this status as exception is an anomaly; they consider the brevity of the teaching of philosophy a handicap in assimilating this new discipline; they overwhelmingly wish to begin earlier. *From the point of view of teachers*: experience leads to the conclusion that it is often only after several months (in February or at Easter) that students (and often even good students) begin to understand what is expected of them, and that they stop practicing philosophy at the very moment they become capable of doing so. The teaching of philosophy has too often been conceived according to the model of the conversion, which would have the student pass from common opinion to the philosophical spirit all at once and all of a sudden. The teaching of philosophy should rather be envisaged as an apprenticeship that takes place through a methodical acquisition that is progressive and adapted to the rhythm of students and the knowledge and skills required to conduct true philosophical reflection.

B. Despite everything in the history of philosophy that might have claimed to justify putting philosophy in a position overhanging the other disciplines, this relation of hegemonic exteriority is essentially a relic; it is less fruitful and less tenable than ever. Philosophy is not above the sciences and the humanities; it follows their approaches by posing its own questions. That equally supposes that it goes along with them at different levels at which they are learned. The teaching of philosophy must be conceived no longer as a final crowning *but as a series of constitutive moments indispensable for all intellectual development starting from a certain level of knowledge and culture.*

That is why we propose to reorganize philosophical training by structuring it in three stages:

1. A period of *introduction*, beginning in the Première, within the framework of interdisciplinary teaching.

2. A period of *training*: the Terminale should remain the high point of the teaching of philosophy. Now taught in all sections of classical and technical lycées, philosophy must retain a timetable sufficient for effective training, which excludes dilution, fragmentation, or reduction. *This timetable should in no case be inferior to the present one.*

3. A period of *specialization* in the first cycle of the universities, not only in literary but also scientific, legal, medical, and other studies, allowing students at once to broaden their philosophical culture and to consider more specifically what they are studying and their future professions (for example, for future doctors, questions of medical and biological ethics and of the epistemology of biology).

Before venturing a few proposals on the forms and contents of the teaching of philosophy outside the Terminale, we should recall the spirit in which such an innovation is conceived, in other words, say why it seems necessary and what the principal and minimal conditions are, outside of which it not only would become meaningless but could even have negative effects.

In our opinion it is obviously a matter of enhancing and developing philosophical reflection and knowledge by ensuring the teaching of philosophy an extension, a space, a time, and a consistency, that is to say, a *coherence*. For a long time, these rights have been recognized for all the so-called basic [*fondamentales*] disciplines. *No basic discipline is confined to a single academic year.* We therefore radically disapprove of every interpretation or implementation of our project that would not move in the direction of this development and this increased coherence. That would be a serious misappropriation. Nothing ought to compromise, and everything must, on the contrary, reinforce, indissociably, the unity of the discipline of philosophy, the originality of the modes of questioning, research, and discussion that have constituted it throughout history, and thus the professional identity of those who teach it. The proposals that follow should in no case, under the pretext of interdisciplinarity or of the necessity of opening philosophy to other disciplines and vice versa, give rise to a process of division, dispersion, or dissolution.

For the same reason, the concrete and intolerable conditions suffered by so many teachers of philosophy (too many classes with a limited timetable, too many students in each class, and so forth) should be transformed profoundly. The proposals we are making would be meaningless, and would have no interest, no chance, they would meet legitimate opposition from all teachers, were they not implemented in a new context.

Among all the elements of this innovation, an absolute priority thus falls to these two conditions: a reduction of the course load or the number of students in each class and of the maximum number of classes for which each teacher is responsible. What is more, it would be desirable for a teacher's work to be defined not only in terms of the number of hours of class, as is currently the case, but also in terms of the number of students and classes for which they are responsible.

Although we cannot recall here all the research and experiences that seem to us to justify the presence of the teaching of philosophy before the

Terminale, we are certain that the access to philosophy is not and should not be conditioned by an "age" (which, moreover, would vary from one student to another as they pass from the Première to the Terminale), nor by the borderline between two classes.[4] The roots of this old bias have now been widely and publicly acknowledged, analyzed, called into question. This bias is today more harmful than ever.

It is important that the basic [*fondamentaux*] teachings, whether scientific or not, and especially when they contribute to the education of responsible citizens, trained to be vigilant in reading, language, interpretation, and evaluation, be linked with a critical and philosophical culture. We are speaking here of the French as well as the European citizen. What is more, "some philosophy" is taught or inculcated, without a "philosophy teacher," before the Terminale and outside of France, in an undeclared form, through other disciplines, and it would be better to be aware of this fact and of these problems. We propose to treat them explicitly, in theory and practice, instead of avoiding them.

On the other hand, we must stress once again that, whether it is a matter of aptitude, desire, or demand, many students are ready to tackle philosophy before the Terminale and are surprised that this access is not given them officially. All the more so (a very serious argument for a democratic teaching), since the numerous students who do not reach the Terminale are thus refused *all* access to philosophy.

It indeed seems that many problems encountered by philosophy teachers and by their students in the Terminale stem from this lack of preparation and from the necessity, which is also the impossibility, of concentrating the wealth of programs in too short a period of time.

To have any chance of becoming effective, the introduction to philosophy in the Première should be undertaken with the utmost determination. It should be the object of a profound structural decision, and therefore should in no case have the status of a precarious and optional experiment. This experimental status should be reserved for the extension of the same project, according to the same model, in the years to come, before the Première and outside of France. Whatever its premises and actual state, the presence of philosophy in French secondary education is, let us never forget, a historical opportunity whose survival, but also whose conditions of development and success, it is our duty to ensure.

Let us recall another indispensable condition: it concerns the inscription of this new teaching in an organic cycle over at least three years, from the Première in the lycée to the first year of university or preparatory classes for the grandes écoles.[5] It is in particular necessary to link closely the programs of the Première and the Terminale and to orient the training of the teachers in all the disciplines concerned in this direction.

The consequences of this innovation will have to be drawn ambitiously and systematically in regard to everything concerning the theoretical and pedagogical training of teachers, whether in the competitive entrance exams for the écoles normales[6] or in the Instituts Universitaires de Formation des Maîtres or, more generally, in competitive examinations for recruiting teachers.[7]

It is important to bring together, first, teachers of philosophy in secondary and higher education, then these latter and representatives of the other disciplines concerned to reflect together on establishing and renewing programs. This would take place, on the national scale, in regards to the generality of norms and programs, and on the regional scale, of the academies and lycées, in regards to more specific choices and determinations. This would be one of the tasks confided to the standing committee on the revision of programs.

National norms and prescriptions will also no doubt be indispensable, whether they concern the content or the form of these new teachings. But they will have to leave a lot of room for initiative on the part of teachers, in the university and the lycées, then within each establishment, where contractual practice should bring together, in flexible and renewable fashion, teachers of several disciplines. This would be a privileged, indeed exemplary, space in which to inaugurate or develop transdisciplinary teachings and to train students as well as teachers.

SECOND PRINCIPLE: **To link philosophy more closely to the other disciplines so that it contributes to the unity and coherence of education, without losing any of its specificity.**

The need is making itself felt to give coherence and unity to programs, to show that, while areas of study and approaches differ, each student's education is a global process that one must endeavor to make as coherent as possible (see the Bourdieu-Gros report).[8]

Philosophy has an essential role to play in unifying education, not because it would dominate and totalize all fields of knowledge, but because it is also, if not only, a critical reflection. Since philosophy has always fed on problems, concepts, debates born in diverse places of knowledge and culture, it has traditionally been the privileged space in which the categories of knowledge or culture can be constructed, assimilated, questioned, and discussed.

We propose:

A. On the one hand, that at the different levels of education, philosophy be more closely associated with the other disciplines. This makes sense only if philosophy affirms and brings to light *the specificity of its approach*, and this presupposes that at all levels, those who teach philosophy would indeed be philosophers themselves (see proposal 1 below).

B. On the other hand, that philosophy be integrated more closely into the training of teachers of all disciplines and of all levels, as has already been the case for the training of elementary school teachers since 1986 (see proposal 6 below).

THIRD PRINCIPLE: **To specify more rigorously what is required of students.**

The philosophy course is in particular, or should be at any rate, the place where the practice of free thinking is learned. That is why the instructions that govern the teaching of philosophy today give teachers complete freedom in how they conduct their teaching, as long as it is authentically philosophical; accordingly, these teachers define a program based on notions,[9] conceived not as successive chapter titles but as "directions in which research and reflection are invited to engage," the study of notions always being "determined by philosophical problems whose choice and formulation are left to the initiative of the teacher." Philosophy teachers all very legitimately cling to this freedom, the guarantee of the really philosophical character of their teaching, which, while it must obviously provide solid knowledge in the history of philosophy and of the human sciences or the history of science, cannot be reduced to them.

This conception, which was expressed most clearly and firmly in the 1973 program reform, should not, in our eyes, be put into question.

But all the evidence we have gathered shows that applying this conception, particularly at the moment of the baccalauréat, leads to a series of abuses whose negative effects have already made themselves felt in the Terminales. In the end, these abuses risk discrediting philosophy and putting in question the teaching of philosophy in the lycée.

The legitimate concern, in other words the good intention, to avoid simple questions drawn from courses leads to the following:

—extremely diverse questions are posed without students having had the possibility to prepare effectively for them;

—the connection between these questions and the program is so oblique that students are forced to completely invent the very framework for their reflection, which cannot reasonably be expected of an average Terminale student;

—the formulation of the questions themselves is often so enigmatic that most of the students are incapable of even identifying the problem posed;

—the philosophical meaning of the texts submitted for commentary, independently of any context, reference, or questions (and often in a language that in fact, whether intentionally or not, is difficult for current students to penetrate) is rigorously impenetrable to most of the candidates.

In short, the current conditions of the philosophy part of the baccalauréat assume a rhetorical ability and a general culture that are well beyond what can reasonably be demanded of Terminale students. This is closer to the kind of aptitude traditionally demanded of those in the *khâgne*.[10]

Operating in such a fashion is disastrous when forty percent of the students in an age group take the "bac." Were this practice to be perpetuated when sixty or eighty percent have access to the bac, it would be simply suicidal for the teaching of philosophy in secondary education.

The consequences of this situation are well known to teachers:

—confusion among students; a feeling of powerlessness and the impression that the philosophy part of the bac is a "lottery" (see "La loterie philosophique," in *Le Monde de l'Éducation*, April 1989);

—discouragement and a strong devalorization of philosophy, particularly in the scientific sections (not to mention the technical ones);

—cramming by the most serious students, who need to reassure themselves and who, in order to prepare for the unpreparable, see in the notions on the program, contrary to its spirit, the chapter headings of a course to be covered, then launch into all kinds of manuals or handbooks varying in quality, all of which treat the program chapter by chapter;

—the compromising of instructors *as teachers*, torn as they are between trying to train students in reflection and the constraints of cramming;

—the compromising of instructors *as examiners*, since most exams satisfy neither the minimum demands of the essay nor those of philosophy homework; the average is too low (abnormal for an *examination*), and the grading becomes rather unpredictable. It is not right for students who are simply average and who have studied seriously not to be assured of getting close to a passing grade.

Official instructions need to determine with sufficient precision the skills that one has the right to demand of students finishing the Terminale. Even if it is true that every teaching of philosophy must contribute to the training of students to practice personal reflection, we still cannot put them in the situation of having to construct a problematic on questions with which they have not previously been familiarized directly or to which the course they took during the year was only obliquely related. Nor can we put them in the situation of having to propose an answer to a philosophical problem without being certain that they have been able, during the year, to study seriously doctrines and theories that constitute appropriate solutions to this problem. Nor can we put them in the situation of having to undertake the hypothetical reconstruction of the thought of a philosopher with whom they are not supposed to be familiar with from twenty lines cut off from all context.

A student does not have to be original, nor able to draw from his own resources what he has never been taught; he is not a budding philosopher or a thinker in embryo.

Knowing how to recognize in a text a philosophical problem that has already been encountered, being able to reproduce ideas and arguments studied previously in a relevant manner, being capable of establishing a connection between a known philosophical idea and an example drawn from one's culture or personal experience: these are eminently philosophical abilities, constitutive of an aptitude for reflection, and which, moreover, can be acquired methodically and evaluated seriously.

In this regard, the expression "to learn to think on one's own," which often sums up the ambition of our teaching, is ambiguous to say the least:

—its indetermination seems to allow one to pose all kinds of questions for which the students have not been prepared directly and that presuppose something quite different from an intelligent application of acquired knowledge;

—its radicality places students before an impossible task and produces confusion that is expressed by students both looking for recipes and giving up;

—its generality, although justified in many regards, makes the tasks of grading and evaluation quite hazardous and makes teachers who want to prepare their students seriously for the exam very uncomfortable.

Whatever one thinks of the Kantian sentence according to which one does not learn philosophy but to philosophize, and however one interprets this sentence, this expression cannot serve to justify the current situation, in which, treating students like little philosophers, one ends up no longer finding any philosophy in their work.[11] Whether one speaks of learning to philosophize or of learning philosophy, it is always a matter of learning, and one must therefore be able to determine with sufficient precision, as in every other discipline, the knowledge and skills that can be demanded.

In this regard, it is strange that the epithet "scholastic" [*scolaire*], in secondary teaching in general and in that of philosophy in particular, has become systematically pejorative. Doesn't the shame of the scholastic too often lead to subjects that are inordinately ambitious and to unreasonable demands?

That part of an exam or the work handed in by a student is "scholastic" in nature should not lead one to discredit them. What is to be demanded of an exam if not that it allow one to verify that a certain amount of knowledge and skill has been acquired thanks to school, that is to say, scholastically [*scolairement*]? What is to be demanded of students if not that they be able to reconstruct correctly and to use intelligently a certain amount of knowledge and of modes of reasoning assimilated scholastically? The contempt generally shown in regard to questions from the course is in no way justified if by "questions from the course" we mean, not encouraging students to recite what was said in class, but simply questions with which they have been familiarized and which they have already considered.

It seems to us that the "scholastic," which cannot be confused with cramming, should be brought back to favor. Cramming is the superficial and hurried accumulation of knowledge intended to delude [graders] on the day of the exam. Scholastic learning is what renders one capable of re-producing and using discriminatingly concepts and distinctions that one has not necessarily invented, of recognizing problems and ideas that one has already encountered. If certain students are original, creative, culti-vated, or brilliant on top of that, all the better. But the teaching of phi-losophy need not be ashamed of being and admitting that it is scholastic.

That is why, while conserving the framework and spirit of the current program, we feel it is urgent to modify profoundly the modalities of the philosophy part of the baccalauréat, at once for it to run better and for the positive effects that will result in the teaching itself.

FOURTH PRINCIPLE: **To think through, finally, the specific problems of the teaching of philosophy in technical sections, where the situation is frankly unacceptable for teachers as well as for students.**

The teaching of philosophy in technical sections constitutes a decisive stake. Nevertheless, the problems it raises have been systematically under-estimated or ignored for the last twenty years; it is in a situation of crisis today that calls for urgent and profound reforms.

With the multiplication of the number of classes in section G, and the extension of its teaching in section F, philosophy has reached an audience it has never previously had either in number or in terms of its social ori-gin, cultural heritage, and scholastic training.[12] This is a *historic opportu-nity* for it that until now was completely lost. The teaching of philosophy in technical sections has in fact never been conceived other than as the mechanical transposition, with a reduced timetable, of the program, exer-cises (essays), and methods (essentially lectures) of the philosophy class.

The inadequacy of this model is manifest: the poor quality of the bac-calauréat exams makes it impossible to evaluate them; most students oscil-late between discouragement and contempt, between believing they are in-capable of doing philosophy and finding that it isn't worth an hour's bother; teachers have the feeling they are being assigned a mission impossible and of simply being unable to practice their profession. Certain of them come to doubt that teaching philosophy makes sense in these sections.

The experience of the extension of the teaching of philosophy to sec-tion F is significant: founded on a legitimate principle (the right to phi-losophy for all), this measure today ends in failure: it is rejected by a large majority of students; philosophy is discredited; teachers become bitter.

The divorce between these students and the current forms of the teaching of philosophy is so profound that it would be perfectly illusory to think of facing it merely by adjusting the timetable (even if this is in fact indispensable).

Along with a majority of the teachers of these classes, we are convinced that the students in these sections are perfectly capable of philosophizing, on the condition that one has the desire and the means to elaborate for and with them a different model of teaching that on the one hand would rely more upon their questions, preoccupations, and motivations, and on the other hand would appeal to a diversified range of better-adapted exercises and work, both written and oral. Faced with the difficulties they encounter, many teachers have sought, individually, to invent different pedagogical practices. It is urgent that these experiments be brought together, circulated, and that collective reflection on the reforms to be undertaken be organized.

Below we propose some measures that might, for the time being, help free up the situation.

But we must be well aware that if we do not decide to think through seriously and rapidly what the teaching of philosophy in technical sections might be, it will be discredited and sooner or later will disappear; many people will conclude from this that "those students" were not made for it. This is therefore an absolutely urgent task, both from the democratic and the philosophical points of view.

Let us add that, if certain difficulties are altogether specific to the technical classes, many others are only the accentuated and magnified version of what teachers of philosophy already encounter to different degrees in all the other sections. On many points—notably everything concerning "tutorials," individual attention for students, organizing group work, in short, a pedagogy less exclusively centered around lectures—what would be undertaken in technical teaching could be useful in improving the teaching of philosophy in the classical sections: after all, the new classes [*couches*] of students who, in the coming years, are going to enter the classical sections are likely, in their behavior and their culture, to resemble current students in sections F and G more than they do future students in the *khâgne*.

Proposals

FIRST PROPOSAL: **To create an "interdisciplinary introduction to philosophy" in the Première.**

This teaching would have a triple objective:

1. To contribute to the acquisition of the fundamental categories of thinking, to the assimilation of the basic logical tools necessary to elaborate discourses, reasoning, and argumentation in all disciplines: the categories of cause, consequence, purpose or end [*finalité*], schemas of demonstration, refutation, concession, and so forth.

2. To give students the elementary and indispensable knowledge about a few decisive and constitutive moments in the history of our culture by showing the connections between the religious, social, scientific, political, and philosophical dimensions of these events: merely as examples, the fifth century in Greece, the advent of Christianity, the Galilean revolution, Darwinian theory, and so forth.

3. To familiarize students with the philosophical approach by showing at once its specificity and its connection with approaches with which they are more accustomed.

This teaching would be organized by the philosophy teacher, but he would share the responsibility for it with teachers of the other disciplines. They would define together the amount and modalities of their contribution (alternating teaching, team teaching in groups of two or three, half or full days organized together, and so forth).

The number of hours on the timetable would be set on an annual basis. At least to begin with, it would not be less than seventy-five hours (or the equivalent of two hours per week). Below this level, such teaching would risk losing its coherence and effectiveness. (From the administrative point of view, and so as not to weigh down students' schedules, we can imagine each discipline making a few hours in the year available for this shared teaching. This "common pool" could represent half the timetable; the other half would represent the equivalent of the introduction of one hour per week of philosophy.)

The organization of this timetable should be flexible and mobile; it would be established at the beginning of each year through consultation between the teachers of the different disciplines and the philosophy teacher.

One distribution could be proposed in three quarterly modules of twenty-five hours each, entitled respectively:

1. Philosophy / Science (logic, mathematics, physics, and biology).

2. Philosophy / Social Sciences (history, geography, sociology, law, economics, politics).

3. Philosophy / Language (rhetoric, translation, languages, arts, and literatures).

In each of these three groups the philosophy teacher would be responsible and have the means for an introduction specific to philosophy as
such (the experience of philosophy as such, its typical attitudes and demands, its modes of questioning and argumentation, its ontological,
metaphysical, or ethical dimensions, the history of its canonical texts,
learning how to read them, and so forth).

It will no doubt be difficult, but all the more necessary, to take into account at once this philosophical specificity and the reciprocal provocation
between philosophy and the other disciplines.

Generally, in the choice of subjects, as well as in their treatment, one
should stress in particular, over the course of this first year:

1. questions of *ethico-political responsibility* (in their most modern and
urgent form, in particular in terms of examples, but also in fundamental
and historical perspectives);

2. learning *logic*, the rules of critical argumentation, and the modes of
appropriating language (speech, writing, translation, instruments of
archiving, information, the media).

The content that might be taught in the framework of this joint contribution would be defined in a national program established in an interdisciplinary fashion. This program would propose a relatively broad range
of possibilities from which teachers would choose according to what
seems to them to meet the needs and interests of their students, as well as
their own competences.

SECOND PROPOSAL: **To focus the main portion of the philosophy part of
the general baccalauréat on a special program defined annually in each
academy, while conserving a general program, established nationally, as
a long-term frame of reference for the teaching of philosophy in the
Terminale.**

*It seems indispensable to maintain a general program, defined long-term
nationally, that could at once constitute the frame of reference for the teaching
of philosophy in the Terminale and provide the material for questions on the
baccalauréat.*

*As is now the case, this would be a program of notions. But it would dis-
tinguish:*

*—A group of notions selected from among the most fundamental in the tra-
dition and in philosophical practice (for example, consciousness, truth, justice,*

and so forth); the number of these notions would be markedly reduced com-
pared to the current program: by one third or one half.

—A group of methodological notions, corresponding to fundamental tools
of theoretical reflection; learning to use these correctly would be more impor-
tant than being able to define them without any context (for example: deduc-
tion, dialectics, analysis, and so forth).

Respect for the unity of philosophy and its globalizing aim forbids a
fragmentary presentation that would limit it to certain of its "parts"; af-
firming its specificity as scholastic discipline demands that a national,
long-term program framework be maintained. A general program of notions must therefore be maintained.

But the number of notions on the current program (more than forty in
A, about twenty in C),[13] all of which could be the point of departure for the
most diverse questions on the baccalauréat, generally leads students to read
them like chapter headings that should be studied successively, as one does
in mathematics or history. The teachers, not wanting to leave any blanks in
preparing their students for the exam, are often led to adopt the same attitude, with all the risks of cramming or skimming that result from it.

It should be noted that nearly all the handbooks and collections of texts
published for the Terminale—which, whether we like it or not, are not
without their influence on the idea that students and teachers form about
what a philosophy course should be—are put together according to the
same model. Thus the scholastic routine and the weight of the baccalauréat tend to transform the list of notions to choose from and to divert the
program from the spirit in which it was conceived: providing an authentically philosophical framework within and on the basis of which problems should be defined and taken up.

It is therefore important that the description of the program, as well as
its content, encourage, more than they do today, teachers and students to
be less concerned with the number, scope, and diversity of chapters to be
treated successively than with the quality of both in-depth reflection and
of knowledge about a few essential philosophical questions.

That is why we propose, on the one hand, to reduce markedly (by one
third or one half) the current program by reorganizing it around the most
fundamental concepts in the philosophical tradition; and, on the other
hand, to establish a list of conceptual tools that we should be able to demand that students have learned to use; finally, to define this program

clearly as a general, long-term framework for the teaching of philosophy in the Terminale, and thus to distinguish it carefully from the special academic program. A small portion of the philosophy part of the baccalauréat should consist in questions about this general program (see proposal 3 below).

But the main part of the philosophy exam (essay or textual commentary) would focus on a special program, established annually in each academy. It would include:

—Two or three fundamental philosophical problems, formulated very explicitly, and closely linked to one or several notions on the general program. These problems could be classical philosophical problems (for example, those of the relation between the State and freedom or between soul and body), or philosophical problems linked to certain contemporary investigations (the evaluation of the idea of progress, for example, or philosophical questions linked to bioethics).

—Between one and three great philosophical texts, or texts of incontestable philosophical significance, classics or works from the twentieth century, whose study would give food for reflection on the problems in question.

Implementing a program of this type should make possible:

A. an improvement in the functioning of the philosophy part of the baccalauréat and of its grading;

B. a positive change in the way students prepare;

C. teachers organizing the school year more intelligently and more freely.

A. If the large majority of bac exams today do not satisfy the minimal demands of philosophy, it is mainly because students, having had to anticipate everything, were not able to prepare anything, and, generally lacking basic knowledge on the questions posed them and the most elementary familiarity with the problems given, do not understand what is demanded of them, and at any rate do not have the theoretical tools to respond to these questions.

If students could focus their learning of philosophy on two or three problems, one could then hope that they would acquire the necessary knowledge during the year, that they would learn to situate certain problems, that they themselves would construct their own reflection, and therefore that they would be able to put together an exam that, while perhaps scholastic, is respectable, that is to say, represents a certain intellectual work.

One could therefore hope, in these conditions, that reading the exams would allow one to distinguish without too much risk of error those who have done the work and assimilated it from those who have done or learned nothing; the not totally unjustified reputation of the philosophy part of the baccalauréat as a "lottery" would essentially be removed.

B. While they do not form a system, the notions constitutive of a philosophy program are nonetheless interdependent: one does not study consciousness without also reflecting upon truth or freedom; one does not study art without also reflecting upon the imagination or language. As long as the problems on the annual program are chosen appropriately, no serious candidate will be able to dispense with knowledge of the entire general program (and all the more so since the "short-answer questions" part of the exam will focus on the general program). But in preparing, candidates will be able to emphasize problems that are clearly circumscribed.

One can thus hope to avoid two pitfalls: on the one hand, preparation that is "all over the place," as in the current system, which leads to cramming and to glossing everything superficially; and on the other hand, preparation that is narrowly limited to too precise an area, which would create a different form of cramming and a technicity that should be absolutely forbidden at the level of the baccalauréat. One can hope, on the contrary, that, while they prepare effectively for an exam with a clearly delimited content, students will be able progressively to discover the scope of the field of philosophical reflection.

C. Relieved of the worry of having to "deal with everything in depth," teachers will be able to conceive of their teaching as a training in philosophy in general, focusing each year on different problems.

They will have all the more freedom to determine the progression of the class according to their students' potential, to choose to tackle problems from the point of view that seems most appropriate to them, to allow their students to discover and practice philosophy on the basis of previously determined notions, problems, and texts.

The role of short-answer questions among which students choose, which is currently too limited ("because-we-already-don't-have-time-for-the-whole-program"), could, in such a context, be reevaluated seriously, which would contribute usefully to broadening students' culture and to diversifying pedagogical approaches.

These special programs would be established annually in each academy by a committee of a few teachers of philosophy. The members of this committee would change regularly, in such a way that, over a few years, all teachers in the academy would have the possibility of participating in it. Thus elaborated in close connection with teachers' experience, these special programs would be better adapted to the preoccupations and potential of the students. Structured around the general program—the guarantee of their philosophical tenor and insurance against arbitrariness—they could show the wealth, diversity, and relevance of philosophical reflection, and would favor renewal and innovation in classes.

THIRD PROPOSAL: **To reorganize the written part of the general baccalauréat by adding short-answer questions to the essay question (or** *commentaire de texte*).

The new exam (four hours in length, as at present) would therefore include two parts:

1. A series of questions whose aim is to evaluate students' assimilation of the knowledge required to practice philosophy with a minimum of seriousness. These questions would focus on basic philosophical vocabulary (define "empiricism" or "abstraction"), elementary conceptual distinctions (distinguish "juridical law" and "scientific law," or "essence" and "existence"), and essential points of reference in the history of philosophy (Who was Socrates? What is Enlightenment?). They would cover the entire general program. Each question would call for a brief but precise response (of ten to twenty lines), supported by examples. The candidates would be posed six questions and should choose three. This part of the exam should be able to be completed in one hour at most.

The existence of this exercise would lead teachers of philosophy to define progressively which knowledge constitutes the minimum that can be demanded of Terminale students—and which does not. It would help all students realize the necessity of acquiring a body of basic knowledge. It would reassure the students who have difficulties with the rhetoric of the essay and would guarantee those who have studied that they have not worked for nothing. It would contribute to relativizing the role of the essay in our teaching and would encourage turning to different and complementary exercises.

2. The second and main part of the exam would consist in an essay or commentary in which candidates would show their ability to reflect, to analyze, to elaborate an argument, and to understand philosophical problems. It would focus exclusively on the philosophical problems and works in the special program.

There again, the forms of this work should be diversified: the essay topic can be given alone (as it is now) or accompanied by a text (or two, potentially contradictory, texts) on the problem in question; the text to be commented upon can be accompanied by no instructions (as it is now) or followed by a series of questions, some comprehension questions, others more open, asking students to reflect upon the text.

In any case, it is imperative that the statement of the subject meet two conditions: on the one hand, its relation to the questions on the program should be obvious for all students; on the other hand, it must be worded in the most explicit manner without trying to be original or brilliant and without any taste for paradox or allusion.

FOURTH PROPOSAL: **To conceive modalities of teaching philosophy that are really appropriate to the students in technical education.**

In order to confront the critical situation of philosophy in the technical sections, three types of proposal seem possible, concerning

A. its organization;
B. the program and the evaluation of students;
C. its concrete modalities.

A. Even more than the others, students in technical education need forms of teaching other than lectures (work in small groups, individual attention, and so forth) that demand very small class sizes. Dividing the class, for at least one hour (two hours for the student, three hours for the teacher), a demand that has already been put forward by several unions and associations, seems to be necessary. At first, this division could be made mandatory in all classes with more than twenty-four students, as is already the case in other disciplines.

In parallel fashion, to avoid splitting up teachers' work catastrophically and diluting philosophy here and there among the other subjects, we propose that the teaching of philosophy in technical sections be organized according to semesters: four hours (or five hours with divided classes) over one semester, instead of two hours over the year, as is currently the case. Thus no philosophy teacher would have more than four (or five) classes simultaneously.

B. It does not seem realistic to want to evaluate students and organize teaching according to a test—the philosophy essay—which we know perfectly well the vast majority of students are incapable of passing (let's say that, in the best case, the time necessary to prepare them properly for it would amount to demanding for philosophy in sections G and F a timetable comparable to that of the literary sections. . . .).

We propose that at the beginning of every year, teachers define with their students, from a range of notions broader than the current program, the precise questions they will take up together; that during the year they have them do a certain number of diverse exercises, both oral and written, assessing their knowledge and reflection; that students, near the end of the year, devote several weeks to putting together a dossier on the question of their choice. Based upon this, two scenarios can be envisaged: Either the organization of the baccalauréat is modified and part of the test takes place in continuous assessment; it would then be desirable that evaluation in philosophy, in technical education at least, be done in continuous assessment. Or the organization of the baccalauréat remains more or less as it is, and we propose that in the technical baccalauréat philosophy be the object of a mandatory oral exam in which the candidates would present and defend their dossier.

C. Collective reflection on the forms of teaching most appropriate for students in technical education is necessary, which implies meetings among teachers with experience in these classes, preparing young teachers for this type of teaching, and so forth.

FIFTH PROPOSAL: **To organize systematically, within the body of teachers of philosophy, reflection and exchanges on the didactics of their discipline.**

Organizing this would depend on a network of lycée philosophy teachers (one per academy, for example) assigned part-time and for several years (three to five maximum), that is, teachers who maintain real contact with teaching, on the one hand, and who intend to return to it full-time, on the other. They would work in close collaboration with certain Instituts Universitaires de Formation des Maîtres, which could be specialized in reflection on philosophical didactics.

The mission of this network of teachers would be:

—to organize, among the 2,500 philosophy teachers, reflection on the problems and methods of the teaching of philosophy;

—to ensure the circulation of information, an exchange of ideas, and a dissemination of experiences among teachers, who are often isolated and who currently have few means of communication;

—to organize the publication of documents that might help teachers, and in particular new teachers, in their work (bibliographic information, reference texts and articles on a given subject, examples of how a certain question is treated, and so forth);

—to encourage publishers to publish books and collections that could be tools appropriate for students (handbooks and textbooks different from the poorly adapted or mediocre instruments most often at their disposal today), but also for teachers (collections of articles that allow one to keep up with the current state of a question; books summarizing areas teachers must be solidly informed about although they cannot in general have access to the specialized literature, in particular concerning the current state of knowledge in the natural sciences, as well as in the human sciences);

—to contribute to the continuous training of teachers of philosophy by helping them remain informed at once about the state of contemporary philosophical reflection and about the state of the sciences;

—to organize colloquia and fact-finding or documentation missions abroad, to invite foreign colleagues, and so forth.

SIXTH PROPOSAL: **To include instruction in philosophy in the training of teachers of all disciplines.**

Teacher training should give all future teachers, without distinguishing among them, the possibility of acquiring the professional qualities that will allow them to complete the tasks expected at every level of school and the lycée. Moreover, it should offer the means for a constructive and critical reflection on the practice of teaching itself.

Mastering a body of knowledge necessarily leads to envisaging the possibility and conditions of its transmission. All future teachers should be able to question and put into perspective the diverse points of view that exist on the didactics of the disciplines, on the diverse pedagogical practices, and, finally, on the psychological dimension of the educative act. Conscious, however, that learning to teach cannot consist in acquiring recipes or in blind faith in a current dogma, future teachers should work to consider the necessarily problematic aspect of the act of teaching, which, paradoxically, alone reveals positivity.

That is to say, whatever the disciplines they are preparing to teach, all young teachers should be able to benefit, within their area of specific training, from instruction in philosophy. This instruction would integrate the fundamental contributions of the human sciences into a questioning about education and into the very old tradition of thought linked to it.

To conceive such instruction, one would have to take as a model the training of elementary school teachers, as redefined by the decree of May 20, 1986. In the écoles normales, all elementary school teachers today receive, in addition to training in their discipline, instruction in the "philosophy, history, and sociology of education, general pedagogy, and psychology," which, comprising three hours a week, is necessarily given by a philosophy professor. The remarkable success of this encounter between philosophy and professional training, attested to by the vast majority of students and teachers in the écoles normales, would encourage extending its scope to all teacher training, that is, to the CPR, ENNA, ENS, and obviously to future Instituts Universitaires de Formation des Maîtres.[14]

Training conceived in this way would have the advantage of revealing the community of problems shared by teachers in primary and secondary education, teachers in classical and technical lycées, and those in professional lycées, and of bringing to light the diversified unity of their practices.

In addition to their basic training, future teachers of philosophy should be prepared (1) to follow the most significant evolutions in contemporary knowledge, and (2) to master new pedagogical practices called for by the preceding proposals.

SEVENTH PROPOSAL: **To reorganize the first cycle of the universities.**

1. The current climate and the general principles guiding our work do not, of course, go in the direction of an authoritarian programming, decided upon at the national level and imposed upon the universities. The principle of the autonomy of universities will certainly be reaffirmed and reinforced, and we have no reason to regret this. A university that would not feel the need to have a department of philosophy would not give it the necessary attention and means if it were forced to keep or create one. What can be defined at the national level is a set of demands that are simply hypothetical and very general in character: if a Department of Philosophy exists at the University of X, then it [the department] must respect a minimum of conditions. Moreover, since these conditions cannot be met if the State does not contribute at least partially to providing the means for it (teaching, administrative, and technical personnel; equipment; space, etc.), the method to be followed should normally take the form of a contract between the State and the universities, as is provided for by the project of the decree of March 13, 1989 (summarized in *Le Monde*, March 21, 1989).[15]

2. With this procedure, the risks that an excessive regionalization of the universities would entail should be avoidable. The French university, as a whole, has often deplored its own "provincialism"; it would be regrettable to see this provincialism pass from the singular to the plural, and each university concern itself only with responding to the local demands of students or of their potential future employers. State interventions are not the only remedies imaginable to guard against this. One could also consider:

—In every possible way encouraging universities to exchange, in a continuous and institutional fashion, information, experiences, and projects, first among themselves, of course, but also with institutions and associations at the level of secondary education. (It would no doubt be interesting for us to obtain information on the activities of the "Promosciences" association, "an association reflecting and offering proposals on the whole of post-baccalauréat scientific education," which was founded following two conferences on reforming the first cycle in the sciences at the university, and which is currently directed by Michel Bornancin, president of the University of Nice.)

—Developing procedures of evaluation and "auditing," not only at the level of the Comité National d'Évaluation (National Evaluation Committee), which is forced by its multidisciplinary function to limit itself to generalities, but also by means of ad hoc committees specializing in philosophy and including, if possible, *foreign* as well as French members. (In general, it seems that we should recommend the institutionalization of inviting experts from other universities, both French *and foreign*, for a whole series of collective, and even individual, problems: the organization of studies, the acquisition and management of equipment, career development, and so forth.)

3. Philosophy can benefit from the "renewal of the humanities" that is currently taking shape, after decades of domination by mathematics, technologies, and rationalized management (see *Le Monde*, April 22, 1989). This "promising wave" nevertheless involves obvious dangers: by allowing itself to enroll in the camp of the "Letters," or of the "Humanities," in order to thwart the "Sciences" and "professionalism," philosophy risks finding itself asked only for a vague "supplement of soul" and losing in the deal a good deal of its specificity. It is desirable finally to respond to the "demand" for philosophy that today issues from the most diverse circles (the exact sciences, the human sciences, technical disciplines, medicine, law, management and administration, cultural activities, and so forth); but this demand will be satisfied in the correct conditions only if the professional character of philosophy itself remains vigorously affirmed in the contacts it can make outside and, at the same time, in teaching in the universities. The specificity of philosophy, a watchword that everyone agrees upon and that is no less ambiguous for this, will prove itself not through self-affirmation but through the discipline's work upon itself, and through a dialectic of communication and cooperation with what it is not.

4. If it is desirable that, beginning in the first cycle of university, the teaching of philosophy become more technical and professionalized than, it seems, it currently is, this result should not be obtained at the price of a dangerous division between the purely scholastic techniques that are good for students (learning to write an essay, to do a *commentaire de texte*, and so forth) and the prestigious practice of philosophical activity reserved for teachers (lectures, open seminars,[16] and so forth). To break down this distribution of tasks, it would no doubt be good to prompt the universities to encourage innovation in the exercises proposed to students, by inventing other formulas than the traditional couple essay / *commentaire de texte*,

by developing techniques for the analysis of concepts, arguments, reasonings, textual strategies, systematic structures, and so forth. What is more, these new types of exercises could also make room for themselves in the continuous assessment of students and even in the exams. And a major transformation of the lecture course would be set under way if French professors distributed to their students, in the form of a "syllabus," a list of the questions they would deal with, week by week, and of the texts that the students should read in advance in order to prepare to listen to the course actively: this practice, frequent in foreign universities, changes the pedagogical relation considerably by allowing students to understand better how the course has been constructed, on the basis of a group of texts with which everyone has been able to familiarize themselves, and to pose relevant questions to the instructor.

5. The current plans we know of, concerning the first cycle of the universities, seem to lead toward the disappearance of DEUGs specialized by discipline and the creation (or resurrection) of a sort of propaedeutic, in the form of a single DEUG (of two years) for each large disciplinary sector, for example Letters-Languages-Human Sciences. In the perspective of such a project, which we have no reason to reject in principle (while, naturally, emphasizing our commitment to the existence of a licence and a maîtrise in philosophy), it seems that we should demand, and obtain:

—On the one hand, that philosophy be present as a mandatory subject in the whole of the first cycle, with a proportionately reasonable space (for example, one quarter of all the courses) and an absolutely specific qualitative content (which does not exclude that, within this philosophical "hard core," students could still be offered, besides a certain number of mandatory teachings, partial choices corresponding to their interests and their own plans).

—On the other hand, that the whole include a certain number of "open slots" that each student could fill as he sees fit; a student who from the outset is very motivated to study philosophy could, for example, fill these "open slots" with complementary disciplines at varying distances from the philosophical "core" (for example, epistemology and the history of the sciences, aesthetics and sciences of art, psychology, sociology, linguistics, ancient languages, the history of religions, and so forth, but also the exact sciences, law, economics, a second modern language, and so forth). It would be important for the instructors who take these students

in to "shape" their teaching, if possible, for an audience whose central interest remains philosophy.

It would no doubt be useful to indicate that the disappearance of a specific DEUG in philosophy need not imply—quite to the contrary—that
philosophy instructors (and especially professors) feel less concerned by
the new first cycle than by the old one. Philosophy departments, represented by their chairs, should negotiate the necessary arrangements with
the other disciplines concerned; and one could no doubt envisage demanding that professors take part in this new first cycle, at once as administrators and as active instructors.

6. The university reforms that are most inspired, from the point of view
of the organization of studies, programs, and the assessment of knowledge, will perhaps weigh less heavily in the destiny of the French university than a certain number of transformations that are apparently prosaic
and modest although they are sometimes expensive, and that could in the
long term profoundly modify the work habits of teachers and students,
pedagogical relations, and the social and scientific productivity of the university milieu. We are thinking, for example:

—of the precarious situation of university and departmental libraries,
which are often underused because of insufficient acquisitions budgets,
lack of space for readers, and lack of a methodical introduction to their
use (see the alarming report by André Miquel);[17]

—of the general absence of proper offices assigned individually to instructors, which would allow them, with a bit of encouragement perhaps,
to work at the university for at least part of their time and to see students
at set times that are posted;

—along the same lines, of the general absence of meeting rooms that
could be used by instructors and students;

—of the insufficiency or underutilization of office personnel and material;

—of the impossibility, in practice, considering the insufficient budget
and the unwieldy procedures, of inviting French, and even more, foreign
colleagues for short visits (seminars, lecture series, participation on thesis
examination committees, and so forth);

—of the all too well known, and scandalous, GARACE norms, which
in calculating the obligations of instructors in terms of the number of
hours they work, take into account only the number of hours during

which they have class, that is, in short, temporarily stop working. We should demand that what makes up the daily life of academics (preparing courses, research, documentation, directing dissertations and theses, more or less institutionalized "tutorials," participating on examination committees and in colloquia and conferences, intellectual exchanges of all kinds, and so forth) officially be taken into consideration, if only symbolically and without any financial impact.

Implementing the organic teaching of philosophy over three stages, as we propose (see principle 1), would mean that the barrier that today cuts off the lycées totally from the universities would be removed. Two demands follow from this:

1. Teachers should be given the opportunity to circulate between the lycée and the university. It would be desirable for professors to be able to contribute *statutorily*, and not merely as lecturers [*chargés de cours*], in training students in the first cycle. This would mean that these teaching hours at the university would be an integral part of their position.

2. Research (DEA, theses, and so forth) that lycée teachers are involved in should be recognized not as a luxury or a strictly personal matter, but as a contribution in its own right to the collective research in philosophy and as part of continuous training that is directly beneficial to the quality of teaching. This assumes, among other things, recognizing a status as teacher-researcher that would give them the right, for a specific period of time, to release-time from teaching and to flexible hours.

P.S. This report—this goes without saying, but we emphasize this once again—constitutes only a group of proposals submitted for discussion. Moreover, it remains to be completed. It will be completed, no doubt, in conditions to be determined during the weeks or months to come, and taking into account discussions that are bound to take place during the colloquia planned by the Ministry. These complements should concern, in particular, certain points of articulation between secondary and higher education, broadening the list of authors and texts to be studied, the relations between the history of philosophy and contemporary philosophy in the teaching of philosophy in general and in the training of teachers in particular.

As an appendix to the considerations and proposals on the training of teachers, see the attached text, which currently regulates the program of the teaching of philosophy in the écoles normales.

Appendix

I. General theoretical and practical pedagogical training.

II. Philosophy, history, and sociology of education, general pedagogy, psychology (250 hours).

The objective of the teaching grouped under this rubric is to offer student teachers [*élèves-instituteurs*] the means for a reflection that is at once constructive and critical. It is a matter of helping them master and put into perspective the particular pedagogical activities and the actual professional practices they will discover and construct in the framework of the disciplinary teachings properly speaking. This group of fields of knowledge and reflections must allow them, in a precise fashion, to find the foundation and to grasp teaching conditions that are social and institutional, as well as human and technical. In general, it is a matter of clarifying how every pedagogical problematic concerning the school makes sense only in relation to fulfilling the fundamental mission of instruction and education.

That is why the contents this rubric defines derive essentially from a philosophical approach and must be taught by a professor of this discipline. Sometimes this derivation is direct, as regards, of course, philosophy, and sometimes it is indirect, as regards the human sciences, the different pedagogical practices and techniques, but also the programs and instructions in elementary school and all the texts governing nursery school.

1. Philosophy (100 hours)

Freedom. Duty. Autonomy.
Human Rights. The Republican State.
School and the State. Public instruction. National education.
The ends of education.
Understanding and learning.
Knowledge and information.
Explaining and demonstrating.
The idea of method. Analysis and synthesis.
The elements of knowledge: categories, concepts, principles.
Parole. Langue. Langage. What is reading?

The experience of the beautiful. Taste. Artistic creation.
Mathematical thinking.
Experimental knowledge.
Historical knowledge and rational knowledge.
The idea of technology.
The body.

2. History and Sociology of Education (25 hours).

The study of the education system and its history will be taken up in chapter 3.11 of the training program. Here, on the other hand, we will study the history of the ideas and conceptions that have accompanied, founded, or followed the evolution of the school.

From the Ancien Régime to the École de la République; the implementation of the primary institution (1800–1880).

School under the Third Republic (1880–1940).

Society and school: contemporary problems.

3. General Pedagogy (55 hours)

By general pedagogy, we understand here not the statement of a formal and universal approach, but all the questions and conceptions that relate to teaching and education. All dogmatism is excluded. Here, facts and concepts are considered in view of their application—for example, the notion of elementary knowledge, the notion of discipline, the notion of interest, the notion of activity, the notion of example, class, childhood, and so forth.

The principal pedagogical conceptions and methods, current research.

The question of experimentation and innovation in pedagogy.

Philosophy, pedagogy, and the sciences of man.

The study of two works, at least one of which will be chosen from the following list:

Plato: *Meno, Phaedrus, Republic* (Book VII).
Montaigne: "De l'institution des enfants" (from *Essais*).
Descartes: *Discourse on Method* (first and second parts).
Locke: *Some Thoughts Concerning Education.*
Rousseau: *Emile, or Of Education.*
Kant: *On Education.*
Hegel: pedagogical texts.

Bergson: "Intellectual Effort" (in *Spiritual Energy*).
Alain: *Propos sur l'education.*

4. Psychology (70 hours)

The methods of psychology. The great conceptions of psychology. The idea of psychogenesis (unity and diversity in child development, psycho-genetic causality).

Perception.
Attention.
Memory.
Imagination.
Play.
Intellectual activity.
The notion of motivation.
Imitation. Social learning.

Nursery School (70 hours)

The objective of this training is to give all student teachers a basic un-derstanding of nursery school and the official texts that govern it. It is a matter of understanding its role in current society and in relation to the family, its place in the school system, the nature of its educative activity. Knowledge of children from birth up to about six or seven years of age, and from their first experiences to the end of the pre-elementary period, allows one to understand the problem of educative continuity between nursery school and the preparatory course and the necessity of giving chil-dren the means to adapt rapidly to elementary school.

Understanding children from birth up to about six or seven years of age.
This understanding must be founded on diverse human and biological sciences and on spending time with and observing children. It concerns the following points:

The characteristics of growth.
The importance of physiological rhythms, hygiene, and physical well-being.
The importance of affectivity and of the structuring of personality.
—Translated by Jan Plug

Notes

A number of notes in the French publication of *Du droit à la philosophie* were provided by Elisabeth Weber. They are indicated here by the designation "—EW." Notes added by Jan Plug for this translation are indicated by "—J.P." Otherwise, translators' notes have been supplied by the translator of the given text and are indicated by "—Trans."

Translator's Foreword

1. The CAPES and the agrégation are national competitive examinations that certify for a teaching position in a lycée (secondary school) or university.

2. "Actes Premiers," in Greph, *Qui a peur de la philosophie?* (Paris: Flammarion, 1977), p. 427. "Un Tableau Noir" (in Jacques Derrida, *Who's Afraid of Philosophy?: Right to Philosophy 1*, trans. Jan Plug [Stanford, Calif.: Stanford University Press, 2002]) details the reduction of positions.

If There Is Cause to Translate I

The four texts that comprise the second part of *Du droit à la philosophie* (Language and Institutions of Philosophy) were first given as lectures at the Fifth International Summer Institute for Semiotic and Structural Studies, May 31–June 25, 1984, held at Victoria College, University of Toronto. The fourth lecture in the series was given as part of the colloquium Semiotics of Literary Translation. The lectures were then published in revised form in *Recherches Sémiotiques / Semiotic Inquiry* 4.2 (1984): 91–154. The translations for that publication were revised by Gabriel Moyal and David Savan under the general editorship of Joseph Adamson. They have been further revised for this volume.—J.P.

1. Descartes, *Oeuvres*, Librairie Philosophique (Paris: J. Vrin, 1964–69), vol. 6, pp. 77–78. Hereafter cited in the text by volume and page number.

2. See *Cours de linguistique générale*, chapter III. *Course in General Linguistics*, ed. Charles Bally et al., trans. Roy Harris (La Salle, Illinois: Open Court, 1983).

3. J. L. Austin, *How to Do Things with Words* (Cambridge, Mass.: Harvard University Press, 1962).

4. On the National Conference on Research and Technology, called for by then minister of research Jean-Pierre Chevènement, see "In Praise of Philosophy" in this volume.—JP.

5. Cited in Marcel Cohen, *Histoire d'une langue: Le français* (Paris: Éditions Sociales, 1967), p. 159.—EW.

6. *Langue de référence*: a benchmark, the language to which others are referred.—JP.

7. Brunot, *L'histoire de la langue française, des origines à 1900,* vol. 2 (Paris: Librairie Armand Colin, 1906). Hereafter cited in the text by volume and page number.

8. Renée Balibar and Dominique Laporte, *Le français national* (Paris: Hachette, 1974); Renée Balibar, *Les Français fictifs* (Paris: Hachette, 1974).—EW.

9. Marcel Bataillon, "Quelques idées linguistiques du XVIIᵉ siècle, Nicolas Le Gras," *Langue, discours, société* (Paris: Seuil, 1975).—EW.

10. See Jacques Derrida, "La langue et le discours de la méthode," in *Recherches sur la philosophie du langage* (Cahiers du Groupe de recherches sur la philosophie et le langage 3) (Grenoble and Paris: 1983), pp. 35–51.—EW.

11. See Jacques Derrida, "Tympan," in *Margins of Philosophy*, trans. Alan Bass (Chicago: University of Chicago Press, 1982).

12. Montaigne, "Des prières," in *Essais*, ed. André Tournon, 3 vols. (Paris: Imprimerie Nationale, 1998), 1: 502–3. Cited in Brunot 2.24. The translation, slightly modified, is from *The Essays of Montaigne*, trans. E.J. Trechmann, ed. J.M. Robertson (New York and London: Oxford University Press, 1946).—JP.

13. Michel de Certeau, Dominique Julia, and Jacques Revel, *Une politique de la langue: La révolution française et les patois: L'enquête de Grégoire* (Paris: Gallimard, 1975).

14. Cited in Brunot 9.180–81 and de Certeau et al., *Une politique*, p. 295.

15. Cited in de Certeau et al., *Une politique*, pp. 160, 300ff.

16. A reference, no doubt, to Heidegger's *Unterwegs zur Sprache* (On the Way to Language): the German *Weg* is translated in French as *chemin*, path.—JP.

If There Is Cause to Translate II

1. Adrien Baillet, *La vie de Monsieur Descartes* (Geneva: Slatkine, 1970), p. 428.—EW.

2. *Lettres de M. Descartes. Où sont expliquées plusieurs belles difficultés touchant ses autres ouvrages*, vol. 2 (Paris: Charles Angot, 1659).—EW.

3. *Descartes: Philosophical Letters*, ed. and trans. Anthony Kenny (Minneapolis: University of Minnesota Press, 1981), p. 34; Descartes, *Oeuvres*, Librairie Philosophique (Paris: J. Vrin, 1964–69), 1.353. All further references to these editions are made in the text and are designated by *Letters* and *Oeuvres* respectively. The translations have often been modified.—JP.

4. Descartes, *Oeuvres*, vol. 1, pp. 353–54. English translations from the *Discourse on Method* are adapted from *Discourse on Method and Meditations on First Philosophy*, ed. David Weissman (New Haven: Yale University Press, 1996), and have often been modified.—JP.

5. See "*Geschlecht*, Différence ontologique, différence sexuelle," *Cahiers de l'Herne: Martin Heidegger*, ed. M. Haar (Paris, 1983), reprinted in *Psyché: Inventions de l'autre* (Paris: Galilée, 1987); "Geschlecht: Sexual Difference, Ontological Difference," *Research in Phenomenology* 13 (1983): 65–83.

6. *Doutes sur la langue françoise* (Brighton: University of Sussex Library, 1971), p. 27.—EW.

7. Quoted in Brunot, *L'histoire de la langue française, des origines à 1900*, vol. 2 (Paris: Librairie Armand Colin, 1906). 3.46.—EW.

8. *Roman* translates as both "novel" and "romance."—JP.

9. Descartes, *Principles of Philosophy*, trans. Valentine Rodger Miller and Reese P. Miller (Dordrecht, Boston, and London: D. Reidel, 1983), p. xxiii.

10. Jean-Luc Nancy, *Ego sum* (Paris: Flammarion, 1979).

11. *Oeuvres philosophiques*, ed. Ferdinand Alquié (Paris: Garnier frères, 1963–73), pp. 342ff.—EW.

12. Kafka, *Parables and Paradoxes* (New York: Schocken Books, 1966), pp. 36–39.

13. See "Plato's Pharmacy," in *Disseminations*, trans. Barbara Johnson (Chicago: University of Chicago Press, 1981).

14. See *Of Grammatology*, trans. Gayatri Chakravorty Spivak (Chicago: University of Chicago Press, 1976), chapter 2.

15. See Roger Dragonetti, *La vie de la lettre au Moyen Age* (Paris: Seuil, 1980), especially the chapter "Rhétorique et roman."

Vacant Chair

1. Immanuel Kant, *The Conflict of the Faculties* (New York: Arabis Books, 1979). Hereafter references will be to this edition and will be made in the text and designated by *Conflict*. Translations have sometimes been modified.—Trans.

2. *Religion within the Limits of Reason Alone* (New York: Harper and Row,

1964), p. 8. References to this work will be to this edition and will be cited parenthetically by the designation *Religion.*—Trans.

3. See that text and "Mochlos, or The Conflict of the Faculties" in this volume.

4. In addition to "well-being" and "safety," the French *salut*, like the German *Heil*, has the religious sense of "salvation."—JP.

5. See the "General Observation" in Book One of *Religion within the Limits of Reason Alone.*

6. Kant, *Critique of Pure Reason* (London: Macmillan, 1958), p. 657.

7. *La* philosophie, emphasizing its apparent unity and uniqueness.—JP.

8. See "The Principle of Reason: The University in the Eyes of its Pupils" in this volume. There, Derrida differentiates research that is "end-oriented" or *finalisée* from applied research as follows:

> In France, for some time, this debate has been organized around what is called the "end-orientation" [*finalisation*] of research. "End-oriented" research is research that is programmed, focused, organized in an authoritarian fashion *in view of* its utilization (in view of "ta khreia," Aristotle would say), whether we are talking about technology, economics, medicine, psycho-sociology, or military power—and in fact we are talking about all of these at once. There is no doubt greater sensitivity to this problem in countries where the politics of research depend closely upon state-managed or "nationalized" structures, but I believe that conditions are becoming more and more homogeneous among all the technologically advanced, industrialized societies. We speak of "end-oriented" [*finalisé*] research where, not so long ago, we spoke—as Peirce did—of "application." For it is growing more and more obvious that, without being immediately applied or applicable, research may pay off, be usable, end-oriented [*finalisable*], in more or less deferred ways. And what is at stake is not merely what sometimes used to be called the techno-economic, medical, or military "by-products" of pure research. The detours, delays, and relays of "end-orientation," its random aspects as well, are more disconcerting than ever. Hence the attempt, by every possible means, to take them into account, to integrate them in the rational calculation of programmed research. A term like "orient" is preferred to "apply," in addition, because the word is less "utilitarian"; it leaves open the possibility that noble aims may be written into the program. (p. 141).—JP.

9. See *New Essays Concerning Human Understanding*, trans. and ed. Peter Remnant and Jonathan Bennett (New York : Cambridge University Press, 1997).

10. *La* philosophie, literally *the* philosophy, emphasizing its apparent unity and uniqueness.—JP.

Theology of Translation

This text was first given as a lecture at the University of Toronto during a conference on *The Semiotics of Literary Translation* and was also the concluding lecture in the series entitled "Languages and Institutions of Philosophy" at the Fifth International Summer Institute for Semiotic and Structural Studies. It appeared in *Texte* 4 (1985) and then in *Qu'est-ce que Dieu? Philosophie/Théologie: Hommage à l'abbé Coppieters de Gibson* (Brussels: Publications des Facultés de Saint-Louis, 1985).—EW. The details of the first English publication are given on pg. 283.—JP.

1. See "Des tours de Babel" in Joseph F. Graham, ed., *Difference in Translation* (Ithaca: Cornell University Press, 1985), pp. 209–84.

2. Roman Jakobson, "On Linguistic Aspects of Translation," in *Selected Writings*, ed. S. Rudy (The Hauge: Mouton, 1971), pp. 260–66.

3. Johann Wolfgang von Goethe, "Übersetzungen," in *Werke*, vol. 2 (Munich: Deutscher Taschenbuch Verlag, 1981), pp. 255–58.

4. Antoine Berman, *L'épreuve de l'étranger: Culture et traduction dans L'Allemagne romantique* (Paris: Flammarion, 1984); *The Experience of the Foreign: Culture and Translation in Romantic Germany*, trans. S. Heyvaert (Albany: SUNY Press, 1992). Hereafter references will be made parenthetically, the first page number corresponding to the English translation, the second to the French.—Trans.

5. F.W.J. Schelling, *On University Studies* (Athens: Ohio University Press, 1966). Further references will be made parenthetically and will be designated by *University*. Translations are sometimes modified.

6. See the Sixth Lecture; with Schelling as well as with Kant, something would have to be said about the alternate recourse to Latin or German words.

7. The French *former* and *se former* are rendered literally as *to form* and *to form oneself* here. Like the German *bilden*, they also refer to "education," "cultivation," and "culture."—JP.

8. See "Vacant Chair" in this volume.—JP.

9. There is something more Schellingian than Kantian about the proposals that have been made to the State and to the French government in view of the creation of an Collège International de Philosophie: a fundamental place reserved for the international difference of languages and the problematic of translation, a place of poetics and of artistic performativity, of departitioned philosophy, and so forth. But there is something very anti-Schellingian about them as well. For the principle of uni-formation or uni-totality can also be worrisome, both from Kant's point of view and from our own present perspective. As we will see, the State can surreptitiously recover in such a principle all its power, the very power of totality.

10. See Nietzsche and his critique of Kant.

11. Goethe, "The Apotheosis of the Artist" (1789).

12. On Derrida's use of the term *finalisé*, see note 8 in "Vacant Chair" above.—JP.

Mochlos, or The Conflict of the Faculties

This paper was delivered in English on April 17, 1980 at Columbia University, for the centenary of the founding of its graduate school and after Derrida had been given an honorary doctorate. It first appeared in French in *Philosophie* [(April 2, 1984) (Paris: Minuit)] and in English in *Logomachia*, ed Richard Rand (Lincoln: University of Nebraska Press, 1992), pp. 1–34.

1. Immanuel Kant, *The Conflict of the Faculties / Der Streit der Fakultäten*, trans. Mary J. Gregor (New York: Abaris Books, 1979), p. 23. Translations modified throughout. Hereafter cited parenthetically as *Conflict*.

2. See, for example, *Of Grammatology*, trans. Gayatri Chakravorty Spivak (Baltimore: Johns Hopkins University Press, 1976), notably p. 54; "Plato's Pharmacy" (in *Dissemination*, trans. Barbara Johnson [Chicago: University of Chicago Press, 1981], p. 128); "Signature Event Context," in *Margins of Philosophy*, trans. Alan Bass (Chicago: University of Chicago Press, 1982); and *Glas*, trans. John P. Leavey, Jr., and Richard Rand (Lincoln: University of Nebraska Press, 1987).

3. *La* deconstruction, literally *the* deconstruction, to emphasize its apparent unity and uniqueness.—JP.

4. "Whereas the utility the higher faculties promise the government is of secondary importance. We can also grant the Faculty of Theology's claim that the Faculty of Philosophy is its handmaid (though a question remains, whether the servant is the mistress's torchbearer or trainbearer [*ob diese ihrer gnädigen Frau die Fakel vorträgt oder die Schleppe nachträgt*]), provided it is not driven away or silenced. For her very modesty—merely being free, and leaving others free, to find the truth for the benefit of all the sciences and to set it before the higher faculties to use as they will—must commend it to the government as above suspicion, indeed, as indispensable." Second Section, "The Concept and Division of the Lower Faculty," *Conflict*, p. 45.

5. "Insofar as the sciences attain actual objective existence in and through the state and become a power, they are organized into so-called faculties. A few remarks are necessary concerning their relative rank—especially since Kant in his *Conflict of the Faculties* seems to have treated the question from a very one-sided point of view. Clearly, theology, as the science in which the innermost core of philosophy is objectified, must have the first and highest place. Since the ideal is a higher potency or level of the real, it follows that the law faculty has precedence

over the medical. As for philosophy, I maintain that there is no such faculty, nor can there be, for that which is all things cannot for that very reason be anything in particular." Friedrich Schelling, *On University Studies*, trans. E.S. Morgan (Athens: Ohio University Press, 1966), p. 79. See "Theology of Translation" in this volume.

6. See, for example, the works and struggles of Greph in *Qui a peur de la philosophie?* (Paris: Flammarion, 1977). See also *Les États généraux de la philosophie (16 et 17 juin 1979)* (Paris: Flammarion, 1979). [Derrida's contributions to these publications are reproduced in this volume and in *Who's Afraid of Philosophy?: Right to Philosophy 1*, trans. Jan Plug (Stanford: Stanford University Press, 2002).—JP.]

7. *En mal de* signifies both longing or yearning for and short of or lacking. It should also be noted that *mal* can also mean ill or evil.—JP.

8. Or, "right of right," or "right of law." Throughout the following pages, the word *droit*, which means both "right" and "law," is translated as "law."—JP.

9. *Conflict* 193. Redundancy. Let us repeat here the name of Polyphemus. *Mochlos* is also the name for the "wedge" or wooden lever that Ulysses—or the ruse of No One, *outis*, *Metis*—puts into the fire before driving it into the pupil of the Cyclops (*Odyssey* 9.375–88).

Punctuations

Given during the thesis defense for the *doctorat d'état* (based on published works), June 2, 1980 at the Sorbonne. The jury consisted of MM Aubenque, de Gandillac, Desanti (thesis supervisor), Joly, Lascault, Levinas. First appeared in English as "The Time of a Thesis: Punctuations," in *Philosophy in France Today*, trans. Kathleen McLaughlin, ed. A. Montefiore (Cambridge: Cambridge University Press, 1983) and in Spanish as "El tiempo de una tesis: Puntuaciones," trans. P. Peñalver, in *Anthropos* 93, "Jacques Derrida" (February 1989).—EW.

1. The agrégation is one of the national competitive examinations to certify for teaching positions in a lycée or university.—JP.

2. See *Le problème de la genèse dans la philosophie de Husserl* (Paris: Presses Universitaires de France, 1990).

3. *De la grammatologie* (Paris: Minuit, 1967); *Of Grammatology*, trans. Gayatri Chakravorty Spivak (Baltimore: Johns Hopkins University Press, 1974). [The thesis for the third cycle is the equivalent of a doctoral dissertation.—JP.]

4. See *L'origine de la géométrie* (Paris: Presses Universitaires de France, 1962).

5. *Of Grammatology*; *L'écriture et la différence* (Paris: Seuil, 1967) (*Writing and Difference*, trans. Alan Bass [Chicago: University of Chicago Press, 1978]); "*La voix et le phénomène*": *Introduction au problème du signe dans la phénoménologie de*

Husserl (Paris: Presses Universitaires de France, 1967) (*Speech and Phenomena and Other Essay on Husserl's Theory of Signs*, trans. David B. Allison [Evanston: Northwestern University Press, 1973]).

6. *Marges—de la philosophie* (Paris: Seuil, 1972); *Margins of Philosophy*, trans. Alan Bass (Chicago: University of Chicago Press, 1982).

7. In *Margins of Philosophy*.

8. *La dissémination* (Paris: Seuil, 1972); *Marges—de la philosophie* (Paris: Seuil, 1972); *Positions* (Paris: Minuit, 1972) (*Positions*, trans. Alan Bass [Chicago: University of Chicago Press, 1981]).—JP.

9. *Glas* (Paris: Éditions Galilée, 1974); *Glas*, trans. John P. Leavey and Richard Rand (Lincoln: University of Nebraska Press, 1986).

10. *Éperons: Les syles de Nietzsche* (Paris: Flammarion, 1978); (*Spurs: Nietzsche's Styles*, trans. Barbara Harlow [Chicago: University of Chicago Press, 1979]); *La carte postale: De Socrate à Freud et au-delà* (Paris: Flammarion, 1980) (*The Post Card: From Socrates to Freud and Beyond*, trans. Alan Bass [Chicago: University of Chicago Press, 1987]).

11. First appeared in *Glyph* 2 (1977) and reprinted as *Limited Inc* (Evanston: Northwestern University Press, 1988).

12. The "Avant-Projet" is published in *Who's Afraid of Philosophy?: Right to Philosophy 1*, trans. Jan Plug (Stanford: Stanford University Press, 2002), pp. 92–98. On Greph and the historical context of its work, see the Translator's Foreword to this volume.—JP.

13. *La vérité en peinture* (Paris: Flammarion, 1978) (*The Truth in Painting*, trans. Geoff Bennington and Ian McLeod [Chicago: University of Chicago Press, 1987]).

14. See, for example, *Fors*, preface to Nicolas Abraham and Maria Torok, *Cryptomanie: Le verbier de l'homme aux loups* (Paris: Flammarion, 1976).—EW.

The Principle of Reason

The French publication of this talk, first given and published in English, is accompanied by the following note.

This inaugural lecture for the Andrew D. White Professor-at-large chair was given in English at Cornell University (Ithaca, New York) in April 1983. I did not believe it either possible or desirable to erase everything that related to the circumstance, to the places, or to the history of this university. The talk's structure has an essential relation with the architecture and site of Cornell: the heights of a hill, the bridge or "barriers" above a certain abyss ("gorge," in English), the common site of so many uneasy discourses on the history and rate of suicides ("gorging out," in the local idiom), among professors and students. What must one do to avoid throwing oneself to the bottom of the gorge? Is it responsible for all these suicides? Must barriers be built? For the same reason, I thought it preferable to leave certain passages in English. In certain cases, their translation poses no difficulty. In other cases, it would be quite simply impossible without very lengthy commentaries on the meaning of this or that idiomatic expression.

Originally appeared, under this title, in *Diacritics* 13.3 (1983): 3–20; then in Spanish, "El principio de Razón: La universidad en los ojos de sus pupilo/as," trans. B. Mazzoldi and R.P. Díaz, *Nomade* 3 (June 1984), and in French in *Le cahier du Collège International de Philosophie* 2 (Paris: Osiris, 1986). A more literal translation of the title would give "The Pupils of the University: The Principle of Reason and the Idea of the University."—JP.

1. James Siegel, "Academic Work: The View From Cornell," *Diacritics* 11:1 (Spring 1981): 68–83; the quotation, on page 69, is taken from Kermit Parsons, *The Cornell Campus: A History of Its Planning and Development* (Ithaca: Cornell University Press, 1968). Hereafter cited in the text as "View."

2. In regard to this "naturalism" (a frequent, but not general phenomenon that Kant, for example, eludes at the beginning of the *Conflict of the Faculties*), and also to the classic motif of interdisciplinarity as an effect of the archetectonic totality, see, for example, Schleiermacher's 1808 essay "Gelegentliche Gedanken über Universitäten in deutschem Sinn, nebst einem Anhang über ein neu zu errichtende." A French translation of this text appears in a noteworthy collection, *Philosophies de l'université, l'idéalisme allemand et la question de l'Université*, ed. Perry, Pesron, Renault (Paris: Payot, 1979).

3. For an English translation of Schelling's text, see F.W.J. Schelling, *On University Studies* (Athens: Ohio University Press, 1966). The passage quoted here (p. 11 of the English translation) has been translated in view of the translation used by Derrida.—JP.

4. What American English calls "the faculty," those who teach, is in French *le corps enseignant*, the teaching corps (just as we say "the diplomatic corps") or teaching body.—Trans.

5. "View" 69. The quotation is taken from Parsons, *The Cornell Campus*.

6. "Un discours propédeutique et préventif": propedeutical remarks, to use the word German took over from Greek to designate the teaching that comes before teaching.—Trans.

7. About national idioms and idioms which, like Latin, aspire to greater catholicity: Leibniz's *rationem reddere*—a phrase by no means his exclusive property, but common to philosophy at large—is easily carried over into ordinary French as *rendre* raison, *rendre raison de quelque chose*; but in English, today, "render reason" sounds outlandish. The Oxford Dictionary shows that English had the idiom at one time; setting aside a willfully archaic and dialectical sentence from Walter Scott, the most recent example adduced is from *An Exposition*

of the Creed, by John Pearson, bishop of Chester, published in London in 1659, and it is an example not without interest for our purposes. "Thus," says Pearson as he expounds Article IX, "the Church of Christ in it's [*sic*] primary institution was made to be of a diffusive nature, to spread and extend itself from the City of *Jerusalem*, where it first began, to all the parts and corners of the earth. This reason did the ancient fathers render why the Chruch was called Catholick" (*An Exposition*, [Ann Arbor, Michigan: University Microfilms, 1968], p. 697). He then goes on to say that for a second reason the church is called catholic because it teaches everything, or at least everything necessary to Christian faith. Apparently, there was a whole teaching of diffusion and dissemination well before our own time. To judge from the quotations given by the OED, *to render reason* (to give it back, as it were) worked in exchange and concert with *to yield reason* and *to give reason*; any one of the three could mean to give grounds for one's thoughts and assertions, but also, to give an account of one's acts or conduct, when summoned to do so: to be held accountable and to speak accordingly. In 1690, writing not of reason but only of understanding, Locke argued that we rank things under distinct names "according to complex ideas in us," as he says, "and not according to precise, distinct, real essences in them." We cannot denominate things by their real essences, as Locke puts the matter, for the good reason that "we know them not." Even the familiar objects of our everyday world are composed we know not how; they must have their reason, but we cannot give it back to them. Thus, for all his practical bent, Locke is drawn to say, and I quote him once again, "When we come to examine the stones we tread on, or the iron we daily handle, we presently find that we know not their make, and can give no reason of the different qualities we find in them" [*An Essay Concerning Human Understanding*, III, vi, 8–9]. In English, as in French or Latin, at one time people could give reason, or render it, or not be able to render it.—E.P.M.

8. In this quotation from Peirce's *Values in a Universe of Chance* [(Stanford: Stanford University Press, 1958), p. 332], in addition to the last sentence, I have italicized the allusion to *desire* in order to echo the opening words of Aristotle's *Metaphysics*. Weber's article appeared in a double issue of *The Oxford Literary Review* 5: 1–2 (1982), pp. 59–79.

9. Here is but one example: "Rationem reddere heißt: den Grund zurück-geben. Weshalb zurück und wohin zurück? Weil es sich in den Beweisgängen, allgemein gesprochen im Erkennen um das *Vor*stellen der *Gegen*stände handelt, kommt dieses "zurück" ins Spiel. Die lateinische Sprache der Philosophie sagt es deutlicher: das Vorstellen ist re-praesentatio. Das Begegnende wird auf das vorstellende Ich zu, auf es zurück und ihm entgegen praesentiert, in eine Gegenwart gestellt. Gemäß dem principium reddendae rationis muß das Vorstellen, wenn es ein erkennendes sein soll, den Grund des Begegnenden auf das Vorstellen zu und d.h. ihm zurückgeben (reddere). Im erkennenden Vorstellen

wird dem erkennenden Ich der Grund zu-gestellt. Dies verlangt das principium rationis. Der Satz vom Grund ist darum für Leibniz der Grundsatz des zuzustellenden Grundes." *Der Satz vom Grund* (Pfullingen: G. Neske, 1957), p. 45. What would resist this order of epochs and, consequently, the entire Heideggerian thinking of epoch-making? Perhaps, for example, an affirmation of reason (a rationalism, if you will) that, at the same instant (but what, then, is such an instant?) 1) would not submit to the principle of reason in its Leibnizian form, that is, that would be inseperable from finalism or the absolute predominance of the final cause; 2) would not determine substance as subject; 3) would propose a nonrepresentative determination of the idea. I just named Spinoza. Heidegger speaks very rarely and very briefly of him and never does so, as far as I know, from this point of view and in this context.

10. In "Vom Wesen des Grundes," *Wegmarken* (Frankfurt am Main: Klostermann, 1976), pp. 60–61.

11. "And yet, without this all-powerful principle there would be no modern science, and without such a science there would be no university today. The latter rests upon the principle of reason (*Diese gründet auf dem Satz vom Grund).* How should we represent that to ourselves (*Wie sollen wir uns dies vorstellen*), the university founded, *gegründet,* on a sentence (a primary proposition: *auf einen Satz*)? Can we risk such an assertion (*Dürfen wir eine solche Behauptung wagen*)?" (*Der Satz vom Grund, Dritte Stunde,* p. 49).

12. See Immanuel Kant, *Critique of Pure Reason*, trans. Norman Kemp Smith (New York: St. Martin's Press, 1965), p. 633.—JP.

13. For this passage, see *Der Satz vom Grund*, pp. 198–203.—EW.

14. *Informatique* has to do with computer programs and programming; thus *informatisation* might also be translated as computerization.—JP.

15. Among many possible examples, I will mention only two recent articles. They have at least one trait in common: their authors are highly placed representatives of two institutions whose power and influence hardly need to be recalled. I refer to "The Crisis in English Studies" by Walter Jackson Bate, Kingsley Porter University Professor at Harvard (*Harvard Magazine*, Sept./Oct. 1982), and to "The Shattered Humanities" by Willis J. Bennett, chairman of the National Endowment for the Humanities (*Wall Street Journal*, Dec. 31, 1982). The latter of these articles carries ignorance and irrationality so far as to write the following: "A popular movement in literary criticism called 'Deconstruction' denies that there are any texts at all. If there are no texts, there are no great texts, and no argument for reading." The former makes remarks about deconstruction—and this is not by chance—that are, we might say, just as unnerved. As Paul de Man notes in an admirable short essay ("The Return to Philology," *Times Literary Supplement*, December 10, 1982), Professor Bate "has this time confined his sources of information to *Newsweek* magazine. . . . What is left is a matter of

law-enforcement rather than a critical debate. One must be feeling very threatened indeed to become so aggressively defensive."

16. In his posthumous writings.

17. Heidegger, *What is Metaphysics?* (*Was ist Metaphysik?* [Frankfurt am Main: Klostermann, 1960].)

18. "The Self-Affirmation of the German University." [Published in English as "The Self-Assertion of the German University," in *The Heidegger Controversy: A Critical Reader*, ed. Richard Wolin (Cambridge: MIT Press, 1993).—JP.]

"In Praise of Philosophy"

We publish under this title an interview between Jacques Derrida, Didier Eribon, Robert Maggiori, and Jean-Pierre Salgas published in *Libération* (Saturday and Sunday, November 21 and 22, 1981). It is worthwhile reproducing here the introduction then proposed by the newspaper for this interview as well as the presentation given of the "project of Greph."—E.W.

For the context in which Greph was created and then fought for the teaching of philosophy, see the Translator's Foreword to this volume.—Trans.

1. For further details on the situation of the teaching of philosophy referred to here, see the Translator's Foreword to this volume.—Trans.

2. See Mitterrand's letter to Greph in the appendices of this volume.—Trans.

3. In France the lycée provides the final three years of studies—the Seconde, the Première, and the Terminale—leading to the State examination, the baccalauréat.—Trans.

4. *Qui a peur de la philosophie?* and *Les États Généraux de la philosophie (16 et 17 juin 1979)* both appeared in the series entitled Collection Champs, from Flammarion (Paris), in 1977 and 1979 respectively. Derrida's contributions are collected in Jacques Derrida, *Who's Afraid of Philosophy?: Right to Philosophy 1*, trans. Jan Plug (Stanford, Calif.: Stanford University Press, 2002), and in this volume.—Trans.

5. "The long second cycle" refers to the final three years of lycée instruction leading up to the baccalauréat. In some sections of lycée instruction—for instance, the professional sections—students complete a short second cycle and do not take the baccalauréat.—Trans.

6. Alice Saunier-Séité, former minister of universities.—Trans.

7. A habilitation is the accreditation to supervise research.—Trans.

8. The Inspection Générale is the administration of central education in France. There is an *inspecteur d'académie* for each *département*, or region, in the nation.—Trans.

9. The adjective *performant* refers to economic performance, profitability.—Trans.

The Antinomies of the Philosophical Discipline

This text reproduces the preface to *La grève des philosophes: École et philosophie* (Paris: Osiris, 1986). This book collects the lectures and discussions from the conference "École et philosophie" that was held at Université de Paris-X, Nanterre, October 20–21, 1984.

1. The Terminale is the final year of the lycée in preparation for the baccalauréat.—J.P.

Popularities

This text was first published as the foreword to *Les sauvages dans la cité: Auto-émancipation du peuple et instruction des prolétaires au XIXᵉ siècle*, ed. J. Borreil (Seyssel: Éditions du Champ Vallon, 1985).

1. See "Privilege," in Jacques Derrida, *Who's Afraid of Philosophy?: Right to Philosophy 1*, trans. Jan Plug (Stanford, Calif.: Stanford University Press, 2002), as well as note 1 to that text, pp. 193–94.—Trans.
2. Immanuel Kant, *The Metaphysics of Morals*, trans. Mary Gregor (Cambridge: Cambridge University Press, 1996), pp. 3–4.
3. One English translation of this passage reads, "[It] should be capable of being popularized (i.e., of being made sufficiently intelligible for general communication)." This may be more intelligible, but it blurs the point being made here about the intelligible/sensible distinction; see "Preface to Part I," in Immanuel Kant, *The Metaphysical Principles of Virtue*, trans. James Ellington (New York: Bobbs-Merrill, 1964), p. 4.—Trans.
4. Kant, *Metaphysics of Morals*, p. 10.
5. In Derrida's "Vacant Chair: Censorship, Mastery, Magisteriality," in this volume.

"Who's Afraid of Philosophy?"

Shortly after the Estates General of Philosophy were held, the journal *Esprit* organized a round table published in February 1980 under the title "Who's Afraid of Philosophy?" I participated in that round table with Roland Brunet, Guy Coq, Vladimir Jankélévitch, and Olivier Mongin. While reproducing only my own contributions here, I nonetheless keep the titles given by the review to the different moments of the discussion.

1. The national competitive examinations referred to here are the CAPES

(Certificat d'Aptitude Professionelle d'Enseignement Sécondaire) and the agrégation, both of which certify candidates for teaching positions in lycées or universities. The écoles normales are the "grandes écoles" for the training of teachers.—Trans.

2. On the Haby Reform, see the Translator's Foreword to this volume.—Trans.

3. The Appeal has been published in Jacques Derrida, *Who's Afraid of Philosophy?: Right to Philosophy 1*, trans. Jan Plug (Stanford, Calif.: Stanford University Press, 2002), pp. 186–87.—Trans.

4. In France the lycée provides the final three years of studies—the Seconde, the Première, and the Terminale—leading to the State examination, the baccalauréat.—Trans.

5. Derrida's contributions to *Qui a peur de la philosophie?* (Paris: Flammarion, 1977) are collected in Derrida, *Who's Afraid of Philosophy?*—Trans.

6. The word *ébranlement*, translated here as "disturbance," signals a shaking, weakening, or destabilizing.—Trans.

7. Régis Debray signed the report to the Estates General of Philosophy produced by the work group on teaching and the media. See Greph, *États Généraux de la philosophie (16 et 17 juin 1979)* (Paris: Flammarion, 1979), pp. 157–67.—Trans.

8. Greph, *États Généraux de la philosophie.*

Letter from François Mitterrand to Greph

The May 28, 1981, letter from Mitterrand to Greph appeared, along with the commentary following the letter, in *Le Monde* under the title "The Teaching of Philosophy Should Be Extended to the Whole of the Second Cycle."—Trans.

Titles

To clarify my argument at this point, I believe it is useful to reproduce here a chapter of the report for the foundation of the Collège International de Philosophie, the chapter carrying precisely the title "Titles." I want to recall that, as opposed to "Sendoffs" (below), this chapter belongs to the part of the report that was accepted and signed by all the members of the committee that I was officially in charge of coordinating. [Further details on the history of the Collège are given in the head note to "Sendoffs" and in the Translator's Foreword to this volume.—Trans.]

1. The Terminale is the last year of lycée studies in preparation for the State

national examination, the baccalauréat. Members of the Collège de France are appointed by the president of France and give lectures open to all. The Centre National de Recherche Scientifique (CNRS) provides positions for researchers who do not necessarily teach within the framework of the institution.—Trans.

2. Immanuel Kant, *The Conflict of the Faculties / Der Streit der Fakultäten*, trans. Mary J. Gregor (New York: Abaris, 1979).

3. The word *ébranlement* refers to a shaking, weakening, or destabilizing.—Trans.

4. A reference, again, to the "nonphilosophical" departments of the university in Kant's *Conflict of the Faculties.*

5. Cited by Fernand Braudel. I take the term out of context here, even turning it against its obvious presuppositions: God, "the guarantor of *interscience*, as is Spinoza's God-Substance."

6. The adjective *performant* refers to economic performance, productivity, or profitability and resonates with performative language in speech-act theory.—Trans.

7. Here the problems and programs of the Collège will be able to intersect with those of the Centre d'Études des Systèmes et des Technologies Avancées (CESTA). From the moment of its creation, the Collège will have to follow up on discussions already under way in this direction and to plan organized exchanges with CESTA.

8. The French here is simply *exploration aux limites*, literally "exploration at/to the limits," which could, of course, be the limits not only of philosophy but of other approaches as well.—Trans.

9. The Faculty of Philosophy comprises the group of disciplines that are themselves subordinated to the discipline of pure rational science—pure mathematics, pure philosophy, the metaphysics of nature and of morals.

10. In Kant's day, theology, medicine, and law, but this list could be modernized.

11. See Derrida's "Theology of Translation," in this volume.—Trans.

12. See "Philosophy and Its Classes," in Jacques Derrida, *Who's Afraid of Philosophy?: Right to Philosophy 1*, trans. Jan Plug (Stanford, Calif.: Stanford University Press, 2002).—Trans.

13. See President Mitterrand's letter to Greph in the appendices of this volume.—Trans.

14. Let us recall that at its creation, the Collège de France was named the Collège des Trois Langues (College of Three Languages), for the study of Latin, Greek, and Hebrew.

Sendoffs

"Coups d'envoi" was published in *Collège International de Philosophie: Sciences, Interscience, Arts,* as part of a "Rapport présenté à M. Jean-Pierre Chevènement, Ministre d'Etat, Ministre de la Recherche et de l'Industrie, par Françoise Châtelet, Jacques Derrida, Jean-Pierre Faye, Dominique Lecourt," dated September 30, 1982, 105–55. Portions of the report, including "Coups d'envoi," were also reprinted in a booklet titled *Extraits d'un rapport pour le Collège International de Philosophie,* prepared by the Collège in the fall of 1983, and parts of "Coups d'envoi" were excerpted as "Légitimité de la philosophie," in *T.E.L. (Temps Économie Littérature)* 8 (November 25, 1982): 1, 7.

Châtelet, Derrida, Faye, and Lecourt made up a French government "mission" charged with investigating the possibilities and conditions of an International College of Philosophy. The idea for such an institution had grown to some measure out of the militant struggles of the Groupe de Recherches sur l'Enseignement Philosophique (Greph) and the Estates General of Philosophy—in which Derrida played a major part—against the attempts made by conservative governments to eliminate or restrict the teaching of philosophy in French schools. A year after François Mitterrand's election as president and the victory of a Socialist parliamentary majority in May 1981, the mission was formally created by Jean-Pierre Chevènement, the new minister of research and industry. On May 18, 1982, Derrida circulated on behalf of the mission an open letter to interested parties worldwide, citing Chevènement's instructions and inviting potential participants in the Collège to identify themselves and to propose research and projects (the letter was widely disseminated; see, for instance, *La Quinzaine Littéraire* 374 [July 1–15, 1982]: 29, and *Substance* 35 [1982]: 80–81). Four months later, after extensive consultations and evaluation of more than 750 replies to the open letter, the mission recommended the establishment of the Collège as an autonomous but State-funded teaching and research institution, aimed principally at encouraging and organizing work on (quasi-)philosophical research themes or objects not sufficiently studied in existing institutions. Their report, a somewhat technical government document, outlined in its first hundred pages the mission's collective recommendations for the definition, the regulating idea, and the constitution of the Collège. This was followed by four individual "projections," one by each of the four philosophers, "Coups d'envoi" being Derrida's contribution.

The Collège was officially founded in Paris on October 10, 1983 and began operating that semester, with Derrida as its first director, followed by Jean-François Lyotard, Miguel Abensour, and others. Today it offers, free and open to the public, without prerequisites, a wide range of courses and research programs, as well as frequent colloquia and lectures, by scholars in its six "intersections": philosophy/science, philosophy/art and literature, philosophy/politics, philosophy/psychoanalysis, philosophy/internationalities, and philosophy/philosophy. It is directed by an Assemblée Collégiale. Its work, particularly the work of its seminars, is documented in a regular series of *Cahiers*. Requests for schedules and other information can be addressed to the Collège at: 1, rue Descartes, 75005 Paris.

Helpful discussions of the Collège in English can be found in Steven Ungar, "Philosophy after Philosophy: Debate and Reform in France since 1968," *Enclitic* 8, nos. 1–2 (1984): 13–26, especially the appendix on the Collège; and in Vincent Leitch, "Research and Education at the Cross-Roads: A Report on the Collège International de Philosophie," *Substance* 50 (1986): 101–14.

Along with the work included in this volume and in *Who's Afraid of Philosophy?* other work by Derrida on the College includes: "On Colleges and Philosophy," Discussion with Geoff Bennington, *ICA Documents* 5 (1986): 66–71; and the interview with Imre Salusinzky in *Criticism in Society* (New York and London: Methuen, 1987), pp. 8–24, especially 14–18. In French, see "Philosophie au collège," interview with Jean-Luc Thébaud, *Libération* 692 (August 11, 1983): 15–16; and "Cinquante-deux aphorisms pour un avant-propos," in *Psyché* (Paris: Galilée, 1987), 509–18.—Eds.

[This translation was published in *Yale French Studies* 77, *Reading the Archive: On Texts and Institutions*, ed. E.S. Burt and Janie Vanpée, 1990.—JP.]

1. At the end of every chapter of this "projection," I will multiply the numbered references to the contributions addressed to us during the course of the mission. All of these documents will be collected as we have indicated, and attached to the final report. They have extremely diverse forms and functions (letters of support, advice, suggestions, offers of participation or association, very elaborate projects). They have been addressed by individuals (teachers, researchers, students, artists, experts, or practitioners), by groups or institutions, from France and abroad. Without picking and choosing from among the different types of correspondence [*envoi*] in my references, I have allowed myself to be guided simply by a classically thematic principle. Of course, it could not be rigorous, given the intersections to which we have appealed from the outset. Certain references will have to appear several times. Nonetheless, it seemed useful to constitute this kind of thematic index, however approximate. It might help the first readers of the report to form an image of the ensemble of contributions and exchanges to which the mission has given space. Its interest and scope will be more obvious, and the consultation of the adjoined dossier may be facilitated. Especially, beyond this first reading, and if the Collège is created, such an instrument could be indispensable when the time comes to make our first initiatives and it is necessary to make contact again with all our correspondents. [In the absence of the supporting documents, these notes have been deleted from the translation.—Eds.]

2. Maurice Godelier, *Les sciences de l'homme et la societé* (Paris: Documentation française, 1982), 2 vols.—Trans.

3. See Marcel Mauss, "Essai sur le don" (1925), in his *Sociologie et anthropologie* (Paris: Presses Universitaires de France, 1980); trans. Ian Connison as *The Gift: Forms and Functions of Exchange in Archaic Societies* (New York: Norton, 1967).—Trans.

4. See Denis Hollier, ed., *Le Collège de Sociologie 1937–1939* (Paris: Gallimard, 1979); trans. Betsy Wing, as *The College of Sociology (1937–1939)* (Minneapolis: University of Minnesota Press, 1989).—Trans.

5. The Centre National de Recherche Scientifique (CNRS) provides positions for researchers who do not necessarily teach within the framework of the institution.—Trans.

6. CESTA, the Center for the Study of Advanced Systems and Technologies, and CREA, the Center for Research on Autonomous Epistemologies, are both housed in the same buildings as the Collège, 1–5 rue Descartes, the former École Polytechnique. The Direction du Livre is a subsection of the French Ministry of Culture that supervises, supports, and studies various aspects of book production and distribution. It is affiliated with the Centre National des Lettres, a semiprivate organization run by both the Direction du Livre and publishers, which supports such activities as the publication of journals and the activity of small presses, etc.—Trans.

7. See Placide Tempels, *La philosophie bantoue,* trans. A. Rubbens (Élisabethville: Éditions Lovania, 1945); *Bantu Philosophy*, trans. Colin King (Paris: Présence Africaine, 1959). And see Paulin J. Honntondja, *Sur la "philosophie africaine"* (Paris: François Maspero, 1976); *African Philosophy*, trans. Henri Evans with Jonathan Ree (Bloomington: Indiana University Press, 1983), especially chapters 1–3.—Eds.

8. See the collective volume from Greph called *Qui a peur de la philosophie?* (Paris: Flammarion, 1977) and the proceedings of the June 1979 *États Généraux de la Philosophie* (Paris: Flammarion, 1979). Minister Chevènement's letter is quoted in Derrida's "lettre circulaire" of May 18, 1982 (see headnote). Derrida's contributions to these volumes are collected here and in *Who's Afraid of Philosophy?: Right to Philosophy 1* (Stanford: Stanford University Press, 2002).—Eds.

9. The complete French text can be found in *Qui a peur de la philosophie?*; English translation in *Who's Afraid of Philosophy?*, pp. 92–97.—Eds.

10. Two years of post-baccalauréat preparation for the entrance examination of the humanities section of the Écoles normales supérieures.—Trans.

11. The Centre National de Recherche Scientifique and the Fondation Thiers, independent though closely linked, provide permanent and part-time positions for researchers, who do not necessarily teach within the framework of these institutions.—Trans.

Report

We reproduce here the beginning of the "Preamble to the *Principles for a Reflection on the Contents of Education*," published in March 1989: "A committee to consider the contents of teaching had been created, at the end of 1988, by the minister of national education. Chaired by Pierre Bourdieu and François Gros and composed of Pierre Baqué, Pierre Bergé, René Blanchet, Jacques Bouveresse, Jean-Claude Chevallier, Hubert Condamines, Didier DaCunha Castelle, Jacques Derrida, Philippe Joutard, Edmond Malinvaud, and François Mathey, its mission was to revise the fields of knowledge taught, while reinforcing the coherence and unity of these fields of knowledge.

In the first phase of their work, the members of the committee gave themselves the task of formulating the principles that would have to govern their work. Conscious of and concerned about the implications and practical applications, in particular the pedagogical applications, of these principles, in order to ground them they endeavored to obey only the properly intellectual discipline that follows from the intrinsic logic of the fields of knowledge available and the anticipations or questions that can be formulated. Since their mission was not to intervene directly and in the short term in the definition of the programs, they wanted to outline the large orientations of the *progressive* transformation of the contents of teaching that is indispensable, even if it must take some time to follow, and even get ahead of, as much as possible, the evolution of science and society.

Having accepted these principles, specialized working committees will continue or begin to reflect more deeply on each of the large regions of knowledge. They will try to propose, in preliminary notes that could be submitted in June 1989, not the ideal program of an ideal teaching, but a group of precise observations, bringing out the implications of the proposed principles."

One of these committees (Philosophy and Epistemology)—cochaired by Jacques Bouveresse and Jacques Derrida, and composed of Jacques Brunschwig, Jean Dhombres, Catherine Malabou, and Jean-Jacques Rosat—submitted the "Report of the Committee of Philosophy and Epistemology" to the minister in June 1989.—E.W.

1. SGEN: Syndicat Générale des Enseignants; SNES: Syndicat National des Enseignements de Second Degré; SNESUP: Syndicat National de l'Enseignements Supérieur.—Trans.

2. University education in France is divided into cycles. The premier cycle, or first cycle, is composed of a two-year DEUG (Diplome d'Études Universitaires Générales—Diploma of General University Studies). The second cycle includes

the licence, obtained at the end of the third year of study, and the maîtrise, at the end of the fourth year. The third cycle comprises higher degrees such as the DEA (Diplome d'Études Approfondi) and the DESS (Diplome d'Études Supérieures Spécialisées), both of which precede the doctorat, and the doctorat itself. Instituts Universitaires de Formation des Maîtres are the university institutes for teacher training. The collège covers the years from the sixième to the troisième (students are approximately eleven to fifteen years of age), and the lycée the final three years of secondary education, from the Seconde to the Terminale, the final year completed in preparation for the national examination, the baccalauréat. The Inspection Générale is the administration of central education in France. There is an *inspecteur d'académie* for each *département,* or region, in the nation.—Trans.

3. The administration of education in France divides the country into areas known as academies, each of which is administered by a rector.—Trans.

4. On the relation of age and philosophy, see, for example, "The Age of Hegel" and "Philosophy and Its Classes," in Jacques Derrida, *Who's Afraid of Philosophy?: Right to Philosophy 1*, trans. Jan Plug (Stanford, Calif.: Stanford University Press, 2002).—Trans.

5. The grandes écoles are prestigious institutions of higher education. Admission to them is controlled by competitive examinations, a factor distinguishing them from the traditional universities.—Trans.

6. The écoles normales also train future teachers, but as grandes écoles have entrance examinations.—Trans.

7. The CAPES (Certificat d'Aptitude Professionelle d'Enseignement Sécondaire) and the agrégation are competitive examinations that certify candidates for teaching positions. In principle, those who pass these examinations are guaranteed a teaching position for the rest of their careers.—Trans.

8. See above, the headnote to this report.—Trans.

9. In proposing a restructuring of the teaching of philosophy, Derrida relies upon three terms: a *programme de notions* (program based on notions), *questions de cours* (questions drawn from the course), and an *exercice de questions* (short-answer questions). The objective is to prepare students to grasp some of the fundamental notions in philosophy and its history and to evaluate their ability to apply this knowledge. Thus, rather than presenting the students with material they are unfamiliar with or asking them to construct an argument they are unprepared for, Derrida proposes to ask them questions that, while not identical to what was covered in class, clearly draw upon what was learned there. He also proposes to relativize the role of the essay by devoting part of exam time to short-answer questions.—Trans.

10. The *khâgne* is the second year of a two-year preparatory course for the arts section of the École Normale Supérieure. (The *hypokhâgne* is the first year.)—Trans.

11. See Derrida's "Vacant Chair: Censorship, Mastery, Magisteriality," in this volume.—Trans.

12. Students in French lycées specialized in one of a number of "sections": sections G and F were "technical" sections for *technologie gestion* (management) and *technologie électronique* (electronics) respectively. The system has since been changed, along with the designations. Today, students complete a "bac L" (literary), for example.—Trans.

13. The literary (A) and scientific (C) sections.—Trans.

14. CPR: Centre Pédagogique Régional; ENNA: École Normale National d'Apprentissage; ENS: École Normale Supérieure.—Trans.

15. The *Le Monde* article summarizes the policy of a contract between the Ministry of Education and the universities. The ministry encouraged universities to renew their programs in view of new teaching technologies and of the needs and demands of current university students, and called for a DEUG that would be "more open" in that it would be organized according to four broad disciplinary sectors: letters and languages; medical disciplines; economics, law, and sciences; and math, physics, and chemistry. The ministry also called for a coherent plan to maintain university campuses and to develop university libraries.—Trans.

16. What Derrida calls "open seminars" (*séminaires libres*) are seminars whose content has not been determined by a program—national or otherwise—or by the university.—Trans.

17. André Miquel submitted a report on the condition of university libraries to then minister of national education Lionel Jospin. Entitled *Les bibliothèques universitaires: Rapport au ministre d'État, ministre de l'Éducation Nationale, de la Jeunesse et des Sports* (Paris: La Documentation Française, 1989), the report famously states that university libraries in France "constitute one of the disaster zones" in the university. The report documents the general conditions of university libraries: too few personnel; a poverty of materials, beginning with books; too little space (for those materials, as well as readers); restrictive opening hours; and general underfunding. Because of these conditions, university libraries are underused and discouraging to university students.—Trans.

MERIDIAN

Crossing Aesthetics

Jacques Derrida, *Eyes of the University: Right to Philosophy 2*

Maurice Blanchot, *Lautréamont and Sade*

Giorgio Agamben, *The Open: Man and Animal*

Jean Genet, *The Declared Enemy*

Shosana Felman, *Writing and Madness: (Literature / Philosophy / Psychoanalysis)*

Jean Genet, *Fragments of the Artwork*

Shoshana Felman, *The Scandal of the Speaking Body: Don Juan with J. L. Austin, or Seduction in Two Languages*

Peter Szondi, *Celan Studies*

Neil Hertz, *George Eliot's Pulse*

Maurice Blanchot, *The Book to Come*

Susannah Young-ah Gottlieb, *Regions of Sorrow: Anxiety and Messianism in Hannah Arendt and W. H. Auden*

Jacques Derrida, *Without Alibi*, edited by Peggy Kamuf

Cornelius Castoriadis, *On Plato's 'Statesman'*

Jacques Derrida, *Who's Afraid of Philosophy? Right to Philosophy 1*

Peter Szondi, *An Essay on the Tragic*

Peter Fenves, *Arresting Language: From Leibniz to Benjamin*

Jill Robbins, ed., *Is It Righteous to Be? Interviews with Emmanuel Levinas*

Louis Marin, *Of Representation*

Daniel Payot, *The Architect and the Philosopher*

J. Hillis Miller, *Speech Acts in Literature*

Maurice Blanchot, *Faux pas*

Jean-Luc Nancy, *Being Singular Plural*

Maurice Blanchot / Jacques Derrida, *The Instant of My Death / Demeure: Fiction and Testimony*

Niklas Luhmann, *Art as a Social System*

Emmanual Levinas, *God, Death, and Time*

Ernst Bloch, *The Spirit of Utopia*

Giorgio Agamben, *Potentialities: Collected Essays in Philosophy*

Ellen S. Burt, *Poetry's Appeal: French Nineteenth-Century Lyric and the Political Space*

Jacques Derrida, *Adieu to Emmanuel Levinas*

Werner Hamacher, *Premises: Essays on Philosophy and Literature from Kant to Celan*

Aris Fioretos, *The Gray Book*

Deborah Esch, *In the Event: Reading Journalism, Reading Theory*

Winfried Menninghaus, *In Praise of Nonsense: Kant and Bluebeard*

Giorgio Agamben, *The Man Without Content*

Giorgio Agamben, *The End of the Poem: Essays in Poetics*

Theodor W. Adorno, *Sound Figures*

Louis Marin, *Sublime Poussin*

Philippe Lacoue-Labarthe, *Poetry as Experience*

Ernst Bloch, *Literary Essays*

Jacques Derrida, *Resistances of Psychoanalysis*

Philosophy

Completing the translation of Derrida's monumental work *Right to Philosophy* (the first part of which has appeared under the title *Who's Afraid of Philosophy?*), *Eyes of the University* brings together many of the philosopher's most important texts on the university and, more broadly, on the language and institutions of philosophy.

In its most immediate context, *Eyes of the University* is invaluable for the light it throws on an underappreciated aspect of Derrida's engagement, both philosophical and political, in struggles against the stifling of philosophical research and teaching, in the France of the late 1970s in particular. As a founding member of the Research Group on the Teaching of Philosophy and as one of the conveners of the Estates General of Philosophy, Derrida was at the forefront of the struggle to preserve and extend the teaching of philosophy as a distinct discipline, in secondary education and beyond, in the face of reforms of the educational system. As one of the founders of the Collège International de Philosophie, he worked to provide a space for research in and around philosophy that was not accepted in other institutions.

Documenting and reflecting upon these and other engagements, *Eyes of the University* collects some of the most important and incisive of Derrida's interventions. At the same time, Derrida's essays always have broad philosophical and political concerns. Thus, in addition to considerations of the implications for literature and philosophy of French becoming a state language, of Descartes' writing of the *Discourse on Method* in French, and of philosophies of the university from Kant and Schelling to Heidegger, the volume reflects on the current political and institutional conditions of philosophy, questioning the growing tendency to orient research and teaching toward programmable and profitable ends. In his formulation of these issues and questions, in his responses to them, Derrida elaborates what he calls a "university responsibility."

Jacques Derrida is Director of Studies at the Ecole des Hautes Etudes en Sciences Sociales and Professor of Humanities at the University of California, Irvine. Among his many works published in English are Who's Afraid of Philosophy? Right to Philosophy 1 *(Stanford, 2002)* , Negotiations *(Stanford, 2002), and* Without Alibi *(Stanford 2002).*

STANFORD UNIVERSITY PRESS

www.sup.org

ISBN 0-8047-4297-9

9 780804 742979

900

Cover design: Rob Ehle